OPERATION
SEA LION

Also by Leo McKinstry

Fit to Govern? (1996)
Turning the Tide (1997)
Boycs: The True Story (2000)
Jack and Bobby: A Story of Brothers in Conflict (2002)
Rosebery: Statesman in Turmoil (2005)
Sir Alf: England's Greatest Manager (2006)
Spitfire: Portrait of a Legend (2007)
Lancaster: The Second World War's Greatest Bomber (2009)
Hurricane: Victor of the Battle of Britain (2010)
Jack Hobbs: England's Greatest Cricketer (2011)

OPERATION SEA LION

THE FAILED NAZI INVASION
THAT TURNED THE TIDE OF THE WAR

LEO McKINSTRY

THE OVERLOOK PRESS
New York, NY

This edition first published in paperback in the United States in 2016 by
The Overlook Press, Peter Mayer Publishers, Inc.

141 Wooster Street
New York, NY 10012
www.overlookpress.com

For bulk and special sales, please contact sales@overlookny.com,
or write us at the address above.

Cataloging-in-Publication Data is available from the Library of Congress

Manufactured in the United States of America

ISBN 978-1-4683-1256-0
2 4 6 8 10 9 7 5 3 1

This book is dedicated to the fond memory of
Katharine Kinney (1959–2013)
adventurer and heroine

Contents

Introduction

'He is coming!'

———

THE ATMOSPHERE INSIDE the Berlin Sportpalast was electric that early September afternoon in 1940. The arena was packed to its 14,000 capacity. Amidst hysterical cheering, the Führer marched onto the stage, his impassive mien in graphic contrast to the frenzied enthusiasm that greeted his arrival. He started his speech in a low-key, almost conversational manner, with jibes at Winston Churchill and the British war effort. As his address continued, he grew more agitated, his passion whipping up the crowd to ever greater paroxysms of adoration. At one point he had to stop, so prolonged and delirious was the applause.

Warming to his theme of an escalation in the Reich's aerial assault on Britain, he proclaimed, 'When they declare that they will increase their attacks on our cities, then we will raze their cities to the ground.'[1] He went on: 'The hour will come when one of us will break and it will not be Nationalist Socialist Germany,' to which the crowd responded with ecstatic cries of 'Never! Never!'[2] Finally, he turned to the issue that was gripping the imagination of the British public: the imminent threat of invasion. With his compelling mix of menace and sarcasm, the Führer said, 'In England, they're filled with curiosity and keep asking, "Why doesn't he come?" Be calm, be calm. He is coming! He is coming!'[3]

The Wehrmacht was certainly preparing with characteristic efficiency to invade Britain. As Hitler fulminated at the Berlin Sportpalast on 4 September, a huge build-up of German military forces was under way in north-western Europe, ready for the strike against England. Along the coasts of France, Holland and Belgium, the Kriegsmarine was gathering a mighty armada to transport the initial assault force of nine divisions across the Channel, which would be followed by heavy reinforcements once the bridgeheads were established. On the very day of Hitler's speech, the shipping section of the German naval staff reported that no fewer than 1,910 barges, 419 tugs, and 1,600 motorboats had been requisitioned for the invasion fleet.[4] The plans for the operation, code-named Sea Lion by the German

High Command, were ambitious in their scale and thorough in their details. Thirteen hospital ships had been commandeered for the wounded; there would be seventy-two guard dogs to protect the snipers. In the same spirit, the army had developed 250 amphibious tanks, complete with snorkels and waterproofed cannon.

After the rapid conquest of France, the Low Countries, Denmark and Norway in 1940, the confidence of the German army could hardly have been higher. As Alexander Hoffer, a rifleman in a mountain regiment recalled, 'The operation was going to be simple, a mopping up detail. The enemy was as good as defeated anyway, weak in numbers and morale. The English, so we were told, were a badly armed army which had been shattered at Dunkirk. The Tommies would be in no position to interfere seriously with our landing.'[5]

On the other side of the Channel, as reconnaissance and intelligence revealed the extent of the German invasion preparations, the British sensed that Hitler's threats were all too real. The intensification of the air war was regarded as a prelude to a certain assault on England's southern coast. According to a report from the headquarters of the army's Home Forces, written the day after the Führer's Sportpalast speech, 'If Hitler thinks that he can achieve a fair measure of air superiority over the next few days, then a full scale invasion may be attempted on a wide front. The attack will be carried out ruthlessly with every means available.'[6] The commanding officer of those Home Forces, General Alan Brooke, wrote in his private diary on 4 September, 'Indications of an impending attack before 15 September are accumulating,' while three days later he recorded, 'all reports look like the invasion is getting nearer.'[7] Churchill himself, who had been highly sceptical throughout the summer of claims that the Germans would invade, grew more convinced of the likelihood of attack, as he warned in one of his celebrated speeches. 'No one should blind himself to the fact that a heavy, full-scale invasion of this island is being prepared with the usual German thoroughness and method and that it may be launched at any time now.'[8]

Yet Hitler never came. He ducked the challenge of conquest. His threats turned out to be bluster, his rhetoric hollow. All the preparations were in vain. The invasion fleet was gradually dispersed through the autumn of 1940; the troops returned to their German bases or were sent to forward positions on the eastern front. After the war it became fashionable, especially among surviving Reich commanders, to claim that Hitler never really intended to invade, that Operation Sea Lion was all a gigantic bluff to demoralise Britain. In one post-war interview, General Gerd von Rundstedt, who was to have led the German army across the Channel in 1940, dismissed the whole concept of invasion as a 'game' and described Sea Lion as 'rubbish',[9] while the Luftwaffe commander Albert Kesselring wrote in 1957 that 'Hitler was only half-heartedly tied to the idea of an invasion of England.'[10]

This argument is undermined by the reality of the Reich's intensive planning for Sea Lion. Indeed, the Kriegsmarine's assembly of the huge invasion fleet in a short timescale was not only a phenomenal feat of logistics but also a direct contradiction of the idea that the Germans were never serious about crossing the Channel. Moreover, Hitler knew that failing to conquer Britain carried the risk of a long war, with Germany potentially forced to fight on two fronts once he invaded Russia in the summer of 1941. In his more bullish moments, Hitler told his military chiefs that talk about breaking Britain quickly through an economic blockade or an assault on her empire in North Africa was mere wishful thinking. 'A positive result can only be achieved by an attack on England,' he said at the end of July 1940,[11] an outlook that he still maintained in September. As Admiral Erich Raeder, the head of the Kriegsmarine in 1940, recorded: 'A landing is, now as before, regarded by the Führer as the means by which, according to every prospect, an immediate crashing end can be made of the war.'[12]

Another common argument is that Hitler's failure to invade can be explained, not by his lack of seriousness, but by the RAF's victory in the Battle of Britain. According to this hypothesis, Britain owed its survival in the autumn of 1940 entirely to the heroic men of Fighter Command, who prevented the Luftwaffe gaining air superiority over the southern English coast and thereby made a Channel crossing too dangerous for the Germans. Bolstered by the grandeur of Churchill's eloquence, the triumph of the Few has become central to Britain's romantic wartime story. It is undoubtedly true that the Hurricane and Spitfire pilots played a vital role in thwarting the Reich's invasion plans, for mastery of the air was regarded as an essential prerequisite of any assault on the beaches. Thanks to the RAF, that goal was never achieved. But this is far from the whole story. The emphasis on the fighter crews unfairly downplays the crucial importance of the wider British resistance to Hitler in 1940, which permeated the armed forces and the home front. The whole nation was galvanised for the fight. When Hitler abandoned his plans for invasion, it was a victory for the many, not the few.

Wartime legend has presented the heroics of the RAF as an exception to an otherwise desperate military performance by Britain in 1940. In this narrative, there is a chasm between the daring and efficiency of Fighter Command and the woeful inadequacy of most other parts of the British war effort. Defeat was inevitable if the RAF was overwhelmed, according to the traditional account, which portrays Britain as hopelessly ill equipped in the face of the Nazi war machine. It was a supposed weakness highlighted by the paralysis in the civil service, the chronic shortages of men and weaponry in the regular army, the lack of modern vessels in the navy and the country's feeble home defences. The might of Hitler's Reich, which had blitzed its way through Poland, Scandinavia and Western Europe, would hardly have been deterred by some hastily erected pillboxes, rolls of barbed wire and lightweight guns. The ultimate symbol of Britain's alleged vulnerability in 1940 was the Home Guard, that makeshift force of volunteers whose very nickname, 'Dad's Army', was so redolent of its antiquated nature in the savage new age of total war. Made famous for future generations by the television comedy series of the 1970s, the Home Guard appeared more likely to provoke laughter than fear in the invader. The image of Home Guardsmen, devoid of rifles or uniforms, performing their pointless drill routines with broomsticks and pitchforks, has long been held to characterise how badly prepared Britain was. This outlook is encapsulated in a remark made by a volunteer from Great Yarmouth when his unit was inspected in the summer of 1940 by a senior army officer, who asked: 'What steps would you take if you saw the Hun come down in parachutes?'

'Bloody long ones,' came the reply.[13]

But the commonly held belief in Britain's defencelessness in 1940 is hardly matched by the historical facts. The Few of Fighter Command were not an exception but part of a national pattern of resolute determination and thoroughness. In almost every aspect of the war effort in 1940, Britain was far better organised than the mythology suggests. The Royal Navy's Home Fleet, guarding every part of the southern and eastern coastlines, represented a formidable obstacle to German ambitions. Between Sheerness and Harwich alone, the navy had thirty destroyers. RAF Bomber Command relentlessly pounded the invasion fleet, weakening the morale of the German forces. Similarly, the British army had gained enormously in strength and equipment since the fall of France. In September 1940, when the invasion threat was at its height, there were no fewer than 1,760,000 regular troops in service, many of them led by tough-minded figures like Alan Brooke, Claude Auchinleck and Bernard Montgomery. The same is true of the Home Guard, whose broomsticks had by then largely vanished. Most of the volunteers were armed with highly effective American rifles, which were superior, in some respects, to those used by the regular soldiers. Outside the military sphere, the British home front was just as impressive. Aircraft production was much higher than that in Germany, factory hours longer. Major operations, like the evacuation of children from areas at risk of attack, the removal of gold from the Bank of England vaults, or the transfer of national art treasures to remote shelters in Wales, were carried out with superb efficiency.

What is so striking about the British authorities at this time is their ruthlessness. Everything was geared towards the struggle against Germany. Sensitivities about civil liberties, personal privacy, international legal conventions and property rights were all ignored under pressure for survival. During his leadership of V Corps, in the front line of the army's southern command, Montgomery set out his creed to his officers. 'We had got to the stage where we must do as we like as regards upsetting private property. If a house was required as an HQ it must be taken. Any material required to improve the defences must be taken.'[14]

This ruthless attitude was applied far beyond the army. In the wake of Germany's western offensive, Churchill's government took unprecedented emergency powers over the life of the nation. The peacetime structure of democracy was swept aside. Mass internment of Germans, Austrians and Italians was introduced, the programme executed in such an uncompromising manner that many refugees from Nazism ended up in British camps. Home-grown political suspects were also detained without trial, while the government created a powerful security apparatus to root out the slightest signs of treachery or defeatism. Even more aggressively, Churchill's War Cabinet planned to use poisonous gas and chemical weapons extensively against the invader, in defiance of the Geneva Convention. Large stockpiles of gas bombs were developed, and rigorous training was given to the RAF pilots who dropped them during low-level missions over the coast. As Churchill put it in May, 'We should not hesitate to contaminate our beaches with gas if this would be to our advantage. We have the right to do what we like with our own territory.'[15] Ruthlessness was backed up by the British gift for innovation, as displayed in the breaking of the Germans' Enigma code.

The saga of Britain's resistance to invasion began with an act of cold resolution that became typical of Britain's stubborn attitude throughout those fateful months.

1

'Walking with destiny'

———

THE NORWAY CAMPAIGN seemed like a military disaster for the Allies, but without it Britain might have been conquered in 1940. The Germans' triumph in the North had left the Kriegsmarine so badly damaged after its clashes with the Royal Navy in Scandinavian waters that its strength was drastically diminished for the remainder of the war. As a result, it could not hope to provide the naval protection required for a safe crossing of the Channel by invasion forces. More importantly, public fury in Britain over the ineptitude shown by the War Cabinet during the Norwegian campaign brought about the downfall of Neville Chamberlain's government and the arrival in Downing Street of Winston Churchill, the only politician with the vision, drive and will to halt the advance of the Reich.

The German coup of seizing Denmark and invading Norway had been extremely risky, given that the Royal Navy was far stronger than the Kriegsmarine. During the Norwegian campaign, the Germans lost four cruisers, ten destroyers, three U-boats and one torpedo boat. The Royal Navy was also badly hit, losing the aircraft carrier HMS *Glorious*, two cruisers, nine destroyers and six submarines. But the British Navy's sheer size meant that these losses were sustainable; that was not the case with Kriegsmarine. As Admiral Raeder later admitted, 'The losses the Kriegsmarine suffered in doing its part weighed heavily upon us for the rest of the war.'[1] Immediately after Norway, the Germans had just 10 operational destroyers, compared to the Royal Navy's 169.

Yet even the comparative success of the Royal Navy could not distract from the catastrophe of the military campaign. The limited Allied forces, which had landed under heavy attack from both the ground and the air, were forced to evacuate central and southern Norway before the end of the month, and the isolated garrison at Narvik was also withdrawn at the end of May. It was ironic, however, that the Norwegian fiasco should have strengthened the political position of the man most directly responsible for the bungled campaign.

Far from enduring the blame as First Lord of the Admiralty, Winston Churchill saw a surge in his popularity. For most of the public, the long-term wisdom of his warnings about the menace of Germany, the folly of appeasement and the failure to rearm prevailed over the immediate setbacks of Norway. Moreover, he was seen as the only senior figure in the government who had shown any willingness to fight, instead of indulging in endless procrastination while hiding behind the bureaucratic machinery of Whitehall. General Ironside, the Chief of the Imperial General Staff, commented on 7 April, 'I cannot think that we have a War Cabinet fit to compete with Hitler. Its decisions are slow and cumbersome. We still refer the smallest thing to a Committee. The Prime Minister [Chamberlain] is hopelessly unmilitary.'² Churchill, on the other hand, full of restless energy, was excited rather than depressed by war. In a letter written in February 1940 about the latter's plans for mining Norwegian waters, the First Sea Lord Sir Dudley Pound told a colleague, 'I have the greatest admiration for Winston and his good qualities are such and his desire to hit the enemy so overwhelming that I feel one must hesitate in turning down any of his proposals.'³

But to his enemies, Churchill's enthusiasm often degenerated into impetuosity. Within Whitehall, the Conservative Party and parts of the services, he was regarded by many as dangerously unreliable, well past his prime, and overly fond of drinking and adventurism. The military historian Sir Basil Liddell Hart, who had extensive contacts in the navy, recorded in his diary, 'Most of the naval staff are very critical of Churchill. They complain that he is slow and confused. It is suggested that the deterioration is due to too much old brandy. They say he alternates between recklessness and panic.'⁴ However, in the wake of the Norwegian debacle, concerns about Churchill's character were outweighed by despair over Chamberlain's leadership.

On 10 May 1940, the political situation was suddenly transformed by the sensational news that in the early hours the Germans had invaded Holland and Belgium. After nine months of the Phoney War in the West, Hitler's long-awaited attack on the western front had begun. Immediately British and French forces moved towards Belgium in an attempt to confront the Wehrmacht's sweeping offensive, for which 135 divisions had been mobilised. The commander of II Corps of the British Expeditionary Force, Lieutenant General Alan Brooke, recognised the significance of what had happened, noting in his diary: 'It is hard to believe that on a most glorious spring day with all nature looking quite its best . . . we are taking the first step towards what must become one of the greatest battles in all history!'⁵ Back at home, General Ironside found London far less ready for the titanic conflict. Summoned to a Chiefs of Staff meeting in the Admiralty at 7 a.m., he was forced to waste time just listening to rumours telephoned through from France for half an hour. Then, when he tried to leave the Admiralty building, he found he 'could not get out again. All the night watchmen away and the day's men not there. Door double and trebled locked. I walked up to one of the windows and opened it and climbed out. So much for security.'[6]

Having been politically mauled in the Norway debate in the House on 7 and 8 May, when even usually loyal Tories had rebelled against his government, Chamberlain had initially hoped that the start of the western blitzkrieg forty-eight hours later might save his premiership. The reverse was true. With all his closest allies deserting him, the prime minister knew he was finished and on 10 May he offered his resignation.

That same evening Churchill was summoned to Buckingham Palace and asked by George VI to form a new government. After days of tumultuous activity, Churchill had finally gained the premiership. Only two years earlier, at the height of political consensus for appeasement, he had been a despised, marginalised figure, supported by only a handful of MPs. Now the nation's fate lay in his hands. As he came away from his audience with the King, Churchill spoke to his bodyguard Walter Thompson, who left a vivid account of their conversation.

'You know why I have been to Buckingham Palace, Thompson?'

'Yes, sir,' replied the detective, giving the new prime minister his congratulations before adding, 'I only wish that the position had come your way in better times, for you have an enormous task.'

Tears then came into Churchill's eyes. 'God alone knows how great it is. I hope that it is not too late. I am very much afraid it is. We can only do our best.'[7]

But Churchill was not overwhelmed by the responsibility he had been given. As he recalled in his memoirs, when he finally retired to bed at three o'clock the following morning after lengthy discussions about the construction of his new government, 'I was conscious of a profound sense of relief. At last I had the authority to give directions over the whole scene. I felt as if I were walking with destiny, that all my past life had been but a preparation for this hour and this trial.'[8]

Churchill's arrival had an immediate impact on the machinery of Whitehall. The mood of vacillation evaporated, replaced by an invigorating new sense of purpose. Contrary to his image as a whisky-soaked bon viveur, he had a phenomenal work-rate, putting in over 120 hours a week and even dictating letters in the bathtub. His slogan 'Action This Day', which he attached to a deluge of instructions that emanated from Downing Street, became symbolic of his energetic style of governance. Of Churchill's arrival in power, Ironside wrote that 'it was as if an electric current had run through the war office, tightening up everyone's muscles. Answers were given to questions. Decisions were made.'⁹ This sentiment was echoed by one of Churchill's doctors, Sir Charles Wilson. 'The job was made for him. He revelled in it. The burden of a Prime Minister is formidable in peace; in war it may well crush a man in the prime of his life. Winston in reckless delight doubled the weight he had to carry by his approach to the duties of office. Now his appetite for work was voracious. He turned night into day.'¹⁰ Churchill's grasp of strategy was as strong as his fascination with detail, as was noted by the senior civil servant Sir Norman Brook. 'He was like the beam of a searchlight ceaselessly swinging round and penetrating into the remote recesses of his administration so that everyone, however humble his range or his function, felt that one day the beam might rest on him and light up what he was doing.'¹¹

The overthrow of Chamberlain was the first act in a catalogue of ruthlessness that was to develop over the coming months, as the fight for national survival intensified. The swiftness and resolution of the step left much of the political class stunned. For some it appeared like a coup, utterly against British Parliamentary traditions, as voiced by the diplomat Sir Alexander Cadogan: 'How beastly the House of Commons is! With what delight they jump on a good man when he is down!'¹² The wealthy American sophisticate and Tory MP Henry 'Chips' Channon wrote: 'Oh the cruelty of the pack in pursuit . . . I am disgusted by politics and human nature.'¹³ Others were doubtful whether Churchill could fulfil the role. The prominent Tory Sir Cuthbert Headlam expressed the anxiety of many in his party about the new prime minister: 'So at last the man has gained his ambition. I never thought he would. Well, let us hope he makes good. I have never believed in him. I only hope my judgement of the man will be proved wrong.'¹⁴

2

'Last Desperate Venture'

—

FOR CENTURIES THE idea of immunity from foreign invasion had been woven into the fabric of Britain's island story. In the romantic narrative, her insular maritime position and the rugged independence of her people combined to form an impregnable barrier against invaders. With the invention of manned flight, however, Britain's position as an island was no longer so unassailable. The Royal Navy, the stalwart protector of England's coast, could do nothing against the bombing of cities. 'The bomber will always get through,' declared the Tory leader Stanley Baldwin in 1934.[1] Four years later, as the Luftwaffe mounted a series of deadly bombing raids during the Spanish civil war, experts at the Air Ministry warned that the first month of any forthcoming conflict with Germany could see 1 million casualties, 3 million refugees and the destruction of most of London. It was this understandable fixation with aerial attack that led the British government of the late 1930s to concentrate its rearmament drive on the RAF and its civil defence programme on air-raid precautions.

The predictions of an apocalypse from the air proved wildly exaggerated once war broke out in September 1939. As months passed without any sign of German preparations for mass bombing, the more traditional fears about an invasion or coastal raids were reawakened, along with anxiety about the possible weakness of British defences. Within weeks of the declaration of war, Sir John Slessor, the head of planning at the RAF, warned of the dangers of 'a picked parachute regiment' landing on the coast. He told the Home Office:

> I do not want to be unduly alarmist and I hope we should succeed in defeating such an attempt by our fighters, but no one can say definitely that it might not succeed — for instance by crossing the sea at very low tide where the RDF [radio-direction finding: the technical name for radar] is not fully effective. Are you quite satisfied that if it were tried there would in fact be suitable reserves standing by at a 'fire brigade' readiness, with the necessary transport to take them quickly to the scene and with the necessary organisation and communications to tell them where to go?[2]

Just as uneasy was Winston Churchill, then the First Lord of the Admiralty, who wrote to the First Sea Lord Sir Dudley Pound, in late October 1939, soon after the sinking of the battleship the *Royal Oak* inside Scapa Flow and a Luftwaffe attack on Royal Navy vessels in the Firth of Forth: 'I should be the last to raise those invasion scares which I combatted so constantly during the early days of 1914–15. Still it might be well for the Chiefs of Staff to consider what would happen if, for instance, 20,000 men were run across and landed, say at Harwich or Webburn Hook [a village near Sheringham on the Norfolk coast], where there is deep water close to the shore. The long dark nights would help such designs.'[3]

With characteristic ambition, Churchill believed that the putative threat could be met by the formation of a new army of volunteers, along the lines of the Volunteer Training Corps in the First World War or Britain's defence force of Napoleonic times. Such a concept of a sturdy English yeomanry, uniting all classes to beat off an invader, appealed to his romanticised version of history. He wrote enthusiastically to a Cabinet colleague: 'Why do we not form a Home Guard of half-a-million men over forty (if they like to volunteer) and put all our elder stars at the head and in the structure of these new formations. Let these five hundred thousand men come along and push the young and active out of their home billets. If uniforms are lacking, a brassard will suffice.' However, he was badly mistaken in his view that there would be sufficient weapons for such a force, as would become apparent the following year.[4]

Churchill's appeal in 1939 for a new voluntary movement was ignored. Most senior army figures from General Ironside downwards believed that the threat of invasion was overblown, given the distance to England from German ports and aerodromes. As the Committee of Imperial Defence reported in late 1939, 'The likelihood of organised attack on a large scale on the shores of Britain is very small.'[5] Sir Walter Kirke, the commander-in-chief of Home Forces, was particularly dismissive of the idea of invasion and believed that the most useful role for the army was in the British Expeditionary Force (BEF), fighting the Germans in France. As a paper from his headquarters argued at the end of 1939, 'We wish to avoid the mistake made in the last war of raising and maintaining units and formations designed only for home defence and with no overseas role. It is a reasonable assumption that if and when all Field Army divisions have left this country, the risk of invasion, if it exists at all, will have been seriously diminished.'[6]

Kirke, a tough, experienced officer who had served in the Indian empire and on the western front in the First World War, was described by the military historian Basil Liddell Hart as 'Energetic, shrewd and an exceptionally good speaker, though he tends to resist any ideas that he does not originate.'[7] Nevertheless Kirke and the Chiefs of Staff were compelled by political pressure to draw up a defence plan that autumn to combat a possible invasion. This became known as the 'Julius Caesar plan', a rather unfortunate name, given that the Roman leader was one of the few foreign conquerors of England.

The scheme was based on the assumption that the Germans might try to land 20,000 seaborne troops on the coast somewhere between the Humber and Harwich, conveyed in about twenty-five ships, along with 4,000 parachutists and another 15,000 airborne men, armed with light automatics and landed by air transports or gliders. To deal with this imagined scenario, Kirke deployed six Territorial divisions on the east coast, with three further Territorial divisions in reserve. In addition, 400 concrete pillboxes were erected in key defensive positions on the coast over the six months from October 1939, while arrangements were also made to commandeer commercial buses to transport the mobile reserves. Although the army units were short of field guns and transports, Kirke was still convinced that an invasion was unfeasible. According to one study by his GHQ in January 1940, 'Enemy troops landed either by air or sea or both could only achieve local successes and their position should rapidly become untenable.'[8]

Kirke stuck to his position throughout the Phoney War. He dismissed occasional intelligence reports about German planning for invasion as nothing more than black propaganda or dirty tricks designed to undermine morale at home and hinder efforts to reinforce the BEF. This confidence about the emptiness of most rumours was fully justified, as shown by an almost comedic incident in February 1940. An urgent naval message was sent from Devonport to the War Office that 'toy balloons are being strewn by the enemy. They contain gas that is highly dangerous and explodes on touch. Police and coastguards should be informed if any are found.' On investigation, the message turned out to be baseless. Kirke's HQ believed it had been 'deliberately circulated as a scare by an ill-disposed person or persons'.[9]

But others were not as sanguine as Kirke, fearing that the British defences were too weak to cope with an invasion. In February 1940, Sir Auckland Geddes, one of the twelve regional commissioners appointed to run the civil side of the home front, exploded with rage at the inadequacy of military preparations. 'This army business is worse than could have been believed. The rubbish we have got here is appalling and the officers, my God! But the really frightening thing is the way the conscripts are being rotted. No discipline, no training, apparently no equipment. I had no idea Walter Kirke was so bad and the CIGS [Ironside] doesn't seem to be much better.' Geddes, who was commissioner for the vital south-eastern region, concluded with some prescience, 'This phoney war stuff is likely to end with the spring and then look out for squalls.'[10]

The predicted squall turned into a storm when Hitler followed up his assault on Scandinavia with his offensive in the West. As the panzers swept through the forest of the Ardennes, the prospects for invasion were transformed. Not only did the Germans now occupy bases in Norway, within reach of Britain across the North Sea, but there was a real chance that they could soon hold aerodromes and ports on the north-eastern European coast. Furthermore the German method of blitzkrieg – where elite paratroopers were dropped in advance of an attack to capture vital points, with the Luftwaffe being used as a lethal form of flying artillery against ground positions – challenged all orthodox thinking about defensive warfare.

A report by the British air staff painted a dispiriting picture of how this new German approach had been highly successful in the attack on Holland. 'Beaches, football grounds and aerodromes were seized and used. Bombing attacks were carried out around the aerodromes first and this was immediately succeeded by the landing of parachute troops . . . Some one hundred troop carriers were employed over a period of a few hours each day, arriving in waves of 20 to 30 aircraft with fighter protection.' The report went on to warn of 'the tremendous hitting power and moral effect' of the Luftwaffe's striking force.[11]

To Henry Tizard, one of the government's chief scientists, the whole thrust of Hitler's two-pronged campaign in the West and in Scandinavia was ultimately aimed at Britain. He told Hastings 'Pug' Ismay on 16 May, 'What Hitler will try is to land a great force from the air, on service aerodromes, emergency landing grounds and any sufficiently large flat place, particularly country near aircraft factories. He will thus short-circuit the Navy, of which he is justifiably afraid, and deal only with our dispersed land forces in England, mostly only partly trained.' Tizard went on to add, 'Is it not possible that the prime object of the Norwegian adventure and perhaps also of the fighting now going on in France and Belgium is not merely to gain possession of aerodromes nearer our coast and of additional petrol supplies, but to draw off as many of our trained men and as much of our first-class equipment as possible?'[12]

The Julius Caesar plan was beginning to seem dangerously outdated, for it had been predicated on the theory that the Channel and the Scandinavian coasts would remain in friendly or neutral hands. In the new climate of bellicosity, the government was inundated with rumours and warnings about the possibility of German landings. At the end of April, for instance, the Foreign Office passed on a message from the Lithuanian legation in

Paris, which had been told by the Italian military attaché that Hitler had given Mussolini an outline of his plans for

an all-out air attack upon Great Britain, by which our key points would be bombed and our naval, air and military forces and internal communications would be thrown into such disorder that the way would be open for an invasion which would, in fact, take place. The British coast was so extensive that landings in force would be easily possible. Germany still had enough naval forces to convey the expedition and cover would be provided by the air force. The Italian military attaché also stated that the Germans had a network of agents in this country [who] would come into action at the crucial moment to assist the invaders.[13]

In the same vein, the British embassy in Helsinki reported that one of their military sources had revealed that 'the Germans plan to use parachutists against England by landing them in county Galway and Connemara where they would join forces with the IRA who are expecting them. Air bases would be established in Eire and aircraft conveying parachutists would carry British markings.'[14]

Soon after the attack in the west, an intelligence report reached the War Office from Norway that 'the Germans are moving troop-carrying planes to Stavanger. This may indicate intention of an airborne attack on the Shetlands or the Orkneys. Please warn garrisons to be on their toes.'[15] A further picture of the nervous mood can be gleaned from a report of 14 May to the headquarters of the army's Southern Command, based in Salisbury, outlining 'suspicious incidents' the previous day:

At 1835 hours three men in a blue saloon car seen acting suspiciously near military post near Claydon [a village near Banbury, Oxfordshire]. Two suspicious characters at Blounts Hotel, 27 Clifton Road, Folkestone, were asking questions about the locations of troops. At Gillingham a man was seen moving suspiciously in the vicinity of Gillingham tunnel. A shot was fired by the sentry and search made. Nobody was found, however, although the grass in the vicinity was much trampled.

This report also contained several alleged sightings of enemy parachutists during the night, coming down over Ramsgate, Gerrards Cross, Broadstairs and the Medway, as well as 'unaccountable lights', flashes and coloured flares in various districts. There was also a disturbing case of interference on radio sets in north Essex, where a voice was heard to say '31 calling all detachments', followed by the slogan 'Heil Hitler'.[16] Equally frantic was a message on 11 May to Kirke's GHQ: 'Admiralty considers attack on Southend Pier a possibility. Information had been received from an anonymous Nazi agent, who displayed strong anti-Nazi feelings.'[17]

As had happened the previous autumn, Churchill was also caught up in the invasion disquiet. Shortly before he became prime minister, he pushed for 'at least one highly trained division' to be brought home from France 'to meet a German landing'.[18] The army chiefs, still certain of Britain's impregnability, refused, Sir Henry Pownall, the head of the BEF general staff, dismissing the demand as nothing more than 'a home defence flap started by Winston'.[19] Churchill kept up the pressure once he gained the premiership in the wake of Hitler's western offensive. 'The scene has darkened swiftly,' he told President Franklin Roosevelt, with whom he had maintained a fruitful correspondence since his return to the Admiralty in 1939. 'We expect to be attacked here ourselves, both from the air and by parachute and airborne troops in the near future and we are getting ready for them.'[20]

On his very first day in Downing Street, 10 May, he set up a new Home Defence Executive, headed by Kirke and including representatives of the three services and the Ministry of Home Security, to coordinate local anti-invasion schemes and update the Julius Caesar plan. He again pressed for the Home Forces to be improved in both quality and strength, this time bringing in six regular battalions from India, with Territorials taking their place in the east. After some prevarication, the India Office agreed to this proposal, although the Secretary of State Leo Amery was dubious about the move, writing in his diary, 'Winston, I fear, is too chiefly concentrating on home defence.'[21] But in the febrile atmosphere of early May, such a focus was both inevitable and necessary.

The Chiefs of Staff, shaking off their earlier complacency, now embarked on a series of immediate measures to bolster the country's defences. New telephone lines were installed between the searchlight detachments of anti-aircraft command and the local headquarters of the army companies. The number of armed guards at aerodromes was increased. A programme of recon-ditioning 150,000 rifles for home battalions was started at the Woolwich arsenal. Wireless sets from the RAF were lent to the army in East Anglia and Kent. A massive reconnaissance effort was undertaken to survey all open spaces within 5 miles of eastern ports and inland power stations, airfields, and radar bases, with a view to creating obstructions that would prevent German landings. Work also began on plans to blow up bridges, dock gates, viaducts and harbour facilities in the event of invasion. More transport in eastern coastal areas was hired for the army's use in the event of an emergency, although this was often of a highly makeshift nature, comprising vehicles like butchers' vans, coal carriers and builders' lorries. Equally makeshift were some of the roadblocks that were quickly installed in early May, with material varying from derelict cars to tree trunks.

Some of the impulse for this defence activity came from civilians keen to do what they could to defend their island. 'There is a mood of belligerency and resolve,' reported the Ministry of Information, which conducted comprehensive daily surveys of public opinion throughout the tense summer months of 1940. One pub landlord in Lambeth told the ministry surveyor, of his customers, that 'their tails are up. They say, "The Germans will never get here, but if they do, we'll show them".'[22]

Apart from improvised roadblocks and transport, popular determination to help the national cause was most clearly manifested in the clamour for the government to create a volunteer defence force, as had happened during previous conflicts. Indeed, ever since war had broken out in September 1939, there had been moves to set up local volunteer units. In Essex, Worcestershire, Cambridgeshire and Northamptonshire, unofficial companies had been formed to keep a lookout for enemy parachutists and to guard vital sites, while the coasts of Dumfriesshire in Scotland were regularly patrolled by volunteers on bicycles. The formidable artist and equestrian enthusiast Lady Helen Gleichen established her own band of seventy guardsmen on her estate of Much Marcle in Herefordshire. Known as the Much Marcle Watchers, the men were armed with ancient pikes and flintlocks taken from the walls of her rambling family home, although Lady Helen also unsuccessfully asked the local Shropshire Light Infantry for the loan of some rifles and 'a couple of machine guns if you've got any'.[23]

The real impetus behind the public demand for a volunteer force arose from reports, often exaggerated, about the deadly effectiveness of the German paratrooopers in Holland. This new peril from the sky not only showed that the sea no longer offered sufficient protection for the British people, but was also held to epitomise the lethal, unchivalrous nature of German aggression; German parachutists were, falsely, said to have come down onto Dutch soil disguised as policemen, priests and peasants. In one *Daily Express* report, whose sensational quality was unmatched by its veracity, 'the steward of an English ship said that he and the crew had watched parachutists descend in women's clothing. They wore blouses and skirts and each carried a sub-machine gun.'

Officialdom helped to fuel the alarm. On the day of the German invasion of Holland, the under-secretary at the War Office, Lord De La Warr, told Parliament that Germany could land 100,000 troops from the air. This prompted public agitation, exacerbated by the military authorities' unintentionally misleading advice about the tactics of the imaginary legions of German paratroopers. 'Information from Norway shows that German parachute troops, when descending, hold their arms above their heads as if surrendering. The parachutist, however, holds a grenade in each hand. To counter this strategy parachutists, if they exceed six in number, are to be treated as hostile and if possible shot in the air.'[24]

Concern about enemy parachute landings was central to the demand for a new volunteer army. Reflecting public feelings, the National Liberal MP for East Fife, Sir James Henderson-Stewart, asked the War Secretary Anthony Eden on 11 May 'if he would consider the immediate formation of a voluntary corps of older, responsible men to be armed with rifles and Bren Guns and trained for instant action in their own localities'.[25] Eden responded that the matter was under urgent consideration. There was also political pressure from the some elements of the radical left, which saw a volunteer force as a vehicle for extending democracy and challenging the outdated, class-ridden establishment.

The government, while eager to strengthen Britain's fighting capability, was firmly against the growth of a revolutionary or unauthorised militia, not least because of the scope for chaos if large numbers of citizens 'took the law into their own hands', to use Kirke's phrase.[26] The War Office and the army therefore decided that they had to take the lead over the development of a voluntary army. Two separate plans were soon under urgent consideration by officials.

One was the work of the adjutant general Sir Robert Gordon-Findlayson, who proposed that groups of volunteers, recruited by the British Legion, should be attached to the searchlight companies run by the RAF's anti-aircraft command. The other, more comprehensive and straightforward plan, drawn up by Kirke and his senior staff officer William Cardon Roe, was adopted. It provided for a force raised in villages, towns and cities for the defence of immediate localities, ultimately overseen by the army but under the control of the Lords Lieutenant at county level.

Frenetic activity followed this decision, as the arrangements for a recruitment drive were put in place. One issue quickly settled was the name of the new force, to be known as the Local Defence Volunteers, although this title would raise violent objections from Winston Churchill later in the summer. Some senior government officials, still living with the leisurely routines of the Phoney War, were appalled at the rushed nature of the force's launch. At one stage Cardon Roe was summoned by Sir Frederick Bovenschen, the severe, bespectacled deputy under-secretary for war. According to Cardon Roe's account, Sir Frederick told him that 'the whole thing was a most irregular and thoroughly slapdash scheme. Was it realized that it had taken many years of planning and an Act of Parliament to form the Territorial Army? In addition to the financial side that required Treasury sanction, there was the legal status of the LDVs which would have to be carefully explored. Why all this precipitancy? I lost my temper and said, "In order to try and avoid losing the war."'[27]

Because of this sense of haste the government decided to announce the creation of the Local Defence Volunteers on 14 May 1940, despite the fact that Whitehall's arrangements were incomplete. In his BBC broadcast that day, Eden stressed that the primary role of the new force was to deal with the threat from German paratroopers.

The response was remarkable. Within twenty-four hours, no fewer than 250,000 men had registered. By the end of May, the total had climbed to 400,000, reaching 1,456,000 by the end of July. The launch had been a huge popular success, capitalising on the enthusiasm and determination of the British public to stand up to Germany and indicative of their determination to fight. 'I rushed to join it. I would have got in if I'd only had one leg,' recalled Bill Scully, a volunteer from Bradford.[28] William Kellaway, who ran a removals business in Devon and signed up for the LDV immediately, said that 'there was such a great response because people wanted to do their bit. They actually thought that the Germans were coming. In fact there were rumours that some had landed in Cornwall. People were arming themselves with pitchforks.'[29]

Pitchforks were one of the few types of weapons that the first volunteers possessed. Nearly all the operational rifles and guns held in Britain in May 1940 were in the hands of the regular army, which also received most of the output coming off the production lines. So the volunteers had to make do with a bewildering variety of weapons, including shotguns, muskets, blunderbusses, swords, axe handles, truncheons and even golf clubs. One Lancashire unit was armed with Snider rifles that had been held in Manchester Zoo and had last been used during the Indian Mutiny of 1857. Another unit, based in London, took pikes from the props department at the Theatre Royal, Drury Lane, while in the East End of the capital a platoon made improvised 'hand grenades' from potatoes filled with razor blades. In one Hertfordshire platoon, the only rifle was an elderly German one taken from an enemy officer by a British veteran during the East Africa campaign during the First World War.

All this improvisation lingered in the public memory long after the volunteers were properly equipped, feeding the myth of Britain's hopeless desperation in 1940. But it would be wrong to exaggerate the depth of the arms famine. In keeping with the government's spirit of urgency, huge orders were placed with the USA to purchase reliable weapons for the volunteers, which would start to arrive in July, while as early as 5 June 94,000 rifles from Britain's own resources had been distributed.

At first the LDVs were just as short of uniforms as they were of rifles. In fact, all each volunteer was given to signify his status was an armband, or brassard, imprinted with the black letters LDV. To resolve this difficulty quickly, the government ordered uniforms made of coarse denim, which began to be issued from the end of May but were of poor quality and often ill fitting. A volunteer in Plymouth was officially issued with a safety pin to hold up his trousers, which were 10 inches too wide round the waist. Joseph O'Keefe from Gateshead said of his jacket that 'you needed a neck like a horse to get a snug fit.'[30] There was also a severe shortage of tin helmets in the early months of the LDV, and the field service caps provided by the War Office did not offer much protection. One volunteer was persuaded by his wife to turn up for patrol duties with an enamel pot on his head, held in place by a scarf. Again, this was not the whole story. From the late summer onwards, guardsmen were issued with smart, well-fitted battledress uniforms and helmets of the type used by the regular army.

Given the volunteers' initial lack of equipment, the role of the LDV in those early weeks was necessarily limited. In the House of Commons on 22 May, Sir Edward Grigg set out the three primary tasks of the new force as: 'observation and information' in the event of an attack, providing details swiftly to the regular army; 'obstruction of movement' through roadblocks and denial of access to motor vehicles; and protection of vulnerable points through patrol and guard duties. The defensive, restricted nature of these functions led to the fashionable jibes in early 1940 that LDV really stood for 'Look, Duck, Vanish' or 'Last Desperate Venture'.[31]

Such mockery was reinforced by reports of the LDV's practice drills, which even to many recruits seemed exercises in pointlessness. Bill Hall from Dorset remembered that a Welsh NCO 'put us through our drill, saluting, marching, turning, halting, presenting arms, sloping arms but nothing with which to combat paratroopers who at that time were imminent. We didn't even have ammunition and were left to our own ideas as to what use we would put our bayonets.'[32] George Beardmore, an engineer based at the BBC headquarters in London, became exasperated by drilling with broomsticks, feeling that the 'LDV were likely to serve no useful purpose whatever should the Germans appear in Upper Regent Street'.[33] In some places, cynicism towards LDV training routines was further fuelled by the fact that their rhythms seemed to be linked to the local pub. 'It was a constant source of amazement to me,' said Edward Pearce, a volunteer in Derbyshire, 'that no matter what the training consisted of and no matter where we went to on a Sunday morning, the Old Soldier in charge never failed to dismiss us at precisely one minute to opening time outside the Nag's Head pub.'[34]

The disorderly conduct of some volunteers could provoke the ire of those who prided themselves on discipline, such as John Bevis, a student at Loughborough University where there was a particularly well-organised LDV unit under the command of ex-army officers. When he returned home to Norfolk and joined the local village platoon, he was shocked at the sight that greeted him on his first morning of drill with his new comrades. 'Most wore battledress, some wore great coats, some had tin hats, some had ammo pouches . . . About twenty past ten we were asked to fall in. There was no inspection; the roll was not called. Some arrived even later and just joined the parade without a word.' Bevis said that he was 'disgusted with the whole outfit – the appalling quality of the instruction, the lack of discipline, the absence of effective leadership, the low morale. That pack of yokels could not have stood up to a patrol of German girl guides. Needless to say I didn't trouble to attend any more of their parades.'[35]

There was also some popular derision over the perceived elderly status of recruits, hence the nickname of 'Dad's Army', later immortalised by the television series, although in truth the average age of volunteers in 1940 was only thirty-five and many were far younger. Nevertheless, a significant proportion of the older recruits were military veterans, most of them from the First World War but some from even earlier conflicts. The oldest officially recorded volunteer accepted for service in May 1940, far beyond Eden's limit of sixty, was Alexander Taylor of Crieff in Perthshire, aged seventy-eight, a former sergeant major in the Black Watch who had taken part in the campaign to relieve General Gordon in 1885.

As with Churchill's arrival in the premiership, the creation of the LDV had shown that Britain was resolved to fight. This burgeoning sense of confidence was epitomised by the experience of Don Evans, who was just sixteen when he joined the Salisbury LDV. Out on patrol one day in the early summer, he and his fellow volunteers came across a German airman who had been forced to bail out of his aircraft. 'He had landed in the midst of a thorn bush and was covered in scratches. He was crying and had messed himself. He was convinced he would be shot.' Having handed over the Luftwaffe crewman to the police, Evans felt invigorated: 'I must confess that I had always been afraid of the Germans. I had always imagined them to be 17-stone, six-and-a-half footers with a square head and an iron fist. Seeing this young lad in front of me snivelling and stinking did me good. I was no longer afraid of Germans.'[36]

3

'These persons should be behind barbed wire'

T HE LOCAL DEFENCE Volunteers were established largely to counter the external threat of German landings, but in the wake of Hitler's offensives in Scandinavia and the West there was just as much concern about the internal threat. During those anxious days, the British authorities and public grew increasingly worried about the enemy within. In this tense atmosphere, traitors and German agents were seen everywhere, ready to conspire in Britain's downfall.

Developments on the continent helped to fuel these suspicions. The German invasion of Norway had led to an attempted coup by the pro-Nazi politician Vidkun Quisling, the leader of the Norwegian fascist party Nasjonal Samling. Some feared that a home-grown Quisling might be lurking within Britain, either in establishment circles or on the fascist right. The Foreign Office civil servant Sir Alexander Cadogan saw the Tory politician and arch-appeaser Sir Samuel Hoare, known as 'Slippery Sam', in this perfidious role, and was delighted when Churchill removed him from the Cabinet and sent him as the new British ambassador to Madrid, commenting: 'The rats are leaving the ship. The quicker we get them out of the country the better. But I'd sooner send them to a penal settlement. He'll be the Quisling of England when Germany conquers us.'[1]

Another prime suspect was Sir Horace Wilson, whose administrative gifts had made him the most powerful civil servant of the late 1930s but whose dogmatic pursuit of appeasement invoked the bitter hostility of Chamberlain's critics. Among them was Winston Churchill, who is reported to have said on 10 May, as he ordered Wilson's expulsion from Downing Street, 'Tell that man that if his room is not cleared by two o'clock, I will make him Minister for Iceland.'[2]

A more obvious candidate was the leader of the British Union of Fascists, Sir Oswald Mosley, a wealthy aristocrat of soaring ambition, oratorical brilliance and malevolent impatience. Certainly his hatred of democracy, rampant anti-Semitism and authoritarian instincts made him Hitler's ideological soulmate. Hitler's own view of Mosley, which he related to his army adjutant Gerhard Engel in mid-June 1940, was that he did 'not think much of him as a personality; on the other hand he is the only Englishman to understand the German-European idea'. Although Mosley could never become 'a real leader' like himself, the Führer said, 'his role was not yet over,' an ominous statement that justified British concerns about the activities of the fascist leader.[3]

Another feature of Hitler's military success that fed fears about the internal threat was the alleged German tactic of using a sophisticated network of spies and collaborators to undermine an enemy's defences from within. The members of these networks were known as 'Fifth Columnists', a term that was first coined during the Spanish civil war by the Nationalist leader General Emilio Mola. With his characteristic gift for spreading psychological terror, Hitler had played on this widespread foreboding about a German fifth column in an interview he gave in 1939: 'When I wage war in the midst of peace, troops will suddenly appear, let us say, in the streets of Paris. They will wear French uniforms. They will march through the streets in broad daylight. No one will stop them. Everything has been thought out to the last detail.'[4]

Reports coming back to London from the crumbling front lines in Europe seemed to confirm this sinister German approach. The *Daily Express*, then Britain's best-selling newspaper, gave this vivid account on 13 May: 'As machine guns came out of the sky like unnatural lightning peppering the streets below, the Fifth Column crept out of their homes in German uniforms, heavily armed. Holland had combed out the Fifth Column for weeks before but as the doors opened at 3am the men who had been proclaimed anti-Nazis and refugees from Germany held rifles.'

The Reich propaganda machine was delighted at the mood of fear created by the fifth column threat, as was demonstrated in the infamous broadcasts of the Irish-American fascist William Joyce, whose sneering nasal drawl earned him the nickname Lord Haw-Haw. Having been the deputy leader of the BUF until Mosley sacked him in 1937, Joyce had remained on the extreme fringe of British politics until 1939, even starting his own tiny Nazi party called the National Socialist League. A violent alcoholic and fixated anti-Semite who opened his League meetings with a cry of 'Sieg Heil', Joyce had escaped to Germany just before the war after receiving a tip-off that he was about to be arrested under Defence Regulations. At the peak of his radio career in the summer of 1940, his Nazi broadcasts on English-language stations reached an estimated 6 million regular listeners in Britain and 18 million occasional ones. He would mention specific geographical details, such as a stopped church clock in a Norfolk village or the number of barrage balloons in Bristol, implying that in Britain a vast web of Nazi agents was feeding him information. These details were wholly bogus, but most listeners could not know that. His apparent omniscience and authenticity stoked the flames of the fifth column fire that swept through Britain from early May.

The government added to the heat by urging extra vigilance. One leaflet from the Ministry of Information stated in unequivocal terms, 'There is a Fifth Column in Britain. Anyone who thinks there isn't, that "it can't happen here", has simply fallen into the trap laid by the Fifth Column itself. For the first job of the Fifth Column is to make people believe that it does not exist. In other countries, the most respectable and neighbourly citizens turned out to be Fifth Columnists.'[5] Given such a context, it was inevitable that the country was soon awash with dark rumours and conspiratorial tales.

One of the most common was that elite German soldiers had already landed and were moving through English society disguised as nuns, although they could be spotted by their hairy forearms. According to a report in the *Daily Herald*, a woman travelling by train from London to Aylesbury became highly suspicious about two nuns sitting opposite her, one of whom dropped her book and then went to pick it up. According to the newspaper, 'From the folds of her habit emerged a hairy, muscular indubitably masculine hand.' The *Herald* went on to relate that the woman had later reported the incident to the police, who gave her £10 as a reward.[6]

Some of those in authority doubted that the fifth column was really as big a menace as was feared. The Home Secretary Sir John Anderson – a Scottish-born Independent MP and former civil servant whose emotional coldness was matched by his intellectual and administrative rigour – was the last man to be swayed by the gusts of public opinion. Because of his judicial outlook, mixed with his innate Caledonian restraint, he was repulsed by the idea of taking punitive action against the entire German and Australian population within Britain, despite the growing threat from Nazism. Public hostility towards aliens appalled him, as did the growing demands for mass incarceration. He remarked at the height of the fifth column scare, 'There is a whispering campaign going on which puts the witch-hunts of the Middle Ages completely in the shade. Everyone now tends to looks askance at this neighbour – very unfortunate, I think.'[7]

Besides, he argued, ever since the outbreak of war sufficient steps had been taken to deal with dangerous aliens and home-grown extremists. In September 1939, there were 73,353 Germans and Austrians aged over sixteen living in Britain, roughly a third of the entire population of foreigners in the country. With his usual efficiency, Anderson had quickly set up 122 Home Office tribunals to examine all their cases, a process that resulted in each enemy alien being placed in one of three separate groups.

Those deemed to be the greatest security risk, of whom there were

569, were classified as Category A and were interned within days of war being declared. Category B was for the borderline cases and recent arrivals. The 6,782 Germans and Austrians who fell into this class were allowed to retain their freedom on certain conditions: they were subject to a curfew; had restrictions imposed on their travel movements; and were banned from owning bicycles, maps, cameras and wirelesses. Category C, which involved no controls at all, covered the other 66,802 cases, with refugees from Nazi Germany making up the overwhelming majority. To Anderson, this outcome combined respect for individual liberty with a recognition of national security demands.

An even more sparing approach was adopted towards British political hardliners. No action at all was taken against the Communist Party, despite the Nazi–Soviet pact of August 1939 that gave Hitler a free hand in Eastern Europe. Nor was Mosley's British Union of Fascists, which had 20,000 members at the outbreak of war, banned outright, despite the concerns of MI5 and the security services. Just a handful of ultra pro-Nazis were imprisoned under Clause 18b of the 1939 Defence Regulations, which allowed the internment of suspects without trial. Among them was T. Victor Rowe, who ran not only a business importing kitchen equipment from Germany but also a fanatically racist outfit called the Nordic League, which was so extreme that Mosley himself refused to have anything to do with it. But, in another indicator of Anderson's liberal regime, Rowe was released after just three months.

Throughout the Phoney War, even as the British Union of Fascists' attacks on the government became ever more brazen, Anderson resisted calls for more toughness, stating in April, 'It is extremely difficult to interfere with these actions without contravening the traditional principle of allowing free speech and free association for political objects.'[8]

However, after Hitler's offensive in Western Europe, such a stance was no longer tenable. Judicial niceties had to be sacrificed to the hard reality of war. Not only were the public and the press demanding a crackdown, so were Winston Churchill, the Chiefs of Staff and the security services. According to a Cabinet minute of 15 May, the prime minister believed that 'there should be a very large round-up of enemy aliens and suspect persons', since it was 'much better that these persons should be behind barbed wire'.[9]

As the calls for action became louder, Anderson was gradually forced to move away from his purist liberal position. On 11 May, he agreed to the detention of all male Germans and Austrians aged between sixteen and sixty who were living in coastal areas between Scotland and Hampshire, a total of around 2,000 enemy aliens. This limited step did nothing to quell the pressure, so on 17 May he ordered the internment of all Category B aliens, regardless of where they lived. He refused, however, to go any further, as he explained in a lengthy memorandum to the Cabinet that same day. Having pointed out that 'the great bulk' of Category C aliens were 'refugees from Nazi oppression who are bitterly opposed to the German regime', he argued that mass internment would soon backfire.[10]

Many in government thought the Home Secretary's policy of forbearance wholly inappropriate for the magnitude of the challenge facing Britain. The War Secretary Anthony Eden wrote in exasperation that he 'did not want a lecture from Sir John Anderson on the liberty of the subject',[11] while even more scathing was the senior MI5 officer Guy Liddell, who met Anderson on 21 May to press for more detentions, especially of the fascists. As he had done with others, Anderson told Liddell that 'he needed to be reasonably convinced that the BUF would assist the enemy and unless he could get such evidence, he thought it would be a mistake to imprison Mosley and his supporters, who would be extremely bitter after the war when democracy would be going through its sternest trials.' That evening Liddell recorded in his diary, 'Either he is an extremely calm and cool-headed person or he has not the slightest idea of the present situation. The position of a serious invasion of this country would seem to be no more than a vague suggestion.'[12]

However, at that very moment Anderson's hand was forced by dramatic new twist in the saga: the discovery of a wide-ranging plot in the heart of London, with tentacles stretching across the globe to Berlin, Moscow and Washington. It was a genuine conspiracy that meant he could no longer dismiss talk of extremist treachery as nothing more than empty scaremongering.

The outline of the plot, which aimed not only to give support to the Nazi enemy but also to bring about the downfall of President Franklin Roosevelt, was as audacious as its cast was outlandish. At its heart were three contrasting, unconventional figures: Anna Wolkoff, a vivacious White Russian who relished underground subversion and yearned for the triumph of the Third Reich; Tyler Kent, a louche US foreign service clerk with a fondness for high society, female company and anti-democratic politics; and Captain Maule 'Jock' Ramsay, a backbench Conservative MP, Eton-educated Scottish aristocrat and heroic war veteran whose patriotism had been eclipsed by his virulent anti-Semitism. United by their hostility to the British war effort, they aimed to change the course of history.

Central to the activities of this eccentric trio was the Right Club, a shadowy organisation set up by Ramsay in May 1939 to spread his anti-Jewish dogma, its goal being to influence the political establishment from the inside. Like all political extremes throughout history, the British far right in the late 1930s was prone to endless splits and schisms, a reflection of their ideological differences as well as of the fanatical, unbalanced nature of their adherents. A myriad of different groups, each with a tiny membership, competed within this narrow orbit. Some were pro-German, like the Anglo-German Fellowship and the Link, founded by the distinguished but deranged ex-Royal Navy commander Sir Barry Domvile. Others were violent, quasi-mystical pro-Nazis, like the Militant Christian Patriots, Victor Rowe's Nordic League, and the White Knights of Britain led by E.H. Cole, among whose wild utterances was a description of Hitler as 'that Man of God across the sea, that great Crusader for whom one would be proud to die'.[13]

There were also, in addition to Mosley's BUF, several other fascist outfits, including William Joyce's National Socialist League, John Beckett's British People's Party and the Imperial Fascist League, founded in 1929 by the veterinary surgeon Arnold Leese, who deeply resented Mosley's fame, sarcastically calling him a 'kosher fascist'.[14] As early as 1936, Leese openly advocated the mass extermination of Jews, an incendiary remark that led to a spell in jail.

Throughout the 1930s, as the clouds of war began to loom, political extremists in Britain were kept under close surveillance by MI5 and the Metropolitan Police. The unit in MI5 that monitored subversion, known as B5b, was headed by the enigmatic former naval officer Captain Maxwell Knight, often said to be the model for 'M' in Ian Fleming's Bond novels. Keen to acquire more inside information, Knight penetrated the Right Club's membership which was heavily tilted towards the aristocracy and London society, with three undercover female agents posing as right-wing zealots. The three were: Marjorie Amor, a middle-aged secretary separated from her husband; Hélène de Munck, a Belgian mystic who shared with Knight an interest in the occult; and Joan Miller, the youngest and most glamorous of the trio.

During the spring of 1940, these three women became trusted lieutenants of the Right Club. It was through their access to Ramsay's inner sanctum that MI5 began to grasp the full scale of the pro-Nazi scheming of Right Club member Anna Wolkoff. A naturalised British subject, she had little allegiance to her adopted country. Her prime political impulse was, as she admitted, her 'inborn hatred of Jews'.[15] During the 1930s she had set up business as a dressmaker and for a time had enjoyed some success, even numbering Wallis Simpson, the Duchess of Windsor, among her clients. But when that enterprise failed, she fell back on her favourite activity of indulging in far right subversion. She regularly boasted that among the friends of her family were the long-serving Director-General of MI5, Major General Sir Vernon Kell, and the Chief of the Imperial General Staff, Edmund Ironside, claims that were to cause lasting damage to both men in the summer of 1940.

What eventually compelled the government to act against her was her friendship with the American embassy clerk Tyler Kent, who had long been plotting against western democracy. A rancorous anti-Semite, he had displayed his treachery in his first diplomatic posting, to Moscow in 1934. One CIA document, written a decade later, stated that he was 'actively engaged in espionage for the Russian Government'.[16] Tellingly, when Kent was transferred from Moscow to London in October 1939, he strongly objected to the move, informing the State Department that he would rather go to Berlin, which he saw as the natural alternative to Moscow. Contrary to the conventional wisdom that Kent trumpeted anti-Communist views, he was quite open about his preference for Russia or Germany over Britain. 'I consider life in the totalitarian state more interesting than in a democracy,' he said in 1939, explaining why he preferred a posting to the Soviet or Reich capitals.[17]

Whatever side Kent was really supporting, it was certainly not the Allies'. At the time of his arrival in London, much of America was in a deeply isolationist mood, desperate to avoid any entanglement in a European conflict. That outlook was shared by the US ambassador Joseph P. Kennedy, a self-made millionaire of Irish stock who had been given the London post by President Roosevelt as a reward for heavily backing the Democrats. However, by 1940 Kennedy's politics had diverged drastically from the president's. Where Roosevelt wanted to give Britain and France as much support as he legally could without breaching US neutrality, Kennedy was antagonistic to the Allies, not least because he regarded their cause as doomed.

The atmosphere of anti-British feeling created by the ambassador was perfectly suited to Kent, who was criminally exploiting his position as a cipher clerk. Since his early days in Moscow, Kent had been in the habit of privately collecting copies of diplomatic correspondence. In London the material to which he had access was even more sensitive, particularly the telegrams between Roosevelt and Churchill that covered not only political developments but also military operations and ship movements.

His plotting took on another dimension when he became embroiled with Anna Wolkoff and the Right Club. His introduction to her circle had arisen through his interest in the Soviet Union and his facility as a Russian speaker. Inevitably, Anna's admiration for Kent soon led to a meeting between him and Captain Ramsay, who was immediately taken with the American's personality and politics. Kent, Ramsay and Wolkoff were now swimming in deadly waters. The Right Club and its associates were shifting from disloyalty to outright treason.

Keen to gather as much hard evidence as he could of Wolkoff's willingness to communicate with Germany, Maxwell Knight decided to set an elaborate trap for her. In early April 1940, he concocted a letter in code to William Joyce, otherwise known as Lord Haw-Haw. Full of defeatist gossip and advice on how to improve Nazi radio propaganda directed at England, this letter purported to come from close friends of Joyce. One piece of advice read: 'Churchill not popular, keep on at him . . . as war-theatre-extender-sacrificer, Gallipoli etc. Stress his conceit and repeated failures with ex-proselites [sic] and prestige.' Another was: 'Butter ration doubled because poor can't buy admitted by Telegraph. Bacon same. Cost of living steeply mounting. Shopkeepers suffering.' Perhaps the most interesting passage was about the CIGS. 'Ironside believed very anti-Jewish, not so anti-German. Possible future British Franco if things reach that stage here,' words that reflected distrust of Ironside within intelligence circles.[18]

Having crafted this convincing fake, Knight passed it to James McGuirk Hughes, a professional double agent who did a lot of freelance work for Special Branch. Following Knight's instructions, on 9 April Hughes introduced himself to Wolkoff at the Russian tea rooms run by her White Russian parents and asked her whether she 'would be prepared to do something that would really help the cause of anti-semitism'.[19] He then handed her the letter addressed to Joyce, telling her that it contained 'some good anti-Jewish stuff'.[20] In her excitement at this development, Wolkoff immediately showed the envelope to her confidante Hélène de Munck in whom she now had complete trust. The deception had worked.

British Intelligence were certain that the coded letter, which Knight sent through his underground network to Berlin, reached Joyce because in his subsequent broadcast to Britain on 27 April he used the word 'Carlyle' in reference to the great Victorian philosopher, which was a coded signal to the conspirators that the letter had arrived.

Even after this cast-iron confirmation of Wolkoff's treachery, Knight refrained from action, believing that he needed more evidence against Ramsay and Kent. By early May the bonds of conspiracy between the two men were becoming tighter, with Kent accepted into full membership of the Right Club. Indeed, so impressed was Ramsay with Kent that, fearing his own London home might be raided by security services, he entrusted him with the club's membership book. In return for this gesture of confidence, Kent showed Ramsay a selection of the documents he had stolen from the embassy, including the Churchill–Roosevelt telegrams. Apart from the thrill of intrigue, Kent's motivation for revealing this material to Ramsay was his desire to spread the word about Roosevelt's supposed breach of neutrality. Kent's theory was that if these telegrams were mentioned in the Commons, the subsequent scandal could drive the president from office.

By the third week of May 1940, the war was going badly for the Allies. French lines were collapsing. Holland was fully occupied by the Germans. The British Expeditionary Force was in near constant retreat. Belgium was on the verge of surrender. Faced with the prospect of Nazi hegemony on the continent, Churchill's correspondence with Roosevelt assumed a more urgent tone. On 15 May, the prime minister set out in stark and detailed terms the support that Britain needed from America. The list included 'several hundred of the latest types of aircraft', large quantities of steel, and 'anti-aircraft equipment and ammunition'. Above all, Churchill wanted the loan 'of 40 or 50 of your older destroyers to bridge the gap between what we have now and the large new construction we put in hand at the beginning of the war'.[21]

As always throughout 1940, Roosevelt had to strike a delicate balance between the requirements of American neutrality and his desire to support the fight against Nazi tyranny. So in his reply of 17 May, all he could offer were warm words and the vague promise to give 'the most favourable consideration' to the sale of steel, planes and other equipment. But he warned Churchill that there was little hope of lending the destroyers, not only because of America's own defence needs but also because 'a step of that kind could not be taken except with the specific authorisation of Congress and I am not certain that it would be wise for that suggestion to be made to Congress at this moment'.[22] Churchill refused to be downcast at this response, telling Roosevelt on 18 May, 'We are determined to persevere to the very end whatever the result of the great battle raging in France may be.'[23]

Both Wolkoff and Ramsay were particularly interested in Churchill's telegram of 15 May about the request for destroyers and military equipment, which they saw as irrefutable evidence that America was being pulled into hidden support for the war. That week Wolkoff was seen dining with the Duke del Monte, the Italian military attaché, at which she passed him some photographed material from Kent. Later that month, British Intelligence intercepts of radio signals from Rome to Berlin indicated that some of the Churchill–Roosevelt telegrams had indeed reached the Italians.

Her conspiracy to exploit Kent's material was further extended to include another Right Club member, Christabel Nicholson, a fanatical pro-Nazi who was a qualified medical doctor and the wife of former naval chief Admiral Wilmot Nicholson. In her outlook, she was an illustration of how unhinged and extreme the Right Club's membership really was. Such was her devotion to Hitler that she had even been invited to the Nuremberg rally of 1938, where she met the Führer. 'A cunning Austrian with beautiful manners,' she later recalled.

Given Ramsay's status as a Member of Parliament and Kent's diplomatic immunity, the question of intervention was a highly sensitive one, but MI5 knew they could not delay any longer. At 3 p.m. on Saturday 18 May, Knight went to see Herschel Johnson, the US embassy's head of intelligence. Johnson was appalled as Knight recounted the details of Kent's subterfuge and his links with Wolkoff and Ramsay. According to Knight's note of their meeting, 'Mr Johnson was profoundly shocked' and told Knight that he 'felt his Government would regard the whole affair as extremely serious'.[24] In response Knight explained that MI5 and the police were planning to arrest Wolkoff on the morning of 20 May, but they wanted to synchronise this step with a raid on Kent's flat, for which they needed the US government's permission.

Johnson promised that he would urgently seek this from Ambassador Kennedy, who, much to the disgust of the British and in keeping with his defeatist image, had taken up residence in Windsor in anticipation of the Luftwaffe's bombing of the capital. It was a reflection of how badly the security of the US embassy had been compromised that Johnson did not dare phone Kennedy directly, fearing that the information might leak and reach Kent. Instead, he drove out to Windsor the next morning to give his report. Embarrassed and outraged by what he heard, Kennedy immediately agreed to the raid and even told Johnson that he was 'prepared to take the responsibility of waiving any diplomatic privilege which Tyler Kent may have'.[25] That night, Sunday 19 May, Johnson told Knight of this decision. At the same time, MI5 obtained authority from the Home Secretary Sir John Anderson to detain Anna Wolkoff under Section 18b of the Defence Regulations. The conspiracy was about to be blown apart.

The next morning, 20 May, a police car drew up outside the Russian tea room in Kensington. Four detectives got out, marched inside, arrested Wolkoff, bundled her into the car and took her to Rochester Row police station. In a fascinating twist of history, the arrest was witnessed by the eleven-year-old Len Deighton, later the author of a host of gripping spy novels, among them SS-GB about life in Britain under Nazi occupation after a successful German invasion. Meanwhile, in nearby Marylebone, a group that included Maxwell Knight, several men from Scotland Yard and a representative of the US embassy, strode into the fashionable mansion block at 47 Gloucester Place and knocked on Tyler Kent's door.

The extent of his plotting was even wider than MI5 had feared. Having searched Kent's flat, Knight was astonished at the wealth of material taken from the US embassy, made up of files, telegrams, photographic negatives and written copies of documents. There was also a set of keys to the US embassy's file room and a 'leather-covered ledger with a brass fastener',[26] which subsequently turned out to be the Right Club's membership book.

Kent disclaimed any knowledge of what was in Ramsay's book, professed ignorance about Wolkoff's disloyalty to Britain, and said he had kept the embassy documents purely for his 'own interest'.[27] The next day, however, his self-confidence was undermined when Washington cancelled his diplomatic immunity and sacked him from the embassy staff. Contrary to his hopes of bringing down the Roosevelt administration and rallying the isolationist cause, he had succeeded only in destroying his own career.

The US government, incensed that Kent had exposed the woeful inadequacy of their own vetting and coding systems, were willing to show no tolerance towards him. Ambassador Kennedy himself told the Home Office that Kent 'ought not to be allowed at liberty for one moment. If it should turn out that you cannot prosecute him here, then we will prosecute him in America.'[28] William Bullitt, by then the US ambassador to France and once Kent's employer in Moscow, went even further, telling a Foreign Office contact, 'I hope you will shoot him and shoot him soon. I mean it.'[29]

The round-up of the plotters continued. On 23 May the police, led by J.W. Pearson, turned up at Captain Ramsay's elegant town house in Onslow Square to arrest him. According to Pearson's account, having been shown the order signed by the Home Secretary, Ramsay launched into a tirade against the 'Jew-ridden and Jew-controlled Government', claiming that 'the war had been engineered by the Jews' and that he was only 'being removed to prison' because he had attacked government policy.[30] Three days later, Dr Christabel Nicholson was taken into custody, after her maid, who had long been concerned about her mistress's fanatically pro-German outlook, went to the police with an envelope containing a pencil copy that Nicholson had made of the Churchill–Roosevelt telegram of 15 May.

Thanks to MI5's coolness and judgement, the conspiracy had been broken. But the implications of the arrests went far beyond the Right Club, for this dark episode served as a catalyst for a much wider apprehension of extremists and aliens. The Tyler Kent case was like a breach in the dam of resistance to tough government action against the enemy within. In the subsequent flood, concerns about traditional civil liberties and peacetime justice were swept away.

A War Cabinet meeting, held at 10.30 a.m. in Downing Street on 22 May, reflected the government's transformed mood. Even Sir John Anderson had been forced to abandon his liberal stance. Having outlined the Right Club plot, he then won the Cabinet's approval for an additional new clause to the Defence Regulations that gave him sweeping new powers to detain without trial any member of an organisation that was 'subject to foreign influence or control' or 'had sympathies with the system of government' of the enemy.[31]

That night, armed with this new authority, Anderson signed orders for the internment of Mosley and thirty-three other leading British Union of Fascists members. The arrests took place early the next morning, with all the fascists hauled off to Brixton prison. The British public was strongly in favour of the move, as recorded by the Ministry of Information: 'The arrest of Mosley and other fascists has overwhelming approval. Our observers report that they seldom found such a high degree of approval for any government action. The most frequent comment is that it should have been done long ago.'[32]

These arrests were just the start. The new climate of firmness resulted in a series of other steps. At the same meeting on 22 May the Cabinet also agreed to introduce new Emergency Powers legislation, which passed through Parliament in a single day. An extension of the 1939 Emergency Powers Act, this measure 'gave the government practically unlimited authority over British citizens and their property', to use the words of A.J.P. Taylor.[33] Houses could be compulsorily seized by the army for defence purposes; men could be directed by the Ministry of Labour into certain industries; machinery and vehicles could be requisitioned.

Just after the Act had been passed by Westminster, Churchill's private secretary John Colville wrote in his diary, 'Yesterday the Government obtained permission from the House to take over fuller powers than any British Government has ever possessed. The purpose is largely that if we are invaded or otherwise in extremis, the rights of individuals and institutions must not be allowed to stand in the way of the country's safety . . . In a totalitarian war, even a democracy must surrender its liberties.'[34]

On 23 May, Parliament passed a new Treachery Act, which widened the definition of treason and enabled the government to proceed against foreigners 'who are not normally resident within the King's jurisdiction', a clause designed to catch non-British plotters like Kent.[35] Furthermore Anderson ordered that all female enemy aliens in Category B should be interned. He also imposed much stricter controls on the aliens in Category C, most of whom were Jewish refugees and had been relatively free until then. One of their number, Klaus Ernst Hinrichsen, who had fled to Britain from Lübeck in 1939, later recalled the experience:

> We had a curfew at night and couldn't have a radio or a bicycle or a camera. We even had to hand in maps of England and we could not travel outside a certain radius. The difficulty was to convince the population that you were harmless. It was almost impossible to speak German in the tube because by

this time some sort of neurosis had developed and every German was a Nazi. Some of the papers, particularly the *Daily Express*, had it in for aliens and really misrepresented the position. We were the enemy in the midst.

Hinrichsen, who lived in Hampstead in north-west London, witnessed one incident that showed the anxious mood in May 1940. 'A family of refugees put out their eiderdowns in the garden to air on warmer days, as was the German habit. Their neighbours were convinced that this was a secret signalling system for the Luftwaffe. Denunciations could be serious, particularly because rumours were difficult to disprove.'[36]

Yet many in the government and the military wanted to go much further and lock up all enemy aliens, no matter what their status. They felt that Anderson, for all his new vigour, was still not being tough enough. The Home Secretary argued that 'the essence of a sound security policy is wise discrimination. A violent policy fitfully administered is not nearly as effective as a more moderate policy firmly and consistently applied.'[37] Such theorising only invoked the anger of others involved in national defence, including Churchill, as the senior intelligence officer Guy Liddell noted in his diary for 25 May: 'It seems that the Prime Minister takes a strong view about the internment of all Fifth Columnists at the moment and has left the Home Secretary in no doubt about his views. What seems to have moved him more than anything was the Tyler Kent case.'[38] Liddell himself was just as frustrated with the Home Secretary: 'The liberty of the subject, freedom of speech etc were all very well in peacetime but they were of no use fighting the Nazis. There seemed to be a complete failure to realize the power of the totalitarian state and the energy with which the Germans were fighting a total war.'[39]

The Chiefs of Staff, led by the head of the RAF Sir Cyril Newall, took the same robust line. In a paper of 25 May entitled 'British Strategy in a Certain Eventuality', the certain eventuality being the defeat of France and a German attack on Britain, the chiefs recommended that 'the most ruthless action should be taken to eliminate any chance of Fifth Column activities'. This should encompass the 'internment of all enemy aliens and all members of subversive organisations, which latter should be proscribed'. According to their paper, 'if we are to survive total war, it is essential to organise the country as a fortress on totalitarian lines.'[40]

The Cabinet was unable to settle the dispute between the chiefs and the Home Secretary, so, in an attempt to break the deadlock and strengthen the official machinery against subversion, Neville Chamberlain, now Lord President of the Council, established a new body, headed by Lord Swinton and called the Home Defence Security Executive, to deal with the problems of aliens and fifth columnists. Swinton already had a

number of formidable achievements to his name, most notably the introduction of the Spitfire and Hurricane fighters into RAF service when
he was the pre-war Secretary of State for Air. Now his executive got to
work with alacrity.

At its first meeting on 28 May, it agreed to recommend the internment
of another 345 British Union of Fascist members, as well as the closure of
Mosley's newspaper *Action*. In the same urgent spirit, the executive introduced stricter landing controls at British ports, required every British seaman
to carry an identity card, imposed censorship of mail from Ireland and
ordered the shutdown of the Communist paper the *Daily Worker*, believing
it had been fomenting discontent and spreading defeatist propaganda.

Swinton also met Ernest Bevin, the Minister of Labour, to discuss possible
fifth column subversion in the munitions factories. According to a report
sent to the prime minister, 'Mr Bevin has at once set about using the
machinery of the trade unions and the shop stewards to watch and report
on the activities of suspected persons. The trade union movement has agreed
to this action generally, having already started something of the kind in
several factories working for the Ministry of Supply.'[41] On the vexed
question of enemy aliens, the executive quickly took several steps, such as
raising the age limit for internment from sixty to seventy, and ordering
the removal of aliens from all vulnerable areas with vital factories.

For the Right Club plotters, the war was over. Kent and Wolkoff were
tried at the Old Bailey in October 1940 on charges of violating the Official
Secrets Act and assisting the enemy. Both were found guilty. Kent was
given a sentence of seven years, but was released at the end of the war and
deported back to America. Anna Wolkoff, sentenced to nine years, was
released in 1947.

Captain Ramsay was never tried, but instead was held under the
Section 18b of the Defence Regulations until September 1944. He officially remained an MP throughout his incarceration and even managed
to put down some Parliamentary questions from his cell before returning
to the Commons after his release, although he did not defend his seat
in the 1945 General Election. Utterly unrepentant and more anti-Semitic
than ever, in 1952 he published a characteristically irrational book titled
The Nameless War, which not only attempted to justify his actions but
also explain that the Jewish goal of world domination was a central
thread of mankind's history. According to Ramsay, even that staunch
Puritan, Oliver Cromwell, turned out to be a 'paid agent of the Jews'.[42]

4

'Facing up to the possibility of invasion'

—◆—

THE FURTHER THE Germans advanced through northern France towards the Channel coast, the deeper grew concerns in England about the prospects of invasion.

In one of its summaries towards the end of the month, the Joint Intelligence Committee noted that 'press and broadcasting reports from 25 to 29 May, inspired by German sources, stressed the employment of fast MTBs [motor torpedo boats] for the invasion of the Thames estuary, Straits of Dover and the Channel', while the same document explained that a Zeppelin airship 'left on night of May 24th for north Germany. Rumoured it is to be used for landing troops in England.'[1] On 28 May, Neville Chamberlain, the Lord President of the Council, gave an ominous warning to the War Cabinet that 'there had been reports of troop movements from east to west in southern Norway', which could indicate that 'the Germans might perhaps be intending a raid on Scotland.'[2] So frequent were the reports about possible German operations that at the end of May the government decided to set up an 'Invasion Warning Sub-Committee' to filter the intelligence.

Much of this information, particularly the allegations about fifth column-ists, was unsubstantiated, merely reflecting the climate of anxiety that had descended on Britain. As General Edmund Ironside himself wrote later in the summer, 'It is extraordinary how we get circumstantial reports of a 5th Column and yet we have never been able to get anything worth having. One is persuaded that it hardly exists.'[3] Indeed, for all the discussion about the German threat, throughout May many of the military chiefs remained sceptical about invasion, none more so than Sir Walter Kirke, the commander-in-chief of Home Forces, who was still strongly of the view that the most effective way to protect Britain from Germany was by supporting the BEF in France.

Interestingly Winston Churchill, who is usually portrayed as the arch-Francophile, was uneasy about this policy. His belief in the need to bolster the Home Forces was reflected in his hesitations about sending the whole 1st Armoured Division to France, complete with 135 light tanks and 160 cruiser tanks, as he told Ismay on 18 May: 'I cannot feel that we have enough trustworthy troops in England, in view of the very large numbers that may be landed from air[craft] carriers preceded by parachutists . . . The Chiefs of Staff might consider whether it would not be well to send only half of the so-called armoured division to France. One must always be prepared for the fact that the French may be offered very advantageous terms of peace, and the whole weight be thrown on us.'[4]

But the Chiefs of Staff were insistent that the whole of the brigade should go, for its arrival in France 'may have results of the utmost importance' for the immediate outcome of the war on the western front.[5] The continuing dispatch of men and equipment was a severe drain on British Home Forces, especially as the LDV at this stage was still effectively unarmed. By the third week of May there were just fourteen divisions available for the Julius Caesar plan, and most of them had received only the most basic training. Moreover they were poorly equipped. Each division had only between twelve and eighteen field guns, when they should have had seventy-two, while across the entire fourteen divisions there were only thirty-three two-pounder anti-tank guns.

Churchill's determination to galvanise the Chiefs of Staff into greater preparedness on the home front resulted in his instruction to embark on a study 'of possible German methods in an attack on this country. The technique employed in Norway had differed from that employed in Holland and there was no doubt that the Germans would attempt to spring new surprises. It would be advisable therefore to study all reports which had been received, however fantastic, so that we could adapt our defences to meet any method which the enemy might employ.'[6] It was in response to Churchill's prodding that on 25 May the Chiefs of Staff produced their candid, rather gloomy paper entitled 'British Strategy in a Certain Eventuality', setting out 'the means whereby we would continue to fight single-handed if French resistance were to collapse completely'. The paper argued that three factors were crucial to Britain's survival in these circumstances: 'the capacity to resist invasion'; the continuation of food and material supplies; and the ability of the public 'to withstand the strain of aerial bombardment'.

Much would depend on the success of fighter and anti-aircraft defences in dealing with the Luftwaffe's bombers. Should the Germans obtain 'a high degree of air superiority', then 'this would enormously increase our difficulties in maintaining the normal life of the country and in meeting invasion.' Nor were the chiefs confident that the navy could protect Britain against the mighty German war machine. 'Whether we shall be able to maintain effective naval forces in bases on the east and south coasts in the face of very heavy scale air attack is uncertain; if we cannot do so, the chance of intercepting enemy forces before they reach our shores will clearly be less.'

There was even greater pessimism about the Home Forces. 'Germany would have ample troops (70 divisions or more) for the invasion of this country even after providing for the occupation of conquered territory,' the paper stated. 'Should the Germans succeed in establishing a force with its vehicles in this country, our army forces have not got the offensive power to drive it out.' Civil defence was seen as another serious weakness. 'As long as the present quasi-peacetime organisation continues there is no guarantee that this country could hold out. The present Home Security Organisation was constituted to deal with air attack only and the volume of such attack was estimated on the basis that the enemy aircraft would be operating from Germany.'[7]

After a lengthy discussion, this paper was accepted by the War Cabinet on 27 May, although Churchill felt that the Chiefs of Staff were being unduly negative about the forthcoming air battle and expressed his doubts about their claim that the Luftwaffe had four times as many operational planes as the RAF.

Given the military disasters in France and the disturbing intelligence reports, the idea of a German assault could not be dismissed as mere fantasy. Nor could the position of figures like General Kirke, with his focus largely on propping up the BEF, be maintained in the face of the domestic threat. Home defences had to be strengthened, coastal areas fortified. The recognition of the challenge meant that a change was needed in the leadership of the Home Forces. Kirke was seen as too old and intractable to remain in charge, especially given his powerful scepticism about the likelihood of invasion and his fierce opposition to a defensive mentality.

The first candidate that Churchill considered as Kirke's successor was Lord Trenchard, the founder of the RAF and former Commissioner of the Metropolitan Police. But Trenchard, always something of an autocrat, quickly fell from favour after setting extravagant conditions on his acceptance. 'He demanded enormous powers which would have rendered him virtually independent of my and the Cabinet's authority,' wrote Churchill later.[8] After this explosive clash, Churchill's thoughts turned to General Ironside, whose perceived qualities of resolution and charisma had made him Britain's most famous soldier in the run-up to war. Ironside perfectly fulfilled the public's image of what a military hero should be like, with his distinguished record, bristling moustache and solid build. Indeed, thanks to his height, he was given the ironic nickname of 'Tiny' within the army. From September 1939, he had been the Chief of the Imperial General Staff, a role for which Churchill had thought him ideally equipped because of his experience and fine military brain, but he turned out to be a severe disappointment: often indiscreet and seized by bouts of glum introspection. His judgement proved as poor as his administration. His dwindling reputation was noted by Liddell Hart in his diary for 7 May: 'The younger members of the other service staffs who see him at committees describe him as gaga.'[9] Ironside's standing as CIGS was further diminished by the failed campaigns in Norway and France, while there were also whispers about alleged links with right-wing extremism, mainly because of his friendship with the military strategist and British Union of Fascists member Major General John 'Boney' Fuller.

By the last week in May the pressure on Ironside had become intense, and he was desperate for a move back to a command. Knowing that Kirke was finished, he told Churchill that he was willing to resign as CIGS and take charge of Home Forces, a proposal that immediately appealed to Churchill, as he later wrote: 'Considering the unpromising task that such a command was at the time thought to involve, this was indeed a spirited and selfless offer.'[10]

It might seem strange that the prime minister was keen to give the general such a vital post, in view of his failure on the general staff, but there were three powerful arguments for the move. First, it allowed Ironside's highly regarded deputy, the hard-headed, less moody Ulsterman Sir John Dill, to be promoted to CIGS, which was generally welcomed. Second, Ironside, like Kitchener in 1914, was a familiar face to the public and therefore could provide a boost to morale at a time of crisis. Third, Ironside was deeply engaged by the subject of home defence and, indeed, was already head of the Home Defence Executive, set up on 10 May.

Elevated to the rank of field marshal and given greater powers than Kirke as Home Forces commander, Ironside believed that he would be helped in his role by the new national mood of urgency. 'Kirke was very sorry to go, poor chap. He has done a lot, but has been hampered by people not taking the defence of England seriously. Now they do, which will make it much easier for me.' He also felt home defence fitted his talents better than the general staff. 'I must confess that it is much more my line than the other. I am now in command and not hampered by a machine that was made for peace conditions and was not fit to function in war.'[11]

Ironside moved with his staff officers into the headquarters of Home Forces at Kneller Hall in Twickenham, a mock-Elizabethan building that had formerly been used as the Royal Military School of Music. His arrival led to an immediate galvanisation in home defence precautions. Given the limited size of his forces and their lack of equipment, particularly in tanks and guns, he urged the creation of a network of internal fortifications against the invader. Under his influence, the War Office embarked on a large-scale programme of works that transformed the landscape of Britain in 1940, as huge swathes of the country were studded with pillboxes, road-blocks, machine-gun nests, trenches, barricades, coastal batteries and tank traps. Fields were strewn with obstacles to prevent airborne landings; beaches were decked with barbed wire and scaffolding to ward off approaches from the sea. The detailed layout of these barriers continued to evolve over a number of weeks in June and July, developing into what became known as 'the Ironside plan' to replace the outdated 'Julius Caesar plan'. Work on the installations, however, started immediately.

Pillbox construction was at the centre of this drive. Almost as much as the Home Guard, these concrete shelters, designed to protect defensive troops from enemy fire, became symbols of Britain's defiance in the summer of 1940, which was ironic, given that the pillbox was essentially a German idea first used on the western front in 1917. The War Office instructed Major General G.B.O. Taylor to oversee the design and building of hardened defences across Britain. Capturing the new spirit of urgency, Taylor's directorate quickly came up with a series of seven basic pillbox designs – ranging from Type 22 to Type 28 – of varying strength, shape and purpose.

By far the most common was the Type 24, capable of accommodating eight men. Its walls formed an irregular hexagon, each with an embrasure, or opening, for a Bren gun, one of the British army's standard light machine guns used throughout the war. It also had a rifle loop on either side of its door, and an interior, centrally placed, Y-shaped wall to prevent bullets ricocheting. Two main variants were built: one to a bullet-proof standard with walls at least 12 inches thick; the other with walls at least 36 inches thick to withstand shells.

The second most common pillbox was the slightly smaller Type 22, which could accommodate six men and whose shape was a regular hexagon. There was also the rectangular Type 23, the circular Type 25 and the square Type 26. Much larger and less common were the last two variants. The Type 27 was octagonal in shape, could accommodate ten men, and had an open well in the centre so it could be used for anti-aircraft defence. The Type 28, the biggest of them all, was almost 400 feet square, with walls at least 42 inches thick and was designed to take two-pounder or six-pounder anti-tank guns, which could be wheeled through its large rear entrance.

Apart from these standard pillboxes, there was a huge range of other fortifications, many of them unique to their locations or developed outside the remit of the War Office, reflecting the drive for improvisation so prevalent in 1940. There were lozenge-shaped pillboxes built into the seawalls of Essex, cantilevered pillboxes constructed around airfields, D-shaped structures erected only in Northumberland, and three-bay oblong boxes built solely in Lincolnshire. Some of the emplacements made imaginative use of existing structures. In Salisbury, for instance, rifle loops were installed in the medieval city walls. At Minismere in Suffolk, a well-hidden pillbox was established in the ruins of a medieval chapter house, while the harbour-master's office at Caernarvon had two snipers' lookouts built into its roof. One of the more eccentric designs was the 'Alan Williams turret', named after its inventor, the managing director of a company manufacturing metal windows. The turret, whose steel dome, mounted on rollers, could be rotated through 360 degrees, was large enough for two men armed with rifles or light machine guns.

Equally ingenious but of limited practicality was the Pickett-Hamilton 'disappearing pillbox', a cylindrical concrete structure used for the defence of airfields. Designed by the Kent engineer Francis Pickett and the London architect Donald Hamilton, the device could be lowered into the ground when aircraft were operating so that its top was flush with the runway. But if needed for action against the enemy, it could be raised 2 feet 6 inches above the surface, allowing its two-man crew to fire from any of its three loopholes. Eventually 335 Pickett-Hamilton forts were built, partly on the insistence of Winston Churchill, who, having seen a demonstration of one, wrote to Ismay on 12 June, 'What is being done to reproduce and install small circular pillboxes which can be sunk in the centre of aerodromes and rise by means of a compressed air bottle to two- or three-feet elevation, like a small turret commanding the aerodrome?'[12] Unfortunately, the Pickett-Hamilton forts turned out to be unreliable, prone to flooding and unable to bear the weight of RAF heavy bombers rumbling over them.

One further unorthodox structure used at airfields was the Bison armoured lorry, effectively a concrete pillbox on wheels. The Bison was the brainchild of Charles Matthews, the director of the Leeds-based company Concrete Limited, who was prompted by the army's shortage of tanks and armoured vehicles to take a number of old lorry chassis and build on them fighting compartments complete with walls 6 inches thick and gun loopholes. Given its weight, the vehicle could only lumber from one spot to another, but the Air Ministry was sufficiently impressed to order around 300 of them.

The standard War Office pillboxes were generally straightforward to construct, an essential factor in the anxious days of 1940. They were built either by the Royal Engineers or by private contractors, both contingents showing tremendous dedication to the task, often working seven days a week during late May and June. The total number of pillboxes built during the war, most of which went up in 1940, is estimated to have been around 18,000. On one 50-mile stretch alone of the east coast, 200 were constructed in just three weeks by a single contractor. By the end of June, so much cement had been used that there was a national shortage and the War Office told contractors to reduce the quality of concrete by replacing some of the cement with sand. In typical wartime spirit, a large variety of scrap metals were used in makeshift reinforcement for the concrete, including park railings and bedsprings. The pillboxes were usually sited at important defensive locations surveyed and chosen by the War Office, such as bridges, harbours, road junctions, and entry points into towns and villages.

Because their effectiveness was thought to depend on their remaining hidden until the enemy came into range, many pillboxes were cleverly concealed, either through blending into the local scenery or through being disguised as another type of building, particularly in urban areas. In some cases camouflage screens were used, made from wire netting that was sprayed with paint and covered with chicken feathers, although alternative materials were sometimes tried: at Taunton, six pillboxes were coated with cow manure and then topped with straw to provide a suitably rustic cover. Elsewhere, the concrete structure itself might be painted in camouflage patterns to blend into the countryside.

Pillboxes were also disguised as public lavatories, petrol stations, bus shelters, harbour cranes, roadside cafés, sports pavilions and municipal huts. At the seafront in Margate, an apparent W.H. Smith bookstall hid a pillbox within, while in Bournemouth an attractive summerhouse, complete with painted windows and a pyramidal roof, was so well built that even local visitors to the beach did not realise its true nature. Some of the structures were more extravagant. At the entrance to the stately home of Dillington Park in Somerset, the designer Oliver Messel used imitation stone from Elstree Film Studios to build a castellated pillbox that was an exact replica of the estate's gate lodge. The camouflaged structures could also serve as an outlet for humour. One pillbox in Woodbridge, Suffolk, was emblazoned with the advertising slogan, 'Hotel Continental: Warm Reception for Visiting Troops'. Another in Eastbourne, which was put up by a local firm called Martin and disguised with a canvas screen to resemble part of an old Roman wall, had a fake ancient plaque with an inscription that proclaimed the builder to be 'Martinus Maximus'.[13]

Apart from pillboxes, a host of additional fixed defences were installed from May 1940. Ironside's command regarded anti-tank obstacles and roadblocks as vital to the task of halting or delaying the enemy's advance. There was an air of desperation about some of the early barricades: in Margate, old bathing carts and beach chairs were filled with sand and pushed into defensive positions; at Newing Green in Bromley, roadblocks were fashioned out of an iron steam boiler, a water tank, a refuse truck and a wreck of a car. One slightly less primitive form of anti-tank obstruction was a simple V-shaped ditch, which the War Office stipulated should be at least 12 feet wide and 5 feet 6 inches deep, with a sloping bank at the front of the same height. In practice, this meant an advancing German tank, going up the ramp and then falling into the ditch, would face a drop of 11 feet.

Other more sophisticated anti-tank barriers were also developed, many of them using solid concrete blocks that could be cylindrical, pyramidal, or conical in shape, 4 or 5 feet high. Thousands were often installed in long lines, sometimes several rows deep, at vulnerable points near beaches or further inland.

Concrete blocks were widely used on roads with the aim of halting enemy traffic or funnelling it into narrow passageways overseen by checkpoints or pillboxes. The obvious problem with such heavy, semi-permanent barriers, however, was that they also inhibited the movement of Home Forces traffic. So the War Office developed removable obstacles that could be pushed into position in the event of an invasion. One of most widely used types consisted of two massive concrete buttresses, placed either side of a road, with holes or slots made in their walls. In an emergency, girders, railway lines or thick steel cables could be inserted within a few minutes into these openings, making it impossible for tanks to force their way through. Similar buttresses were also placed beside the tracks of railway lines.

Two types of removable metal barriers were developed on similar principles. One, known as 'hedgehogs', comprised simple vertical lengths of railway line or rolled steel joints (RSJs). The other, called 'hairpins', was made of railway lines or RSJs bent at an angle of 60 degrees with the point facing upwards. Both were plugged into concrete sockets created in the roads. When the hedgehogs or hairpins were not in use, the sockets were covered with lids or filled in with wooden caps.

Reginald Titt, a member of the Salisbury Local Defence Volunteers, later recalled that two or three men from his unit could block a road 'in about half a minute' with movable barriers made from angled pieces of railway line or heavy steel girders. 'We had little prospect of holding the attackers off for long, but if they could be delayed significantly at every block, the cumulative effect of the delays was expected to allow mobile Army units to get to the scene. In effect, we were trained and equipped to fight and almost certainly lose a nasty little battle that might last half an hour.'[14]

In order to strengthen the defensive impact of roadblocks, army commanders planned in some places to install anti-tank mines in the sockets rather than just metal segments. Although there was a severe shortage of such mines in the early summer of 1940, demand ensured that production of them was rapidly increased to 80,000 in June. To halt the passage of German motorcyclists, the War Office recommended a 'single strand of heavy fencing wire or light steel wire rope stretched between trees or houses at a height of three feet six inches above the road level'.[15]

Other steps were taken to prevent enemy movement. In many parts of the country, road and rail bridges that gave direct access to ports were prepared for demolition, with military guards being increased at these sites to prevent sabotage. The Ministry of Transport also drew up a detailed scheme to shut down the rail links to the coast in the event of a German attack, not only by blocking trunk lines and tunnels but also by immobilising locomotives, destroying exits from the ports, cutting off power supplies at marshalling yards and removing breakdown cranes.

The aim of all the plans for pillboxes, roadblocks, bridge demolition and train immobilisation was to tackle the ground advance of the enemy, but the government recognised that it was just as vital to stop the invader from landing either by sea or by air. Much of the fortification programme, therefore, had to be focused on beach defences, an approach opposed by Sir Walter Kirke, who felt that such efforts were a waste of time and that the War Office should concentrate on training and strengthening the army.

Meeting on 25 May, Ironside's Home Defence Executive argued that 'in the present circumstances, the possibility of an attempt at invasion on the whole of the east and the south coasts from the Shetlands to Swanage cannot be ruled out. The area of greatest danger of invasion proper is between the Tyne and Flamborough, and between the Wash and Newhaven.'[16] So from late May, large gangs of labourers and men from the Royal Engineers began to install pillboxes, gun emplacements, mines, barbed-wire fencing, anti-tank blocks and metal obstructions around the most vulnerable beaches.

As the concern about invasion mounted, so did the demand for barbed wire. In May alone, 251,000 coils of what was known as Dannert concertina wire (named after its German inventor) and 100 tons of ordinary British wire were issued for beach defences, figures that rose in June to 291,000 Dannert coils and no fewer than 2,000 tons of British wire.

However impressive these figures might seem, barbed wire on the beaches would not stop German invasion vessels reaching the shore, so the government ordered that sections of scaffolding be installed along 300 miles of the coastline. By far the most widely used of this type of structure was Admiralty scaffolding, also called Obstacle Z1, which was a frame made up of steel tubes, reaching around 20 feet in height. Each section was pre-assembled on land, then taken by labourers or servicemen to be fixed in the sea at the half-tide mark and fitted with explosive booby-traps.

The government had considerable faith in these scaffolding defences, but that confidence was badly misplaced, as a later official experiment demonstrated. At the port of Felixstowe on 15 December 1940, in the presence of a group of senior military and naval officers observing from the shoreline, a self-propelled barge was sent into a line of Admiralty scaffolding. To the dismay of the service representatives, the vessel just smashed its way right through the obstacle and was soon aground. Not a single booby-trap went off.

Fortunately, there were other forms of obstruction around the coast from May 1940. In an attempt to prevent German craft from entering the ports of Dover, Plymouth, Harwich and Rosyth, or penetrating into the Thames or the Humber, heavy anti-boat booms were installed at these sites. Similarly, just outside many open beaches, specially commissioned naval vessels put in place more than 100 miles of a lighter form of boom, consisting of horizontal wire nets supported by floating tubes of canvas filled with kapok, a natural fibre from the tropics with a buoyancy even greater than that of cork. On some shorelines, heavy concrete slabs with metal stakes were embedded in the sand below the water's edge at low tide, with the aim of ripping through the hulls of any enemy barge that tried to run aground. Another 80 miles of coast was protected by mines attached to wire jackstays, with the crucial area of the Wash in East Anglia guarded by a light boom 5 miles long as well as a defensive minefield.

More complex was the creation of a long chain of gun emplacements all the way from Scotland to the south coast, a task that might have taken several years in peacetime but, with the invasion threat looming, was completed in a matter of weeks. The Emergency Battery Programme was started in May, when the Royal Navy offered 150 6-inch guns that had been taken from its old First World War cruisers and kept in naval arsenals. Once renovated, these guns were placed in pairs in a network of coastal batteries, each of which consisted of two solid gunhouses set into a concrete-lined pit and covered by camouflage netting. Every battery site was equipped with searchlights, generators, ammunition stores, garages, workshops, guardrooms and accommodation large enough to house a crew of at least sixty men, half of whom were gunners.

As with most vulnerable points in the summer of 1940, the sites were protected by rings of barbed wire, trenches and pillboxes, while the permanent buildings also had loopholes for rifles. Despite their substantial size, their construction was carried out with remarkable speed by contractors, the Royal Navy and the Royal Engineers. By 12 June, no fewer than forty-six of them had been completed in locations stretching from Sullom Voe in Shetland to Worthing in Sussex. It is interesting that two-thirds of these were sited north of the Thames, reflecting the fact that, in the early summer of 1940, the military planners considered the east coast to be more vulnerable to the German invasion threat than the south.

Over the next few months the number of heavy coastal batteries doubled, as more guns became available and defences were strengthened. Additionally, in an echo of the Bison pillboxes for the aerodromes, around fifty ex-naval 4-inch guns were mounted on the backs of commercial lorries to provide mobile batteries around the coast.

The Royal Navy's Emergency Programme was largely aimed at protecting the beaches, but just as crucial was the defence of the ports and fleet bases. Heavy gun emplacements were also built at these sites, usually in the form of six-pounder twin batteries, based in revolving turrets, or close-defence (CD) 6-inch batteries or counter-bombardment (CB) 9.2-inch batteries, although some of the guns were even larger. A dozen mighty rail-mounted 12-inch and three 13.5-inch howitzers of First World War vintage were released from stores, reconditioned in railway works at Derby, and then taken to some of the most vital ports. On the personal instructions of the prime minister, the batteries at Dover were fortified by two immense, 14-inch-calibre guns, given the nicknames Winnie and Pooh. Despite their impressive size and range of over 20 miles, enough to reach the continent, they were more effective as morale boosters than deadly weapons, being inaccurate with a slow rate of fire. However, though little used, Winnie had the distinction in August 1940 of becoming the first British gun of the war to land a shell on the soil of occupied Europe.

As a last resort in the event of an emergency, the government made plans to immobilise several of the key ports in the event of a seaborne German force reaching Britain. The country's willingness to consider drastic self-destruction, in order to thwart the enemy, was further highlighted by the War Office's bold plan in May 1940 to flood a large part of Romney Marsh, the vast wetland area straddling more than 100 square miles of southern Kent and Sussex, by deliberately demolishing the dykes along the Royal Military Canal and letting in the sea water if the Germans invaded.

Throughout the summer of 1940, the threat from the air was perceived to be just as great as that from the sea. The fear was not only of German parachutists landing, but also of enemy transport aircraft coming down on British soil, either at aerodromes or, worse still, in the open countryside, or that the Germans would use gliders, as they had done in Belgium. The vital task, therefore, was to deter such landings by the use of obstructions, no matter how primitive or makeshift.

This prompted a nationwide drive to prevent the Luftwaffe from using fields and green spaces as improvised airstrips, since military experts believed that any hostile troop-carrying aircraft required a runway of no more than 300 yards to make a safe landing. Advice from the War Office to local authorities included lists of a wide variety of materials that could be used as obstacles, such as 'lines of felled trees', 'concrete blocks in lines', 'low rough stone walling', 'fencing of various types, as long as it is strong and firmly fixed', and 'ditches dug criss-cross at 200 yard intervals. These should be at least four feet wide and three-and-a-half feet deep. They need not be continuous provided that the spoil from the ditches is heaped in the gaps to form embankments. Certain types of excavator machine can produce a good ditch of this sort very quickly.'[17] The digging of defensive ditches in open spaces was exploited by Goebbels' propaganda machine, which feverishly claimed that 'a revolt against plutocratic cricketers' had taken place. 'The people tried to destroy the playing grounds at night and this led to a state of war between the population and the English sports clubs.'[18]

As usual in the summer of 1940, the mood of improvisation flourished. A traveller, passing through Kent, recorded that in a single field he saw obstacles in the form of a car, a hayrick, a harrow, an old kitchen range and a bedstead. One ingenious idea, used by Southern Command, was to plough grassland so that it appeared from above to be intersected with stone walls. The headquarters of Southern Command in Salisbury, in a circular to district units, explained: 'It was found that a ridge of three furrows up and three furrows back in the opposite direction gave a very satisfactory imitation of a stone wall when seen from the air. The shallow top soil in this area exposes the stone underneath. It is an easy and cheap expedient and within the scope of any farmer to carry out without difficulty.'[19]

Priority in the installation of anti-landing obstacles was given to the London Metropolitan region or any area within a 5-mile radius of an aerodrome or a major port along the eastern and southern coasts. However, so great was the task that at the height of the summer of 1940 many open spaces remained untouched.

The government's concern over aerial landings extended to the possible use of main roads by the enemy, but again a balance had to be struck between inhibiting the invader and allowing the free movement of domestic traffic. This requirement gave rise to the extraordinary sight that summer of huge metal hoops 20 feet high arching over some trunk roads in parts of southern England, as well as concrete columns, steel scaffolding poles and upright girders standing by roadsides. The Ministry of Transport, which was responsible for the road network, advised on 25 May how other obstructions could be used, both on the ground and overhead.

> The placing of obstacles down the straight lengths of road (80 yards long or over) to prevent the landing of aircraft should be undertaken as soon as practicable. Angle iron pickets driven into the crown of the road to divide it into up and down traffic are better than nothing but one of the heavier types of obstacle is required to be really effective. Heavy fencing wire or steel wire stretched from telegraph posts to other posts on the other side of the road at sufficient height to clear all normal road traffic will also serve to deter traffic from landing on the roads.[20]

Aircraft landings by water were another threat that the British authorities had to consider, for Germany had an impressive record in maritime aviation. Faced with the potential menace of seaplanes, particularly troop-carrying flying boats, the War Office urged local commands to establish water-bound obstacles in lakes, reservoirs, stretches of river or estuaries. Owing to the shortage of steel and timber, suggested materials included sleepers, logs, boats, barges, rafts or fencing stretched between stout posts with wire concertinas on top – or even ropes slung between piles.

As the fortifications increased from late May, so the appearance of England gradually began to change. Precautions against invasion became part of everyday existence. Sandbags could be seen throughout cities and towns. Barrage balloons hovered overhead. Pillar boxes carried a square of yellow paint that would change colour if gas was detected in the vicinity.

One highly visible consequence of the new mood of defensive alertness was the government's decision, taken at the end of May, to remove as many public markers as possible that might provide geographical information to the enemy. Signposts were taken down and milestones uprooted. Place names were erased from shopfronts, advertising hoardings, delivery vans, public buildings and church notices. Neither buses nor trains were permitted to carry destination boards or even route numbers. Within a matter of weeks, more than 30,000 village and road signs put up by the Automobile Association over the previous decades had disappeared.

For E.J. Rudsdale, a curator at the Colchester Museum in Essex, the action was not only panicky but pointless, as he recorded in his journal on 31 May: 'There is a great scare now – we are going to be invaded by Germans, landing by parachutes, so in order to confuse them every place-name in Britain is to be obliterated. I can see that this would have some value in rural districts but I really cannot believe that it is possible for the Germans to reach Colchester without knowing where they were. It doesn't seem to occur to anybody that the Germans have maps. Corporation men were running around tonight taking down all the signposts or boards with the name "Colchester" on them.'[21] Rudsdale's scepticism may have been justified, for even after this clearout there were still plenty of fixtures that could reveal a location, such as manhole covers embossed with the name of the local authority, or postcards on sale in local shops, or engravings on tombstones.

The impact of the invasion threat was felt by citizens in several other ways. Motorists were required by the Ministry of Home Security to immobilise their vehicles when they left them unattended, either by the removal of the distributor arm or by the attachment of a locking device to the steering wheel or one of the tyres. Car owners who failed to do so found that the police not only deflated their tyres but also mounted vigorous prosecutions, with fines of up to £50.

On 28 May, the government gave instructions under the Emergency Powers Act, banning all wireless sets from private cars. Radios had to be removed and surrendered to the police. With the danger of Luftwaffe aerial attacks ever present, householders were told to keep buckets of sand and stirrup pumps at the ready to deal with fires caused by German bombing. The blackout was more rigorously enforced than ever, with fines of up to £1 for any breaches, a big sum when the average weekly wage for an agricultural labourer was only £2 10s (£2.50). Since the start of the war, 38 million gas masks had been distributed and regular demonstrations were given in how to use them.

The government also encouraged families to install Anderson shelters in their gardens for protection against air raids. First devised in 1938 and named after Sir John Anderson, the politician who oversaw their introduction, these basic but highly practical shelters were huts made of corrugated, galvanised steel, with six curved panels for the roof and three straight sheets for either side. Having been bolted together by its owner, the hut was buried in the ground to a depth of about 4 feet, and its top covered with 18 inches of soil, in which flowers, plants and vegetables often began to grow. Able to accommodate up to six people, the Anderson shelters proved remarkably resilient in action since their structure was more shock absorbent than some types of concrete. But they were also claustrophobic and damp, a problem made worse by the widespread habit of draping a sheet of sackcloth across the doorway in the belief that it would lessen the effects of poison gas. Despite this drawback, the Andersons were an essential part of life on the domestic front in 1940. More than 3.5 million were issued to homes during the first two years of the war, lower-income households receiving them free, the more affluent paying £7.

All these home defence measures, from the roadblocks to the Andersons, reflected the national mood of defiance as German forces moved closer to the Channel. As the Ministry of Information's daily opinion survey reported on 30 May, 'Many more people are facing up to the possibility of invasion and many . . . speak of it as certain.' Nevertheless, the ministry found that 'morale remains good. There is no defeatism and a general confidence in ultimate victory.'[22] This was the determined outlook that Churchill and his supporters wanted to foster throughout the government. On 25 May, Sir Alexander Cadogan, the permanent under-secretary at the Foreign Office, sent a powerful message to his fellow officials warning against any defeatism. 'It is as unpatriotic to be pessimistic as it is to be optimistic. Both attitudes weaken and paralyse efforts. We may in our own minds face very unpleasant truths and possibilities, but we have no right to let our friends or acquaintances assume from a chance word or an attitude of depression the anxiety we may feel.'[23]

Yet at the very moment that Cadogan wrote this, the spirit of defeatism was lurking in the heart of the Cabinet, fomented by his own chief, Lord Halifax. Posing as the champion of hard-headed realism in the face of indulgent romanticism, Halifax was to force Churchill into a titanic political struggle whose outcome would decide whether or not Britain continued the fight against the Reich.

5

'Bring England to its knees'

———

IN THEIR URGENT preparations against invasion during the last weeks of May 1940, the British military and civil authorities laboured under a profound delusion. At this time, the Germans had no detailed plans whatsoever to invade England. When the Chiefs of Staff warned on 28 May that 'an attack is imminent' they were mistaken.[1] All the energies of the Wehrmacht were concentrated on the defeat of France and the Low Countries. Operations across the Channel by sea or air had never come under serious consideration before the western offensive was launched on 10 May.

The lack of any comprehensive German strategy for invasion reflected Hitler's own ambivalence towards England, which oscillated between hatred and admiration. On one hand he saw Britain as potentially the biggest obstacle to his dreams of European domination. On the other, he cherished a deep respect for Britain's achievements, especially in building her empire and defeating her continental enemies, and was inclined to see the British establishment, including the class system, Oxbridge and the elite public schools, as a bulwark against Bolshevism. On one occasion, the German army's chief of staff General Franz Halder entered the Führer's office to find him happily leafing through a copy of the *Illustrated London News*. Hitler looked up from the magazine and said, 'That we have to make war against such personages, isn't it a pity?'[2] Mixed with this high regard for Britain's record was his belief, so characteristic of his racially fixated ideology, that the Anglo-Saxon people were essentially of the same ethnic stock as the Germans.

Apart from his contradictory attitudes towards British nationhood, there were two more practical factors that had prevented him developing any invasion plan during the first nine months of the war. One was his lack of interest in naval policy. Filled with visions of conquest by land to expand the *Lebensraum*, or living space, for the German people, he treated the army and the Luftwaffe as far greater military priorities than the Kriegsmarine. On a personal level, Hitler felt little attraction to nautical activities. Forests and mountains were where he liked to relax, not by the sea, which he regarded as alien, even intimidating territory. 'On land I feel like a lion but at sea I am a coward,' he once admitted.[3] Just as importantly, he believed that Britain would capitulate if France were defeated. With the Reich all-powerful on the continent, he did not see any reason why the war would continue since Britain's cause would have become so hopeless. The collapse of France would force the British government to seek terms. Indeed, one of the key goals of the western offensive, he said, was 'to bring England to its knees'.[4]

According to Hitler, if Britain refused to surrender in the event of France's collapse, then she could be strangled into submission by cutting off her supplies, making invasion unnecessary. He told a conference of his commanders in May 1939, 'Britain can be blockaded from western France at close quarters by the Luftwaffe, while the Navy with their submarines can extend the range of the blockade.'[5]

When the commander-in-chief of the Kriegsmarine, Grand Admiral Erich Raeder, met Hitler on 23 September 1939 to discuss naval operations in the West, the Führer again made no reference to any amphibious land-ings on the English coast, urging instead an aggressive naval blockade if the war continued against France and Britain. 'The quicker the start and the more brutal, the quicker the effect and the shorter the war,' he told Raeder.[6] Nevertheless, for all Hitler's indifference, Raeder recognised that the Reich might well have to mount an invasion.

Ambitious, eccentric and puritanical, the grand admiral was also method-ical and well organised. What he feared was a sudden demand from Hitler or the Wehrmacht Chief of Staff for the provision of an invasion fleet, complete with troop transports and convoy protection. Although the pos-sibility of invasion might seem remote, Raeder felt he should be prepared for it, particularly since, throughout the autumn of 1939, Hitler was plotting an assault on France, code-named Case Yellow. As Raeder later wrote of the preliminary analysis by the naval war staff:

> It was clear to us that studies should be made in case developments of the war suddenly presented us with a new twist to the English problem . . .
> Although the British people had been haunted from the first by the spectre of invasion, there had been not the slightest thought of this on the German side. It was only natural, however, that this problem would one day be given attention by the armed forces command, and I wanted to have some soundly reasoned particulars on hand when that time came, so that the thinking could at least begin on a firm basis. The Navy would be the first of the armed forces to be concerned with an invasion, since it would be a question of overseas transport on a colossal scale.[7]

To carry out this technical study, on 15 November Raeder appointed a small team under Rear Admiral Otto Schniewind. The naval planners went to work with speed rather than enthusiasm. Within a fortnight they had produced the tentative outline of an invasion scheme, code-named Study Red, which envisaged a landing area about 60 miles wide on the southern English coast between Portland in Dorset and Yarmouth. The attacking force, which was to number only 7,500 men carried in about fifteen ships, could theoretically embark from the French Channel ports if they had been seized, but that would leave it highly exposed to enemy fire, as well as depriving it of the element of surprise. Therefore, said the planners, embarkation from Germany would be preferable, despite the longer sea route, although an alternative would be to use Antwerp and Amsterdam.

Study Red was essentially pessimistic, with a strong emphasis on the difficulties that any invading force would encounter, such as the strength of British coastal artillery, the mobility of defensive British troops, the threat from Royal Navy submarines, the large amount of shipping required and, above all, the need to establish air superiority over the RAF. As the naval planners pointed out, the paradox was that if all the conditions were achieved to make an invasion possible, especially the defeat of the RAF and the Royal Navy, then Britain would have already been beaten: 'thus a landing, followed by occupation, will scarcely be necessary.'[8]

This negativity was important, setting the tone for the naval staff's attitude towards Operation Sea Lion. Throughout the summer of 1940, Raeder and his senior officers remained highly dubious about the whole enterprise, always pushing for a postponement in the invasion or the use of an alternative strategy to subjugate England. Halder noted in his diary on 30 July 1940 after one unproductive conference, 'The navy in all probability will not provide us this autumn with the means for a successful invasion.'[9] However, the army was more bullish, as was shown when Schniewind sent his Study Red to the Oberkommando des Heeres (OKH), the supreme command of the German army under Field Marshal Walther von Brauchitsch.

In late 1939, having received the naval plan, von Brauchitsch ordered a counter-study to be conducted by one of his officers, Helmuth Stieff, who was renowned for his organisational skills, although Hitler disliked him, calling him 'a poisonous little dwarf'.[10] Adopting a more optimistic, less hesitant approach than the naval staff, Stieff drew up an invasion plan, code-named Study North-West, which proposed a series of landings, not on the southern coast, but on the East Anglian shoreline between the Thames Estuary and the Wash. Speed and surprise were the scheme's key elements. The proposed initial assault would be made up of three or four infantry divisions, along with the 7th Parachute Division, followed by a second wave of two panzer divisions and one motorised division. There would also be a diversionary attack by two divisions north of the Humber to draw British troops away from Norfolk and Suffolk. As the first two invasion strikes moved inland from the coast, a third wave of troops would be landed in East Anglia to ensure the defeat of the British army and to help cut off London from the rest of the country. In contrast to the small invasion force proposed by the Kriegsmarine, Stieff's plan involved roughly 100,000 men.

The response to his proposal demonstrated the serious lack of unity within the top echelons of the German military, something that was to hinder the preparations for Sea Lion in the months ahead. Raeder's staff regarded the OKH scheme as completely unrealistic, both in scale and in geography.

As they explained in their reply of 8 January 1940, they believed that the East Anglian ports of Lowestoft and Great Yarmouth were too small for major unloading operations, as well as being heavily defended by the Royal Navy. Moreover, the idea of a diversionary operation in the north would only further weaken the Kriegsmarine's already limited resources. Indeed, the fleet stipulated in Stieff's plan far exceeded German maritime strength. 'The transport required for the forces specified by the General Staff amounts to 400 medium-sized steamers, with in addition a large collection of auxiliary vessels of the most varied nature, some of which must first be constructed.'[11] The Kriegsmarine estimated that it would probably take a year for such construction work. What made the OKH plan even less feasible, declared Raeder's staff, was the power of the Royal Navy. 'The British Home fleet will always be able to appear in greater strength than our own fleet, if the will is there.'[12]

Just as dismissive of Stieff's scheme was the Luftwaffe, headed by the gargantuan, egocentric figure of Herman Goering. Even more than the Kriegsmarine, the Luftwaffe was always averse to the concept of invasion, partly because Goering, an ideological believer in the pivotal influence of modern air power, thought that his own force could single-handedly overwhelm Britain. This same attitude prevailed in December 1939, when the Luftwaffe staff responded to Stieff's scheme: 'The planned operation can only be considered under conditions of absolute air superiority, and even then only if surprise is ensured.' In conclusion, the Luftwaffe argued that 'a combined operation with a landing in England as its object must be rejected. It would only be the last act of a war against England which had already taken a victorious course, as otherwise the conditions required for the success of a combined operation do not exist.'[13]

In the month following the Norway campaign of April 1940, the speed of the German advance through the Low Countries and France revived the concept of a British invasion. By 20 May the panzer force led by General Heinz Guderian, the pioneering tank commander and one of the architects of blitzkrieg warfare, had reached Abbeville at the mouth of the Somme. This remarkable dash to the English Channel had brought German troops within sight of the White Cliffs of Dover. Concerned that the Führer, fired by his success on land, might impulsively want to send his victorious divisions across the sea, Raeder sought a private meeting with him. As he later explained: 'The time had come when I had to raise the question of an invasion with Hitler. I was afraid that otherwise some irresponsible person would make the obvious suggestion to invade. Hitler would take up the idea, and the Kriegsmarine would then suddenly find itself faced with an insurmountable problem.'[14] Hitler agreed to Raeder's request. The next day the grand admiral travelled to the Felsennest (or 'rocky eyrie'), the Führer's remote, craggy headquarters in the Eifel mountain range of western Germany.

Some of Hitler's generals remember him as hesitant and anxious at this time. As Halder wrote in his diary for 16 May, 'An unpleasant day. The Führer is terribly nervous. Frightened by his own success, he is afraid to take any chances and so would rather pull the reins on us.'[15] In another entry, Halder recorded that Hitler 'rages and screams that we are about to ruin the whole campaign and that we are leading up to defeat'.[16]

At the meeting, Raeder set out his deep reservations about the possibility of invading England, stressing the strength of the Royal Navy, the lack of open ports and the need for absolute command of the air. He also put forward another argument that had not previously been aired. 'The diversion of a huge percentage of Germany's ocean, coastal and river shipping for transport of the invasion troops, I pointed out, would greatly impair Germany's domestic economy.'[17] Adopting a non-committal, almost indifferent attitude, Hitler seemed to accept this, telling the grand admiral that once France had fallen, he would strangle England through the submarine war and aerial bombardment. It was wise to get ready for a long war, the Führer said, although he believed that England 'would soon come round to peace'.[18] To Raeder's relief, he ordered that no preparations for an invasion should be made for the time being.

At the very moment when the Felsennest meeting was under way, in England invasion fever was reaching new levels of intensity, as reflected in the surge of recruits to the LDV, the round-up of enemy aliens, the creation of makeshift roadblocks, the establishment of coastal batteries and the spread of barbed wire across the beaches. Little did the British military staff and politicians know that the idea of invasion was far from the Führer's mind, which was then wholly focused not on a future campaign in Britain but the present one in France. To Hitler, so aggressive yet so paranoid, the sheer speed of the German attack brought its own dangers and doubts. From his deliberations with a few of his generals emerged one of the most extraordinary decisions of the early war, one that was to have a huge influence over Britain's ability to survive.

By 21 May, with the leading German units surrounding them at the coast, the British Expeditionary Force was isolated and facing defeat. Churchill's private secretary John Colville noted in his diary, 'The situation in France is extraordinary. Owing to the rapid advance of armoured troops, the Germans are in many places behind the Allied lines,' adding ominously, 'Preparations are being made for the evacuation of the BEF in case of necessity.'[19] Ironside, in his last week as Chief of the Imperial Staff, thought that the only hope was for the BEF to counter-attack by moving southwards. However, during a visit to see General Gort, the commander of the BEF, he was disturbed by the lack of fighting spirit among the French, writing in his diary on 21 May, 'Situation desperate . . . God help the BEF, brought to this state by the incompetence of the French.'[20]

On that same day, due to the Allies' disorganisation and poor communications, a planned major counter-offensive against the Germans fizzled out after a brave strike near the north-eastern French town of Arras by two divisions and a tank brigade under Major General Harold Franklyn. But the Germans soon regrouped, forcing the BEF into headlong retreat towards the Channel ports of Calais and Dunkirk. Trapped in the northernmost corner of France, short of supplies and air cover, Gort's force looked doomed as the panzer divisions seized the port of Boulogne on 23 May just south of Calais, thereby depriving the Royal Navy of a vital facility for any evacuation. 'I cannot see that we have any hope of getting the BEF out,' wrote Ironside that night,[21] an opinion shared by Lieutenant General Alan Brooke, the Commander of II Corps, who recorded, 'Nothing but a miracle can save the BEF now and the end cannot be far away.'[22]

Yet just as disaster appeared to be inevitable, the British were to be given a glimmer of hope by Hitler and some of his generals, who were suddenly gripped by uncertainty. That evening, Generals Heinz Guderian and Paul von Kleist were leading their panzer forces in a blitzkrieg-style pursuit of the BEF towards Dunkirk when they suddenly received an order from Field Marshal Gerd von Rundstedt, the head of Army Group A, to halt for thirty-six hours. Guderian was furious, believing that a chance to annihilate the BEF was being thrown away. After the war, he wrote, 'My repeated protests went unheard. On the contrary, the cursed order became repeated. The order allowed the British army to escape for if we could have continued our rush on Dunkirk, we would have probably been there before the British.'[23]

Von Rundstedt's decision was driven by concerns about overextended supply lines, the strain on the panzer divisions, the risk of exposing his divisions at the rear and the need to conserve his armour for the final push south against the French. His stop order was endorsed by Hitler, who visited Army Group A headquarters the following morning, 24 May.

After the war, it became common among the surviving German generals to heap all the blame on Hitler for the move. He had acted entirely against their wishes, they said, which just indicated how poor he was as a military strategist. General Wilhelm von Thoma, head of the tank section, said that he 'begged for permission to let the tanks push on', but his appeals were fruitless because of the Führer's influence. As he wrote in 1950, 'You can never talk to a fool. Hitler spoilt the chance of victory.'[24] The panzer commander von Kleist, who was just 18 miles from Dunkirk when the stop order was issued, argued that the BEF were able to reach Dunkirk 'only with the personal help of Hitler'.[25] Similarly the operations officer of Army Group A, General Günther Blumentritt, claimed that 'Hitler was quite alone in his decision to give the order to stop.' Senior officers, said Blumentritt, 'remonstrated strongly but in vain'.[26]

Two vital factors played on Hitler's mind. The first was the role of the Luftwaffe, whose chief Hermann Goering was Hitler's closest ally. Revelling in his pre-eminence but jealous of the army's success in France, he told his leader that, rather than put the German armoured divisions at further risk, given the soft terrain around Dunkirk, the job of annihilating the BEF should be given to the Luftwaffe. The British, he claimed, would be easy prey for his fighters and bombers, declaring grandly, 'The great mission of the Luftwaffe is imminent: to wipe out the British in northern France. All the army has to do is occupy.'[27]

Hitler's willingness to indulge Goering's vanity was partly driven by the second, more political, reason for the stop order, one that highlighted his ambivalence towards the war against Britain. Believing that the British government was anxious to reach a peace deal, he was reluctant to waste his valuable armour in the treacherous Flanders marshes in what he perceived as a pointless fight. Whether the BEF surrendered in the Pas de Calais or returned to Britain as the bedraggled remnant of an army, he was certain that Churchill would have to negotiate terms once France fell, telling his generals at one point, 'It's always good to let a broken army return home to show the civilian population what a beating they've had.'[28]

On a deeper level, because of his respect for Britain, for a moment he lacked the ruthlessness that he usually showed towards his enemies.

Blumentritt later claimed that he and his planning staff had been amazed at their leader's attitude on 23 May. 'He astonished us by speaking of his admiration for the British Empire, of the necessity for its existence and of the civilisation that Britain had brought to the world.'[29] This was also the recollection of von Rundstedt, who said that, at their Charleville meeting, Hitler had explained his hopes to 'make an earlier peace with the England' by letting the BEF escape. According to the general's testimony, written in 1949 with the benefit of hindsight, the Führer said, 'The British empire could not be destroyed even in 100 years. England must only keep her hands off the European continent and return our colonies to us.'[30]

Whatever its justification, the order had a crucial impact on the BEF's chances of survival. By the time it was lifted on 26 May and the German tanks began to move again, much of Lord Gort's force had managed to reach Dunkirk. Added assistance was given to the retreat by the heroic resistance put up by the British garrison at Calais, where units of the King's Royal Rifle Corps and the 30th Motor Brigade under Brigadier Claude Nicholson tied up a large number of panzers and troops. Essentially, Nicholson's brave band was sacrificed in order to protect the BEF, since he was instructed by Churchill not to withdraw but to fight to the bitter end. General Pug Ismay, Churchill's aide, witnessed the prime minister's anguish at this moment. 'It is a terrible thing to condemn a body of splendid men to death or captivity. The decision affected us all very deeply, especially perhaps Churchill. He was unusually silent during dinner that evening, and he ate and drank with evident distaste. As we rose from the table, he said, "I feel physically sick."'[31]

That same evening, as the first Germans came within artillery range of the British and French troops now based in Dunkirk, the War Cabinet agreed to order the start of the evacuation, code-named Operation Dynamo. The following morning Churchill wrote to Gort, his letter revealing his sense of foreboding. 'At this solemn moment, I cannot help sending you my good wishes. No one can tell you how it will go. But anything is better than being cooped up and starved out.'[32] It seemed a forlorn hope at the beginning of Dynamo that many of the BEF troops would indeed be rescued from Dunkirk. Ironside predicted that no more than 30,000 would be saved, little more than a tenth of the entire BEF.

Nor were spirits high among the exhausted and surrounded British troops, their mood darkened by what they perceived to be the lack of air cover, although in reality the Spitfires and Hurricanes of Fighter Command were engaged in ferocious aerial battles with the Luftwaffe high in the sky over northern France. Sandy Frederick, serving in the 2nd Fife and Forfar Yeomanry, left a vivid description of his struggle to reach Dunkirk aboard his unit's Bren gun carrier: 'It was frightening to be under air attack. We didn't seem to have any defence. We were in a real panic. There was no control whatsoever. Wrecks of British vehicles were everywhere. We were getting fired on from every side. By now I had about 20 men hanging on to my Bren carrier as we retreated.'[33]

For Lieutenant General Alan Brooke, the commander of II Corps, the scenes of chaos on the road to Dunkirk were all too indicative of the madness that gripped France as she faced collapse under the German onslaught. Passing through a heavily bombed town, he came across a group of inmates from a mental asylum that had been demolished. 'With catastrophe on all sides, bombarded by rumours of every description, flooded by refugees and a demoralized French army, and now on top of it all lunatics in brown corduroy suits standing at the side of the road, grinning at one with an inane smile, a flow of saliva running from the corner of their mouths and dripping noses! Had it not been that by then one's senses were numbed with the magnitude of the catastrophe that surrounded one, the situation would have been unbearable.'[34]

Brooke's sense of despair would have been all the greater had he known that, at the very moment the BEF was trying to reach safety, back in London a faction within the heart of the British government was plotting to give up the fight and negotiate a settlement with the Reich. For all the retrospective condemnation heaped on him by some of his generals, Hitler had been partially correct: there was indeed one very senior British politician who was all too anxious to reach a peace deal. Convinced that the BEF was lost, that the triumph of Germany was inevitable and that Churchill was hopelessly deluded, this self-styled realist believed that the continuation of war would ultimately destroy the empire. The retreat to Dunkirk was his opportunity to strike. While the British troops hoped for salvation, one of their political masters plotted surrender. And it took all of Churchill's skill and determination to outmanoeuvre him.

6

'We shall fight on'

—◄

W HEN THE FRENCH prime minister Paul Reynaud flew to London on 26 May, he warned Churchill that his country's position was desperate. The morale of the French army was in free fall. The Germans outnumbered the northern French divisions by more than three to one. A vast exodus of refugees was under way. Marshal Pétain, the First World War hero who had been brought into the French Cabinet to strengthen its resolve, was now openly defeatist. Churchill urged Reynaud to continue the struggle but declared that 'whatever happened, we were not prepared to give in. We would rather go down fighting than be enslaved to Germany.'[1] His defiant stance certainly represented the overwhelming view of the British public, particularly the working class. Opinion polls during the summer of 1940 showed that on average 78 per cent of people approved of his premiership.

But this tough-minded attitude was not shared by all of Britain's political leaders. Although the prime minister's standing in the country was high, the same was not true of his relationship with the Conservative Party, many of whose MPs still regarded him as a reckless adventurer of erratic judgement and drink-fuelled romanticism.

Doubts about Churchill extended to the top of the Cabinet, where the Foreign Secretary Lord Halifax abhorred the prime minister's belligerence. Even after the German invasion of Norway and the end of the Phoney War, he maintained his reluctance to fight. His pessimism was mirrored by his deputy minister at the Foreign Office, the sophisticated, evasive Tory Rab Butler whose heart was not in the war in 1940, whatever he might have claimed afterwards in his memoirs.

On the night of 23 May, Churchill's intelligence aide Desmond Morton wrote to tell him that Sir Robert Vansittart, the government's chief diplomatic adviser, 'has had a private communication from the Italian Embassy here, which leads him to suppose that if we can save a major disaster in France, the Italian Government will make some overture to us of a pro-Ally and anti-German character.'[2] Halifax and Butler seized on this information, ostensibly because it could keep Italy out of the war, but more importantly because it might help to open up a channel of mediation with Germany.

With the sceptical approval of Churchill, Halifax arranged to meet the Italian ambassador, Giuseppe Bastianini, on 25 May to sound him out. It was an interview that showed the lengths to which Halifax would go in order to end the war. Judging by what he told Bastianini, the Foreign Secretary seemed to regard Munich not as a shameful disaster but as the template for another round of capitulation to the threat of force. He went far beyond his remit of finding out Italy's intentions and, in a display of pusillanimity, contradicted all Churchill's tough public rhetoric, even developing a plan to make a direct appeal to Il Duce himself. More certain than ever that the continuation of the war was folly, he now tried to swing the War Cabinet around to his viewpoint and away from Churchill's. The stage was set for a bitter political struggle over three days of Cabinet meetings.

Another key War Cabinet member was Neville Chamberlain, who served as the Lord President of the Council. Churchill knew that if Chamberlain sided with Halifax, then the Tory Party would turn against his premiership, making his continuation in office almost impossible. That was partly why Churchill had been so solicitous towards the elder statesman since succeeding him as prime minister just a fortnight earlier, on 10 May. In response, Chamberlain showed Churchill increased loyalty and admiration, while decreasing his natural allegiance to his colleague Halifax. As the debate intensified within the government, Chamberlain's position became ever more crucial.

Halifax put forward the question of Italian-led negotiations to his Cabinet colleagues at a series of lengthy meetings on Sunday 26 May. Churchill was profoundly hostile, arguing that any concessions would only undermine the war effort. He also used the impending Dunkirk evacuation, which was sanctioned that same day, as a justification for his antipathy to talks, since the outcome of Operation Dynamo would have a considerable bearing on Britain's military capacity to resist.

The next day, 27 May, the War Cabinet met three times, against the backdrop of the beginning of Operation Dynamo. On the first day of the evacuation, 7,669 troops had been taken from Dunkirk harbour, although the men were forced to leave behind their equipment. Within the Cabinet, the chasm between Halifax and Churchill had deepened overnight. Halifax again put the case for talks with Italy, but Churchill now adopted a much harder stance. He was backed up by two senior Labour figures, the deputy leader Arthur Greenwood and his chief Clement Attlee, who said that any appeal to Mussolini would be 'very damaging to us': the humiliating equivalent of asking Il Duce to 'intercede to obtain peace terms for us'.[3] Similarly Chamberlain now started to side with Churchill, declaring that the proposed approach to Italy 'would not serve any useful purpose'.[4]

The hour of reckoning had almost arrived. Halifax, conscious of 'profound differences of points of view',[5] decided that he had to use all his political authority to force the issue. During the War Cabinet meeting that began at 4.30 p.m., he dramatically told his colleagues that if they maintained their refusal to countenance an approach to Mussolini, he would have no alternative but to resign.

With Dunkirk at a critical point, Churchill could not allow his government to be destabilised and the Tory Party thrown into turmoil by Halifax's departure. He therefore suspended the Cabinet and asked the Foreign Secretary to join him for a walk in the Downing Street garden. As they strolled together, Halifax again threatened to resign. Despite his antipathy to the prime minister, however, he did not carry through his threat. Churchill's government remained intact.

The tide now began to shift against Halifax, his demand for peace talks seeming a woefully inappropriate response to Britain's military crisis. The next day, Tuesday 28 May, was to prove decisive. The news from the western front could hardly have been grimmer. At 4 a.m. the Belgians formally surrendered to Germany, their forces having been in a state of collapse for days. The decision prompted a wave of anger in Britain, with the Belgian king accused of cowardice and perfidy.

On top of Belgium's capitulation the reports from the BEF were also desperate. Although another 18,000 men were lifted from the beaches and harbour that day, around 200,000 British and 160,000 French troops were still encircled by the enemy. Indeed, the situation at Dunkirk appeared so gloomy that Churchill was forced to address the House of Commons that afternoon on the subject. In his speech, he admitted that the BEF, although fighting with 'the utmost discipline and tenacity', were in 'grievous peril' and that the House 'should prepare itself for hard and heavy tidings'. But, in characteristically defiant language, he concluded that 'nothing which may happen in this battle . . . should destroy our confidence in our power to make our way, as on former occasions in our history, through disaster and through grief to the ultimate defeat of our enemies.'[6] In contrast to the Foreign Secretary, most MPs, especially those outside the Tory ranks, were fully behind the prime minister.

Buoyed by this support, Churchill then went into yet another meeting of the War Cabinet, no longer in any mood to put up with a lack of resolution. He launched his strongest attack so far on the idea of negotiations, asserting that in any talks Britain would be completely at Hitler's mercy, whereas 'we should get no worse terms if we went on fighting, even if we were beaten, than were open to us now.'[7] With a historical flourish, he told his colleagues, 'Nations which went down fighting rose again, but those which tamely surrendered were finished.'[8] Perhaps the most crucial intervention came from Chamberlain, who urged that the proposal for talks was 'a considerable gamble' and should be rejected.[9] There was no formal vote, but it was obvious that Halifax was badly isolated.

The prime minister's next move completed the rout of the Foreign Secretary. Soon after six o'clock on 28 May, the War Cabinet members left Churchill's room at the Commons, their place taken by a much larger group of ministers outside the Cabinet. After days of fraught negotiations, Churchill was exhausted. But he knew this meeting was a vital opportunity to cement his policy of resistance, and he brilliantly exploited it to the full in one of his most forceful interventions of the war. As the twenty-five ministers crammed into the room, he used all his renowned eloquence, historical allusions and bulldog defiance to set out his case in a compelling address, telling his ministers that whatever happened with Operation Dynamo, 'we shall fight on.'[10]

The most vivid, detailed account of the meeting was provided by Hugh Dalton, the fiercely anti-German socialist and Minister for Economic Warfare. Churchill had been 'quite magnificent', he wrote, 'the only man we have for this hour'. Of the call for negotiations, he was delighted to find Churchill contemptuous, saying, 'We should become a slave state, though a British Government, which would be Hitler's puppet, would be set up under Mosley or some such person. And where would we be at the end of all that?' Churchill finished with a highly personalised, dramatic passage, using lines that would reverberate throughout 1940. 'I am convinced that every man of you would rise up and tear me down from my place if I were for one moment to contemplate parley or surrender. If this long island story of ours is to end at last, let it end only when each one of us lies choking in his own blood upon the ground.'[11] At that closing remark, the ministers sent up a tremendous cheer.

The meeting entirely changed the atmosphere at Westminster. Churchill's position became unassailable. Through his rhetoric and the sheer force of his personality, he had bent government policy to his will. Soon afterwards, at seven o'clock, there was yet another session of the inner War Cabinet, the ninth in the last three days, but by now Halifax's scheme had little credibility, especially after Churchill informed his colleagues that the wider government 'had expressed the greatest satisfaction when he told them that there was no chance of our giving up the struggle. He did not remember having ever before heard a gathering of persons occupying high places in political life express themselves so emphatically.'[12] The game was up. Despite his reputation for cunning, Halifax had been comprehensively outmanoeuvred by Churchill.

Barely more than a fortnight since he had assumed office, the prime minister had overcome the greatest political challenge of his early premiership. If Halifax had prevailed, the entire course of the war and of modern history would have been different. As it was, the Foreign Secretary's authority was fatally diminished. Within less than six months, he was out of the Cabinet for ever.

Churchill's determination to continue the struggle was infectious. With each passing day, as the Royal Navy battled across the Channel along three separate routes between Dunkirk and Dover while the RAF fought in the skies, growing numbers of troops were taken off the beaches and the harbour. On 29 May, 47,000 men were evacuated, the total rising to 54,000 on 30 May and 68,000 on the last day of the month. Altogether during the evacuation, the RAF flew 4,822 sorties over Dunkirk and claimed to have shot down 240 German aircraft in return for 177 losses of their own.

Operation Dynamo was overseen by Vice Admiral Bertram Ramsay, an officer of remarkable coolness, stamina and authority who had retired from the navy in 1938 but had been coaxed out of retirement by Churchill after the start of the war and appointed flag officer commanding Dover. Working tirelessly from an underground network of tunnels beneath Dover Castle, high above the Channel coast, Ramsay masterminded the massive logistical task with consummate skill and very little sleep.

Captain William Tennant, a distinguished veteran of the Gallipoli and Jutland campaigns during the First World War, was appointed by the Admiralty to take charge of evacuation from the French coast. On his arrival at Dunkirk on 26 May, Tennant sent a signal to Ramsay asking for 'every available craft' on the south coast to be mobilised and sent across the Channel.[13] With his gift for organisation, Ramsay quickly accomplished this job. At the start of Dynamo, he had just 42 destroyers and 35 transport ships. In a couple of days, he could call on a fleet of over 850 vessels, including 230 fishing boats, 208 motor boats, 27 yachts, and numerous lifeboats, tugboats and barges. The miracle of Dunkirk could never have been achieved without these 'little ships' acting as makeshift ferries during those climactic days.

But contrary to mythology, this was a secondary method of evacuation. Throughout the entire operation, marginally less than a third of the troops, a total of 98,671 men, were taken directly from the beaches. More vital was Captain Tennant's other innovation, which addressed the problem of the inner harbour at Dunkirk having been destroyed, making it impossible for vessels to dock in the normal fashion. In a highly unorthodox move he decided to utilise one of the two huge concrete breakwaters, or moles, that had been built in front of the harbour. The manoeuvre worked superbly. The destroyers and transports were able to exploit the deep water to come right up against the structure at the eastern side of the port. Moreover, because the east mole was connected to the beaches by a causeway, the men were able to march directly to the waiting ships.

With the Royal Navy operating in relays, the numbers of the rescued began to rise dramatically. By the use of this method alone, on 28 May, 11,874 men were lifted from the harbour, increasing to 33,558 on 29 May and 47,081 on 31 May. As Patrick Barrass, a soldier in the Essex Regiment who fought at Dunkirk, recalled, 'Most of the fighting troops were taken off the Mole. It was crucial but has too often been ignored by historians.'[14]

The patient restraint of the troops, which helped to make Dynamo possible, was all the more remarkable given the carnage and chaos that enveloped the port. A vivid account of the scene on 1 June, when the evacuation was at its height, was left by Lewis Ricci, a retired naval captain and BBC correspondent aboard one of the destroyers. That day fifty-two bombs had fallen on the ship, yet she still made it back to Dover crammed to capacity. Ricci then returned to Dunkirk that night on another vessel. 'We riddled our way through the minefields till we were nearing Dunkirk. The oil tanks were still blazing furiously, and there was an occasional sound of distant gunfire. Once a shell landed in one of those blazing tanks and a huge red glare blazed up almost to the zenith. It died down again and the moon came out from behind a cloud, giving the sea and the sky a queer semblance of peace in contrast to the blazing inferno ashore.' The moon was bright enough for Ricci 'to see, assembled on the whole length of the Mole, thousands of men of the British Expeditionary Force waiting patiently for embarkation'.

Ricci explained how the men came on board once his destroyer had docked: 'It was nearly low water, and the top of the Mole was level with our bridge. Scaling ladders were lowered, and down they came as fast as fully equipped, fully armed men could climb.' The embarkation continued calmly even when a German bomber appeared and attacked the mole. Then, packed beyond capacity, Ricci's ship departed for the journey back to England. 'The English Channel was an extraordinary sight as the sun rose. It looked something like Henley Regatta, as if every craft on the south coast that could float was heading for Dunkirk . . . On board our ship every inch of space on deck and below was crammed with men. Already, many of them were asleep where they lay.'[15]

Some witnesses at Dunkirk contradicted this tale of patriotic heroism in adversity, nor did all maritime operators rally to Vice Admiral Ramsay's call or show the highest courage. Two lifeboat crews on the south Kent coast failed to set sail for Dunkirk and their vessels had to be requisitioned by the Royal Navy. Soon afterwards Buller Griggs, the coxswain of the Dungeness lifeboat, and his brother Dick, the boat's mechanic, were dismissed from the RNLI's service for acting as the ringleaders of this minor revolt. Similarly, on 28 May, the steamer *Canterbury* refused to cross the Channel, and the Admiralty had to put an armed naval unit on board to strengthen her resolve. More shamefully, on 29 May, the tugboat *Conquest* was run aground by her crew to avoid the crossing. The next day, three passenger steamers failed to set out from Folkestone in defiance of their orders.

Some elements in the army also lost their composure, as Sandy Frederick of the Fife and Forfar Yeomanry recalled. He managed to make it on board the drifter *Loughgarry*, but found the journey back to England 'a nightmare. It was like Dante's inferno. The Stukas were bombing us. On the boat I was crying, I was so frightened. I did not think we would make it home. It was a terrible, awful experience. Some of the boys on board were going berserk, screaming. We were wee laddies: untrained, underpaid, under-officered.'[16]

Nevertheless, Operation Dynamo far exceeded all expectations. The mood within the prime minister's office was transformed, as Jock Colville noted on 31 May, 'Everyone is elated by the progress of the evacuation.' On 1 June another 64,000 men were lifted from the beach and the harbour, among them Lieutenant General Alan Brooke, the commander of II Corps, who recorded in his diary, 'Finally arrived at Dover at 7.15am. Wonderful feeling of peace after the last three weeks.'[17] This was followed by more than 26,000 troops on each of the next three days, until the operation was formally brought to an end at 2.23 p.m. on 4 June.

One of the last to leave was Major General Harold Alexander, who had been in charge of the BEF's rearguard action. According to the BBC's report, 'He inspected the shores of Dunkirk from a motorboat this morning to make sure no-one was left behind before boarding the last ship.'[18] Those reassuring words were an exaggeration. In fact, 34,000 of the French soldiers who had been in the bridgehead protecting the evacuation were left behind, something that would lead to bitter recriminations and accusations of betrayal. Nevertheless, 123,095 French troops were among the total of 338,226 taken from Dunkirk.

The gallant efforts of all marine forces came at a significant cost. Over 200 Allied sea craft were sunk and an equal number damaged. The Isle of Man Steam Packet Company alone lost eight of its vessels. Of the Royal Navy's fleet, six destroyers and nine other large ships were sunk, and nineteen destroyers were damaged. But even these losses were far lower than had been expected when the evacuation began.

The organising genius behind Dynamo, Admiral Ramsay, rewarded himself on 4 June with a well-deserved round of golf on the course at Sandwich nearby, and, liberated from the strain, proceeded to attain the best score of his life.

British troops had expected to encounter a hostile, demoralised public once they arrived back on English soil, but just the opposite was true. Most people were thrilled by the uplifting reports from the evacuation, as the Ministry of Information's daily survey reported: 'The return of the BEF has given great emotional relief and many observers report extreme elation succeeding the grave depression of the last few days. Reports from nearly all regions show that where men of the BEF have returned morale is stiff-ened.'[19] Apart from the warmth of the public, what also struck the returning soldiers was how well the arrangements for their reception had been organised in Kent, just as the evacuation had been. Again, this contradicts the fashionable historical fallacy that Britain was in a shambolic state in the early summer of 1940.

'When we got back to England, the organisation was superb,' recalled the Scotsman Sandy Frederick. 'There were ladies giving us sandwiches and tea. We were instructed which trains to get. One dear old lady came up to me with a postcard and said, "What's your name and address?" which she took down. Then she asked me to write a few words on the card to tell my parents that I had made it back. So I wrote, "Don't worry, I'm home." My father and mother broke down when they got that postcard.'[20]

The logistics of all this activity were impressive. Doctors and nurses worked flat out to help the wounded. The public provided clothing, blankets and boots through house-to-house collections. Men were fed at stations further inland from the coast with food donated by local shops, bakers and farmers. At the railway junction in the tiny village of Headcorn near Maidstone, trains from Dover were stopped for eight minutes to enable troops to receive their first proper meal in days. On each day at Headcorn during the operation, at least 2,500 loaves were sliced, and 1,000 tins of corned beef or sardines were used for making sandwiches. On one single evening at the peak of Operation Dynamo, 5,000 meat pies and 5,000 eggs were delivered to Headcorn's makeshift kitchen, which were run in tandem by the army and female volunteers. During the evacuation, 145,000 men were fed at this usually tranquil spot.

The shattered condition of the returning troops was all too obvious to others involved in the relief effort. Some of the soldiers were dressed in little more than rags; others were filthy after weeks of struggle through France. 'The stench was terrible,' recalled Joan Davis, a member of the Women's Auxiliary Air Force helping at a camp in Calshot, Hampshire.[21] Lucilla Andrew, who worked as a nurse at a military hospital on Salisbury Plain, left these notes of her experience: 'Men too tired to remember to swallow a mouthful of soup or keep their eyes open, but not to mumble, "Thanks, nurse . . . ta, duck . . . that's great . . . grand, love . . . I say, thanks awfully."'[22]

Some of the relief personnel had a more morbid task. Dennis Mulqueen of the London Irish Regiment was ordered with his battalion to go down to Margate, just north of Ramsgate, as he remembered in a post-war interview. 'At the end of Margate pier there was a big amusement park called Dreamland and that was turned into a mortuary. We put all the dead chaps there. After a few days, we took the bodies, a dozen at a time, and brought them up to the clocktower on the seafront, where the brigadier gave the salute. Then we took them to the cemetery. It took us about a week to deal with them.'[23]

Even with all the casualties and the hardship, the overwhelming public feeling was that Dunkirk had greatly enhanced Britain's chances of surviving the inevitable German onslaught. To a large number of citizens, the defeat in France was a blessing in disguise. The BEF had returned to defend its native land and its survival gave the country a chance to continue fighting. Just as the triumph of Halifax's strategy would have brought Britain's involvement in the war to a swift end, so the nation might have been unable to stand up to the Reich after the disaster of losing more than 200,000 men if the operation had failed. That was the view of Alan Brooke, always a realist, who later wrote, 'Had the BEF not returned to this country, it is hard to see how the Army could have recovered from this blow. Time and again during the years of the war I thanked God for the safe return of the bulk of the BEF.'[24]

Churchill himself felt that the returning army would be a powerful deterrent against invasion, as he explained to Ismay on 2 June. 'The successful evacuation of the BEF has revolutionised the Home Defence position. As soon as the BEF units can be re-formed on a home defence basis, we have a mass of trained troops in the country which would require a raid to be executed on a prohibitively large scale.'[25] It was in this defiant mood that, two days later, he made one of his greatest speeches to the Commons, when he described Dunkirk as 'a miracle of deliverance, achieved by valour, by perseverance, by perfect discipline, by faultless service, by skill, by unconquerable fidelity'. Turning to the invasion threat, he reassured the House that 'we have for the time being in this island incomparably more powerful military forces than we ever had at any moment in this war or the last.' History could be a source of comfort, he said. 'When Napoleon lay at Boulogne for a year with his flat-bottomed boats and his Grand Army, he was told by someone, "There are bitter weeds in England." There are certainly a great many more of them since the expeditionary force returned.'

Surprisingly, Churchill was never a natural speaker and had to take tremendous pains over all his major addresses. He once said that each minute on the floor of the House took an hour's preparation. The benefit of his meticulous approach was that it allowed him to exploit fully his natural gift for uplifting, romantic prose. That quality was on fully display in his inspirational peroration, which embodied his unyielding spirit and became the rallying cry for Britain in 1940, when he told the Commons: 'We shall not flag or fail. We shall go on to the end. We shall fight with growing confidence and growing strength in the air, we shall defend our island, whatever the cost may be. We shall fight on the beaches, we shall fight on the landing grounds, we shall fight in the fields and in the streets, we shall fight in the hills; we shall never surrender.'[26] The effect of Winston's words was electric. In the words of the Labour MP Josiah Wedgwood, 'That was worth 1000 guns and the speeches of 1000 years.'[27] Chips Channon, previously so dismissive, commented: 'He was eloquent and oratorical and used magnificent English; several Labour members cried.'[28]

The British public was just as enthralled when an edited version of the speech was read out by a BBC announcer on the radio that evening. The novelist Vita Sackville-West, wife of the National Labour MP Harold Nicolson, told her husband that the broadcast 'sent shivers (not of fear) down my spine. I think one of the reasons why one is stirred by his Elizabethan phrases is that one feels the massive backing of power and resolve behind them, like a great fortress.'[29] In 1942, the Scottish Unionist MP Walter Elliot revealed to the young John F. Kennedy, then in the US navy, that when Churchill had sat down after his great speech, he had said, 'I don't know what we'll fight them with – we shall have to slosh them with bottles – empty of course.'[30]

Amidst the thrill of defiance, however, the Dunkirk evacuation also prompted a disturbing question: given that the Royal and Merchant Navies had managed to carry a battered, beaten army of 338,000 men across the English Channel from hostile territory under heavy aerial bombardment in just nine days, how much easier would it be for the Reich to transport a well-equipped invasion force from France? In the BEF's salvation lay the potential threat of enemy conquest, as Ironside recognised. 'It is almost fantastic that we have been able to do it in the face of all the bombing and the gunning. It brings me to the fact that the Bosche may equally well be able to land men in England despite the bombing,' he wrote in his diary for 2 June.[31] In the same vein, the novelist Dennis Wheatley wrote a colourful, 12,000-word paper for the War Office in late June, in which, using his gift of creative imagination, he tried to inhabit the German mindset and foresee how the invasion might be mounted. His dramatic account included fifth columnists dressed as British troops, the use of poisonous gas, mass parachute descents, the dropping of delayed action bombs on citizens, the destruction of utilities and landing parties armed with flame-throwers. Still posing as a German invasion planner, Wheatley concluded: 'If the British could bring off 338,000 troops from Dunkirk in a hastily-mustered armada, in spite of continuous attack by our aircraft, there is no reason why we should not transport 338,000 troops to the coasts of Britain in spite of continuous attack from the British navy when we are in a position to launch an armada of at least six times that size in small craft by collecting every available ship, motor-boats and other suitable vessels from every port between Norway and the Pyrenees.'[32]

That is exactly what some German strategists were thinking.

7

'Drown the brutes is what I'd like to do'

—

SOON AFTER DUNKIRK, Churchill said to his Economic Warfare Minister Hugh Dalton, 'We've got the men away, but we've lost the luggage.'[1] It was a typically striking Churchillian metaphor to describe the spectacular loss of equipment that the British army had suffered in the evacuation. One of the many myths of the early war held that the BEF was ill prepared for the French campaign because of the years of appeasement under Chamberlain. In fact, during late 1930s the British army had undergone a programme of modernisation, and the BEF was far more motorised than the Wehrmacht, which still relied heavily on horses for transport; Germany actually used more horses in the Second World War than it had done in the First.

The strength of the BEF's logistical support was reflected in the inventory of what had been left behind by the departing army. This included 2,472 guns, 615 tanks, 63,870 vehicles, 90,000 rifles, 7,000 tons of ammunition, 165,000 tons of petrol, 20,000 motorcycles and vast quantities of other equipment. The sheer scale of this detritus at Dunkirk astonished General Fedor von Bock, the commander of the Reich's Army Group B, when he surveyed the scene. 'Here lies the material of a whole army, so incredibly well-equipped that we poor devils can only look on with envy and amazement.'[2] The Chiefs of Staff claimed that the return of the BEF had 'revolutionised the home defence position', but that was true only of manpower.[3] In practice, a large swathe of the British land forces had been almost disarmed.

Overall, artillery and anti-tank losses in France amounted to about 60 per cent of the army's total stock. Supplies of everything from 25-pounder field guns to armoured fighting vehicles, from anti-tank guns to motorcycles, would have to be manufactured and distributed. In turn, this would require a huge increase in production over the coming months.

So denuded was the British army after Dunkirk that there were widespread fears in political and military circles that Hitler would take the opportunity to launch an assault on Britain. When Montgomery returned from Dunkirk on 2 June, he marched into the office of Sir John Dill, the CIGS, and with typical forthrightness asked, 'Do you realize that for the first time in a thousand years this country is now in danger of invasion?'[4] At the height of the evacuation, on 30 May, the Chiefs of Staff warned the War Cabinet that 'it is highly probable that Germany is now setting the stage for a full-scale attack on England'. The chosen method, said the service chiefs, could be 'a large fleet of fast motorboats carrying 100 men apiece', crossing the Channel 'during the dark hours. These boats would be handled with the utmost boldness and would probably be run up to the beaches without regard to the loss of the craft or casualties to the personnel.' On a pessimistic note, the chiefs concluded, 'we do not consider that by naval or air action we could prevent such a landing.'[5]

On 31 May an urgent telegram was sent by the chiefs to naval, air and army bases around the coast: 'Secret: Urgent Operations. It is considered by the Chiefs of Staff that attack on this country is imminent. All defences will be manned during the hours of darkness. Work on defences will be accelerated to the utmost possible on the Yorkshire, East Anglian, South East and South Coast . . . Commanders will make such changes to their positions as may be necessary to meet this dual threat from sea and air. Air coastal patrol at dawn and dusk has been instituted as from tonight.'[6]

Just two days after the final boat had reached Dover from Dunkirk, the GHQ of Home Forces issued a paper that highlighted the risks of an imminent invasion. Having emphasized that reports from German sources pointed to the possibility of the Reich deploying fast motorboats in an amphibious assault on south-eastern England, the paper then argued that the Germans might use Ireland as a base for invasion, perhaps with the help of the Irish Republican movement: 'Extensive German plans for a descent on Eire have been in preparation for a considerable time', while the potential strength of the IRA was 'estimated to be as high as 15 to 20,000 in the case of a successful invasion. Stores of arms are reported to exist capable of arming up to 5000 men.'[7]

The concerns of the military chiefs were backed up by intelligence, which frequently referred to the growing German menace. On 3 June, the penultimate day of Operation Dynamo, the government's chief diplomatic adviser, Sir Robert Vansittart, wrote to Churchill's aide, Desmond Morton, to tell him that his 'best source in Germany' was certain 'that Hitler means to get on with the invasion as soon as possible'.[8] Indeed, during Dunkirk and its immediate aftermath, the service chiefs found that the barrage of rumours was so great that they decided to beef up the Invasion Warning Sub-Committee and turn it into a stronger Combined Intelligence Committee, made up of the secret services and the military, to 'consider all intelligence matters appertaining to invasion'.[9]

In this tense period, when information from Swedish sources strongly suggested that Norway would be the base for an invading force, Ironside, now in charge of Home Forces, was understandably anxious about what the Germans were planning. In private he speculated that they could land 20,000 airborne troops in East Anglia and another 10,000 in Kent, followed by 'seaborne expeditions pushed forward with the utmost brutality'. He feared that the geography of the English coast was a disadvantage to the defender because, although 'the number of landing places available, beaches, coves, piers and small harbours, is very large', Britain was small in size, so 'armoured troops can penetrate at prodigious speed'.[10]

Given the anxiety about a seaborne or airborne attack in the wake of Dunkirk, his Home Forces stepped up their defence preparations, such as the immobilisation of ports, the establishment of submarine patrols and the obstruction of landing grounds. A comprehensive progress report from GHQ Home Forces sent to all army commands on 4 June, the last day of Operation Dynamo, revealed this new sense of urgency.

The document explained that a huge reconnaissance operation had been completed along the entire coast from Fraserburgh to Southampton, and 'on such beaches as are considered possible for the landing of troops and vehicles, work has commenced and in many places is well advanced on the construction of pill boxes and wiring.' In addition, 50,000 anti-tank mines had been issued for the beaches and orders placed for another 200,000, while the supply of anti-tank obstacles and lighting sets was also under way. To obstruct any airborne assault by the enemy, work had 'started on 90 per cent of possible landing grounds within five miles of specified ports between Yarmouth and Newhaven and 40 per cent of such grounds between the Tyne and the Humber'.

The Air Ministry, it was reported, was carrying out similar work on 'possible landing grounds within 5 miles of all aerodromes in the eastern counties'. In the same spirit, 90 per cent of the preparations to demolish bridges on vital roads from eastern ports had been completed, and the installation of forty-seven batteries, each comprising a pair of 6-inch guns, would be completed within the following week. Every army command was putting up roadblocks, defences posts and barbed-wire obstructions.

The Local Defence Volunteers were gaining in numbers and strength. Around 300,000 men had been enrolled and already 94,000 rifles and 2 million rounds of .22 ammunition had been issued. Moreover, the police were 'collecting all available rifles from private firms and arrangements are in hand for issuing these'.[11]

One aspect of the Dunkirk aftermath that worried the Chiefs of Staff was the danger of returning soldiers undermining morale with tales of disaster in France or criticism of the RAF. There had been incidents of fights between airmen and soldiers, as well as claims that a few downed pilots were barred access to some boats, so deep was the belief that the air crews had failed to provide enough protection to the troops.

The RAF, understandably, profoundly resented this criticism, given the sacrifices made by their crews. Far from feeling any sense of failure, RAF chiefs believed that Dunkirk showed how their planes could play a vital part in defence, not just in taking on the Luftwaffe but also in deterring a seaborne invasion from the occupied continent. Indeed, the vice-chief of the Air Staff, Richard Peirse, urged that the RAF should be allowed to undertake an immediate bombing campaign between Le Havre and Denmark. 'The primary objective of the whole of our air force should immediately be the ports on the other side of the Channel and the North Sea. If really strong air forces were employed on each in succession, before the Germans can launch their air offensive against us, we might succeed in destroying all the shipping and port facilities, and thus completely prevent an invasion.'¹² This was too radical an approach in the early summer of 1940 when Britain was on the defensive, although a version of Peirse's idea would be adopted to some effect several months later.

Fears that Germany might try to take immediate advantage of Britain's post-Dunkirk equipment crisis were not unfounded. According to the American journalist William Shirer, who was based in Berlin during 1940, the German public believed that Hitler was planning just such a move. 'Most people here think Hitler will try now to conquer England. Perhaps. I am not so sure. Maybe he will try to finish France first.'¹³ Several commanders within the Reich's military felt that this was the moment to strike. The humiliation of the French campaign, they concluded, rendered Britain incapable of mounting any effective resistance. It was better to attack now, said some, before the British army was re-strengthened. That was the firm view of the Luftwaffe commander Albert Kesselring, Goering's deputy. 'England's Expeditionary Force had been wiped out. To re-equip it must take months.'¹⁴

Another of those in favour of an assault was the Luftwaffe general Kurt Student. An aggressive, innovative leader, Student had been a pioneer of the use of paratroops as part of the Reich's blitzkrieg approach. He had, however, been badly injured during the invasion of Holland in May 1940 and did not return to action with the German airborne forces until 1941. Like Kesselring, he was firmly of the view that a daring invasion could have worked, observing after the war, 'If I had been on the scene, I should have urged the use of parachute forces against England while your evacuation from Dunkirk was still in progress, to seize the ports where your troops were landing. It was known that most of them had left Dunkirk without their heavier weapons.'[15]

A more influential advocate of early attack was Erhard Milch, the inspector general of the Luftwaffe and therefore deeply involved with German military planning in 1940. Like von Bock, he had been amazed by the wreckage at Dunkirk but, recognising that over 330,000 men had escaped, he feared that Germany had 'no time to waste'. He therefore hatched a daring scheme for an immediate invasion, in which the attack would be spearheaded by paratroopers landing in southern England under the cover of heavy bombing. They would seize a couple of airfields, which could be used to bring in fleets of Junkers Ju52 transports carrying ammunition and weapons. With this bridgehead established, ten infantry divisions could then be shipped across the Channel to break the last remnants of resistance in England's weakened defences.

Milch was so enthused with his own idea that he went to see Goering the same day and set out his plan, declaring that an attack on Britain must be made 'without delay', then adding, 'I warn you, Herr Field Marshal, that if you give England three or four weeks to recoup, it will be too late.'[16] Goering was initially dismissive, saying, 'It can't be done,' but changed his mind overnight. The next day, 6 June, he visited Hitler in Brûly-de-Peche, the Belgian village where the Führer based himself during the final stages of the French campaign. There Goering outlined Milch's scheme, which he claimed was 'a blueprint for victory'.[17] But Hitler was not persuaded. 'Do nothing,' he told Goering.[18] His thoughts were focused on completing his victory over France, not on the conquest of England.

The Führer's dismissal of Milch's plan was understandable. Until his meeting with Admiral Raeder on 21 May, he had not even considered the possibility of an invasion. No detailed preparations had been made for what was bound to be a formidable undertaking, even with Britain's defences in such a precarious state. In the first week of June, the sole planning work then being carried out was a preliminary survey by Raeder's Kriegsmarine of Germany's shipping capacity and the possible development of landing craft. Like Hitler, the general staff of the German army had given little thought to an invasion because, at that stage, it 'considered the carrying out impossible'.[19]

What the sceptics grasped, unlike Milch and Goering, was that although the BEF had been broken, the Royal Navy remained largely intact and was more than ten times the size of the Kriegsmarine. Moreover, the RAF had proved a dangerous adversary at Dunkirk and would be even more deadly over home territory. Nor did the Germans have the transport available for a large-scale attack by airborne troops and parachutists. Even at the end of

June, the Luftwaffe had only 357 Ju52s, each capable of carrying just twelve parachutists. On another level Hitler saw France's downfall, not a direct invasion, as the key to bringing about Britain's surrender. Once the Wehrmacht had marched into Paris, he believed, Churchill would have to recognise that it was futile to continue the war.

The fall of France was not far away. The French army, utterly demoralised, was in ceaseless retreat; the French government under Reynaud was gripped by talk of an armistice. As the Germans advanced towards Paris, Churchill made a series of increasingly dangerous trips by air across the Channel to meet Reynaud and the French government at the Supreme Allied War Council. During these dark hours, the French, particularly General Weygand, urged Britain to throw the entire might of RAF Fighter Command into the battle in a last-minute gamble to turn the tide against the Germans. This demand was too much, even for Churchill. With his usual prescience, he wrote on 9 June,

> It would be wrong to send the bulk of our fighters to this battle and when it was lost, as is probable, be left with no means of carrying on the war. I think we have a harder, longer and more hopeful duty to perform. Advantages of resisting German air attack in this Island, where we can concentrate very powerful fighter strength, and hope to knock out four or five hostiles to one of ours, are far superior to fighting in France, where we are inevitably outnumbered and rarely exceed a two to one ratio of destruction and where our aircraft are often destroyed at exposed aerodromes.[20]

He was determined, however, to provide France with other military support, not only through munitions but also men. Remarkable as it might seem, soon after the evacuation from Dunkirk, British empire troops were on their way back to France, as the War Cabinet decided to send the 52nd Lowland Division and the 1st Canadian Division to join the floundering Allied campaign. These two divisions became part of a reconstituted British Expeditionary Force, known as the Second BEF, comprising 200,000 men and commanded by Alan Brooke.

The lieutenant general was perplexed at his mission, which seemed utterly pointless, more a political gesture than a military operation. He received his instructions on 10 June just as France's slim chances of survival dramatically worsened; the day before, the Germans had broken the final French defence lines on the Somme, and von Rundstedt's panzers had reached Rouen, not far north-east of Paris. Now the French government was fleeing the capital. Paris was made an open city and awaited her fate with a sense of grim inevitability. Long lines of anxious refugees and cars packed with luggage moved along the roads to the south and west, occasionally coming under fire from the Luftwaffe. In the courtyards of government offices, civil servants made bonfires of papers to deny the enemy information or destroy incriminating evidence of political corruption.

The catastrophe was made all the worse by Italy having declared war against the Allies a month earlier, on 10 May. This entirely cynical move, unsupported by military reasons, permitted Mussolini to grab a share of the spoils of conquest without the ordeal of much fighting. For Britain, the long-awaited news was another blow in the depths of crisis. Although Italy's army was nothing like as powerful as Germany's, her navy was the fourth largest in the world and represented a major threat to Britain's position in the Mediterranean, which meant that it would now be harder to reinforce the Home Fleet against a German invasion.

Mussolini's declaration had far-reaching consequences for civic life in Britain. In June 1940, there were about 19,000 Italians living in the United Kingdom, many of them from long-established families. After the western offensive in May 1940, British public opinion turned decisively against immigrants from enemy nations. Italy's entry into the war led to a renewed bout of public hostility towards these aliens, and this time Churchill, now in a much stronger position than he had been in mid-May, was in no mood to engage in a lengthy debate about the civil rights of Italians. 'Collar the lot,' he announced, urging the internment of all Italian males aged between seventeen and sixty with less than twenty years' residence in the United Kingdom.[21] The Home Secretary agreed, and the next day saw the start of the round-ups by the police.

This official crackdown was accompanied by criminal attacks on Italian businesses and sporadic anti-Italian riots in several major British cities. In Glasgow, a group of hooligans marched down a couple of the main roads, wrecking every Italian café, restaurant or ice-cream parlour, while in Edinburgh two premises were so badly vandalised that only the bare walls were left standing. Public fury at the Italians ran through all sections of society. Even at the highest rank of the Foreign Office, Cadogan wrote privately of the political discussion about ice-cream vendors: 'Drown the brutes is what I'd like to do.'[22]

The indiscriminate nature of the attacks and the arrests hardly lived up to the British tradition of fairness. Just as refugees and innocent citizens had been apprehended during the clampdown in May targeted on German nationals, so the anti-Italian net caught a host of entirely loyal people of Italian origin. Among those seized were Luigi Bianchi, the head chef of the Café Royal, and Rene and Burni Manetti, who had been clowns at the renowned Bertram Mills circus for the last fifteen years. But the public and the politicians alike believed that this was not the moment for delicate sensitivities. As in so many other fields in the summer of 1940, ruthlessness was what Britain needed. The War Cabinet had not been impressed by the recent performance of the intelligence services. Even before the round-up of the Italians, ministers had decided that change was needed at the top of MI5. Since the start of the war, the reputation of the director-general Sir Vernon Kell had been plummeting. He had lost the trust of Churchill during the Phoney War, when MI5 had been guilty of several intelligence failures, most notably a serious incident of sabotage at the Woolwich arsenal. Kell had also been tainted by the Captain Ramsay affair, in which Anna Wolkoff had on several occasions invoked his name as a family friend in her bid to escape detention.

On 10 May, Kell was sacked by Churchill, while his ineffectual deputy Eric Holt Wilson also resigned. Kell's successor was Brigadier Oswald 'Jasper' Harker, a former senior officer in the Indian Police who had later become head of MI5's B Division in charge of investigating subversion. Harker, though younger than Kell and more suave, turned out to be scarcely more effective, as recalled by Ashton Roskill, an MI5 wartime agent: 'He was a sort of highly polished barrel which, if tapped, would sound hollow because it was.'[23] However, his weaknesses were not as important as they might have seemed, for in some respects, especially on wider strategic policy, the real power lay with the dynamic chairman of the Home Defence Committee, Lord Swinton, who had executive control over MI5.

By the time of Kell's sacking, France was less than a week away from defeat. Churchill appealed to President Roosevelt to intervene by providing urgent material support to both the Allies. But Roosevelt, bound by the Neutrality Act, the continuing mood of isolationism and the US constitution, which gave Congress the power of declaring war, could offer nothing immediate to France except warm words. On the night of 13 June, the prime minister's private secretary John Colville complained in his diary about the White House's refusal to do more. 'Roosevelt has got to proceed cautiously, but the plain truth is that America has been caught napping, militarily and industrially. She may be really useful to us in a year; but we are living hour to hour.'[24]

Although deprived of American backing Churchill had not exhausted all his options. He now wanted to see the reconstituted Second BEF under Brooke join up with the French, go on the offensive or at least establish an Allied redoubt in Brittany. But it was another forlorn hope. As Brooke told Weygand at Orléans on 14 June, 'I considered the Brittany scheme a wild project that was quite impossible.'[25] That afternoon he rang Dill, the Chief of the Imperial General Staff, to tell him that 'the only course open to us' was to re-embark the BEF. The CIGS appeared to accept this. Later that evening, he telephoned Dill again to discuss the evacuation. To Brooke's surprise, he was put through to Downing Street, where Dill was in a meeting with Churchill. Once more, Brooke made the case for an immediate return to Britain.

'The Prime Minister does not want you to do that,' said Dill.

'What the hell does he want?' replied Brooke.

'He wants to speak to you.'

There followed an awkward half-hour's conversation down a crackling line, during which Churchill stressed the need to make the French feel that Britain was supporting them. 'It is impossible to make a corpse feel,' said Brooke. As the talk went on, the lieutenant general developed the impression that Churchill believed he was 'suffering from cold feet'. This was too much for the BEF commander, who recalled: 'I was repeatedly on the verge of losing my temper.' Gradually he convinced the prime minister of the argument for withdrawal. Churchill said tersely, 'All right, I agree with you,' before giving Brooke the authority to organise the evacuation from the northern and western French ports.[26] Brooke's willingness to stand up to Churchill would later have tremendous personal consequences for the command of Britain's defences.

Yet even when the French were planning a retreat to Bordeaux and a call for negotiations with Germany, the British government clung to the hope that, after mainland France had fallen, the Gallic fight against the Reich could be carried on by sea and from her colonies. In a last-minute gamble, the War Cabinet put forward an extraordinary, outlandish but generous proposal to create a political union between Britain and France. Its aim was partly to stiffen resistance among the French people, partly to strengthen Reynaud's position against the absolute defeatists like Marshal Pétain, and partly to ensure that the vast resources of the French empire, particularly its fleet, did not fall immediately into German hands.

Despite the speed with which it had been drawn up and its brevity at just 300 words, the high-sounding Declaration of Union was astounding in its scope. Britain and France would no longer be separate nations but would become a single entity, with one Cabinet, one Parliament, and 'joint organs of defence, foreign, financial and economic policies'.[27] There would also be joint citizenship for the British and French peoples.

Meeting at 5 p.m. on 16 June, the French Cabinet threw out the proposal. One reason was the suspicion that the whole plan was really a cover for a British takeover of French territory overseas. Another, equally ignoble argument was that the whole scheme was useless because Britain was militarily doomed. 'It is not in France's interest to marry a corpse,' said Pétain.[28] Reynaud resigned, his support in the Cabinet having evaporated. At the age of eighty-four, Pétain became the new leader of the government. Just after midnight on 16 June, he broadcast to the French people: 'It is with a heavy heart I say to you today that it necessary to stop fighting.'[29] France's war was over.

By the time Pétain took office, the evacuation of the Second BEF had already begun, as Brooke had agreed with Churchill. Operation Aerial, as it was known, was an achievement almost on the scale of Dunkirk, although it never became anything like as famous. In fact it was far greater in its geographical range, if not in the numbers saved, than Dunkirk, stretching all the way from Cherbourg on the northern coast to Bayonne near the Spanish border on the south-western coast. Altogether, through another colossal effort by the Royal Navy and the merchant fleet, Aerial saw 191,870 Allied troops taken from France, 144,171 of them British.

However, the operation did not pass without significant casualties. On 17 June the RMS Lancastria, a Cunard liner commandeered by the British government for the duration of the war, was sailing from St Nazaire in Normandy when she came under attack from two waves of German Ju88 bombers. Because of heavy cloud above, which hindered the RAF fighter escorts, the Luftwaffe were able to drop their bombs with precision. In the chaotic scenes of withdrawal, it was not known how many men were aboard the Lancastria but it may have been over 7,000, far beyond the ship's usual capacity of 1,600 passengers and crew. Sergeant Trevor Williams of the Royal Army Ordnance Corps recalled, 'There was a terrific explosion nearby and debris started to fall almost at once on to my steel helmet. I could see nothing but dense smoke and dust through a red-hot glow. Then the ship started listing heavily.'[30] Badly burnt, Williams managed to dive into the water and reach a raft. He was one of the lucky ones.

The Lancastria sank within twenty minutes of being bombed. Over 4,000 died, most of them from drowning, but others from choking on oil or from strafing by the German aircraft. It was the greatest maritime tragedy in British history, significantly worse than the Titanic disaster, and the death toll was the highest for any single British engagement in the entire Second World War. Churchill was so appalled that he used security censorship to ban the press from publishing any report of the sinking.

In addition to the fatalities in Operation Aerial, a large amount of equipment was left behind, some of it needlessly, due to administrative chaos and military indiscipline. Nevertheless, the return from France of a combined total of more than half a million men during late May and June greatly strengthened the home defences against the potential threat from Germany.

That threat loomed larger than ever, now that Germany was free to deploy most of her formidable power against Britain. After all, the Reich now had 2.5 million conquering servicemen standing idle, while the entire continental coast was in Germany's possession. Amidst their triumphalism, it was inevitable that the thoughts of Hitler and the Wehrmacht should turn to England, Germany's still unvanquished foe. Still refusing to recognise the strength of Churchill's determination to fight on, the Führer remained certain that Britain would soon be compelled to accept peace talks. He was therefore in no hurry to push forward with plans for invasion. When Colonel Walter Warlimont, the senior operations staff officer of the Wehrmacht, saw Rear Admiral Kurt Fricke of the Kriegsmarine's Operations Division on 17 June to discuss the logistics of a possible future attack on England, they noted that their leader had not changed his mind with respect to invasion and 'up to now has expressed no such intention since he fully saw the extraordinary difficulties of such an undertaking'.[31]

The Führer's lack of interest in an early invasion was again displayed on 20 June. At a military conference with Hitler and other commanders, Grand Admiral Raeder outlined some of the plans that the Kriegsmarine had already investigated, such as possible routes across the Channel and the laying of minefields, but, with his usual caution, he stressed that the chief responsibility lay with the Luftwaffe, declaring, 'Control of the air is the pre-condition of invasion.'[32] But Hitler, who seemed bored by Raeder's analysis, was not contemplating anything of the kind, as he explained to the head of the German army, Walther von Brauchitsch, in a separate meeting held immediately after the full conference. According to the note of this meeting, 'Von Brauchitsch briefed the Führer on the urgent need either to make peace with Britain or to prepare to carry out an invasion as soon as possible. The Führer is sceptical and considers Britain so weak that, after bombing, major land operations will be unnecessary. The army will move in and take up occupation duties. The Führer comments that one way or another the British will have to accept the situation.'[33]

The Army, with its predictable sense of obedience, embraced Hitler's sceptical position, stating in its official diary on 21 June, 'Execution of landing considered impossible. 20 defending divisions in England so 40 German divisions would have to get over. Air supremacy seems unattainable. The Army General Staff rejects the operation.'[34] The feeling in French military circles was that, if the Germans mounted a swift invasion, British resistance would be ineffectual. At one stage during the final Allied talks, the French generals told Churchill that 'in three weeks England will have her neck wrung like a chicken.'[35]

However, that Gallic feeling of despair was not broadly shared by the British government or people. If anything, the fall of France actually lifted public spirits. Just as Dunkirk, which might have been interpreted as a disaster, was regarded as an act of heroism, so the end of the French campaign had a perverse revitalising effect: no longer weighed down by the burden of continental entanglements, Britain could now concentrate on her defence. It was an attitude well captured by King George VI in a letter to his mother, the imperious Queen Mary: 'I feel happier now we have no allies to be polite to and to pamper.'[36]

Opinion surveys by the Ministry of Information in the wake of France's surrender found an increase in confidence. There was little support for the idea that Britain should give up the fight. The researchers found that 75 per cent of the public said that the war would continue, and only 15 per cent believed that it would end soon. That kind of resolution shone through a letter from Christopher Mayhew, a future Labour minister, then a BEF officer just back from Dunkirk, to his parents on 17 June. 'We have suffered tremendous losses and the Nazis will still be more powerful and confident. But Hitler has a long way to go yet and I've no doubt whatever we're going to see him to the end of the journey if we don't beat him first.'[37]

This was the mood that Churchill sought to reinforce when, on 18 June, he made his renowned 'Finest Hour' speech in the Commons, which was broadcast to the nation that evening. In this inspiring forty-minute oration, one of the most powerful ever made in the English language, Churchill gave the British people the central role in the making of history and the conquest of good over evil. The future of civilisation, he warned, depended on the forthcoming battle against the Reich. 'The whole fury and might of the enemy must very soon be turned on us. Hitler knows he will have to break us in this island or lose the war.' So the nation had to be resolute in the ordeal that now lay ahead. 'Let us therefore brace ourselves to our duties and so conduct ourselves that if the British Commonwealth and Empire lasts for a thousand years, men will still say, "This was their Finest Hour."'[38]

They were magnificent, stirring words that have resonated ever since, but Churchill knew he would need more than just rhetoric to ward off the Germans. During one of their meetings in those anguished days of mid-June, Weygand said to Churchill, 'If we capitulate, the great might of Germany will be concentrated on invading England. And then what will you do?' According to Ismay's account, Churchill replied jocularly that he 'would propose to drown as many as possible of them on the way over' and 'to knock the others on the head as they crawled ashore'.[39] The reality would be very different.

8

'Making bricks without much straw'

———

O N 15 JUNE, the day before Reynaud resigned as French prime minister, Churchill wrote to President Roosevelt in stark terms: 'The changed strategical situation brought about by the possession by the enemy of the whole coast of Europe from Norway to the channel has faced us with a prospect of invasion which has more hopes of success than we ever conceived possible.'[1] It suited Churchill's political purpose to stress the danger that Britain faced, for at that moment he was pushing for more American logistical support, particularly in the form of munitions and naval destroyers. 'The successful defence of this island will be the only hope of averting the collapse of civilisation as we define it. We must ask therefore as a matter of life or death to be reinforced with these destroyers. We will carry out the struggle against whatever the odds but it may well be beyond our resources unless we receive every reinforcement.'[2]

Yet the anxiety about invasion that Churchill professed to Roosevelt did not reflect his convictions. In reality he was sceptical of many of the invasion reports that referred to the threat and in one Cabinet paper of 16 June he wrote, 'We are asked to consider many plans of possible invasion by Germany. Some of these seem to me very absurd.'[3] Although he was privately doubtful about an immediate assault, he believed that the response to the danger galvanised the armed forces and also kept the public in a heightened state of alert.

The army's training, morale and leadership all had to be addressed, but the two biggest, most immediate problems in June 1940 were: first, the appalling lack of equipment; and second, the shortage of manpower, for the units that had just returned from France through Operations Dynamo and Aerial would not be reassembled until the beginning of July.

In early June the British army had only fifteen full infantry divisions in home defence service, plus part of the 2nd Armoured Division. In total, this represented a force of about 170,000 men. There were also more than 300,000 in the Local Defence Volunteers, although at this point many of them were still unarmed since only 94,000 rifles had been issued to them. Eight of the army's regular fifteen divisions were given the role of guarding

Britain's shoreline, with six of them stationed between the Wash and the Hampshire coast. The rear elements of the coastal divisions were deployed to deal with airborne attacks and the defence of airfields, although, as Ironside complained to Dill, the numbers he had at his disposal in the front line were woefully inadequate. 'These divisions are holding some 80 miles of coast and 1,100 to 1,600 square miles behind the coast. As divisions are about 10,000 strong, it is apparent that there are few places in which a German landing can be opposed in strength quickly.'[4]

Of the other seven divisions, four were training formations and three were held in reserve to act as mobile forces, in theory ready to be sent to any area under attack. In practice, however, these reserves were not nearly as mobile as the army planners claimed, for dedicated transport was also in desperately short supply in June and was generally used only for military supplies and field artillery. So the mobile divisions had to use hired motor coaches, which was hardly ideal. Their arrival was later remembered by Patrick Barrass of the 47th Division, based at Hereford.

> Our job would have been to go out and try and hold down parachutists or go further south and serve as a mobile reserve. We weren't actually mobile until I remember one morning waking up and finding a whole lot of red buses with silver tops, single deckers, all parked under the trees by the fields. They were Midland red buses from Birmingham. They were our tactical transport. A couple of days later they had all disappeared under camouflage paint. Troop carriers were not available in any numbers until the next year.[5]

But the drivers could not always be relied upon in a crisis, as Sidney Nuttal, of the Royal Army Ordnance Corps, learnt. Nuttal's battalion was stationed near Newcastle-upon-Tyne and they, too, were provided with civilian buses from the Midlands.

> We had a stand-to when we had to dash to the coast in the middle of the night. These drivers had been living the life of Riley – they had money for food; they had accommodation in hotels and lodging houses. But when it came to the night when we were going to move off to fight, they refused to drive the buses. 'We didn't come here to get killed.' That's exactly what they said to us in real Brummie accents. We threw them off the buses and anybody that could drive climbed in and I drove a Midland Red bus up to the coast. We got there and were deployed but of course it was a false alarm.[6]

Even where there enough troops, all types of equipment, from tanks to rifles, were in extremely short supply in early June. The dire situation was spelt out in an official memorandum,[7] dated 13 June, on the strength of Britain's defences, which revealed that the Home Forces had 'a few' 2- and 3-inch mortars, just 163 medium and heavy guns, and 37 armoured cars. Each division should have had 72 field guns but in total there were only

420. The supply of Bren guns was a little better, with 2,300 available. The memorandum also highlighted the shortages of tanks, with a total of just 500 across the country. The majority were Vickers Mark VI light tanks, which had been outgunned by the powerful German Panzer IIIs in France. According to this official document, the army could muster just 33 Cruiser tanks, which were in fact ineffective in battle, although in his history of the Second World War Churchill claimed that there were 103 of them in Britain after the fall of France. Similarly, the official inventory showed that the entire army possessed just 50 two-pounder anti-tank guns, whereas each division alone should have had 48 of them.

In early June, according to the historian David Newbold, the majority of divisions had 'at most 47 Boys anti-tank rifles', less than a sixth of the officially required number.[8] The Boys rifles were weapons with a powerful recoil that could penetrate half an inch of metal at 300 yards. Each division on average had only 3,000 Mills bombs, which had been the British army's standard hand grenades since they were developed by the explosives engineer William Mills in 1915. The same deficiencies could be found in shells, bullets and mortar rounds.

It was hardly surprising, then, that throughout the army there were complaints about shortages. The 55th (Lancashire), based in Suffolk, and the 18th (East Anglian) in Norfolk, had only twelve field guns between them to guard the entire shoreline stretching from the Wash to the Thames. Incredibly, the East Anglian Division had no anti-tank guns at all. The story was just as worrying in Kent, the most vulnerable part of the coast.

When Winston Churchill inspected the beach defences at St Margaret's Bay near Dover towards the end of the month, the local brigadier told him that he had just six rounds of ammunition for each gun and then 'asked, with a slight air of challenge, whether he was justified in letting his men fire one single round for practice in order that they might at least know how the weapon worked'. According to his own account, the prime minister replied that the army 'could not afford practice rounds, and that fire should be held for the last moment at the closest range'.[9] In nearby Ramsgate, Peter Ewood was part of a unit protecting a gun battery. 'In the event of invasion, the defence of that line was down to us. With six rifles and a dozen or so pickaxe handles, the chances of any spirited resistance seemed rather on the thin side. Our officers instructed us that should paratroopers land, we were to rush at them with pickaxe handles, stun them and grab their guns.'[10]

Further along the south coast, which was just as vulnerable to landings, it was the same picture, as Claude Auchinleck, the head of V Corps in Southern Command, wrote at the end of the month: 'I am making bricks without much straw; two divisions on a hundred mile front.'[11] Auchinleck's chief Alan Brooke, who had been appointed head of Southern Command on his return from France, was just as disturbed. A fortnight after his return from France, he made a tour of coastal bases in Dorset. 'The more I see the nakedness of our defences, the more appalled I am! Untrained men, no arms, no transport, and no equipment.'[12]

As Alan Brooke's diary entry revealed, the threat of invasion cast a looming, constant shadow throughout June. Whatever Churchill thought, the idea that the Germans were planning to land gripped the authorities. Tension was permanently in the air. Most officials and military leaders believed that Britain was on the verge of a climactic struggle for national survival.

This pressure was exacerbated by the almost daily intelligence of the Germans' menacing plans towards England. On 22 June, the Combined Intelligence Committee reported that 'a large number of barges' that appeared to be 'in excess of trade requirements' had been sighted by RAF reconnaissance along the Belgian and Dutch coasts, commenting, 'They could be used for invasion purposes and must therefore be treated as a threat.' The Committee also noted that the Germans were building aerodromes around Calais.[13]

The same day Major General Philip Whitefoord of the Directorate of Military Intelligence wrote to GHQ of Home Forces with two alarming reports. One came from a source in Switzerland, claiming that 'the invaders will land (apparently from the air), 35,000 at a time and that disembarkations from the sea will support these operations. Troop-carrying aeroplanes will also carry some kind of tank and artillery. They will fly very low, approximately 1000 feet. Gas will be used. There will be several hours of preliminary bombardment.' The other report came from Norway and warned that 'considerable quantities of tanks and heavy guns are being collected at Stavanger and Bergen. New aerodromes are being prepared in the neighbourhood of these two towns for the use of giant, troop-carrying machines, which are stated to carry 50 men each.'[14] Only five days later, on 27 June, the Combined Intelligence Committee was told that the Germans were researching the development of amphibious tanks in an experimental base in the Baltic. And there was a further report that some of the barges in the Low Countries now had 'German patrol recognition markings', consisting of a white stripe across the bows.[15]

By the end of the month, the Foreign Office had picked up a definitive date for invasion. On 30 June, Lord Halifax passed on to Churchill and other senior ministers a letter from August Zaleski, the Polish ambassador to London, who reported that his counterpart in Berne had ascertained 'from reliable German sources connected with the German Military Attaché' that 'an attack on England is to take place between 6th and 8th July'.[16]

The growing siege mentality imposed a heavy burden on the regular troops, who had to man the defences and keep a constant lookout over the coast and skies. When the *Daily Telegraph* journalist Leonard Marshland Gander went down to the Sussex coast in June, he came across a sergeant who said that so long were his hours on duty, he had not been able to take his boots off for three days. Ernie Faulkner of the Devonshire Regiment had this memory of that same period when he was stationed in the West Country:

> They kept us moving along the coast because they did not know where the invasion would take place. You had to learn a different password every night when you were on guard in the pillboxes on the coast. I felt that the Germans could have invaded at any moment. We had very old equipment. In the pillboxes all we had were old Lewis guns and Maxim machine guns from the First World War. That's all we had, apart from our rifles. You had to stay in the box on duty, two hours on, four hours off. Also when we went on patrol, we had just a canister of soup or a flask of tea.[17]

It was no surprise that, in this tense atmosphere, nervous soldiers did not always exercise restraint. The less experience and training the men had, the more inclined they were to be jumpy. H.V. Cusson, a member of the Buffs Regiment who was put on coastal duty manning a machine-gun nest near an airfield after just two days' training on a Lewis gun, later admitted, 'My nerves was so bad that anything approaching the airfield was fired at. I let rip at a plane once and must have frightened the pilot as he circled round to see who the culprit was. It was one of ours.'[18] At times this trigger-happy behaviour had fatal results, especially where the Local Defence Volunteers were in charge of roadblocks. On the night of 2/3 June, the LDV units accidentally killed four motorists at separate locations, claiming that they had failed to stop when ordered to do so, although in the blackout it was not easy for drivers to see checkpoints.

Some people complained about the authoritarian instincts of too many LDVs, who appeared to revel in their power and in their ability to demand compliance with even the pettiest regulations. As one member of a London platoon recalled, 'It was the LDVs' greatest delight to pull up all policemen and ask them for their identity cards.'[19]

In June 1940, incidents provoked by LDV overreactions were just part of civic life. Normality in all areas was suspended. Everywhere there were indicators of the invasion threat, from the absence of signposts to the presence of pillboxes, from barrage balloons in the sky to air-raid shelters in the ground. When the new American military attaché General Raymond Lee arrived in London in mid-June, he was immediately struck by the intensity of the preparations: 'What areas have not been dug up for trenches have been ruined with piles of earth to prevent their use as landing fields,'

Issued by the Ministry of Information   in co-operation with the War Office
and the Ministry of Home Security.

If the
INVADER
comes

WHAT TO DO — AND HOW TO DO IT

THE Germans threaten to invade Great Britain. If they do so they will be driven out by our Navy, our Army and our Air Force. Yet the ordinary men and women of the civilian population will also have their part to play. Hitler's invasions of Poland, Holland and Belgium were greatly helped by the fact that the civilian population was taken by surprise. They did not know what to do when the moment came. *You must not be taken by surprise.* This leaflet tells you what general line you should take. More detailed instructions will be given you when the danger comes nearer. Meanwhile, read these instructions carefully and be prepared to carry them out.

I

When Holland and Belgium were invaded, the civilian population fled from their homes. They crowded on the roads, in cars, in carts, on bicycles and on foot, and so helped the enemy by preventing their own armies from advancing against the invaders. You must not allow that to happen here. Your first rule, therefore, is :—

(1) IF THE GERMANS COME, BY PARACHUTE, AEROPLANE OR SHIP, YOU MUST REMAIN WHERE YOU ARE. THE ORDER IS "STAY PUT".

If the Commander in Chief decides that the place where you live must be evacuated, he will tell you when and how to leave. Until you receive such orders you must remain where you are. If you run away, you will be exposed to far greater danger because you will be machine-gunned from the air as were civilians in Holland and Belgium, and you will also block the roads by which our own armies will advance to turn the Germans out.

II

There is another method which the Germans adopt in their invasion. They make use of the civilian population in order to create confusion and panic. They spread false rumours and issue false instructions. In order to prevent this, you should obey the second rule, which is as follows :—

(2) DO NOT BELIEVE RUMOURS AND DO NOT SPREAD THEM. WHEN YOU RECEIVE AN ORDER, MAKE QUITE SURE THAT IT IS A TRUE ORDER AND NOT A FAKED ORDER. MOST OF YOU KNOW YOUR POLICEMEN AND YOUR A.R.P. WARDENS BY SIGHT, YOU CAN TRUST THEM. IF YOU KEEP YOUR HEADS, YOU CAN ALSO TELL WHETHER A MILITARY OFFICER IS REALLY BRITISH OR ONLY PRETENDING TO BE SO. IF IN DOUBT ASK THE POLICE-MAN OR THE A.R.P. WARDEN. USE YOUR COMMON SENSE.

The threat of invasion becomes a dark reality for the British public. This leaflet, issued by the Ministry of Information in June 1940, was written by Sir Kenneth Clark, director of the National Gallery, with the help of the National Labour MP and author Harold Nicolson

he wrote, adding that 'London seems dark as a pocket, with various familiar streets barricaded and barbed wired.'[20]

The danger was explicitly brought home to British citizens when, on 19 June, the Ministry of Information produced a leaflet entitled 'If the Invader Comes'. Sent to every household in the country, it warned the public that 'The Germans threaten to invade Great Britain' but promised that 'If they do so they will be driven out by our Navy, our Army and our Air Force.'

The civilian population, however, would have 'their part to play' in the response to invasion.

To avoid hampering the army's effectiveness by clogging up the country's main arteries, the 'first rule' was that if the Germans come 'you must remain where you are. The order is "Stay Put".' The leaflet further warned against spreading rumours. 'If you see anything suspicious, do not rush around telling your neighbours all about it. Go at once to the nearest police station or military officer.' There was also a warning against providing even the most basic assistance to the enemy.[21]

If the leaflet was meant to reassure the public, it did not entirely succeed. The ministry's own pollsters found that it had 'created alarm in some quarters', such as East Anglia, where the wording was said to be 'too frightening'.[22] Some felt that the advice, especially about not feeding the German invader, was laughable. The writer and artist Frances Faviell stuck the pamphlet up on a wall to cheer herself up, saying, 'It never failed to amuse me when I was depressed.'[23]

Those living on the southern and eastern coasts were particularly affected by invasion preparations when the government announced on 20 June that the entire strip of coast from the Wash to Rye in Sussex, extending 20 miles inland, was to be a 'defence area'. Not only was a curfew imposed from 5 p.m. until 5 a.m., but also, according to the official declaration, 'all persons entering the area are liable to be questioned by the police or military as to the reasons for their entry or their presence in the area. If they are unable to produce satisfactory evidence that they are engaged in business or have similar good reasons, they will be asked to leave.'[24] On 6 July, the coastal defence zone was extended from Sussex to Dorset. So draconian was this regulation that no private vehicles were allowed on the roads within the restricted zone, while 'owners of seaside bungalows' were told that 'they will not be allowed to visit them for holiday purposes. They will have to satisfy the police or military authorities that the purpose of their visit is purely of a business character connected with the maintenance of their property.'[25]

All this represented a major restriction on liberty but it could occasionally have a lighter side. In the West Country village of Wilmington, which was just inside the defence zone, a courting couple were becoming amorous inside their parked car one evening. Unfortunately for them, their vehicle was spotted by a guardsman, who marched over and banged on the window on the driver's side.

'Yes?' asked the man.

'You've just entered a prohibited area.'

'Oh no he hasn't,' replied the woman with indignation.[26]

Another precaution that had a heavy impact on normal English life was the decision by the government to impose a ban on the ringing of church bells for the remainder of the war. From 13 June, they would be rung solely by the police or the military to signal that the invasion had started. As Sir Auckland Geddes, who was regional commissioner for the South-East, recalled: 'The signal at the time was supposed to be used only in the counties of Kent and Sussex and in the rural areas, but somehow or other the order became more or less sacrosanct and spread all over the country.'[27] *Ringing World* magazine described the ban as 'a stunning blow to ringing from which, even when the war is over, it will take a long time to recover'.[28]

The heightened awareness of a possible invasion inevitably gave rise to frequent scares and false alarms. Suspicions could be aroused by an unfamiliar face in a rural village or a strange accent in an urban pub. A flock of swans descending on a lake could be mistaken for German paratroopers; the wind through the trees could be misinterpreted as a low-flying aircraft.

By far the biggest invasion scare in June was a near farcical incident that later became ironically known as the 'Battle of Bewdley'. At 4 p.m. on 30 June the police in this Worcestershire town received a report from two members of the public that enemy parachutists had landed nearby. The police passed on the information to the LDVs who went eagerly into action. Roadblocks were established. Several platoons of volunteers scoured the woods and fields. A Bren carrier was sent to Bewdley from the local regular army barracks. At 5.30 p.m., in the neighbouring town of Stourport-on-Severn, the church bells rang out to warn that the invaders had landed. In the mounting excitement and fear, the local branch of the Territorial Army placed explosive charges under the main bridge into Bewdley.

Leonard Burrows, a young volunteer from nearby Kidderminster, was told to collect his uniform and rifle. Amidst the 'pandemonium', his sergeant then 'gave me a clip of five bullets; he said, "make them all count".'[29] The official history of the Bewdley LDV battalion later described the scene in the town when the scare was at its peak: 'Civilians thronged every point of military activity through the action; roads and bridges were so crowded that troop movements and road checks were virtually impossible. High Street, Stourport and Load Street in Bewdley were both solid with people and matters were made worse by the fact that in both places there were motor coach trips due to return.'[30] Yet after almost twelve hours of frantic searching, not a single German had been found. At 4 a.m. the all-clear was sounded. The entire episode had been a false alarm. A few days later the explanation for the scare emerged: some hay in the fields had been caught up in a strong wind and then fallen to the ground when the wind dropped, appearing to some fevered imaginations as descending parachutes.

The sense of apprehension that led to incidents like the 'Battle of

Bewdley' was partly fuelled by the perception that Britain was ill prepared to meet an invasion. Yet the depths of the crisis should not be exaggerated. In the invigorating spirit that was so characteristic of 1940, Britain was already rearming and strengthening its defences. The anxiety over invasion was matched by a determination to provide the means of resistance. It was an attitude reflected not only in increased military production at home but also in imports and innovation.

In June fighter output leapt from 325 the previous month to 446, and in July to 496, far higher figures than the Chiefs of Staff expected, partly due to the volcanic influence of the maverick press baron Lord Beaverbrook, who had been appointed Minister of Aircraft production in May. He had immediately overhauled the management of the aeroplane factories, particularly the vast Spitfire plant at Castle Bromwich in Birmingham, where workforce indiscipline and trade union intransigence had been rife. Other parts of war production saw welcome, if less spectacular, progress during the summer months. The output of infantry and cruiser tanks rose to 123 a month in June, July and August, making up for the losses after Dunkirk. Production of four-wheeled vehicles was an impressive 9,000 a month throughout the summer, while the deliveries of field guns increased from 42 in June to 60 in July, reaching 72 in August.

This was still nowhere near enough, but some of the deficiency was met by the kind of inventiveness at which the British excelled. Laboratories and workshops hummed with daring ideas; the military were bombarded with unconventional plans. Some of the schemes were brilliant, some bizarre, but what united them was a resourceful determination to enhance the capabilities of Britain's defences. One correspondent wrote to *Picture Post* magazine, urging that the army 'utilize the services of British and Norwegian sailors who have worked on whaling ships. A harpoon can be fired with sufficient accuracy to penetrate the vulnerable chinks in a tank's armour.'[31] There were also proposals to hang blankets from wires across the road, thereby blinding enemy drivers, or to set boards with nails on the ground to puncture tyres or feet.

Brigadier Harry Hopthrow, who worked at the Directorate of Fortifications in GHQ Home Forces, recalled having been approached by a military commander with the idea of deterring enemy landing craft through the use of special large trumpets on the beaches, which 'if sounded at the right note, could make people violently sick'.[32] Sir Roger Keyes, the director of Combined Operations, received a suggestion that loudspeakers be installed along the coast equipped with gramophone records in the German language, 'telling the landing craft to return to the bases as the invasion is off. The basis of the idea is the German characteristic of inherent obedience to orders.'[33]

Several of the more unorthodox ideas were dreamt up by the Department of Miscellaneous Weapons Development, which soon acquired the nickname of the 'Department of Miscellaneous Wheezes and Dodges'. The organisation was headed by Commander Charles Goodeve, who had an original mind, once proposing the use of fish as mine detectors. The department was soon investigating a host of unconventional devices. One, called the 'Wroxham Roaster', was a set of cords lying just below the water's surface and connected to large amount of gelignite, which, in theory, would explode when the cords caught the floats of an amphibious plane on landing. Goodeve's department was also inundated with propositions from enthusiastic civilians, from searchlights that could supposedly freeze planes to the placement of high-tension cables on beaches to electrocute invading troops.

A further source of sometimes eccentric creativity was the novelist Dennis Wheatley who, following the success of his first paper for the War Office on a potential German invasion strategy, had been commissioned to consider ideas for countering a German assault. In this 17,000-word paper that he claimed to have written in just fourteen hours, Wheatley came up with a stream of whimsical suggestions, from a 230-mile barrier of fishing nets to foul the propellers of the German landing craft to wind machines that turned back the fire of German flamethrowers. Wheatley also urged experts to devise a 'very strong magnet which upon being lowered from an aeroplane will affect the compasses of the ships beneath it'.[34]

Most of the ideas never advanced beyond the drawing board, but several were put into production. The most primitive was the Molotov cocktail, first developed in the Spanish civil war and used with some effectiveness by the Finns in their fight against Russia in the winter of 1939/40. It was essentially a glass bottle full of petrol and other flammable liquids, with a fuel-soaked rag as the source of ignition. At a meeting with LDV leaders on 5 June, Ironside admitted that production of the Mills bomb did not yet match demand, so he wanted to introduce 'this thing they've developed in Finland called the Molotoff [sic] cocktail, a bottle with resin, petrol and tar which if thrown on top of a tank will ignite and if you throw half a dozen more on it you have them cooked'.[35] By the second week of June 1940, the army staff recorded, 'We have considered the use of such methods and are making a large number of Molotov cocktails.'[36]

Following the example of the army, many householders manufactured their own stores of petrol bombs. The novelist Vita Sackville-West described spending an afternoon with her friends 'filling old wine bottles with petrol, paraffin and tar and finishing them off with two of Messrs Brocks' [the firework manufacturer] gay blue squibs bound tightly to the sides. This novel form of bottle party is conducted with the usual supply of English chaff and good humour. It is quite difficult to detect the underlying grimness.'[37]

A technical advance on the simple Molotov petrol bomb was the 'Self Igniting Phosphorous' (SIP) grenade, also known officially as the No. 76 Special Incendiary Grenade or the A.W. bomb. The SIP grenade comprised a short-necked, half-pint bottle filled with a highly combustible mixture of white phosphorus, benzene, crude rubber and water, then sealed tightly with a cork. The moment the glass was broken, the phosphorus ignited on contact with the air, thereby setting the rest of the mixture alight. Because of their vulnerability and flammability, these grenades were meant to be handled and stored with care by their users, but such safety-consciousness was not always observed in the frantic summer of 1940, as furniture tradesman William Kellaway of the Holsworthy Home Guard from Devon recalled:

> They were like ginger-beer bottles, filled with chemicals and some kind of rubber. Deadly damn things they were. I had to go to the local railway station to collect cases of them. Did not know what the hell they were. I stored them under the staircase of our flat at the shop. I always thought about that later. There would have been a bit of rumpus if they had gone off. You only needed to get air at the stuff. Crack a bottle and it would go up. You did not even need to light them.[38]

Despite these dangers, the SIP grenades were produced on a colossal scale because of their cheapness. By August 1941, 6 million of them had been made, most of them going to the LDVs.

Another, more sophisticated hand grenade, produced in large quantities, was the Anti-Tank No. 74 grenade, colloquially known as the 'sticky bomb'. It was the brainchild of the Ministry of Supply's Military Intelligence Research unit, or MIR, which specialised in the development of sabotage devices. The department later acquired the nickname of 'Winston Churchill's Toyshop', not only because from November 1940 it was subsumed within the Ministry of Defence under the direct control of the prime minister but also because its idiosyncratic work appealed to his mischievous, boyish streak.

From close range, the sticky bomb, which in essence was a glass sphere filled with nitroglycerine, encased in metal and attached to a wooden handle, could penetrate armour up to an inch thick. It had several drawbacks, however, including its fragility and its tendency to leak. Even worse, there was the inherent risk that its explosive, mucilaginous contents could end up being stuck to the thrower rather than the enemy vehicle. One LDV, Geoff Bowery from Suffolk, described the grenade as 'the product of a madman'.[39] Jack Yeatman, who was in the Gloucester LDV, recalled a terrifying incident when his unit was practising with sticky bombs.

> My most vivid memory is of one of my mates swinging his bomb back over his shoulder to get a good throw – and touching his back.
> 'Sergeant!'

A somewhat plaintive voice – two pounds of high explosive were glued immovably to his collar and very white knuckles gripping the now 'live' handle. It proved the efficacy of the adhesive. We had to cut away the back of his tunic.[40]

On 19 June, the War Office placed a provisional order for 1 million sticky bombs, with full-scale production to begin in early July, reaching an output of 20,000 per week by the first week of August.[41] As with both the Molotov cocktail and the SIP grenade, most of the sticky bombs went to the LDV. Altogether 2.5 million of them were produced between 1940 and 1943.

All these bombs and the Mills grenade could be thrown by hand, but to give more range and power to the defences, the government's engineers also worked throughout 1940 on the development of a number of makeshift missile launchers and guns. These included the Northover projector, a primitive cannon that looked like a piece of drainpipe mounted on a tripod. Named after its inventor Major Harry Northover of the Home Guard, it was principally designed to fire the SIP grenade and had an effective range of about 150 yards. Although cheap to produce, each one costing only £10, the projector was unreliable, as Henry Smith, a London LDV, recalled. 'Unless the utmost care was exercised in loading and firing, there was a natural tendency for the shock of discharge to break the glass bottles in the breech, whereupon the gun, and sometimes the gunner and troops standing leeward, were liable to burst into flames.'[42] The War Office was reluctant to put it into production and it was only after Churchill's personal intervention that manufacturing started in October 1940.

He also had a strong influence over the development of the Blacker Bombard. Another product of the MIR team, this was a mortar that could fire a 26-pound anti-tank bomb and had a crew of three. It was demonstrated in the grounds of Chequers during the summer of 1940 in the presence of a distinguished gathering that included the South African statesman Jan Christian Smuts and the French leader Charles de Gaulle. When fired, the missile flew directly into its target, a tree that stood quite near to the VIPs. Churchill was delighted and ordered the MIR team 'to proceed with all speed with the development of this excellent weapon'.[43] As Stuart Macrae, one of the two engineers heading the MIR, claimed later with a note of impishness, the prime minister's enthusiasm had nothing to do with the fact that the missile 'had very nearly wiped out General de Gaulle'.[44]

Another counter-invasion bomb was the Canadian Pipe Mine, also known as the McNaughton Tube, an anti-tank obstacle that was a long piece of pipe, packed with explosives and pushed under the ground. At the end of June, it was demonstrated in action at Chatham to a group of officers from the Home Forces GHQ. Hydraulic jacks and drills were used to bury a network of connected pipes, each of them about 55 feet long, under the soil to a maximum depth of 8 feet. The pipes were then filled with explosives and detonated, creating a huge ditch that no tank could have crossed. The Home Forces leadership immediately saw the potential. The pipe mine could be used not only under roads, railways and airstrips, but also on approaches to bridges and embankments. One of its great advantages over orthodox anti-tank obstacles was that it could not be seen from the air, so it had a large element of surprise. Moreover, its construction did not interfere with the normal use of land. 'A good form of defence' was the verdict of Alan Brooke.[45] Eventually, through the work of the Canadian drillers and the Royal Engineers, about 40,000 feet of McNaughton pipe mines were installed across southern England, filled with over 100 tons of explosive.

The same enterprising attitude was also applied to the creation of make-shift armoured vehicles. Ironside himself was largely responsible for the arrival of the Humber Light Reconnaissance Car, a 3-ton vehicle made of an open-topped armoured body fitted to the chassis of a Humber Super Snipe motor car. Its armament consisted of a Boys anti-tank rifle and a .303 Bren light machine gun. The Humber LRC proved to be longer-lasting than its origins might have suggested. Around 3,600 units were made up to 1943, and the vehicle saw action in Western Europe and North Africa.

Ironside showed some flair for the extempore by ordering a fleet of seventy-six 10-ton lorries to be equipped with obsolete Hotchkiss four-, six- and twelve-pounder guns in order to create a number of mobile batteries along the coast. Another, more primitive, armoured car that took its name from its creator was the 'Beaverette' since it was initially produced for Lord Beaverbrook to defend his aircraft factories. It had a basic metal hull, about half an inch thick, backed by wooden planks and mounted on a commercial car chassis. Open at the top and rear, this ugly vehicle was both heavy and limited in armament, carrying just a Bren gun or twin Vickers machine guns. Nevertheless, in the emergency of 1940, it filled a gap and around 2,800 were produced.

At the peak of the invasion scare, the government decided to create a number of armoured trains to defend the eastern and southern coasts from Land's End right up to Edinburgh. A group of experts was brought together, headed by Sir Nigel Gresley, the London and Northern Eastern Railway's chief engineer who had designed some of Britain's greatest steam trains like *The Flying Scotsman* and *Mallard*. Gresley's team came up with an arrangement that featured a Great Eastern Class F4 locomotive in the centre of the train, with armour covering the water tanks and cab. At each end of the locomotive there were several armour-plated wagons and gun trucks, carrying well-equipped troops and powerful weaponry. Train K, for instance, which operated between Edinburgh and Berwick, carried two six-pounder Hotchkiss guns, six Bren guns, two Vickers sub-machine guns, four Thompson sub-machines and a detachment from the Royal Armoured Corps complete with rifles and 14,000 rounds of ammunition. In total, twelve of these special armoured trains were built by the London, Midland and Scotland works at Derby and the LNER works at Stratford in east London.

All these measures were valuable, but the shortage of rifles and ammunition was still severe in June, particularly for the LDVs. A small part of the deficiency was made up by the import of 75,000 Ross rifles and 60 million rounds of ammunition from Canada. But there were two problems with the Ross rifles: there were not enough of them and they were badly outdated, having been withdrawn from service in 1916 because they were not up to the demands of trench warfare. Britain desperately needed another source of weaponry, for which she had to look to the United States, that great 'arsenal of democracy', to use Roosevelt's famous phrase.[46]

Churchill's government had seen one minor gain in munitions through the fall of France, in that Anglo-French supply contracts placed with American companies went entirely to the British. But these contracts were for aircraft and aero engines rather than the arms that were so badly needed. President Roosevelt, bombarded with telegrams from Churchill, was deeply sympathetic to Britain's plight but continued to be hampered by the USA's isolationism, which had been reinforced by the Neutrality Acts of the 1930s.

But Roosevelt was a leader of supreme resourcefulness. With characteristic imaginative subtlety, he found a way round the political and legislative impediments. His first move was to require the US military to conduct a full audit of their stock and find as much weaponry as possible, especially rifles and ammunition, that was surplus to requirements. General George Marshall, the US Chief of Staff, told Roosevelt that the army could sell Britain 500,000 Lee-Enfield rifles of First World War vintage, plus 250 rounds for each weapon, 25,000 Browning automatic rifles, 900 howitzers, 22,000 machine guns and 500 mortars.

As soon as the official document was signed on 4 June, declaring that all this matériel was not needed by the US Defense Department, a huge logistical operation swung into action. Within days, the weapons had been gathered up from army depots and arsenals all over the country and were on their way by rail to the US army's docks at Raritan, New Jersey, to where twelve British merchant ships were sailing to pick up the armaments. As the 600 freight trains arrived, men worked day and night to unload them.

But there was another legal hurdle to overcome before the weapons could be packed onto the British freighters. Under American neutrality laws, it was illegal for the US government to sell arms directly to any belligerent nation. Only a private company was allowed to do that. So the White House devised another cunning strategy, whereby the weapons destined for Britain were officially purchased from the War Department by the US Steel Corporation, which then signed a contract in Washington with the British government, selling the entire arsenal for $37.6 million. The moment the contract had been signed, a top US army officer phoned the quayside warehouse at Raritan and ordered the loading to begin. The first ship, the *Eastern Prince*, left the docks two days later and arrived in England in early July.

Many in the American military had deep reservations about the White House's artful scheme. Marshall's aide, Major General Walter Bedell-Smith, later said that 'if we were required to mobilise after having to release guns necessary for this mobilisation and were found to be short, everyone who was party to the deal could expect to be found hanging from a lamppost.'[47] For all such concerns, the supply of US arms, along with the return of former BEF troops to the front line, was to transform the capability and morale of Britain's defence forces.

The crucial question for Ironside was how his thin but strengthening forces would be deployed to cope with the invasion threat, an issue with which he had been wrestling ever since taking over from Kirke in late May. His predecessor's Julius Caesar plan was now badly outdated, having been devised when the Reich did not occupy most of the continent. 'It is a race for time to get something organised before we are attacked,' he wrote in his diary for 13 June.[48] Throughout the middle of that month, Ironside worked on the development of his own plan, which would, necessarily, involve much stronger defensive measures than Kirke had ever been compelled to envisage. His greatest fear was deep penetration by the Germans once their armour had broken through the first line of beach defences. It would, he thought, be difficult to stop the Germans reaching British soil 'since our resources will not permit the occupation of defensive positions to cover all possible landing beaches with fire'. The vital task, therefore, was to establish a series of inland strongpoints 'to prevent the enemy from running riot and tearing the guts out of the country as happened in France and Belgium'.[49] It was this belief in the importance of building effective, secure inland defences that became central to his approach – and it ultimately dragged him into fatal political controversy.

Ironside outlined his thinking in a policy paper of 15 June, entitled 'GHQ Operational Instruction No. 3'. Based on the theory that the invasion would probably take the form of a 'seaborne expedition' crossing from the continent 'during the hours of darkness' and landing somewhere 'from the Wash to Newhaven', his plan to repel such an attack was made up of three main elements: first, a series of beach defences along the coast, comprising pillboxes, anti-tank obstacles, barbed wire and 6-inch naval gun batteries; second, further inland, a network of barriers or 'stops', as Ironside called them, which would use geography, fortifications and military hardware to halt the enemy's advance; finally, behind the 'stops', a mobile reserve, which could be sent to the area of greatest danger.

Spelling out in more detail the nature of these inland 'stops', Ironside said that they would fall into two categories. One type would be made of natural obstructions like waterways or steep hills, which could all be rendered more impregnable by the demolition of bridges and crossings, as well as the cratering of roads. The other type would be static, man-made defences, formed by ditches, minefields, roadblocks and pillboxes. These lines of 'stops', not the beaches, would, he argued, be the key to defeating the enemy.[50]

He further explained that his mobile reserve would be made up of three infantry divisions and the 1st Armoured Division, largely dispersed across the Midlands and East Anglia. In the Ironside plan, their job was to support the static defences, not counter-attack along the coast where they would be spread too thinly.

Not everyone was impressed by this focus on inland fortifications. Churchill was concerned that too many soldiers had been diverted into building work that could have been done by civilians, writing angrily to the War Secretary Anthony Eden, apparently shocked that 'only 57,000 men are being employed on these works . . . I fear that the troops are being used in large numbers on fortifications.'[51] Ironside, however, told the War Cabinet that actually 150,000 civilians and 'all the excavating machinery in the country' were employed on the scheme.[52]

These were arguments about logistics, but towards the end of the month Ironside came under more serious attack for the whole philosophical basis of his plan. His difficulties began on 25 June, when he presented it in full to the Chiefs of Staff. Typically, he was in a bullish frame of mind, telling the chiefs that the 'beach defences were progressing well and those in East Anglia were strong. All beaches on which landings might take place had been blocked and wired, and large numbers of anti-tank mines had been placed in position. Concrete blockhouses were being put up by civilian contract. In Kent alone there were some 900.'[53] Again, he outlined the three key elements of his plan, starting with what he called 'a "crust" on the coast acting as outposts', followed by the 'stop lines' with the mobile reserve behind them.

In an illustration of how important the stop lines were to his plan,

Ironside had by now worked them out in considerable geographical detail. Inland from the coastal 'crust' across southern and eastern England, there were a number of secondary divisional, corps or command lines made up of natural and man-made obstacles such as pillboxes and tank traps. So the Taunton Command 'stop line', for instance, ran from the Bristol Channel to Lyme Bay in Dorset, theoretically isolating Devon and Cornwall from the rest of England. The Salisbury East Command line ran through Wiltshire down to Portsmouth, while the Midhurst Corps line went through the centre of Sussex and Kent.

But more significant than these local defences, which varied greatly in strength, was Ironside's principal line of resistance, the real backbone of his plan. Named the General Headquarters or GHQ line, this was meant to be a formidable barrier that would protect London, the Midlands and the industrial North. It ran eastwards from Gloucestershire, passed Aldershot and Guildford, skirted round the south of London down to Maidstone, then continued northwards to Cambridge. From there it went up to York, past Newcastle-upon-Tyne and on to the Forth Estuary. Apart from this principal course, there was also a separate GHQ line around Plymouth, which was seen as a particularly vulnerable point.

The defences in the GHQ zone were to be much deeper than in other stop lines, and the aim was to create a continuous anti-tank shield, reinforced by minefields, ditches, barbed wire, roadblocks and concrete pillboxes armed with anti-tank guns, anti-tank rifles and machine guns. Between the pillboxes, further firepower would come from infantry units based in trenches or behind earthworks at independent sites called section posts. According to Ironside, once these arrangements were completed Britain would have gained a powerful security cordon.[54]

The Ironside plan was not greeted with universal approval. For his critics, the sheer scale of the fortifications was a source of anxiety rather than admiration. To some, it was almost as if Ironside was trying to build his own British version of the Maginot Line, despite all the evidence of that structure's woeful inefficacy against the marauding German army. Even worse, it was argued, he was concentrating all the effort and resources of the Home Forces on static inland defences, when he should have been focused on guarding the coast. Churchill had spoken of fighting on the beaches, yet Ironside seemed only to want to fight elsewhere.

On 26 June, there was a meeting of the vice-chiefs, whose number included Air Marshal Richard Peirse, Vice Admiral Tom Phillips and General Sir Robert Haining of the Imperial General Staff. It was Peirse, later to be head of Bomber Command, who led the denunciations of Ironside. He started by expressing his 'gravest concern' about the plan, particularly the idea that 'the coast was to be held by a crust'. To him, 'it appeared that the main resistance might only be offered after the enemy had over-run nearly half the country and obtained possession of aerodromes and other vital facilities.' In the RAF's view, 'the only policy was to resist the enemy with the utmost resolution the moment he set foot on the shore.' The other two deputies concurred with Peirse. In a harsh conclusion, they declared that the Ironside plan was 'completely unsound and needed drastic and immediate revision'.[55]

So severe was the criticism that the Chiefs of Staff, led by the head of the RAF Sir Cyril Newall, felt compelled to call another meeting later that same afternoon. The vice-chiefs were also present, as was Churchill's representative Ismay. Once again Peirse repeated his dismay that the coast was only 'to be lightly held by the crust'.[56] The Chiefs agreed that the plan was inadequate: the GHQ stop line 'was in places a long way from the coast' and 'too much emphasis had been placed' on anti-tank obstacles, while the mobile reserves were 'some distance back'.[57] As chairman, Newall concluded that Ironside should revise his plan, beefing up his mobile reserves, and giving more attention to the beach defences and training. The following day the chiefs sent him a paper setting out their concerns, which included 'the insufficient beach defences' and his failure to recognise 'the paramount necessity of resisting the enemy by all means in our power during the vital first phase of operations.'[58]

It was at this point that Churchill intervened. As always in 1940, he showed both a profound interest in the detail of military operations and a willingness to air his strong opinions. Interestingly, his main consideration was not the strength of the beach defences, but the size and speed of the mobile reserves. Indeed in mid-June he had advocated the creation of a specialised, highly mobile division on the German model of storm troopers, as he explained to Ismay in a letter of 19 June. 'There ought to be at least 20,000 Storm Troops or "Leopards" drawn from existing units, ready to spring at the throat of any small landings or descents. These officers and men should be armed with the latest equipment, Tommy guns, grenades etc. and should be given great facilities in motor cycles and armoured cars.'[59] Ironside felt that Churchill's idea of a so-called Leopards division was unfeasible because he did not yet have the requisite weapons and transport but, as he explained to the Defence Committee, he was 'proceeding on the principle that there should be a large number of smaller units in the nature of Storm Troops,' including tank hunting platoons and independent companies.[60]

In a further response to the Ironside plan, sent to the Chiefs of Staff on 28 June, the prime minister summed up his own attitude to invasion, which again ran counter to some of his public rhetoric. He admitted that 'no-one can tell' where the Germans might land, although he felt that the south coast was 'less immediately dangerous' than the east because 'no serious invasion is possible without a harbour with its quays, etc'. But it would be useless 'trying to guard all the beaches,' he continued; the 'safety of the country' depended on the mobile brigades that could be directed quickly, in not less than four hours, to where the Germans landed. 'The battle will be won or lost, not on the beaches but by the mobile brigades and the main reserve.'[61]

By now Ironside was exasperated with all this advice, much of which was contradictory. To him, the talk about mobile brigades and coastal strongholds overlooked the reality of his lack of troops and equipment.

At a further meeting with the chiefs on 29 June, which he described as 'unsatisfactory',[62] Ironside warned them in frank terms of the daunting problems he faced: 'the coastline is terrific in length and we may be attacked at any point of it'; air landings 'can take place anywhere in the United Kingdom or Ireland with even less warning than in the case of seaborne landings'; above all, 'the forces we have available in the United Kingdom are both untrained and armed insufficiently, especially in tanks and guns and anti-tank weapons.' He assured them that 'every day gets our preparations better and our troops better armed', particularly with the beach fortifications and the local static defences. Even so, 'we are forced to disperse' while the Germans 'can concentrate on any point or points they have chosen. All the main points are therefore in the Germans' favour.'[63]

He reiterated this argument in a further despairing memorandum to the chiefs on 3 July, in which he complained: 'The fact is that the forces available are inadequate by some eight divisions for the tasks they have to carry out and I have to do the best I can to meet this serious handicap.' Moreover, he added, if he moved his GHQ reserves 'too close in to the coast, their liberty of manoeuvre will be curtailed'.[64]

Ironside may have felt that his policy was realistic, but the row had succeeded only in fuelling the doubts about his authority. Many felt that the monumental effort required to create stop lines was not just a waste of time but was even counter-productive, in that it reinforced a defensive, siege mentality. Ironside's predecessor Walter Kirke wrote at this time, 'The worst feature of all the invasion scares has been the stoppage of training for mobile warfare in favour of digging, wiring and general concentration on static defence. The summer of 1940, which should have been devoted to the higher training of the staff and troops, has been frittered away in creating obstacles and pill boxes.'[65]

Accusations of incompetence were mixed with fears that Ironside had failed to display the right fighting spirit. From the end of June, his days were numbered.

9

'Our backs are against the wall'

———

THE STOICISM OF most of the British public in the summer of 1940 was not a myth created by government propaganda or post-war nostalgia. In the face of the darkest perceived threat to Britain's independence for more than a century, there was little sense of panic or despair. Despite all the recent disasters, belief in ultimate victory over the Reich was widespread. The majority of people shared the optimistic view of the porter at a Pall Mall club who fell into conversation with one member soon after the fall of France.

'Bad news, isn't it? We are all alone now,' said the member.

'Oh no sir, it's not too bad. After all, we are in the final and it is going to be played on the home ground.'[1]

An opinion poll conducted by Gallup in June found that only 3 per cent of the population believed that Britain would lose the war. Even in the areas most vulnerable to seaborne landings, the mood was the same. This calmness was evident in a remarkable incident in Stoke, where a man picked up an unexploded incendiary bomb that had been dropped by the Luftwaffe in one of their raids over England, put it in a bucket and took it to a local police station. 'His only complaint was that the police retained the bucket,' a government pollster noted.[2]

Amidst all the visible features of the wartime emergency, such as food rationing, the gas masks and the blackout, the public tried to retain a semblance of normality. Maintaining some of the rhythms of peacetime society helped to ease the tension and produce an air of defiance. Immediately after the fall of France, cinemas, theatres, restaurants, pubs, hotels and parks largely remained open.

Although the Football League was suspended for the duration of the conflict and many players were called up for national service, a special tournament called the Football League War Cup was devised in 1940 to give the clubs some competition. During just nine weeks from April to June, no fewer than 137 matches were played. The final at Wembley on 8 June between West Ham and Blackburn was attended by 42,400 people, despite attempts by the government to impose a crowd limit of 15,000 for fear of casualties in the event of a Luftwaffe air raid. In addition, some forms of cricket and horse racing continued. Although the Oval, one of England's Test match venues, was taken over by the military, Lord's continued to host cricket fixtures.

Nor was normal political campaigning entirely abandoned. Parliamentary by-elections were still held to fill vacancies in the House of Commons, the results of which demonstrated overwhelming support for the tripartite Coalition and the complete absence of any mood of volatility in the British public. On 22 May, a by-election in the Lancashire constituency of Middleton and Prestwich produced a landslide for the Conservative candidate, Ernest Gates, over his opponent from the British Union of Fascists. On a respectable 49 per cent turnout and backed by the other Coalition parties, the Tories won 98.7 per cent of the vote, a result that remains a record for any British Parliamentary by-election. In fact, it was the last that the BUF was allowed to fight before their leaders were interned.

The summer of 1940 was the British people's first experience of the modern concept of total war, where citizens were as much in the front line as combatants, and where all resources, from manpower to transport, from industrial output to food supplies, had to be mobilised in the national cause. In previous conflicts, including even the First World War, most of Britain's civilian population had not been in direct danger nor given wartime duties by the government, but the twin menaces of invasion and aerial bombardment changed that. The citizenry became an integral part of the home front, not just in the factories and the Local Defence Volunteers, but also through organisations like the National Fire Service, the Women's Royal Voluntary Service, the Police Reserve and the Women's Transport Service. One of the most vital civilian bodies was the vast Air Raid Precautions (ARP) service, which at one stage had more than 1.4 million members in roles such as wardens, messengers and ambulance drivers.

The determination of the state to enrol the populace in defence preparations was also reflected in the creation of local 'Invasion Committees' all over the country. The committees, which were set up even in small villages, included representatives of the local councils, voluntary services, the police and the LDVs, as well as responsible figures such as doctors and churchmen. Their existence was kept secret from the wider public and their task was to make all the civilian arrangements for dealing with any forthcoming emergency. In practice this meant they had to draw up plans for a wide range of measures, like the immobilisation of petrol pumps; the control of traffic; the supply of food and water; the creation of local stores, canteens and medical centres; the recruitment of local labour for emergency construction and clearance; the formation of local messenger services; and, more morbidly, the establishment of makeshift mortuaries. Every committee was required by the government to keep a 'war book' made up of twenty-two foolscap pages, which set out these arrangements, and also listed local assets and contact telephone numbers for key individuals.

An insight into this work is provided by the recollections of Hilda Cripps, who lived in the village of Great Wakering in southern Essex and was asked by her parish council to join her local committee. Over the next few weeks, Hilda and the rest of the committee were heavily engaged in their duties.

> The first thing we expected, before the invasion started, was saturation bombing. So we took delivery of 420 papier-mâché coffins, and they were stored in the loft of a building in the middle of the high street. Then we placed containers of iron rations at strategic points throughout the village . . . We set aside one large house as a possible hospital and an isolation hospital. We took a census of all the livestock, sheep, cows, pigs and chickens. Then we decided the order in which they would be killed for food: pigs and sheep first, then cows – though not, of course, those in milk – then finally the chickens that were not laying.

Hilda's particular job was to organise the water supply for the village. She had all the local wells inspected to see if the water was fit for drinking, then commandeered three farmer's carts for delivering it. 'In those days there were very few mains, certainly out in the country. So the water had to be carried in these carts. Again the atmosphere was, "Our backs are against the wall. There is a war on" . . . In an emergency, the water would have had to be rationed because the wells could not otherwise have coped. We were working on the smallest amount to keep people alive.' But death also hung in the air for the committee. 'We were told that if the invasion did come, six of the committee would be shot as hostages, which was not a very nice thing to hear.'

A more pleasant moment for Hilda and the committee was when they were invited to meet Clementine Churchill as she made a morale-boosting visit to the village. The conversation revealed an intriguing aspect to the prime minister's personal habits, as Hilda recalled.

> She came to our table and asked us how we were getting on with soap rationing.
>
> 'Not very well,' we replied.
>
> She said, 'I understand that. My husband is a terror. He puts a shirt on in the morning. A couple of hours later he will take it off and put another one on. That's how it goes on. I said to our housekeeper, "Now look, these shirts are not dirty and we can't keep washing them. Just iron them and put them back. He won't know." But he did notice. He said to me, "I thought I would do anything for my King and Country, but I won't wear hotted-up shirts."'[3]

In contrast to the determination shown by the likes of Hilda Cripps, some wealthy individuals retreated to Scotland, Wales, the Lake District or the West Country, staying in hotels that euphemistically advertised their qualities in soothing the nerves and alleviating the stress of 'sensitive or artistic types'.[4] To cynics, these places were known as 'funk hotels' or 'bolt holes', their guests as 'gluebottoms' because they did nothing all day but sit on their posteriors while others fought the war.[5] Some rich or talented individuals went even further afield. The writers Christopher Isherwood, W.H. Auden, and Aldous Huxley had all taken up residence in the United States before 1940, much to the public's disgust, as had the composer Benjamin Britten and his partner Peter Pears. It was estimated that, between 1939 and 1940, around 2 million people moved privately from their homes, either by going abroad or by finding accommodation in Britain in hotels or with friends. Many such departures were sanctioned by the government through official evacuation schemes for children, mothers and vulnerable people. The initial large evacuation had taken place at the end of August 1939, shortly before the declaration of war. In this exercise 1.5 million people were displaced from the big cities to what were termed the reception areas, including 827,000 children of school age, 524,000 mothers, and 103,000 teachers and other helpers. Despite all the government's exhortations, however, a significant number of parents in London had refused to send their children away.

More seriously, by June 1940, two other problems had emerged with this large shift in population. First, during the Phoney War many families began to drift back to their homes, believing that the dangers of German attack had been exaggerated. Second, with the fall of France, some of the reception areas on the southern and eastern coasts were no longer safe. Places like Worthing and Ramsgate, to which large numbers of families had been sent, were now in the front line of the invasion threat. The government therefore had to embark on a further round of mass evacuation. From mid-June until early July, another 213,000 people were moved or re-evacuated from the capital and the coastal defence areas.

Once more, it was a massive administrative task, yet it was accomplished with a sustained efficiency that belies the myth of Britain's chaos in the early summer of 1940. Over a period of six days from 13 June, 120,000 children and 10,000 accompanying adults were taken out of London to 222 different railways stations, which served over 500 local authorities that had agreed to receive them. Despite the complexity of the transport arrangements, which required children to assemble at their schools and then be taken by buses to the train stations before embarking on their journeys to

LEAVE HITLER TO ME SONNY – YOU OUGHT TO BE OUT OF LONDON

ISSUED BY THE MINISTRY OF HEALTH

British government propaganda in the summer of 1940 told parents that it was their patriotic duty to send their children out of the capital, both for safety reasons and to avoid creating a burden for the military and civic authorities

their remote destinations, the whole evacuation passed with barely a single problem.

Amidst all the administrative success of evacuation, some individuals could not cope with the trauma of upheaval, either as homesick evacuees themselves or as hosts shocked at the behaviour of the new arrivals. The two youngest sisters of Ethel Robinson, who worked in Littlewoods in Liverpool during the war, were both evacuated to Shrewsbury, where they were housed with a terrifying matriarch. Ethel recalled: 'She was very strict and Victorian, this lady . . . My sisters had to wash outside in the freezing rain water and that sort of thing. When we visited them they looked completely defeated and miserable and really unhappy. They pleaded with us to take them home, it was awful. So my mother did take them home.'[6]

Rose Rosamund, a Londoner with two young children, was persuaded by her husband Bob to leave the capital because of her fear of bombing. But the experience of moving to a small Oxfordshire village was an unpleasant one, as she recalled in a later interview. 'I went down on my own. I was not with a school or anything. The billeting officer dumped me in a council house and I had to borrow a bed from the village. That bed was clean, but the bed my eldest boy had to sleep in was dirty. I cleaned that room and bed with glycol, whatever I could get hold of, because the boy's body was bitten all over with fleas.'[7]

An alternative perspective, from the reception end, came from Mary Whiteman, who was married to the billeting officer for the rural Essex town of Saffron Walden. 'There were some very difficult cases of poor children and families – boys who would pull the wallpaper off looking for bugs or were endlessly bedwetting. So there was a lot of cleaning up that had to be done. There was so much bedwetting that mattresses had to be destroyed.'[8]

The evacuees in mid-June 1940 may have numbered 120,000 children, but there were more than 450,000 in London at that time. The government believed that, if there were an invasion, they would be in the way of the military, either in the defence zones or in the capital, but recognised that there was fierce resistance among many parents to being separated from their young. It was a mood compounded by a false sense of security created by air-raid shelters and barrage balloons, as well as the tales of anguish from earlier evacuees. In an attempt to improve attitudes towards evacuation, the civic authorities embarked on a major propaganda initiative, portraying parents who sent their children away as responsible and patriotic.

The official propaganda was backed up by supportive articles in the press, such as one in the *Star* on 15 June by the feminist Labour MP Dr Edith Summerskill, who had sent her own children to Herefordshire. 'No sensible parent should be influenced by a child's plea to stay at home,' she wrote, condemning the 'pure selfishness' of women who kept their children for company.[9]

Throughout June there were discussions about the introduction of compulsory civilian evacuation schemes for towns along the southern and East Anglian coasts, but the War Cabinet was not convinced. As the Home Secretary Sir John Anderson put it when outlining his objections, 'The complete scheme would involve the evacuation of 250,000 to 300,000 persons and would entail compulsory billeting on a scale never before contemplated. So heavy a burden could be justified in the face of an obvious military necessity, but not as a purely precautionary measure.'[10] Eventually the Cabinet agreed that plans for compulsory evacuation should be completed but would be put into action only in the face of an immediate invasion.

By the beginning of July, much of the agitation from the Chiefs of Staff for compulsion had evaporated. This was because voluntary evacuation from the coast had become so effective. The exodus of women, children, the disabled and the elderly caused a dramatic change in the demography of the traditional seaside resorts of southern and eastern England. Between early June and mid-July, the population of coastal towns in East Anglia fell by 54 per cent from 280,000 to just 129,000. In Kent the picture was even more extreme, with the population in its coastal towns falling by 61 per cent from 207,000 to 80,000. The impact of the voluntary evacuation on individual places was striking. In Dover, at the heart of the front line, the population fell from 36,000 to 16,000. Further up the coast in Broadstairs, the number of local residents dropped by more than two thirds, from 7,500 to 2,000.

One tragic consequence of this change was the mass killing of pets that evacuees could not take with them. Andy Thompson, a vet in Dover, put so many to sleep that he had to hire a lorry to take away their corpses. 'It was both sad and disgusting,' he later recalled.[11] It was the same story in East Anglia. At Walton-on-the-Naze, 70 per cent of the inhabitants shut up their homes and left, and in Clacton-on-Sea there were only 5,000 people in the town by mid-July, compared to the usual 25,000 at the height of summer. As those figures indicate, tourism to parts of the coast was devastated by the invasion threat. The railway companies put up notices to warn that over 700 holiday destinations were now out of bounds for 'holiday recreation or pleasure'.[12] Throughout the entire summer season in 1940, Great Yarmouth in Norfolk had just 750 staying visitors.

The collapse of the tourism trade created a strange atmosphere of desolation in the traditional seaside resorts, as J.B. Priestley recorded for the BBC after a visit in mid-July to Margate. To his shock, he found the once lively town almost deserted:

Everything was there: bathing pools, bandstands, gardens blazing with flowers, theatres and the like and miles of firm golden sands spread out under the July sun. But no people – not a soul. Of all the hundreds of thousands of holiday makers, of entertainers and boatmen – not one. And no sound – not the very ghost of an echo of all that cheerful hullabaloo – children shouting and laughing, bands playing, concert parties singing, men selling ice cream, whelks and peppermint rock, which I'd remembered hearing along this shore. No, not even an echo. It was as if an evil magician had whisked everybody away . . . The few signs of life make the whole place seem unreal and spectral.[13]

Some of the adults who remained in the danger area nevertheless chose to send their own children right out of the country. Usually this was done by private arrangement, as happened in the case of the author Vera Brittain and her husband George Catlin, a well-known academic. They decided to evacuate their two children, one of whom was the future politician Shirley Williams, to America. 'They kiss us and leave us as calmly as though they are departing for a weekend visit to a familiar relative,' wrote Brittain.[14] It has been estimated that around 14,000 British children were privately evacuated overseas, nearly all of them to Canada and the United States, although such decisions could cause resentment and accusations of selfishness. The arrival of Duff Cooper's son in New York provoked this bitter outburst from William Connor in the *Daily Mirror*: 'I was disgusted that millions of ordinary kids, without wealth, without fame, without rank or title or influence have been left without a hope in hell of getting out of range of Hitler's bombers.'[15]

Yet the exodus to foreign parts was not confined exclusively to well-off families. In response to British public demand as well as generous offers from the Dominions of Canada, Australia, New Zealand and South Africa, the War Cabinet established the Children's Overseas Registration Board (CORB) on 19 June to organise an evacuation scheme within the empire. But it soon ran into problems. Within days of its creation, the CORB had received over 200,000 applications for the initial 20,000 places on the scheme, far more than it could handle, which meant that the first ship did not even sail until the end of August when the Battle of Britain was at its height. Within a fortnight of its start, the scheme had to close to new applications.

Nor was there strong political support from the top. Churchill, though embroiled in bigger issues, disliked the whole business, feeling that it 'encouraged a defeatist spirit'.[16] King George VI and his wife Queen Elizabeth also frowned on the scheme, as reflected in their own personal hostility to any suggestion that the royal family should leave Britain for its safety. 'The children won't leave without me. I won't leave the King. The King will never leave,' the Queen famously said.[17]

Moreover, there was the difficulty of providing naval protection to the passenger ships at a time when, as Clement Attlee explained to the House of Commons, the government had to 'concentrate the whole of our naval forces on the task of meeting the overriding demands of national security'.[18] It was this vulnerability at sea that led to a series of tragedies in August and September 1940, which were to finish off the CORB scheme completely before fewer than 3,000 children had been sent overseas.

Evacuations were not the only source of trouble. Throughout this period, there continued to be deep anxieties among the public and the military about clandestine German infiltration into British society, supposedly aided by treacherous fifth columnists and defeatists. With the Wehrmacht just across the Channel, this disquiet was understandable, although occasionally it was carried to extremes. Rodney Foster, a retired colonel and surveyor living in Hythe on the Kent coast, recorded in his diary that he and his wife had sacked their Swiss maid at the beginning of June: 'She exclaimed, "I am not a spy." But we had our doubts. She had made friends with a boarding house keeper near Folkestone harbour, where there was considerable naval and military activity. Twice on her afternoon off she claimed to have missed the last bus and stayed the night there.'[19]

But most of the rumours turned out to be baseless, with the result that political leaders became convinced that the fifth column threat had been exaggerated. It was 'a much less serious menace than had been supposed', Churchill told his secretary John Colville,[20] while MI5 spoke dismissively of 'Fifth Column neurosis' after a false alarm in which an Oxfordshire farmer was falsely accused of working with the enemy.

Despite such scepticism about the existence of a fifth column, there was still deep concern about the number of Germans, Austrians and Italians who remained free in Britain. The crackdowns on enemy aliens since May had been limited in their scope, focused mainly on young men without proven loyalty to Britain or living in the most vulnerable districts. Pressure continued to build for a further, more severe round of internment embracing all foreigners from enemy nations, regardless of their personal status. In a paper of 19 June entitled 'Urgent Measures to Meet Attack', the Chiefs of Staff stated that, 'out of approximately 76,000 male and female Germans in this country, only 12,000 have been interned and, out of 18,000 Italians, about 4,500 have been interned.'[21]

With Churchill lending his backing, the War Cabinet agreed on 21 June that all Germans and Austrians aged over sixteen and under seventy should immediately be interned, with a few exemptions, including: the invalid or the infirm; those 'engaged in work of national importance'; ministers of religion 'other than Ministers of a German Church'; people 'who have a British born or naturalised son' serving in the forces; or large-scale employers whose factories or businesses would have to close down if they were locked up, resulting in 'the discharge of British employees'.[22]

There was no concept of innocence for the targets of the crackdown. What was particularly inhumane was that large numbers of German Jewish refugees, who had fled Nazi persecution, ended up being interned. Some of them committed suicide, unable to cope with this new form of oppression at the hands of a government that was meant to be their protector. The internees' despair was exacerbated by the conditions that many of them had to endure. Under the government's scheme, the men and women were held in large, makeshift camps in England before being sent to more permanent custodial centres, either on the Isle of Man or further abroad to Australia and Canada. The English transit camps were often appalling because they had been created so hurriedly. Some internees were placed on an unfinished council estate in Huyton near Liverpool, several in houses without any furniture or hot water, others just in tents. One group of 500 men was incarcerated in a disused cotton mill in Bury, with a leaking roof and few mattresses but plenty of rats.

The government minister Sir Walter Monckton KC was shaken by the experience of visiting this mill, particularly when he learnt that a pair of inmates had killed themselves: 'The two men who succeeded in committing suicide had already been in Hitler's concentration camps. Against these they held out, but this camp has broken their spirit.'[23] As Klaus Ernst Hinrichsen, formerly a Jewish refugee from Lübeck, working in 1940 for a British publisher, observed when he was detained: 'The refugees had come to England because they had one enemy, and that was the enemy Britain was now fighting.'[24]

For most internees, the picture improved when they were sent to more permanent camps on the Isle of Man, where they had greater freedom and the accommodation was better. Indeed, there were complaints in Parliament and the press that the internees on the island were enjoying an easier life than most of the British working class toiling in the factories or the services. Several of the camps developed their own vibrant communities due to the presence of so many highly skilled, well-educated people. It was an appealing paradox that the government's ruthlessness created a flourishing, sophisticated culture behind the barbed-wire fences on the Isle of Man, something that has tended to be ignored in previous histories. A survey at Onchan near Douglas, the Isle of Man's first internment camp, showed that of its 1,491 inmates, 1,230 of them were Jewish, 121 were writers or artists, 113 were scientists, 68 were lawyers, 67 were engineers, 19 were churchmen and 12 were dentists.

With a powerful sense of autonomy, the inmates elected their own house captains and an overall camp captain, who liaised with the British army commander. As Klaus Hinrichsen, who was interned in this camp, later recorded: 'I think at first the commander was upset, when he saw these bedraggled people arrive instead of smart Nazis. But when he discovered how many had been professors, musicians and artists, he got very proud.' Soon the camp had its own chamber orchestra and informal university, staffed by the many interned lecturers and teachers. 'People were sitting at the professors' feet like a lesson in antiquity. It was wonderful for the professors as well because many of them had been forbidden to lecture in Germany and now they had an audience.'[25]

By the end of June, there were 27,200 alien internees in Britain, prompting government concern about the shortage of accommodation and the diversion of troops from the front line into guarding duties. Fortunately, the Dominions of Canada and Australia generously offered to take some of the internees to lessen the burden, although South Africa declined to do so. Eventually more than 11,000 internees were sent to the Dominions. It was not until August 1940 that the first innocent refugees began to be released, and only in 1941 was the internment programme brought to an end.

Yet there was a profound irony about all this vigorous action against potential traitors and collaborationists, for within the political establishment in June 1940 there still lurked a number of men of questionable loyalty to the national cause. One such politician, remarkably, was David Lloyd George, the victor of the First World War, who by the summer of 1940 had become nothing like the fiery warrior of the past and was consumed by pessimism about Britain's chances of survival. Churchill refused to recognise this decline in his former colleague and kept trying to bring him into office throughout the early summer months of 1940. On 13 May, according to John Colville's diary, the prime minister offered Lloyd George the job of Minister of Agriculture, taking charge of food production. It seems that, rather than giving an outright refusal, the elder statesman dithered over the decision, in a pattern that continued over the next few weeks.

The longer Lloyd George hung back, the more Churchill grew suspicious that he was part of a plot to reorganise the government, perhaps even force a change in the premiership. His suspicions were not entirely baseless. Several ministers outside the War Cabinet, including Leo Amery and the under-secretary for food Bob Boothby, had drawn up plans to refashion both the policy and the personnel of Churchill's administration. The fall of France only fuelled their scheming, one of whose features was a demand for the return of Lloyd George.

When Churchill heard about what became known as 'the Under-Secretaries plot', he was furious, telling Amery, Boothby and their colleagues that they should 'stick to the job he had given them' or resign.[26] Strangely, even after this episode Churchill still did not abandon his dream of persuading Lloyd George to join his government. As late as 6 July, Lloyd George was told, 'Winston increasingly feels he needs you,'[27] and it was not until later in the month that the plan was finally dropped. Yet Churchill's efforts, reflecting his generosity as a statesman, were always doomed simply because, in 1940, Lloyd George had little faith in Britain's chances of survival. What Churchill failed to recognise was the depth of Lloyd George's defeatism, reflected in his belief that Britain had to reach a peace deal with Germany, the very opposite of Churchill's policy of 'never surrender'. The offer to join the government, Lloyd George said privately, was like 'calling in a specialist when the patient's case was well-nigh hopeless'.[28] Indeed, so convinced was he of Britain's inability to resist German might that he came to see himself as a kind of British version of Pétain, ready to serve as a unifying figure for a broken nation.

Even without Lloyd George's presence, defeatism continued to lurk within the heart of the Churchill's government. Those two arch-compromisers, Lord Halifax and his deputy Butler, still clung to their policy of appeasement. If anything, Butler was even more treacherous than Halifax, his private eagerness for peace reflecting his irresolute, duplicitous character. Butler's inconstancy was displayed on the very day that France fell, in an incident that would invoke the justifiable fury of Churchill and cast a shadow over his subsequent career.

On 17 June, while walking through St James's Park, Butler ran into Björn Prytz, the Swedish ambassador to Britain. At the time, the prospects for their respective governments could not have been darker. The peace rumours, allied to the fall of France, had convinced Hitler, triumphant on the continent, that Britain was divided and broken. At the same time Sweden, still a neutral country, faced escalating demands from the Reich to allow her railway network to be used for the transport of armaments and supplies to the German forces of occupation in Norway. On 16 June, the day before Butler met Prytz, these demands had been renewed with more force than ever. Understandably, in deciding their response to this German bullying, the government in Stockholm wanted to be sure of London's intentions. It was this dangerous backdrop that lent such weight to the two men's conversation in St James's Park.

It was not long before Butler asked Prytz to come back to his room at the nearby Foreign Office where they could talk more privately. During the continued discussion there, Butler was briefly asked to see Lord Halifax, who gave him a vital message for the Swedish government.

That night, Prytz sent a telegram to Stockholm with a detailed report of his conversation. According to the Swede's account, Butler said that 'Britain's official attitude will for the present continue to be that the war must go on, but he assured me that no opportunity for reaching a compromise peace would be neglected if the possibility were offered on reasonable conditions and that no "diehards" would be allowed to stand in the way in this connection.' Prytz further explained that, during their talk, Butler had been 'called in to see Halifax, who gave me the message that "common sense and not bravado would dictate the Government's policy",' words that could easily be interpreted as a rebuke of Churchill. The conclusion of his telegram showed how vulnerable Churchill remained: 'It would appear from conversations I have had with other members of Parliament that there is an expectation that, if and when the prospect of negotiation arises, possibly after 28 June, Halifax may succeed Churchill.'[29] It was inevitable that this incendiary telegram should cause a political stir in both Stockholm and London. As the diplomatic row intensified, Prytz was pressurised by Butler into issuing a retraction, claiming that he had misquoted the British minister, while Butler himself claimed that 'the statement attributed to him had been quite inaccurate'.[30]

Churchill's reaction to the affair was one of cold fury. Angrily, he demanded an explanation from the Foreign Secretary, pointing out that there must be not be 'any suspicion of lukewarmness' in the government when the House of Commons had just been assured that 'all its members were resolved to fight on to the death'.[31] Halifax wrote to the prime minister the following day, reassuring him that there could not be any doubt 'about Butler's discretion or his complete loyalty to Government policy'.[32]

After receiving the Foreign Secretary's letter Churchill let the matter drop, although the episode showed that his policy of absolute resistance did not command unanimous support.

It has often been asserted that Butler's notorious remark to Prytz was just an unfortunate indiscretion that reflected his own private, appeasing outlook, but was not part of any wider conspiracy to challenge the prime minister's hard line. Yet the argument against such a claim is that Butler was deeply cautious and calculating, notorious as an intriguer and had never been reconciled to the premiership of Churchill, whom he once disparagingly described as 'the greatest adventurer in modern history'.[33]

On 3 July, a week after this unsettling episode, Churchill sent this ringing message to all military and civil authorities:

> On what may be the eve of an attempted invasion or battle for our native land, the Prime Minister desires to impress upon all persons holding responsible positions in the Government, in the Fighting Services or in the Civil Departments, their duty to maintain a spirit of alert and confident energy.

While every precaution must be taken that time and means afford, there are no grounds for supposing that more German troops can be landed in this country, either from the air or across the sea, than can be destroyed or captured by the strong forces at present under arms. The Royal Air Force is in excellent order and at the highest strength it has yet attained. The German navy was never so weak, nor the British army at home so strong as now. The Prime Minister expects all His Majesty's servants in high places to set an example of steadiness and resolution. They should check and rebuke expressions of loose and ill-digested opinion in their circles or by their subordinates.[34]

'A unified Ireland under the German jackboot'

⁓

THROUGHOUT THE SUMMER of 1940, Britain saw Ireland as a potential threat to her security. Eire was still technically part of the British empire at this time, but, unlike the other Dominions, her strongly nationalist government under Eamon de Valera, Ireland's Taoiseach, refused to back the Allied cause. On the contrary, Ireland adopted a stance of overt neutrality, reflecting her determination to assert her independence from Britain.

This desire for autonomy, long the central theme of Irish politics, had led to the bloodshed of the Easter Rising in 1916 and the bitter conflict of the Anglo-Irish War, which was brought to an end in December 1921 by the treaty that created the Irish Free State and, much to the long-term resentment of Republicans, the entity of Northern Ireland. More importantly, in the context of the Britain's defences, in 1938 the Irish government took control of the three deep-water naval ports, one in Donegal and two in County Cork, that Britain had retained under the treaty.

As the invasion threat deepened in 1940, the British authorities grew increasingly concerned about the presence of an uncooperative Ireland on their western flank. Some leading politicians, including Churchill, saw a graphic contrast between the staunch loyalty of Protestant Ulster, under the veteran prime minister Lord Craigavon, and the sullen hostility of Eire, under de Valera. Anger at the loss of the treaty ports was compounded by the belief that southern Ireland was riddled with Nazi sympathisers, fifth columnists and IRA terrorists who adhered to the traditional doctrine that 'England's difficulty is Ireland's opportunity.'

From the start of the western offensive by Hitler in May, the British government frequently received reports that the Germans were about to land in Ireland and, working in league with the IRA, would overthrow the British garrison in the north before turning the island into a base from which to launch a full-scale invasion of England. Some intelligence reports even claimed that clandestine German operations in Ireland were already under way.

In fact, just as in May 1940 the Wehrmacht had no comprehensive plans to invade England, there was no detailed German blueprint for an attack on Eire. General Günther Blumentritt, the operations officer of Army Group

A, later explained that any thoughts about an early German landing in Ireland 'were quite unreal and they bear no relation to German resources at sea and in the air at the time. It would have been necessary to get there, a much harder task than an attack across the Narrows [the waters outside Oslo]. The British fleet and air force would have crushed any attempt very quickly. Above all, it would have been impossible to transport supplies even if we had got there in the first place.'[1]

Nor was de Valera as hostile to Britain's cause as his critics suggested, claiming that he 'personally had great sympathy for England and recognised that two-thirds of the Irish population were anti-German'.[2] Moreover, since the mid-1930s his government had pursued an increasingly ruthless campaign against Republican extremists, who were regarded as a dangerous threat to the nascent state. Not only was the IRA banned but its members faced internment, military tribunals and even executions. Yet the political reality was that, after decades of the Irish struggle for freedom from British rule, there was little chance that Ireland would join the other Dominions in fighting for Britain. Neutrality was effectively an affirmation of sovereignty, and any declaration of war would have torn apart the fragile unity of the nation.

The negative military consequences of neutrality could also be over-played. If Eire had actually joined the Allied cause, then Britain would have been forced to station large numbers of troops there, thereby diminishing her own defences. And the loss of the treaty ports was not as influential as Churchill claimed. This was partly because the conquest of France gave Germany a number of major ports on the Atlantic coast, but also because advances in German maritime technology meant that their deadly U-boats could roam widely across the seas, reducing the effectiveness of any shelter that the Irish ports could have offered British ships.

Although reluctant to use force against Eire, Britain was willing to contemplate a radical political solution, one that, if it had been implemented, would have changed the course of modern history in the British Isles. Churchill's government knew that mere exhortation would not persuade de Valera to abandon neutrality; something concrete would have to be offered to make him change his policy. With national survival at stake, what Britain proposed seemed to be the fulfilment of the Republican dream: an end to partition, the abolition of the Northern Irish state and the unity of the island under Dublin rule. The build-up to this offer took place in the first two weeks of June 1940.

Selected to represent the British government in talks was Health Minister Malcolm MacDonald, the son of the former prime minister Ramsay MacDonald. He had long experience of negotiations with Dublin, having served as Dominions Secretary in the late 1930s. With mounting rumours of a German invasion of Eire, the War Cabinet felt that the Irish problem could not be allowed to fester. On 17 June he was sent to Dublin to see whether, by his personal intervention, he could make any headway with the Taoiseach, although de Valera remained intransigent. Refusing to give up either neutrality or his claims to Ulster, he insisted that the 'unity of Ireland was an essential and primary condition for the adequate defence of Ireland'.[3] MacDonald returned to London empty-handed.

When he reported on his failure to the War Cabinet on 20 June, British ministers decided a more dramatic step was needed to win over de Valera. Neville Chamberlain put forward the idea that, in return for access to Eire for the British armed forces, the London government would make a declaration 'in principle, in favour of the establishment of a United Ireland'.[4] Even Churchill, instinctively unsympathetic to Ireland's cause and opposed to any coercion of Ulster, went along with the policy, whilst remaining deeply sceptical about the chances of its reaching fruition. Chamberlain observed gloomily, 'I fear he [de Valera] won't be moved until the Germans are in Dublin.'[5]

He was proved right. MacDonald went back to Eire the next day, 21 June, with the new offer but the promise of the declaration did not sway the Taoiseach, who refused to countenance the arrival of British troops on Irish soil or British ships in Irish ports before any German invasion actually took place.

Given the chasm that had opened up between London and Dublin, it might have been expected that the British Cabinet would give up the attempt to win over de Valera, but ministers now went even further by deciding to strengthen the unity proposal. They agreed to put it in a formal document, stating that if Eire entered the war on the side of the Allies, then Britain would 'accept the principle of a united Ireland'. Furthermore, Britain would provide immediate arms supplies to Eire, setting up at once both a Joint Defence Council for the whole of the island and a constitutional committee 'to work out the practical details of the union of Ireland'.[6]

The British government also briefed the US representative in Dublin, David Gray, about the plan, hoping that he could add to the pressure on de Valera. Gray's punchy summary of the proposal was that 'it guaranteed the whole lock, stock and barrel, providing for the immediate setting up of a commission to draft an all-Ireland Constitution but insisting on a declaration of war by Eire.'[7] The document setting out this proposal was drawn up by Chamberlain, then taken by MacDonald to Dublin on 26 June, his third visit to the capital in less than ten days.

At their meeting, MacDonald had to read out the paper to de Valera, whose eyesight was extremely poor. However, the magnitude of the offer did not move the Taoiseach, who instead appeared almost offended by Britain's presumption, as Macdonald reported.

> He could not enter into serious discussions on any basis except the immediate establishment of a united, neutral Ireland. Moreover, the Taoiseach made it clear to Mr MacDonald that Ireland belonged to the Irish people and Great Britain had no right of any kind to attempt to barter the unity of the Irish nation for the blood of her people. Ireland's unity and complete independence would come some day. The Government would defend the country against invasion, but they would not purchase unity by an act which would bring civil war and disaster to the people.[8]

Craigavon, who was just as rigid and inflexible as his old foe de Valera, was incensed. Having been sent a copy of the proposal by Chamberlain, he instantly replied with a 'short but violent telegram', which read: 'Am profoundly shocked and disgusted by your letter making suggestions so far reaching behind my back and without any pre-consultation. To such treachery to loyal Ulster, I will never be party.'[9]

Craigavon believed that instead of trying to win over de Valera, the British should be planning the overthrow of the Eire government. In fact, during the early MacDonald talks in Dublin, he wrote to Churchill, urging the occupation of Eire by British forces under a military governor. But Craigavon, the epitome of Unionist obduracy, was in a weaker position than he might have imagined. This was no return to the famous 1912 Home Rule crisis, when the near-mutinous British army and the irreconcilable Conservative Party had refused to back Liberal legislation to bring Ulster under the governance of Dublin. The attitude within both organisations was very different in June 1940, with far less support for Ulster's resistance.

In a strongly worded call for unity on 20 June, the Chiefs of Staff described 'the continuation of partition' as producing 'a very dangerous military situation'. Therefore, they said, 'the strongest possible pressure should be put on the Northern Irish Government' to reach a deal with the South. 'We suggest that the people of the North should be told in the plainest terms that if we win the war we shall see to it that a united Ireland is ruled within the Empire as a true dominion with all that it implies, but that if we lose the war – as we may well do if the enemy succeeds in subjugating Ireland – they will have a unified Ireland in any event, but unified under the German jackboot instead of the British Crown.'[10]

Interestingly, even within Ulster Unionism, support for Craigavon's stubborn, unchanging stance was far from universal. For some less obstinate politicians, London's push for Irish unity in order to save the British empire had created a conflict between loyalty to the Crown and belief in the union.

Alan Brooke's nephew Sir Basil Brooke, probably the most able member of the Ulster Unionist Cabinet, and soon to become the Prime Minister of Northern Ireland, told a member of the Dublin senate on 25 June that 'if the south were to join the war on Britain's side in return for post-war unification, Craig's cabinet would be split with his own vote favouring a new relationship with the south.'[11]

The paradox of June 1940 was that de Valera's intransigence ultimately maintained partition. Ulster Unionist politicians were never faced with the decision to accept unification or not. The Irish government appeared to regard neutrality as more important than unity. One Irish politician was told by Frank Aiken, Eire's Minister for Defence Coordination, 'Get this into your head. There are no conditions under which we will abandon neutrality.'[12]

After the failure of MacDonald's talks with de Valera on 26 June, the British abandoned any further negotiations on a political settlement. During this fraught period, de Valera cited a number of justifications for his negative approach: he feared that there would be widespread opposition within Eire to any alliance with Britain, perhaps even sparking a civil war; he said that Ulster would never agree to any deal; he had no trust in Churchill; and he believed a post-war British government would renege on any agreement to impose unity.

He even asserted that it was in Britain's military interests for Ireland to remain neutral, for any departure from this policy might provoke a German invasion of the South and thereby threaten Britain. But some thought there was a less edifying reason. With his calculating, often Machiavellian air, de Valera prompted the suspicion that he felt Britain was doomed, so any sacrifices for the Allied cause would be pointless. 'They don't want to be on the losing side,' said Chamberlain after the collapse of negotiations, a remark the reflected some of his own pessimism.[13]

The greatest refutation of the claim that de Valera was secretly pro-German came in the aftermath of the MacDonald negotiations, for the talks had one extremely useful result from the point of view of Britain's military command. Despite its insistence on the outward appearance of strict neutrality, the Irish government was willing to engage seriously in military cooperation in the months that followed the rejection of the unification bid. In fact John Maffey, the British representative in Dublin, was full of praise for Ireland's conduct: 'When it comes to practical measures for caging the Axis, the Irish will co-operate to any length. De Valera has always been anxious to help us to the utmost.'[14]

During discussions between the British and Irish military leaders in the early summer of 1940, a detailed contingency scheme was devised, code-named Plan W, for Britain to come to Eire's aid in the event of a German invasion. The scheme was certainly comprehensive. The 53rd Division, based in Belfast and Lisburn and comprising 14,000 troops, would form the bulk of the British counter-attacking force, with the support of 8,000 partially trained and equipped men from the 61st Division.

There were several other vital elements to Plan W. A brigade of Royal Marines, based in South Wales, would cross the sea and seize the southern Irish port of Wexford to disrupt German supply lines. The RAF would fly three Hurricane squadrons to airfields near Dublin and two Fairey Battle light bomber squadrons to Cork, while British anti-aircraft units would also be sent to southern airbases. The Royal Navy would go into action, ordering all foreign vessels to leave Irish ports and then adopting a 'sink on sight' policy around the southern and western Irish coasts.

Apart from Plan W, cooperation existed on other levels. The Irish allowed the RAF to use a narrow corridor of airspace from County Fermanagh to the western coast in order to carry out reconnaissance patrols over the Atlantic and even provided wireless beacons as navigational aids for British planes. In the same vein, most British airmen who came down on Irish territory were quietly released and allowed to go to Northern Ireland, whereas Germans were interned. It was a similar story at sea. Throughout the war, more than 200 Germans were interned by the Irish, but not a single Allied sailor.

Unlike the USA, which barred its citizens from serving in foreign armed forces during 1940, de Valera made no objections to Irishmen fighting for Britain, and more than 32,000 did so in the British army alone. There was also extensive liaison between MI5 and the Irish Intelligence service, a key reason why the IRA was so ineffectual in 1940. Despite their own shortages, the British also provided limited supplies of military hardware, including six Hawker Hind biplanes, a battery of eight 3.7-inch anti-aircraft guns, twenty-six machine-gun carriers and thirty Beaverette scout cars.

One intriguing, secret agreement between Britain and Ireland led to the creation of a hidden airfield, called Rathduff, in the valley of the River Suir in County Tipperary. Rathduff was to be used as an airbase for British fighter planes should Germany mount an invasion on England; effectively, it would have become a centre for aerial resistance to German land forces. The site was carefully chosen and, because of its top-secret nature, the entire location was kept out of bounds to most military personnel. Indeed, its existence did not even become public knowledge until the publication in 1996 of Donald MacCarron's history of the Irish Air Corps. Rathduff was never used and late in 1941 it was returned to its original use, as a stud farm.

Although the Germans had no plan to attack Ireland in June 1940, they did have ominous designs on another part of the British Isles.

II

'It is repugnant to abandon British territory'

CHURCHILL WAS USUALLY indefatigable in the defence of Britain's realms. When the Channel Islands were first threatened by Germany after the fall of France, he still clung to the hope that they could be defended by the Royal Navy. 'It was repugnant now to abandon British territory which had been in the possession of the Crown since the Norman Conquest,' he told the Chiefs of Staff, who had recommended the demilitarisation of Jersey and Guernsey, effectively allowing their occupation by the Reich.[1] But the Chiefs of Staff were adamant that they should be abandoned, arguing that the Channel Islands were of no strategic use to Britain, nor could any effective resistance there be mounted against the Wehrmacht. Any RAF fighters, anti-aircraft guns or troops sent to the islands would just weaken Britain's home defences for no gain.

At a meeting of the War Cabinet on 19 June, Churchill reluctantly agreed to demilitarisation. The following day, the last remaining British troops were removed by the Royal Navy. In a final act before departure, the British cut the submarine communications cable between Jersey and the French mainland. Within less than a fortnight, all the defenceless Channel Islands had been occupied by the Germans.

Yet Churchill was not content for the initial German occupation in 1940 to be untroubled. Even with Britain's limited resources and her focus on her own defences, he was still determined to make the Reich think that he might order a counter-attack. What he loathed, as he had shown in discussions about anti-invasion measures, was the Maginot mentality, hiding behind static barriers and waiting for the onslaught.

He explained his thinking in a letter to his military aide Pug Ismay just after Dunkirk: 'The completely defensive habit of mind, which has ruined the French, must not be allowed to ruin all our initiative. It is of the highest consequence to keep the largest numbers of German forces all along the coasts of the countries they have conquered and we should immediately set to work to organise raiding forces on these coasts.' He concluded, 'How wonderful it would be if the Germans could be made to wonder where they were going to be struck next instead of forcing us to try to wall in the island and roof it over.'[2]

He proposed the creation of advance elite units of highly trained soldiers to carry sabotage operations in occupied territory, as he explained in another letter to Ismay the following day, 5 June:

> Enterprises must be prepared, with specially trained troops of the hunter class, who can develop a reign of terror down the coasts, first of all on the 'butcher and bolt' policy, but later on, or perhaps as soon as we are organised, we should surprise Calais and Boulogne, kill and capture the Hun garrison and hold the place until all the preparations to reduce it by siege or storm have been made, and then away. The passive resistance war, which we have acquitted ourselves so well in, must come to an end.[3]

Both these missives reached Ismay at an opportune moment, for the army was considering an initiative on exactly the same lines. Lieutenant Colonel Dudley Clarke, a Royal Artillery officer and military assistant to Sir John Dill, the Chief of the Imperial General Staff, had proposed to his superior a plan 'which revolved around the idea of carrying on guerrilla warfare against the enemy, much as the Boers had done in South Africa and the Jews more recently in Palestine'.[4] Dill was attracted by this idea of a guerrilla force and, with Churchill's support, quickly set up the organisation.

A new department in the War Office, known as MO9, was established to run it under Clarke, with the Hollywood actor David Niven serving as one of its liaison officers. Circulars were sent out to all military commands and the police, asking for highly motivated, physically fit volunteers for this special new force, which had been given the title of the 'Commandos', a term first coined by the Boers during their campaign against the British. Dill envisaged that there would be ten Commando units, each of about 500 men. The designations of units No. 1 and No. 2 were left aside for proposed future special airborne forces, so the first proper Commando unit was No. 3, headed by John Durnford-Slater, the adjutant for the 23rd Medium and Heavy Training Regiment.

Having been swiftly raised to the rank of lieutenant colonel, he began recruiting, mainly from Southern Command. The formation of the Commandos was not universally popular among other officers, who were often loath to lose their best men. But, given Churchill's influence, they had no alternative.

While No. 3 Commando was still being established, Dudley Clarke was impatiently plotting the first British guerrilla-style raid on German-occupied territory. This daring exploit was to be a reconnaissance and sabotage mission carried out on a 20-mile stretch of French coast around the port of Boulogne. Clarke created a special unit for the raid, made up of volunteers from the ten specialised, mobile independent companies that had been formed for the disastrous Norwegian campaign. The new formation, Clarke decided, should be given the title of No. 11 Independent Company to reflect the origin of most of its volunteers.

Within less than a fortnight of its creation, the company had embarked on its first assignment, code-named Operation Collar. At two o'clock on the morning of 24 June, 115 of its officers and men set out on the raid, their faces blackened with theatrical make-up. Dudley Clarke was among their number, going along as an observer. They were divided into four groups: two departing from Ramsgate, one from Dover and the other from Newhaven. Their goal was a vague one and their brief broad. Apparently, they were given orders to spend no more than eighty minutes ashore, during which time they were 'to obtain information about the nature of the German defences, destroy any installations they might happen across and bring back what prisoners they could'.⁵

They had no purpose-built landing craft so instead travelled in RAF air-sea rescue boats, which lacked navigation equipment and reliable compasses; their departures were delayed by a couple of menacing RAF fighters that had not been told about the mission. At various points the raid descended into farce: weapons were lost or mishandled; Clarke was the only casualty – whether from friendly fire or falling over in the boat is not clear; the teams returned empty-handed; and when they reached England and tried to dock at Folkestone, the suspicious coastguard would not allow the vessel into the harbour for several hours, since none of them had any identification documents.

Although Operation Collar achieved little in concrete terms, the Ministry of Information tried to use the raid as a morale booster at a time when Britain was under desperate pressure, issuing a press release that declared, with a degree of creativity, 'Naval and military raiders, in cooperation with the RAF, carried out successful reconnaissances of the enemy coastline; landings were effected at a number of points and contacts made with German troops. Casualties were inflicted on the enemy, but no British casualties occurred.'⁶

Despite his injury and the operation's mixed results, Clarke was determined to press on with his Commando initiative and turned his attention to the occupied Channel Islands. Once more, Churchill was thinking on the same lines, as shown by another of his letters to Ismay, this one of 2 July: 'If it is true that a few hundred German troops have landed on Jersey or Guernsey by troop carriers, plans should be studied to land secretly by night on the islands and kill or capture the invaders. This is exactly one of the exploits for which the Commandos would be suited. There ought to be no difficulty in getting all the necessary information from the inhabitants and from the invader.'[7]

Clarke's department acted swiftly on these words, conceiving a scheme whereby a number of agents would be dispatched to Guernsey to investigate the German defences, followed, if feasible, by a Commando raid on the island. One Guernsey citizen, Hubert Nicolle, serving as a lieutenant in the British army, undertook an initial reconnaissance trip, bringing back a report which stated, with remarkable specificity, that the Germans had 469 soldiers on the islands, that machine-gun posts had been erected around the coast and that the main body of the troops were in St Peter Port.

With his usual energy, Clarke decided instantly to implement his plan for an assault on the island. Code-named Ambassador, the operation was to be undertaken on the night of 12/13 July. Its two main elements were explained to Durnford-Slater by none other than David Niven: first, No. 11 Independent Company would attack the island's airfield; second, his own No. 3 Commando would create a diversion in the north of the island by taking out some German strongpoints.

Immediately there were problems. Poor weather meant that the operation had to be postponed for forty-eight hours. More seriously, while Durnford-Slater was making his final preparations, a staff officer arrived from London with a vital message: 'Colonel, the whole plan has been changed. Jerry is too strong. He's been reinforced at some of the places where we intended to land.'[8] Durnford-Slater quickly worked out a new plan but, because of the lack of organisation and intelligence, there was an amateurish feel to the whole enterprise.

It began to go wrong almost as soon as the team left England. Two of the launches broke down with engine failure and could not make the voyage. When the two accompanying destroyers reached Guernsey and disembarked the raiders, one launch went completely off course due to a faulty compass. A second hit a rock, began to leak and, rapidly submerging, had to be towed back to the destroyer by another launch.

Only Durnford-Slater's band of forty men from No. 3 Commando actually made it to dry land. However, partly because the RAF rescue launches had not been designed as landing craft and partly because the tides had been badly misjudged, they became exhausted and drenched in their struggle to the shore. Not one dry weapon was left among them. Then they had to climb a long flight of steps from the beach to the top of the cliff, the weight of their soaking uniforms making it an arduous task. Their targets, a machine-gun nest and a German barracks, were deserted when they found them. Encountering no Germans at all, they contented themselves with cutting three telegraph cables to the empty barracks.

At the end of this disastrously fruitless mission, on the way back down the steep steps from the cliff top to the beach, Durnford-Slater tripped and fell, his cocked revolver going off and making a tremendous noise that at last roused the Germans. Almost at once, a line of tracer machine-gun fire from the top of the cliff found the very spot where the launches were meant to be waiting. Because of an increasingly rough sea, these had had to stay further offshore than originally planned. A small dinghy was sent out instead, but on its return voyage it was hurled against a rock and capsized. All the weapons were lost, while one Commando was presumed to have drowned, although it was learnt later that he had survived and made it back to shore. The rest, having no alternative but to swim back to the launches, waded into the sea, at which point three of them confessed to Durnford-Slater that they could not swim. Furious, he told them he would try to persuade the Royal Navy to send a submarine for them the following night, although they were soon captured and became prisoners of war. Fortunately, those who were able to swim reached the launches and were eventually picked up by one of the destroyers at daybreak.

For all its risks, Operation Ambassador had achieved little. No Germans had been captured; no damage had been inflicted on their infrastructure apart from the cutting of a few telegraph lines. In contrast, one British soldier had been lost and others left behind on the island. The raid had failed so dismally because of poor intelligence, inadequate planning, and lack of men and equipment. Durnford-Slater called it a 'ridiculous, almost comic failure', while Churchill regarded it as a 'silly fiasco'.[9] For a time the whole Commando concept was discredited.

Nor had Guernsey derived any support from Operation Ambassador, rather the exact opposite. The occupation became tougher as the Germans strengthened their defences. In fact, Guernsey's attorney general Ambrose Sherwill wrote to the Home Office on 18 July, asking that the islands be left in peace now that they had been demilitarised and complaining, 'I do not know what the object of the landing was, but to us it seems senseless.'[10]

But if the Germans thought that this botched enterprise was truly indicative of efficiency and determination in the British armed forces and government, they could not have been more wrong, as the events of the coming months were to demonstrate.

12

'To the last ship and man'

—————

GERMANY HAD CONQUERED much of Europe and even seized British territory, but the might of the Royal Navy, still the largest maritime force in the world, continued to represent a formidable obstacle to the Reich's ambitions. Whereas the British army was much weaker and smaller than the German army, the Royal Navy was far stronger than the Kriegsmarine. As Grand Admiral Raeder wrote later of the first serious discussions within the Reich's High Command about Operation Sea Lion,

> A German invasion of England would be a matter of life and death for the British, and they would unhesitatingly commit their naval forces to the last ship and last man, into an all-out fight for survival . . . We in the Navy doubted that we could establish conditions that would guarantee even reasonably safe protection for a crossing of the Channel . . . It could not be expected that our Air Force could make up for our lack of naval supremacy.[1]

The man charged with upholding that supremacy was the uncharismatic Sir Dudley Pound, the First Sea Lord since 1939. A stolid, uninspiring figure, dogged by the poor health that would kill him within three years, he was also dedicated and reliable, having never failed in any of the commands he had held since becoming a captain in 1914.

He had a colossal force under his command. Whereas Britain had thirteen battleships and battlecruisers in mid-June 1940, Germany had just two, the *Scharnhorst* and the *Gneisenau*, both of which had suffered serious damage in Norwegian waters and were undergoing major repairs. The chasm was even wider when it came to destroyers. After the heavy losses of Norway, the Kreisgmarine had just 10 in operation, whereas the Royal Navy could deploy 169. Nor was it just a matter of quantity. Although many of Britain's capital ships were of First World War vintage, they had undergone substantial reconstruction in the 1930s and could be highly effective in combat. Contrary to the fashionable idea that all Britain's armed forces were run down by penny-pinching, appeasing, insular governments during the 1920s and 1930s, Britain's navy had been significantly modernised. In the interwar years, it was building more ships than any other navy: during the period in which the Royal Navy constructed five aircraft carriers, the Germans built none.

Moreover, Britain possessed a tremendously powerful force in its own waters to tackle any invasion threat. At the start of July 1940, the operational Home Fleet comprised five battleships, three battlecruisers, eleven cruisers and fifty-three destroyers, with a further twenty-three destroyers based in Liverpool, which were designated for convoy duties but could be available in an emergency.

Even this is to underplay the Navy's strength. The total potential destroyer force in home waters was actually 115 ships, including vessels under repair and refitting, many of which had sustained damage at Dunkirk but would soon be operational again, as well as those from the Royal Canadian Navy. In support of this were a huge number of other vessels, including 700 armed coastal fast patrol craft, of which between 200 and 300 were always at sea between the Wash and Newhaven, seen as the most likely points for a German landing. There were also 25 fast minesweepers, 20 corvettes (a light, manoeuvrable warship), and 140 minesweeper trawlers operating between Sunderland and Portsmouth. For wider reconnaissance, the Admiralty could deploy 35 submarines, as well as the aircraft of the Fleet Air Arm.

With the invasion threat deepening, the Admiralty expanded the Royal Navy Patrol Service, which was largely staffed by former merchant seamen and trawlermen operating auxiliary vessels for minesweeping, reconnaissance and escort duties. With its headquarters in Lowestoft on Suffolk coast, the RNPS had around 800 adapted trawlers, drifters and other, smaller boats, as well as 100 harbour defence patrol craft that also operated on inland waterways.

Further maritime defences came from the erection of mine barrages. One, stretching along parts of the east coast, was laid 30 to 70 miles offshore and was made up of 35,000 mines. Another barrage of 10,000 mines was laid just outside Dover. By the end of June, the Admiralty had also installed 150 6-inch gun batteries along the eastern and southern coasts, manned by 8,000 naval ratings and Royal Marines.

The officer in charge of the Home Fleet was Sir Charles Forbes, appointed in 1938. Technically able, outspoken and forthright in his views, he was even willing to stand up to Churchill on occasions. In the summer of 1940 a serious controversy arose when his ideas on the disposition of the Home Fleet clashed with those of other senior members of the Admiralty. At the crux of this row was Forbes's reluctance to place a sufficiently strong naval force in the most vulnerable areas along the southern and eastern coasts.

Pound and other senior admirals felt that the Home Fleet had to be ready to strike quickly if the Germans came across the Channel or the North Sea. This meant, in particular, building up strong naval protection in the Nore Command, which covered the English coast from the Humber to Dover. At this point of maximum danger, the Admiralty wanted a minimum of thirty-six destroyers, which were to be divided into four flotillas based at the Humber, at Harwich in Essex, and at Sheerness and Dover in Kent. The Nore Command, which was led by the splendidly named Sir Reginald Plunkett-Ernle-Erle-Drax, was also to be supported by five cruisers and other vessels taken from escort duties, including sloops, corvettes and anti-aircraft cruisers.

But Forbes was less worried about the enemy threat in the south and east; his priorities were the protection of the western approaches to the Atlantic and keeping his fleet, especially the big capital ships, intact. Indeed, it was over the issue of the battleships and battlecruisers that he clashed most fiercely with the rest of the Admiralty.

An original thinker as well as an outspoken one, he fought hard to keep his heavy ships in the far north at Scapa Flow, rather than send them south to Rosyth on the Firth of Forth, as was proposed, closer to areas where, according to the naval staff, the enemy might be expected to land or attack. It was Forbes's profound conviction, however, that the Germans had no intention of mounting an invasion at all, and therefore it would be foolish to put men and resources at risk against a non-existent threat. The naval staff stubbornly believed that if the Kriegsmarine commanders knew that the Royal Navy had 'no heavy ship south of Scapa Flow', they would attack and 'retire long before any equal British force could arrive to bring them to action'.[2] Summing up the Admiralty's view, Captain Cecil Harcourt, the Royal Navy's Director of Operations, urged strongly that the main capital ships be based at Rosyth.

Ever more convinced of his position, Forbes sent a long, three-page memorandum to the Admiralty on 4 June, seeking to justify his deep scepticism about the possibility of a German invasion of England while praising the skill with which the Royal Navy had just evacuated 338,000 men from Dunkirk despite the Luftwaffe's supposed dominance in the air. A far greater, more immediate priority than anti-invasion measures, he concluded, was the protection of supply lines and communications across the Atlantic. 'The enemy has realized that he can only defeat this country if he can sever lines of communication.'[3] With the benefit of hindsight, several historians have held Forbes's document to be a magisterial, cool-headed refutation of the invasion fever that gripped the British authorities in the summer of 1940, though at the time most of his colleagues found him stubbornly complacent.

The dispute raged on, while Forbes continued to show his independence of mind, writing to Pound with a tone of condescension on 15 June: 'I should have thought that the German Army was fully employed in France, Norway, Poland, Czechoslovakia, Holland, Belgium and Denmark and would therefore not be likely to stage an overseas invasion on the East coast during the next few weeks,' and again insisting that most heavy ships remained in the north.[4]

By now the naval situation was rapidly changing because of the collapse of France, which made the southern and eastern coasts even more vulnerable and also raised the possibility that the huge French fleet could fall into the hands of the Germans. Just as disturbingly, Italy was now an enemy in the Mediterranean, while there was a danger that Spain could also opportunistically join the Axis powers, thereby threatening Gibraltar. For the Admiralty as a whole, the developments in Europe made Forbes's strategy for the Home Fleet all the more problematic, provoking further intense debate.

The deepening sense of urgency within the Admiralty about a potential invasion was reflected at a high-level meeting, chaired by Pound, on 30 June, where it was agreed that maritime reconnaissance had to be improved, patrols around Dover reinforced, better liaison with Ironside's Home Forces established, and the destroyer force in the south and east increased. 'Invasion might be attempted during the next fortnight,' warned Pound, ordering his staff to 'sift every commitment or application for destroyers most rigorously, as in his opinion as many destroyers as possible should be made available for anti-invasion duties.'[5] But Forbes's stubbornness also bore fruit. Pound, who had never been as unequivocal about Rosyth as many of his subordinates, now signalled his willingness to reach a compromise, based on the intelligence that on 20 June the Gneisenau, the Kriegsmarine's only operational battlecruiser, had been badly damaged by a torpedo attack and was undergoing repairs in Norway. When asked why the main Home Fleet had still not moved to Rosyth, Pound replied that 'this seemed unnecessary so long as the only effective enemy battlecruiser was believed to be at Trondheim,'[6] an argument that ran counter to everything that most of his colleagues had been saying to Forbes for weeks. Pound had to admit to the Chiefs of Staff on 2 July that the measures 'are not entirely in accordance with those recommended as necessary to meet the invasion': in particular, 'no battleships are at Rosyth' and 'the destroyer force available in the Nore Command is only little more than half the considered necessary number.'[7] Churchill himself said that he was 'a little anxious' at the decision to keep the capital ships at Scapa and 'would prefer to see' two of the vessels at Rosyth.[8] Looking back on the mood in military circles during that period, the historian Basil Liddell Hart remembered that 'the Navy's dispositions did not promise a very prompt intervention in the Channel, for the admirals were almost as anxious about the menace of the German Air Force as the German admirals were about the interference of the Royal Navy.'[9]

Forbes seems to have been completely sure in his convictions, shocking a naval strategy conference in the early summer of 1940 by stating that his heavy ships would not operate south of the Wash 'under any circumstances'. Rather than exploding at this comment, Churchill, who was chairing the meeting, said that 'he never took much notice of what the Royal Navy said they would or would not do in advance of an event.' He continued in this mildly jocular tone: 'Since they invariably undertook the impossible whenever the situation demanded, he had not a shadow of doubt . . . we would see every available battleship storming through the Straits of Dover.'[10]

But Forbes did not get his way over the cruiser and destroyer forces. Throughout the summer, he kept asking for the coastal defences to be reduced so as to provide more support in the western approaches and on the Atlantic routes, a request he made with ever greater urgency as British shipping losses mounted. In June, Britain lost the equivalent of 284,000 gross tons of shipping to German U-boats, followed by 196,000 tons in July and a gross tonnage of 295,000 in August. Pound and the other admirals stuck to their strategy of maintaining as strong an anti-invasion force as possible in the south. From late July onwards, the Nore Command could deploy at least four cruisers, thirty-two destroyers and seven sloops, the bulk of them being out on patrol every night. In the same period, twelve destroyers and a cruiser were stationed at Portsmouth, as well as at least forty vessels, including motor torpedo boats, at Dover, while cruisers continuously patrolled the east coast from the Forth to the Thames. Churchill backed up this policy, stating that 'the losses in the western approaches must be accepted', although this made him press Roosevelt all the more strongly for a large batch of US destroyers.[11]

His case at the White House was helped by one of his most ruthless, controversial decisions of the entire war, reverberating throughout the world and impressing upon both Hitler and Roosevelt the seriousness of Britain's determination to continue the struggle. It was driven by fears that, following France's conquest, the French fleet would be taken over by the Axis nations. Such a step would not only transform the balance of maritime power in Europe but would also increase the potential risk of invasion, since the Kriegsmarine would be massively reinforced by the arrival of Gallic ships.

In June 1940, France still had a potent navy. Led by Admiral Jean François Darlan, it consisted of seven battleships, twenty cruisers, two aircraft carriers and several dozen destroyers. Its flagship, the *Richelieu*, had been launched in 1939 and was one of the biggest, most modern vessels on the seas, weighing 35,000 tons and carrying seventeen 6- and 15-inch guns. For Pound, it was 'the most powerful battleship in the world today'.[12]

As early as 7 June, when it was obvious that the French were heading for defeat on land, the Admiralty had discussed the problem. According to the official note of the meeting, Pound took the view that, in the eventuality of an armistice, 'the only practical way to deal with the matter was to sink the French fleet', since he was doubtful that the French government would 'turn it over to us'.[13] The one other possibility that would help Britain would be a decision by the French to scuttle their own ships.

Through diplomatic channels, the US warned France that if its fleet were to surrender to Germany, the government would lose American goodwill. During the days leading up to the official armistice, Darlan tried to reassure America and Britain that there was no risk of any German seizure of the fleet, declaring, 'I will never surrender it – I do not yet know where it will go or whether it will be destroyed, but the Germans will never have it.'[14] Attempts were made to persuade the French government to send the fleet to British ports, without success, although the French promised that 'the ships would fight the Germans and if necessary scuttle' rather than surrender.[15]

In fact, Hitler, never very interested in naval affairs, viewed the French navy as something of an irrelevance. The agreed peace terms reflected this attitude. The French fleet, with the exception of the vessels based in the colonies, was to be assembled in France's home ports, where the ships would be demobilised or disarmed. Furthermore, under Article 8 of the armistice, the Germans 'solemnly and expressly' declared that 'they have no intention of making any claim to the French war fleet at the time of the conclusion of the peace.'[16]

Soon after the armistice's signing, Churchill told the Commons that Article 8 'makes it clear that French warships pass into German and Italian control while fully armed. What was the value of the solemn declaration that they would not be used for their own war purposes? Ask half a dozen countries what is the value of such a solemn assurance.'[17] Nor did the government have much trust in Admiral Darlan, whose anti-British credentials were later displayed when he became a minister in Pétain's collaborationist Vichy regime.

As concern intensified about French and German intentions, Churchill was inundated with advice about the French fleet. The Irish writer George Bernard Shaw urged him to 'to declare war on France and capture her fleet (which would gladly strike its colours to us) before AH [Adolf Hitler] draws breath'.[18] The unorthodox idea was even put forward of purchasing the fleet, but it was recognised that the money would have gone straight to the Reich.

Rigorous action was required, the Admiralty decided, a view that was increasingly shared by Churchill and the Chiefs of Staff, who said that if the French ships reached their home ports, Britain should be 'under no illusions as to the certainty that, sooner or later, the Germans will employ them against us'. Uncertainty about the French fleet must end so that the Royal Navy could concentrate on measures 'to meet the imminent threat of invasion'.[19]

Importantly, the White House also informed Britain that America would not object to any steps that kept the French fleet out of German control. Following an interview with President Roosevelt, the British ambassador Lord Lothian reported to London, 'I asked him whether this meant that American opinion would support forcible seizure of these ships. He said certainly. They would expect them to be seized rather than they should fall into German hands.'[20]

At this stage, the bulk of the French fleet was widely spread across Europe and North Africa, with by far the most important element being the main striking force or Force de Raid, which was gathered in the Algerian port of Mers-el-Kebir, near Oran. Commanded by Admiral Marcel Gensoul, a figure described by one senior British officer as a 'somewhat pig-headed, negative touchy French admiral who, like many small men in big positions, was rather full of his own importance',[21] the Force de Raid was made up of six destroyers, an aircraft carrier and no fewer than four capital ships, including the modern battlecruisers the *Dunkerque* and the *Strasbourg*. It was the sheer weight of this naval power that convinced the British that they had to act.

Negotiations were opened with Gensoul about the possibility of handing over his Oran fleet to the Royal Navy, but came to nothing. Churchill's government therefore conceived a plan called Operation Catapult, in which the Royal Navy would use its influence to neutralise, by physical coercion if necessary, the French fleet at Mers-el-Kebir. The War Cabinet agreed that, at the same time as Catapult was implemented, the French vessels in Britain and Alexandria would either be seized or disarmed.

By late June, the Admiralty had already assembled a powerful formation, commanded by Vice-Admiral James Somerville and known as Force H, to strengthen the Royal Navy in the western Mediterranean and reinforce the defence of Gibraltar,

When they met at the office of A.V. Alexander, the First Lord of the Admiralty, before Force H sailed, Pound told Somerville that he would have to 'secure the transfer, surrender or destruction of the French warships at Oran so as to ensure those ships did not fall into German and Italian hands'.[22] Alexander later recalled, 'Somerville understood clearly the position and what had to be done. He said to me in my room at the Admiralty, "I quite recognise that, however repugnant this job may seem, the Government know it has got to be done, in the interests of the safety of the nation."'[23]

That night, Pound and Churchill met in Downing Street to agree the ultimatum that Somerville would deliver to Admiral Gensoul once the Royal Navy arrived at Mers-el-Kebir. Four choices were to be given to the French. First, they could 'sail with Britain and continue the fight for victory against the Germans and Italians'. Second, they could 'sail with reduced crews to a British port', after which their men would be quickly repatriated. In both these cases, the British promised to 'restore your ships to France at the conclusion of the war, or pay full compensation if they are damaged meanwhile'. The third option was 'to sail with us with reduced crews to some port in the West Indies – Martinique for instance – where they can be demilitarised to our satisfaction, or perhaps be entrusted to the United States and remain safe until the end of the war, the crews being repatriated'. But the fourth option was far more belligerent. If all these 'fair offers' were refused, then the French would be instructed to sink their ships 'within six hours'. Failing that, Somerville was to warn that he had 'the orders of His Majesty's Government to use whatever force may be necessary to prevent your ships from falling into German or Italian hands'.[24] These instructions were sent by Pound to Somerville the next day, 2 July.

The die had almost been cast, but for Churchill, a lifelong Francophile, the episode was a deeply painful one. That afternoon, he was seen in Downing Street by Beaverbrook, who told the prime minister that boldness was the only course. Beaverbrook later recalled their tense discussion in the garden of Downing Street. 'There was a high wind blowing . . . Churchill declared that there was no other decision possible. Then he wept.'[25]

The climax of Operation Catapult was now approaching, as Force H headed towards the Algerian coast. Further east in Alexandria, Admiral Cunningham, thanks to his easy authority and his close relationship with the French admiral René-Emile Godefroy, was able to negotiate an amicable settlement, whereby the French ships were to be disarmed by having the firing mechanisms removed from their guns and their tanks emptied of fuel. In Britain the takeover of the French ships caused more friction. Most of the Frenchmen surrendered their vessels without any resistance, but the story was very different aboard the submarine the *Surcouf*, where some of the crew refused to obey the Royal Navy's instructions and in the ensuing skirmish four men died.

But the clash aboard the *Surcouf* paled beside the slaughter that was to unfold at Mers-el-Kebir on Wednesday 3 July. The advance part of Force H reached its destination just after dawn, and at seven in the morning Captain Cedric Holland, in the destroyer *Foxhound*, asked for permission to enter the harbour to negotiate with the prickly, status-conscious Admiral Gensoul. Holland handed over the letter with the British government's four alternatives. Somerville, whose entire Force H had arrived at Mers-el-Kebir by noon, sent a signal to Gensoul, warning that no French ship would be allowed to leave the harbour unless the British terms were accepted. To show that this was not a bluff, he ordered a series of magnetic mines to be laid across the harbour entrance by Fleet Air Arm Swordfish biplanes from the *Ark Royal*.

Conflict seemed inevitable. In the early afternoon, Somerville sent a further signal, warning the French that unless the conditions were accepted by 3.30 p.m., he would open fire. The French employed delaying tactics, hoping to spin out discussions until darkness descended, then try to reach Toulon. Meanwhile their ships were raising steam ready to go to sea and all their direction-range finders were trained on Force H. Tensions continued to escalate.

After a further wait, Somerville sent a warning to Gensoul that unless the British terms were accepted by 5.30 p.m., he would open fire. The talks came to an end, with Gensoul confirming his rejection of the ultimatum and Holland returning to his destroyer.

At 5.54 p.m., as soon as the *Foxhound* was clear of the harbour, the three battleships of Force H opened up from a range of 17,500 yards, launching thirty-six salvoes of 15-inch shells at Gensoul's fleet, a total of 144 shells, each of them weighing three-quarters of a ton. It was one of the most concentrated, deafening broadsides in British naval history. The thunderous roar from the guns filled the bay, huge columns of black smoke from the explosions soon rising from the harbour, with the French guns, on board the ships or from shore batteries, making their own contribution.

As Ronald Phillips, a sub-lieutenant on the HMS *Hood*, recalled, 'The destruction wrought in that short period was terrible but necessary and inevitable.'[26] Apart from the sinking of the *Bretagne*, the British shells severely damaged *Dunkerque*, the *Provence* and a destroyer. Amidst the carnage, 1,297 French seamen were killed, a death toll that caused deep regret to some of the English sailors. Others felt differently, such as Morgan Morgan-Giles, an officer aboard the destroyer the *Arethusa*. 'It has always been represented afterwards as a most harrowing thing, that we had tears in our eyes at having to attack our former allies. But the fact is that it was not like that. It was a purely professional thing we had to do.'[27]

But Force H did not completely succeed in its objective. Despite the bombardment, the mine barrier and torpedo attacks from the Swordfish aircraft of the *Ark Royal*, the *Strasbourg*, two destroyers and three frigates managed to reach Toulon, having used the cover of heavy smoke to break out of the harbour.

The importance of Oran was not so much in its practical outcome for the Royal Navy but as a symbol of Britain's ruthless determination to continue with the war. Perhaps even more than Dunkirk, the attack on the French fleet dramatically improved Britain's prospects of survival. Public morale was lifted, Churchill's position was strengthened and the American attitude to Britain's war effort was transformed. The Ministry of Information recorded overwhelming public support for the Royal Navy's action, finding on 4 July that 'this strong action gives welcome evidence of Government vigour and decision'.[28] This mood was also reflected in the Commons, where the attitude of many Tory backbenchers had remained equivocal towards Churchill because of lingering affection for Chamberlain. But by showing his true fighting spirit, the prime minister won over all the doubters. For the first time since taking power in May, he had almost the entire political class behind him. When he reported on the action at Mers-el-Kebir, the reception the House gave him was far more enthusiastic than anything that had followed his great orations in May and June.

John Colville, who watched the performance from the public gallery, recorded in his diary, 'He told the whole story of Oran and the House listened enthralled and amazed. Gasps of surprise were audible but it was clear that the action taken was unanimously approved. When the speech was over all the Members rose to their feet, waved their order papers and cheered loudly. Winston left the House visibly affected.'[29] The MP John Martin, who was also present, recalled that 'there had been nothing like it, people said, since Munich. Churchill himself was quite overcome and his eyes filled with tears.'[30]

The reaction among Americans was just as warm. Churchill's ruthlessness was a source of inspiration rather than condemnation, demonstrating that Britain was willing to take the fight to the Reich. Roger Ingersoll, the editor of *PM* magazine, wrote: 'I want to record what a deep satisfaction it was to me to read the news that someone stood up to Adolf Hitler, taking dangerous toys away from him. When an Allied officer gives an ultimatum and it isn't a bluff, that's news.' Ingersoll concluded, 'I'm all for sending supplies to England as long as it's governed by a Churchill who will fight.'[31]

In political terms, Oran portrayed Britain in a new heroic light, directly contradicting the stream of defeatist opinions that Ambassador Kennedy had continued to relay to Washington. This was crucial because it meant that the White House was now willing to circumvent the neutrality laws in providing all the support it could, particularly in the form of destroyers, aircraft and weapons.

Most important of all, the encounter at Mers-el-Kebir had a dramatic impact on Hitler's attitude towards Britain. No longer could he hold to the belief that the enemy was about to crumble.

13

'We hurl it back, right in your evil-smelling teeth'

———

IN THE DAYS immediately after the fall of France, the Führer was still deceiving himself that Churchill was about to be ousted from power and a new British government, perhaps led by Halifax or Lloyd George, would soon reach a peace deal. The action at Oran disabused him of that idea. He had to recognise that Britain would not submit without a fight, and the knowledge infuriated him. The dream of an easy victory in the West had vanished; the hopes of parley had gone.

According to Karl-Jesco von Puttkamer, Hitler's naval adjutant, the news of the naval engagement created in the Führer's headquarters an atmosphere of 'general consternation and succeeding gloom'.[1] So incensed was the German leader that he even allowed Oran to cloud the Nazis' victory celebrations in Berlin on 6 July after the conquest of France.

The conflict between the impulse to attack Britain and the wish to negotiate was a theme of Nazi policy throughout the early summer of 1940. The Reich might have started preparations for invasion following the French armistice, but, even after Oran, there were still attempts to put out peace feelers to London, some of them grasped by naive figures and credulous diplomats who had no understanding of the Nazi regime's barbarity or Churchill's resolution. Despite all the failures he had experienced, the Foreign Secretary Lord Halifax continued to be wedded to his policy of appeasement, much to the contempt of Sir Alexander Cadogan, who wrote of his superior: 'The Pope is making tentative, half-baked suggestions for agreement. Silly old Halifax evidently still hankering after them.'[2]

A more serious diplomatic effort was made at the beginning of July by the Red Cross's representative in Switzerland, Dr Carl Burckhardt. He visited Berlin, ostensibly to discuss the plight of European refugees from the conflict, but in reality to learn whether there was room for new peace negotiations. He saw several leading Germans, made up of two gauleiters, a general and Baron Ernst von Weizsäcker, the state secretary at the Nazi Foreign Office. What Dr Burckhardt heard from this quartet gave him grounds for encouragement about a potential peace deal, as he told the British

135

ambassador to Berne, Sir David Kelly, on his return to Switzerland. According to the account of Dr Burckhardt's mission that Kelly sent to London on 8 July, German ambivalence about whether to mount an invasion or initiate talks was graphically clear in these discussions.

> All four men told the same story. Hitler had returned to his old idea and hesitated before attacking England because he still clung to the hope of a working arrangement with the British Empire . . . He wanted a European Federation and felt this would be difficult without British co-operation . . . The General said that while they were confident of their ability to defeat England they realized that it might involve much greater sacrifices than had the defeat of the French army, most of whom had put up a very poor show and fought half-heartedly.

Sir David went on to add that Dr Burckhardt had assured him that 'the Germans really were hesitating with the preparations for an attack on England and they were willing to call it off if they could do so without loss of face.'[3] Unlike Rab Butler, Sir David Kelly had no secret anti-Churchillian agenda, telling Dr Burckhardt that any deal was impossible because of Britain's distrust of Hitler and the Nazi regime. Despite a couple of further secret meetings between Sir David and Dr Burckhardt, the idea gained no traction because of Churchill's hostility and determination to 'prosecute the war with the utmost vigour'.[4]

Another plank of Hitler's so-called peace effort was his belief in the power of his own rhetoric. Without connections, wealth, an established party or experience, he had gained dominance in Germany largely through his platform oratory. Just as he had used his messianic gift for language to bend the German political system to his will, so he now planned to compel Britain to submit to his authority through a dramatic speech that would captivate the world and leave the British public eager to reach a settlement. Lacking in any awareness of how much he was despised by the overwhelming majority of British citizens, Hitler thought that, by means of the press, radio and the German propaganda machine, he could get through a message that would end their willingness to continue the war.

As the State Secretary Otto Meissner recorded: 'Hitler spoke repeatedly in his table conversations of this, that he saw the time had arrived for making a peace proposal on a grand and generous scale to Great Britain. He would therefore, in a Reichstag speech, make an offer of a covenanted peace with precise detailed proposals, which would accordingly set forth the basis for a peace treaty. He hoped that the English people themselves, if their government still resisted, would concur with his proposal and thereby exert pressure on the warmonger-led cabinet.'[5] So great an importance did Hitler attach to this speech that he felt he needed time to prepare, 'to weigh every word'.[6] He had originally planned to make his address to the Reichstag on 8 July, but, anxious about the content, decided to postpone it.

The date was soon fixed for 19 July and Goebbels, with his usual sinister skill, began to portray the event as the climactic moment when the British would be compelled to come to terms. But the hype meant that Hitler had to have something distinctive to say. As he considered his address, he was plunged once more into vacillating between aggression towards Britain and placation. Goebbels saw the same indecision as Hitler retreated to his headquarters at the Berghof, on the Obersalzberg above Berchtesgaden, where he felt he would have the tranquillity to ponder his words: 'He is still not ready for the final strike. He will go to the Obersalzberg and think over his speech there, in quiet.'[7]

The problem for the Reich was that at the beginning of July, no detailed, comprehensive scheme for an attack on England had been developed, in contrast to all their other cases of aggressive expansionism. Nevertheless, the German High Command recognised that thorough contingency planning for an assault had to begin immediately. Before the end of the month, naval and army staff held a preliminary, informal meeting to discuss 'certain operational views' in connection with an invasion, while more practical research continued on the development of landing craft and submersible tanks that could be used in an amphibious operation.[8]

Yet given Hitler's continuing belief in the possibility of a peace settlement, such an operation would take place only once other strategies had been exhausted. Indeed, General Alfred Jodl, the Wehrmacht's Chief of Staff, told his deputy, General Walter Warlimont, that he had taken up the issue of invasion with Hitler and found him 'very reluctant'.[9] This attitude permeated an official paper that Jodl produced on 30 June, setting out the latest German thinking on the continuation of war with England.

Essentially, it was a defensive document that gave little encouragement to the advocates, like Warlimont, of an early attack, viewing invasion as 'a last resort'.[10] In its doubtfulness about the need for landings and its stress on other means of defeating Britain, Jodl's paper accurately reflected Hitler's thinking at the time. Even so, it was the first official paper from the Supreme Command to instruct the armed forces to begin devising plans for an invasion in 1940.

Jodl's analysis was made just at the moment when the German army's Chief of Staff General Franz Halder was beginning to warm to the idea of invasion, not least because the conquest of the Channel Islands had proceeded so smoothly at the end of June. Moreover, the German army had gathered on the northern coast of France an impressive force of no fewer than thirteen well-equipped, victorious divisions, backed by 60,000 horses and 38,000 vehicles, enough men and equipment, he thought, to overwhelm Britain's makeshift defences.

On 1 July during a birthday visit to Berlin to see his family, Halder called on Otto Schniewind, the Chief of Staff of the Seekriegsleitung or Maritime Wartime Command. Effectively Raeder's deputy, Schniewind was not only on friendly terms with Halder but was far more enthusiastic about invasion than his chief, as became obvious once the two men began to discuss how such a potential operation might be organised.

Schniewind was already well acquainted with Study North West, the 1939 scheme developed by Raeder largely as a means of showing how difficult such an exercise would be. But rather than focusing on the problems, Schniewind highlighted the opportunities, using the wealth of information he had absorbed, particularly on southern England's geography. Much to the approbation of Halder, who took full notes throughout their talk, Schniewind ran through tide levels, moon cycles, points of departure, navigation and potential landing grounds. Fuelling each other's optimism, they agreed that the invasion should take place between the Isle of Wight and Margate, while the most favourable conditions would be a smooth sea and at least a half-moon to provide clear visibility.

A sense of excitement permeated Halder's notes: 'Underwater threats can be neutralised by net barges. Surface threats can be minimised by mines and submarines supplementing land-based artillery and planes,' he wrote in one passage. 'One hundred thousand men in one wave' could be transported across the Channel in 'a large number of small steamers (sixteen hundred),' he wrote in another, evidently departing from reality, given that there were only 300 such steamers in the whole of continental Europe.[11]

Later that day, still elated with the thought of German troops marching on London, he saw Emil Leeb, the head of the Army Ordnance Office, who seemed surprised at the new enthusiasm for invasion but outlined a number of helpful innovations, including amphibious tanks and new smoke bombs to provide smokescreens for landings.

From the moment of those meetings with Schniewind and Leeb, Halder believed that 'a landing undertaken against England was feasible'.[12] The impetus for invasion was further reinforced the next day, 2 July, by a directive from Hitler himself that mirrored much of what Jodl had said. This was the first time that the Führer had addressed the question in an official document, but it was devoid of the decisiveness and clarity usual in his other campaign instructions.

The directive stated: 'The Führer and Supreme Commander has decided that an invasion of England is quite possible under certain conditions, of which the most important is the gaining of air superiority. For the present, therefore, the time at which it will take place remains an open question. Preparations for carrying out the operation will begin immediately.' The army was asked to provide an estimate of the strength of Britain's coastal artillery and defence forces; the navy was instructed to conduct a survey of 'landing possibilities for large military forces (25 to 30 divisions)' and 'the means by which troops and supplies can be convoyed across with sufficient protection'; Goering's Luftwaffe was required to provide an assessment of the strength of the RAF as well as an indication of 'when a decisive air superiority will probably be attained'. But in case any commanders took the directive to be a commitment to invasion, he made sure the conclusion dispelled any such belief: 'All preparations must take into account that the plan to land in England has by no means taken full shape and that it is a question only of preparation for a possible event.'[13]

In another sign of his detachment, Hitler did not even sign the directive, but left it to Wilhelm Keitel, the commander-in-chief of the Wehrmacht, whose stock-in-trade was his absolute, unquestioning loyalty to the Führer and the Nazis, so much so that he was nicknamed Lackeitel, which translates as 'Lackey Keitel'. Hitler did not admire his sycophancy, once saying that he had 'the brain of a cinema doorman'.[14]

Despite the Führer's coolness, several parts of the armed forces were now caught up with the burgeoning invasion spirit. General Alfred Jacob, the commander of the Pioneers (roughly the equivalent of the Royal Engineers), began to examine the key issue of how to develop effective transport craft. At the same time, the Luftwaffe's Chief of Staff, Hans Jeschonnek, was studying the availability of airborne troops and gliders, while Erhard Milch, the Air Inspector General and an advocate of an early assault on England, continued to press the case for a Luftwaffe-led invasion, with paratroopers seizing coastal beachheads and airfields. The Kriegsmarine, although still as sceptical as ever, set up a planning unit on 9 July to fulfil the directive's requirements.

With more enthusiasm, Halder established a specialist office, known as E (England) Section, in the army staff's Operations Department, to develop the invasion plans. The section soon came up with an ambitious, if sketchy, outline of an assault that would involve a first wave of six divisions, each backed by armoured battalions, landing between the Thames and Lyme Bay, followed by two further waves of troops.

But since no amphibious attack had been undertaken before, there was a host of practical issues to resolve. Here the army staff benefited from the positive results of the recent work on amphibious craft, particularly the creation of submersible tanks which could travel underwater. The Germans knew they would need the firepower of heavy tanks for any amphibious operation, but the problem was that craft capable of transporting such vehicles would be too large to go right up to the beach. The solution, the Germans decided, was to convert some of the tanks so they could be disembarked in shallow coastal waters. Two types were chosen for the experiment: the Panzer III combat tank and the Panzer IV infantry support vehicle. The central aim was to make them completely watertight, which entailed a number of procedures. All openings such as sighting ports and hatches had to be sealed with tape and caulking. Non-return valves had to be fitted to the exhaust pipes, while the engine was converted so it could use seawater as a coolant. Rubber covers were fitted around the guns and a rubber seal placed between the hull and the turret. Once in action, all the coverings and seals could be removed either manually or from the inside by electric detonators. A periscope and a bilge pump were also installed. Fresh air was provided through an 18-metre long thick hose, covered in wire mesh, connected to a buoy floating on the surface. In one final aquatic touch, the submersible tanks were painted the colour of seawater. Fitted out like this, each of them could travel through the water at 5.7 km per hour, going down to a maximum depth of 15 metres. Working with remarkable speed, the conversion unit managed to have the first Panzers ready towards the end of June, and initial trials were conducted in Jade Bay, north of the major port of Wilhemshaven. Paul Zieb, Director of Equipment at Wilhelmshaven, later described how these opening tests were conducted in warm, sunny weather, first in dammed waters no more than 7 metres deep, and then in strong tidal currents in the sea. 'The tank remained firmly on the sandy bottom at every test depth in every position – against, with or diagonal to the current – as long as it was in motion. If it was stopped in the current for tactical reasons, for instance to allow another tank to close ranks, it quickly sank about 20 centimetres in the sand. The diver who was observing this reported via the telephone link that the tank was unlikely to be able to free itself under its own power, and that the exhaust lay on the sand. A floating crane was ordered, but the tank managed to free itself without too many difficulties before its arrival. The lesson learnt during these tests was that the immobile tanks would soon become mired in strong currents.'[15]

A trial on 26 June was witnessed by Dr Fritz Todt, Reich Minister for Armaments and Munitions, who was sufficiently impressed to order that the conversion programme be accelerated. On 13 July, an experimental tank company was formed under the tank commander George-Hans Reinhardt, and by the end of the month there were four battalions with submersible tanks. The trials continued, though not without some setbacks. In several cases the Panzers became flooded and the crews were only saved by rescue divers. On one occasion, when a group of tanks reached dry land, the detonators failed to remove the covers over their openings. As a result, the tanks were momentarily travelling blind as they rumbled up the beach, crashing into several seaside villas and a clump of trees before coming to a halt. By far the biggest problem, however, was that the submersibles could not avoid underwater obstacles, a serious failing given that British beaches were already full of scaffolding and concrete blocks. Eventually Reinhart decided to give the order that, in the event of invasion, these tanks should be disembarked at high tide so that if they became stranded on the seabed they could be recovered once the tide fell. Despite these difficulties, the conversion programme ran with striking efficiency. By 15 July, the first submersibles had been dispatched to the French coast and within another fortnight 130 of them were ready for action. For many German troops, the images of tanks were a morale booster, a symbol of the Reich's superiority over the British, as rifleman Alexander Hoffer recalled. 'We had better equipment. We even had submersible tanks. None of us believed that story until we saw a newsreel which showed a whole group of Panzers completely hidden under water, climb out of a river, then up a bank and halt there. Quick as a flash, the crews were out of the turrets stripping off a sort of rubber covering and clearing the tank guns. In no time at all, or so it seemed, the Panzers were in action. A Sonderführer [specialist leader] who gave us a lecture pointed out that our assault would be accompanied by such submersible tanks. We were all reassured after that.'[16] Altogether 202 of these tanks were developed by the end of August 1940. Produced in smaller numbers was the *Schwimmpanzer* II, a light amphibious tank which, instead of submerging to the seabed, was able to float on the water through the attachment of long rectangular buoyancy boxes made of aluminium and filled with kapok sacks. It was powered by a ship's propeller that was connected to the tank's own tracks by an extension shaft. Like the submersible tank, it could reach 5.7 km per hour but it had the advantage that it could fire its guns during a landing. Its two great drawbacks, however, were that its floats were extremely vulnerable to enemy gunfire and that it was costly to produce. By the end of the summer, only 52 had been made.

Two other early innovative ideas for an assault on England never reached fruition. One, drawn up by Major-General Adolf von Schell, the head of the Army's Mechanised Transport Group, was to use a flotilla of fast boats, powered by aircraft engines and capable of travelling at 50 mph, to transport mobile troops across the Channel. In Schell's conception, the sheer speed would provide the element of surprise for a landing, with the craft roaring onto the English beaches like racing boats. Experimental versions of these boats, which went by the impressive title of *Truppentransporttragflachen-schnellboote*, had been conducted with a degree of success in April, but in late June Raeder's staff, which by order of the Führer had taken charge of all research on landing craft, decided that Schell's boats did not have the constructional strength to cross the Channel, so the project was dropped. More imaginative was a proposal from Professor Gottfried Feder, Hitler's former economic adviser and at this point State Secretary in the Reich Ministry of Economics, for a series of gigantic floating concrete bunkers with powered caterpillar tracks. According to Feder's plan, these vast amphibious beasts, which he called 'war tortoises' or 'war crocodiles', would be 90 feet long, 20 feet wide and 12 feet high. He envisaged that they would be able to crawl along the sea, carrying either tanks or 200 men and then, on reaching the shore, use their tracks to climb up the beaches. Feder was certain that their construction would be 'a simple task for the ferro-concrete expert'[17] and his enthusiasm infected some key figures on the naval staff, including Schniewind. The Naval Ordnance Office had severe doubts about the seaworthiness of the crocodiles and in early July research on the project was permanently shelved.

Much experimentation and planning took place as Hitler and the German High Command had to face up to the reality that, after Oran, Britain was not about to capitulate. With Churchill more defiant than ever, the Führer began to take a deeper interest in the invasion concept, although his priority remained his Reichstag speech. On 10 July, still in his remote Berghof headquarters, he ordered that heavy guns should be installed on the Channel coast to provide frontal and flanking fire for any projected crossing. By early August, there were four 11-inch guns ready to fire at Cap Gris Nez, and three 12-inch guns north of Boulogne. Other batteries were created during the following weeks, so that by mid-September there were no fewer than thirteen huge guns in the area, backed by over 130 other artillery pieces trained on the Channel. This coastal arsenal became something of an obsession of Hitler's during the summer of 1940. In the words of the novelist and historian Derek Robinson, 'shelling the enemy always made him feel more secure.'[18]

However, the installation of the batteries was only an auxiliary measure. The far bigger question was the creation of a credible invasion force. On 11 July, the day after his order on the Channel guns, Hitler held a meeting at the Berghof with Raeder, who reiterated his long-held view that 'invasion should be used only as a last resort to force Britain to sue for peace'. The grand admiral then argued that such pressure on Britain could also be created 'by cutting off her import trade by means of submarine warfare, air attacks on convoys, and heavy air attacks on her main centres, as

Liverpool, for instance'. But he stressed that he could not 'for his part, therefore, advocate an invasion as he did in the case of Norway'.[19] Raeder left the meeting with the impression that Hitler had agreed with him, as he recorded in his report: 'The Führer also views invasion as a last resort, and . . . considers air superiority a prerequisite.'[20]

While Raeder was filled with reservations, Jodl, like Halder, was becoming more positive about the chances of invasion. On 12 July he issued a paper entitled 'First Deliberations Regarding a Landing in England'. Endorsed by Keitel, Jodl's study admitted that 'the landing will be difficult' because of Britain's command of the sea and the vulnerability of any transport fleet to RAF bombing, although neither would make an invasion impossible. Jodl continued: 'The landing must therefore be effected in the form of a large-scale river crossing on a broad front, in which the role of artillery will fall to the Air Force, the first wave of landing troops must be very strong and a sea lane completely secure from attack must be established to the bridgehead.'

The paper then turned to the actual form of the attack, whose detail showed how much planning work had already been done. 'It will be necessary to land the assault elements of seven divisions simultaneously between Bournemouth and Dover,' a broad front stretching over a distance of 143 miles, three times the breadth of the Normandy landings in 1944. The disembarkation harbours, argued Jodl, should be decided by the navy, which would also, under this plan, be responsible for laying two long mine barriers to protect the invasion force, one on the left flank between Alderney and Portland, the other on the right flank between Calais and Ramsgate. Jodl estimated that at least 800 craft would be needed.

As well as protecting the invasion fleet, the Luftwaffe would have to 'overcome coastal defences which can operate against the landing points; break the resistance of the enemy ground troops and annihilate the reserves; and destroy the most important lines of transport necessary for bringing up reinforcements'. But for any chance of success it was vital for a number of preliminary conditions to be met, among these being the establishment of air supremacy, the 'destruction of all naval forces stationed on the south coast', and the creation of sea lanes 'free of mines'.[21] The plan was given the code name Löwe or Lion.

Hitler's exasperation at Britain's continuing defiance was increased on 14 July by another of Churchill's historic radio broadcasts, in which the prime minister prepared the British public for the likely German attack. 'Conscious that we serve an unfolding purpose, we are ready to defend our native land against the invasion by which it is threatened . . . We await undismayed the impending assault. Perhaps it will come tonight. Perhaps it will come next week. Perhaps it will never come. We must show ourselves equally capable of meeting a sudden violent shock or, what is perhaps a harder test, a prolonged vigil.'

Due to the lack of British intelligence, he could not have known that serious German planning had only just started, but he recognised the invasion threat as a powerful unifying force for the nation: 'We may therefore be sure that there is a plan – perhaps built up over years – for destroying Great Britain, which after all has the honour to be his main and foremost enemy. All I can say is that any plan for invading Britain which Hitler made two months ago must have had to be entirely re-cast to meet our new position.' That new position involved the return of troops from Dunkirk, the creation of the LDVs, the construction of defences, and the growing confidence of the RAF and the Royal Navy. With such strength, he concluded, 'the dark curse of Hitler will be lifted from our age.'[22]

Taunted and vilified by Churchill, the Führer ordered the preparations for invasion to be intensified. An attack was no longer to be just a last resort, but a central part of Nazi strategy to overpower Britain. On 15 July, Keitel, acting on Hitler's instructions, informed the naval staff that planning now had to be speeded up so that an invasion could be launched within a month. Raeder found this precipitous demand absurd and twice rang the Wehrmacht operations staff to ask for verification, only to be told that it was indeed true. Written confirmation followed the next day, 16 July, when Hitler issued Directive No. 16, setting out the new, more hostile approach to Britain, although even now, on the eve of his Reichstag speech, there was still a note of hesitation.

The opening paragraph was not a loud, assured trumpet call to smash Britain, but a bland notice of a future possible option. 'Since England, despite its hopeless military situation, still gives no sign of any readiness to come to terms, I have decided to prepare for an invasion of that country and, if necessary, to carry it through. The aim of this operation will be to eliminate England as a base for carrying on the war against Germany and, should it be requisite, completely to occupy it.' The directive grew more forthright as Hitler described the basis of the operation, whose name had now changed, on the suggestion of the Wehrmacht staff, to Seelöwe or Sea Lion to reflect its maritime nature.

The plan was much as Jodl had set out to the Führer four days earlier, although its breadth had now been extended. 'The landing will be carried out as a surprise crossing on a broad front from the neighbourhood of Ramsgate to the area west of the Isle of Wight,' Hitler declared, confirming that 'preparations for the entire operation must be completed by the middle of August.' To emphasise that he was taking charge, he stated that 'the final decision I reserve for myself' and that 'Commanders-in-Chief will direct the forces concerned under my order according to my general directive.'[23]

Perhaps the most crucial practical task was given to Raeder's navy: that of assembling the transport craft on the occupied northern coast in accordance with the army's stated needs. In the coming weeks, it was to prove a huge logistical burden, leading to deepening friction between Raeder and the army.

The conflict between the Reich's army and navy over Sea Lion had its roots in two very different conceptions of the operation. For the army, which had little fear of the British land forces after the experience of the French campaign, it was a straightforward exercise, scarcely more than 'a river crossing' in the phrase that gained currency within the army's general staff in early July. By the time Directive No. 16 was issued, Halder's staff had already worked out an extensive plan, involving an assault on England by thirteen elite divisions across a broad front.

Under this scheme, six divisions from the 16th Army, commanded by General Ernst Busch, would depart from the Pas de Calais and reach southern England between Ramsgate and Bexhill. Meanwhile, four divisions of Adolf Strauss's 9th Army, crossing from Le Havre, would land between Brighton and the Isle of Wight. Further west, three divisions from Field Marshal Walther von Reichenau's 6th Army were to embark from Cherbourg and land around Lyme Bay in Dorset. Reinforcements made up of six panzer and three motorised divisions would quickly follow, with support from airborne troops, either at Lyme Bay or north of the Isle of Wight.

The operation would unfold through three waves of troops, with 90,000 men put ashore in the initial assault and 170,000 more arriving in the next two waves. In addition to the troops themselves, this initial force would be accompanied by 62,000 horses, 34,200 vehicles and 52 light flak batteries belonging to the Luftwaffe. The aim of the 9th and 16th Army divisions was to establish bridgeheads on the coast, then advance towards their first objective, a line from Gravesend to Southampton, while Reichenau's 6th Army would take Bristol. Once the first assault troops had secured the ground, further waves could follow, bringing the total invading force to no fewer than thirty-nine divisions.

The entire operation, it was claimed, would last less than a month. Von Brauchitsch, the commander-in-chief of the army, regarded Sea Lion as 'comparatively easy'.[24] Raeder's staff, however, were far less sanguine, recognising it as a mammoth venture for which the Kriegsmarine was ill equipped when facing a task far bigger than that of the other two forces.

In particular, there were two related problems: first, the sheer scale of the transport required for the crossing; and, second, the question of where the troops would land. A naval staff officer pointed out that the army required 170,000 men to be transported across the Channel in the second and third waves, for which 'we would need 400 ships of 5000 tonnes each; that comes to 2 million tonnes of shipping space!'[25] Yet in July the entire German cargo fleet amounted to only 1.2 million tonnes. Even the inclusion of passenger ships contributed just another 285,000 tonnes. Given these limitations, the deadline Hitler had set of mid-August for the completion of preparations was hopelessly unrealistic.

Nor did the army seem to have taken account of all the factors that would hamper landings in southern England. These included not just the growing strength of the British defences, especially the RAF and the Royal Navy, but also tidal patterns, currents, natural obstructions, the layout of beaches and cliffs, the weather, and the need for harbours to maintain supplies. The German navy, declaring that it was the height of irresponsibility to call Sea Lion a 'river crossing',[26] was opposed to the very concept of a broad front stretching over 160 miles along the south coast of England. That, they claimed, would make the invasion fleet more vulnerable to British attack, whereas it would be easier for the Kriegsmarine to protect the flanks of a far shorter crossing on a narrower front in Kent.

Raeder felt he had a duty to press his case with the army. On 17 July, he met his opposite number there, von Brauchitsch, to discuss Sea Lion. The fact that this was the very first meeting between the two commanders about an invasion of Britain is a further indication of how late the planning had been left and how little cooperation existed between the German armed forces. It was not a profitable exchange.

Two days later, Raeder set out his criticisms of Sea Lion in a highly negative paper of 19 July. 'The task allotted to the Navy in Operation Sea Lion is out of all proportion to the Navy's strength and bears no relation to the tasks that are set the Army and the Air Force,' he began, before highlighting the 'principal difficulties'. Among them were: the 'limited capacity' of the French harbours damaged during the offensive; the treacherous nature of the English Channel; the danger of mines; the lack of proper landing craft; and doubts that the Luftwaffe would be able to destroy Britain's coastal defences. 'The possibility must be envisaged that, even if the first wave has been successfully transported, the enemy will still be able to penetrate with resolute Naval forces so as to place himself between the first wave, already landed, and the succeeding transports.'[27]

The military arguments over Sea Lion were briefly suspended as Hitler prepared to give the Reichstag speech that he thought would change the whole course of the war. In classic Nazi style, the build-up to the event was carefully manipulated to bring the German people to fever pitch and to portray Hitler as the victorious statesman, the master of global events offering Britain the choice of either annihilation or peace. A radio station descended into lurid fabrications: 'In England, men and women feel the urge to raise their courage by resorting to drink. Alcoholism is increasing by leaps and bounds. Press gangs are visiting cinemas, cabarets and tea rooms to enrol young civilians as trench diggers. Fear in England is indeed terrific.'[28]

Three days later, on 18 July, Hitler finally finished writing his speech at the Berghof. He had discussed it in detail with his Foreign Minister, Joachim von Ribbentrop, whose verdict was inevitably a flattering one. 'The Führer is going to make a very magnanimous offer to England. When Lloyd George hears it, he will probably want to fall on our necks. I would not be surprised if we are not all soon seated at a peace conference,' Ribbentrop told Dr Paul Schmidt, the Führer's interpreter, who was going to give a simultaneous translation of the speech in English for overseas broadcasters.[29] After a midday meal at his retreat, Hitler was taken by car from Obersalzberg to Munich's main station, where he boarded his special overnight train bound for Berlin.

After a visit to the Reich Chancellery in the afternoon, he was driven to the Reichstag, where he was due to begin his eagerly awaited speech at seven o'clock, his words to be broadcast not just to the German nation but across the world. The Reichstag itself, once the legislative assembly of Germany, had become a moribund body under Hitler's totalitarian dictatorship, little more than a one-party echo chamber for the acclamation of Nazi decrees, and its home, the drab surroundings of the Kroll Opera House, reflected its diminished status. But the lack of grandeur could not detract from the sense of portentousness that now enveloped the occasion. 'Tonight, the fate of England will be decided,' Goebbels declared.[30]

All the leading figures of the Third Reich were there, with the military commanders filling the most prominent places. To add to the solemnity of the event, the seats of six Reichstag members who had been killed in action were each left empty apart from a simple laurel wreath.

The gargantuan figure of Goering opened the proceedings with a dedication to the fallen, and then, to a rapturous reception, he introduced the Führer to the podium. Moments later, a hush descended on the auditorium as Hitler began to speak. In a departure from his usual demagoguery, he used a quieter, more measured style in keeping with his theme of seeking peace. His aim, he declared, had never been the destruction of the British empire although that would be the result if Herr Churchill insisted on 'the continuation of the struggle'. He explained that he wanted nothing more than an end to the war, in contrast to the bellicose British prime minister. 'My stomach turns when I see such unscrupulous destroyers of entire peoples and states. My purpose was not to wage wars but to build a new social state of high culture. Each year of this war robs me of this work.'

In his climax, the Führer took on the stance of a far-sighted leader, urging Churchill to see sense before it was too late. 'I feel obliged, in this hour, by my conscience to direct once more an appeal to reason to England. I believe I can do this not as someone who has been defeated, but as a victor speaking reason. I see no compelling ground for the continuation of this war.'[31]

It was a lengthy speech, containing over 12,000 words and lasting two hours and seven minutes. The performance was made all the longer by Hitler's triumphalist recitation of the German victories in Europe, as well as his announcement, in the middle of the address, of a glut of honours for commanders, giving twelve of them new insignia as field marshals and Goering the unique rank of Reichsmarschall. The American journalist William Shirer vividly recorded the sight of Goering at this moment: 'Sitting up on the dais of the Speaker in all his bulk, he acted like a happy child playing with his toys on Christmas morning.'[32]

As a piece of oratory, Hitler's speech impressed Shirer because of its restraint. 'His voice was lower tonight; he rarely shouted as he usually does; and he did not once cry out hysterically as I've seen him do often from the rostrum.' Apart from his more measured voice, another surprising physical aspect of Hitler's method struck Shirer. 'I've often admired the way he uses his hands, which are somewhat feminine and quite artistic. Tonight he used those hands beautifully, seemed to express himself almost as much with his hands – and the sway of his body – as he did with his words and the use of his voice.'[33]

The style may have been effective, but the content was not. At the very heart of the speech was meant to be a convincing, appealing peace offer, yet Hitler completely failed to set out his case. Instead of specifics to win over the British, he dealt merely in bland generalities. It was as if he expected Churchill's government to stop fighting just because he said so. He had laboured for days at the Berghof, only to end up with pages of hollow verbiage. Even many Germans, who had been encouraged to expect a dramatic, far-reaching pronouncement, were privately dismayed.

Hitler's interpreter Dr Paul Schmidt, who was in a small studio at the Berlin Broadcasting station, reading out an English version of the text as the Führer spoke, later wrote that he was

profoundly disappointed in the content of the speech. It was interminably long, and enlarged upon the favourable course which events had taken for Germany – to such an extent that even many Germans, not to mention foreigners, said, 'We've had enough of that.' I looked in vain for Ribbentrop's magnanimous peace offer, which was to induce Lloyd George 'to fall on our necks'. It was contained in a single passage, high sounding but completely bereft of substance. Nothing more. Not the slightest hint of any concrete suggestion. I had often noticed at negotiations that precision was not a strong point of Hitler's. Nevertheless, it was incomprehensible to me that he should believe that such a meaningless, purely rhetorical observation would have any effect upon the sober British.

Indeed, Schmidt feared that this 'provocative, vainglorious speech would further strengthen the British will to fight'.[34]

The sense of deflation in Berlin was worsened as soon as the first British response came in, exposing how miserably Hitler had failed. Within an hour of the Führer finishing his speech, the renowned British journalist Sefton Delmer, who was a fluent German speaker, was on the airwaves of the BBC's German service. In a precise, mock-deferential tone, Delmer said, 'Let me tell you what we here in Britain think of this appeal of yours to what you are pleased to call our reason and common sense. Herr Führer and Reichskanzler, we hurl it right back at you, right in your evil-smelling teeth.'[35] Both Delmer's language and the starkness of his rejection shocked the Germans, as Shirer witnessed when he sat listening to the broadcast with a group of high-ranking officers and civil servants. 'They could not believe their ears. One of them shouted at me: "Can you make it out? Can you understand those British fools? To turn down peace now?" I merely grunted.'[36]

What shook the Germans even more was that, used to living under autocracy, they believed Delmer's broadcast represented the official response of the British government, although in reality there had been no time for any such consultation. There was no doubt, however, that his insults represented the overwhelming view of the British press and public, as was confirmed by the Ministry of Information's opinion surveyors, who found: 'On the whole people have treated Hitler's speech less seriously than the press have done. People laughed and jeered.'[37] It was a mocking attitude that was shared by Churchill, who was inclined to treat the Reichstag speech with silent contempt. When asked by the Foreign Office what answer he planned to give, the prime minister said, 'I do not propose to say anything in reply to Herr Hitler's speech, not being on speaking terms with him.'[38]

The Reichstag speech had met with nothing like the response the Führer wanted, yet even in the face of clear rejection he remained indecisive. The hope still lingered that the British public might change its mind or that Churchill would be forced from power. Goebbels wrote, 'The Führer does not yet want to regard England's answer (or lack of answer) as genuine. He thinks of waiting a little longer. After all, his appeal was to the English people, not to Churchill,'[39] a remark that yet again exhibited the Nazis' woeful inability to understand that in July 1940 their leader mirrored the views of the vast majority of Britons.

Hitler's bewilderment at Britain's non-response was highlighted at a full-scale Führer conference held in Berlin on 21 July. In front of his military chiefs, Hitler showed no vigour, no willingness to take charge of the invasion plans. On the contrary, he openly expressed his puzzlement at Britain's reluctance to come to terms despite the utter hopelessness of her position. 'The war has been won by us, and reversal of the prospects of success is impossible,' he declared, yet he was unsure how to proceed. Operation Sea Lion could be an effective means of bringing the war to an end, he continued, but it would be 'an exceptionally daring undertaking'.

Continuing his negative monologue, he stressed the need for 'mastery of the air', control of the Dover Straits and protection by minefields, while issuing gloomy warnings about the coastal climate. 'The time of year is an important factor, since the weather in the North Sea and in the Channel during the second half of September is very bad and fogs begin in the middle of October. The main operation would therefore have to be completed by September 15; after this date, cooperation between the Luftwaffe and the heavy weapons becomes too unreliable.'[40] Hitler concluded that if all the conditions could not be met, it would become 'necessary to consider other plans'.[41]

So confident about Britain's imminent capitulation only a month earlier, the Germans now began to understand that they had a tremendous battle on their hands.

14

'To defend our own little patch of England'

———

BOTH GERMANY AND Britain were hindered by their lack of military or political intelligence throughout the summer of 1940. A central explanation for Hitler's ill-judged speech at the Reichstag was that the Germans had no inside knowledge of the British political scene, and were still relying on the preconceived notion of Churchill as an unpopular plutocrat.

Although the Nazis had cracked some of the Admiralty radio codes, thereby gaining useful information about ship movements, they knew little about the army, the RAF or the strength of Britain's defences. In fact, Hitler once bewailed Germany's ignorance about its enemy, given that she lay only 21 miles away from occupied territory: 'It seems incredible that we do not have a single informant in Great Britain.'[1] British military leaders complained just as bitterly about being kept in the dark, largely because the German occupation had destroyed the Allies' networks of agents across Western Europe and resistance cells had not yet been established.

But Britain did have one advantage over the Germans: the work of the government's Code and Cipher School at Bletchley Park, where the pioneering use of semi-electronic computers was beginning to yield results in decrypting the latest codes employed by the German military on their ferociously complex Enigma machines.

A crucial breakthrough came on 22 May 1940 when the decoders succeeded in unlocking the traffic between Luftwaffe operational units and Goering's headquarters. The intelligence from the Enigma decrypts was known as Ultra and was regarded as so important that it was circulated to only a handful of military and political leaders, including the Chiefs of Staff, Churchill and Ismay.

The Ultra decrypts were personally taken to the prime minister each day by Sir Stewart Menzies, the head of MI6, another indicator of their importance, and were carried in a special buff-coloured box, for which Churchill alone in Downing Street had the key. Indeed, the existence of Ultra was so secret that it was kept from the public until the 1970s, when the retired senior intelligence officer Group Captain Frederick Winterbotham, who was in charge of the Ultra decrypts, published his memoirs. Churchill

151

himself approvingly described the Bletchley Park staff as 'the geese that laid the golden eggs and never cackled'.[2]

In late June 1940, the Bletchley listeners were able to provide one intriguing detail that appeared to indicate that the Germans were planning major landings on the British Isles. The message ran: 'on 20 June, a request from Flakcorps I (anti-aircraft corps) for the following maps to be delivered, among others, immediately to their HQ: i) 800 copies, England and Ireland, scale 1/100,000 and 1/300,000; ii) 300 copies, France and England, scale 1/1,000,000'.[3]

Perhaps even more valuable was an analysis of the decrypts in early July by air intelligence, which seemed to show that German bomber strength was much lower than expected. Instead of the 2,500 front-line bombers previously thought to be held by the Luftwaffe, the estimated number was now believed to be 1,250, or half that. Describing the figures as 'heaven-sent', the air staff said that the forthcoming German aerial offensive could be viewed 'much more confidently than was possible a month ago'.[4] Yet over the coming months, the Luftwaffe traffic did not yield as much solid information as the British government had initially hoped when the Luftwaffe code was broken.

In fact, Ultra was of limited benefit in mid-1940, for two reasons. One was that the German military, including the Luftwaffe staff, tended to use secure telephone landlines rather than the radio throughout their occupied territory. Another was that Goering, puffed up with arrogance, was completely detached from the invasion planning process and had no interest in cooperating with the other commanders, as he showed by his regular non-attendance at conferences.

Given Ultra's limitations in July, the British therefore still had to turn to other sources of intelligence, whose varied quality gave rise to constant empty rumours and false alarms. Indeed, after submitting a report stating that 'a fairly reliable source gives 5 July as the date for invasion', MI14, the German section of British Intelligence, admitted candidly, 'we doubt if any source open to us can be in possession of such accurate information.'[5] Nevertheless, the defence authorities had a duty to consider every piece of data that might shed light on the invasion plans. At the end of June, for instance, Lord Halifax circulated a report from Polish sources in the Turkish capital Ankara, warning that the invasion would be mounted in the second week of July. Partly as a result of this report, speculation grew about the imminence of an attack on 8 July, although such talk was never taken too seriously. 'This is the zero hour for Hitler's invasion of England – the actual date favoured by tipsters being about 8 July,' Sir Alexander Cadogan recorded drily.[6]

When that day passed without incident, Thursday 11 July became the rumoured new date of destiny. John Colville wrote in his diary with a hint of cynicism, 'The invasion and great attack is now said to be due on Thursday.'[7] When the day came and the Channel crossing similarly failed to materialise, he noted that new intelligence pointed to Norway as the possible base for a German assault.

In the same vein, on 10 July, another intelligence report to the committee stated that 'training for combined operations is being carried out in the Baltic', and, even more disturbingly, that 'Germany intends to use poison gas in the attack on Great Britain.'[8] But two days later, in a further sign of how poor the intelligence was, another report admitted that the sudden, recent focus on Scandinavia might have been misleading.[9]

Other information sent to the defence authorities pointed elsewhere. Admiral Drax, the commander of the Nore, circulated to the Chiefs of Staff an ominous rumour he had heard from three Dutch army officers who had escaped from occupied Holland. According to this Dutch trio:

> The German preparations in Holland for the invasion of England are obvious and the German slogan is 'London on 15th July. Every craft that can be made capable of making the crossing is expected to start on 11 July, and one and a half million men are being transported in various small craft. A very large number of parachute troops are in Holland and are continually practising. Large quantities of troops are to be airborne and special underground starting places complete with runways have been constructed. Planes have been specially constructed to land in small places, i.e. – the size of a football ground. The plan for invasion is the launching of a parachutist attack which is intended to withdraw the troops from the coast, thus facilitating the task of the first landing parties which will come from all ports from Norway to Belgium. After the first parties have secured a footing, the main landing force will arrive in larger ships. The Germans estimate there will be a total invasion force of three-and-a-half to four million.[10]

The absurd scale of this supposed operation, as big as Barbarossa if it had been mounted, rightly undermined the credibility of the rumour.

Amidst this miasma of false trails, exaggeration and gossip, there was one unintentionally comedic result. The prime minister decreed that all the intelligence reports and Bletchley decrypts about the potential invasion should be classified under the code name Operation Smith, since the British knew nothing about the German title, Operation Sea Lion. Indeed, it was not until late September that Bletchley discovered that the Germans' invasion plan was called Seelöwe. However, Churchill's choice of name was unfortunate, as the government scientist R.V. Jones later recounted:

> It turned out that the War Office had its own 'Operation Smith' that was concerned with the invasion. It was the code name for the movement of one of its minor administrative branches from its current headquarters in

Tetbury to some place further north if the Germans should have invaded and posed a threat to south Gloucestershire. The result was that when the Bletchley teleprints were received in the War Office, duly headed according to the Prime Minister's instruction, they were immediately sent to a Colonel in Gloucestershire, who no doubt impressed by the service that the War Office was providing but realizing that the material was too secret for general circulation, locked them in his safe and told nobody.[11]

For all the conflicting advice from the continent, the government had to prepare for the worst eventuality. As Churchill said in his radio broadcast of 14 July, perhaps the invasion might 'never come'[12] but he knew Britain could not rely on such blind optimism. Everything possible had to be done to secure the country's defences, since it was in Germany's essential interest to conquer her last remaining foe in Western Europe. Ironside wrote in his diary: 'This looks like the decisive month' for 'there can be no doubt that vast preparations in the way of air and sea invasion are being made'.[13]

Always fascinated by military strategy, the prime minister himself was considering the nature of the invasion threat and the effectiveness of Britain's resources. In a paper of 9 July, he struck a dismissive note about Germany's chances of launching a successful assault, particularly because of the strength of the Royal Navy. 'I find it very difficult to visualize the kind of invasion all along the coast by troops carried in small craft and even in boats. I have not seen any serious evidence of this class of craft being assembled and except in very narrow waters, it would be a most hazardous and even suicidal operation to commit a large army to the accidents of the sea in the teeth of our very numerous patrolling forces.' With remarkable boldness he expressed his disbelief that 'the south coast is in serious danger at the present time', because 'no great mass of shipping exists in the French ports', with the Dover mine barrage acting as a deterrent.[14]

Partly in response to Churchill's paper, the First Sea Lord Sir Dudley Pound produced a more circumspect analysis, setting out his view of the German threat. On the seas, it was true that Britain enjoyed naval superiority, but this could be countered by air power. Following the launch of an invasion, 'large numbers of German air forces will be concentrated on our warships in the narrow seas in an endeavour to prevent them operating against invading forces'. Contrary to Churchill's positive view, he said that it would 'never be possible for the Admiralty to guarantee' that German landings could not take place in the south, partly because of advances in naval technology. 'In the hundred years since invasion of this country was last seriously talked about the Channel and North Sea have become very much narrower because of the greatly increased speed of the craft that might be employed and the crossing of these waters by large numbers of high speed, small boats is now a practicable matter. The whole crossing can now be undertaken in many places in the dark hours.'

Continuing in this pessimistic vein, Pound wrote that the most likely launch points for such barks were between Calais and the Netherlands. 'The enemy may well have prepared a considerable number of these fast craft and it is not impossible that, say, 400 of these vessels, each capable of holding 40 men, may be in readiness.' If these fast vessels were to travel across to England at 30 knots, 'the likelihood of our destroyers being able to get to the spot in time to take any considerable toll is not great. The coastal patrols themselves, being slow and of weak armament, could not be expected to stop more than 20 per cent of such a force.' Taking account of potential embarkation from Nazi-occupied Denmark and Norway, as well as from ports in Germany, Pound believed it was probable that 'a total of some 100,000 men might reach these shores without being sufficiently intercepted by naval forces.' It would be difficult for the invader to maintain supply lines, but, on the other hand, 'he could make a quick rush on London, living off the country as he went, and force our Government to capitulate'.[15]

On seeing Pound's paper, Churchill struck an emollient tone. Rather than dismiss the First Sea Lord's arguments, in his reply of 15 July sent to the Chiefs of Staff, he said he was certain 'that the Admiralty will in fact be better than their word, and that the invaders' losses in transit would further reduce the scale of the attack'. However, he urged the chiefs to review their invasion plans and make sure that they had the land forces to repel a German attack of 100,000 men, which in practice meant at least 200,000 troops in the home defences.[16]

Churchill's demand to the chiefs for a minimum defence force of 200,000 was in fact rather modest in the context of a growing strength at home. Since the dark days of May, when the country seemed hopelessly ill equipped to cope with an assault, Britain's security had radically improved. On every front, the nation was becoming better prepared. Fighter Command, having proved its capabilities over Dunkirk, was rapidly expanding its fleet. Between 29 June and 2 August, 488 Hurricanes and Spitfires came out of the factories. In early May, Fighter Command had an establishment of little more than 600 aircraft. By mid-July the figure had reached over 900, with Hurricanes and Spitfires making up the vast majority of planes. In addition, the radar stations and the Royal Observer Corps, now both fully operational, gave the RAF an invaluable warning system about hostile Luftwaffe activity; while the technically minded head of Fighter Command, Sir Hugh Dowding, had devised a highly efficient command structure for processing information about enemy movements, which meant that fighter resources could be directed to where they were needed most.

Similarly, the Royal Navy was an increasingly strong obstacle against invasion, with the coastal fleet, gun batteries and mines all being reinforced. It was the same reassuring story with the coastguard, which, having been taken by the Admiralty from the Board of Trade, had been 'doubled in strength and armed, so that the maximum patrol beat between posts was only half an hour,' reported Pound to a meeting of government ministers on 15 July. As regards the main Home Fleet, Pound's news was equally heartening. There were now, he said, at least fifty destroyers, thirteen cruisers and nineteen corvettes in home waters.[17]

The army had long been seen as the weakest of the three services, but even here the deficiencies should not be exaggerated. Contrary to the myth that Dunkirk had left the British army hopelessly denuded, the total number of men under arms in the United Kingdom in mid-July 1940 was 1,313,000, and that did not include the 600,000 men who had registered as Local Defence Volunteers. This huge force included 595,000 troops in the regular field army, 42,000 in home defence battalions, 13,000 in coastal defence, 365,000 in training units and 38,000 from the Dominions. However, the real effectiveness of the force was not nearly as impressive as these numbers suggested, since 220,000 were in support organisations and had not been trained to fight, while 150,000 of the soldiers had less than two months' service. In addition, sixteen of Ironside's twenty-eight divisions were still re-equipping and regrouping after their disastrous ordeals in France. Nevertheless, when it came to equipment, the army's position was improving compared to early June. It now had 710 field guns, 198 medium and heavy guns, 263 towed anti-tank guns, 291 tracked light tanks, 10,000 Bren guns and 4,500 anti-tank rifles, although this was all far below the armoury of the Germans in the West.

Static fortifications were the centrepiece of the Ironside plan, made up of trenches, sandbagged strongpoints, roadblocks, mines and tank traps. Allied to natural obstacles like rivers or woods, these man-made barriers formed the local and GHQ 'stop lines' that Ironside hoped would halt the advance of the invader.

While worried about the numbers of troops and the quality of their training, Ironside was pleased with progress on his stop lines and beach defences. 'Our fortifications are getting better every day,'[18] he wrote on 8 July. One indicator of this progress was the delivery of a new, more powerful type of anti-tank mine filled with ammonal, an explosive largely made up of ammonium nitrate and TNT. From mid-July, these were sent to the army commands at the rate of 20,000 a week.

As well as the beach defences and the stop lines, work had continued on obstructing fields that could be used as potential landing grounds for

German airborne troops, although progress here was hampered both by the need to maintain agricultural production and by severe shortages of labour. At the beginning of July, Churchill became concerned that the effort to block open spaces was 'not being pressed with sufficient vigour, particularly in the Western and Midland areas. Local authorities or owners should be made personally responsible for the execution of this work.'[19]

In the mood of wartime emergency, the construction of anti-invasion defences was sometimes accompanied by a degree of ruthlessness, with the normal respect for private property and individual rights often being ignored by the military under Emergency Powers legislation. One of the toughest in this regard was Lieutenant General Bernard Montgomery, who was put in charge of No. 3 Division, based near Brighton, on his return from Dunkirk. Typically, he was quite unashamed about his uncompromising attitude, boasting in his memoirs that his division 'descended like an avalanche on the inhabitants of that area; we dug in the gardens of seaside villas, we sited machine-gun posts in the best places. The protests were tremendous. Mayors, County Councillors, private owners, came to see me and demanded that we should cease our work; I refused and explained the urgency.'[20] Monty's harshness was witnessed by Lieutenant Colonel Brian Horrocks, commander of the 9th Infantry Brigade based in the South-East. 'Monty used to pay constant visits. "Who lives in that house?" he would say pointing to some building which partly masked the fire from one of our machine gun positions. "Have them out, Horrocks. Blow up the house. Defence must come first."'[21]

Sometimes the destructive mood of haste could be counter-productive. According to a report to the Home Defence Executive on 11 July, some soldiers who were trying to obstruct fields near the RAF base at Woodhall Spa in Lincolnshire 'dug up in the course of a few days an aerodrome and eight miles of piping which had taken the Air Ministry 18 months to do'.[22]

Fighter Command's key role in the summer of 1940 was, of course, to prevent the Germans gaining air superiority over the south-east of England, but in July the Air Ministry also drew up plans to use almost every available aircraft in the country, no matter how old, obsolete or ill equipped, in a last-ditch fight against the invader. Code-named Operation Banquet, the scheme essentially meant that all aircraft, apart from those in Fighter Command, would be absorbed into a series of striking forces to bomb the enemy as they landed. Under this operation, even training planes and unqualified students would be sent into action. The most unorthodox element of the plan was a separate initiative called Operation Banquet Lights, by which 350 Tiger Moth biplanes from the Elementary Flight Training School would each be fitted with eight 20-pound bombs and then fly to the landing beaches. Despite its almost suicidal nature, given the planes' slow speed and vulnerability, the plan for Banquet Lights was taken seriously, and trainee pilots at the Elementary Flying School in mid-1940 were instructed in bombing, although shortages of dummy bombs meant that they often had to use bricks during such practice.

Another vital step in invasion planning was to maintain effective and secure communications between the three service headquarters and the front-line forces, made up of the five army area commands (Scottish, Northern, Eastern, Southern and Western), the Home Fleet commands and the RAF Fighter Groups. Normal radio and landline links were insufficiently reliable in an emergency as well as carrying the danger that they might be used by the Germans. So a separate network was developed, code-named the 'Beetle' scheme, which had two main elements for use in the invasion: first, a point-to-point wireless service to pass information from the head-quarters to the commands; second, a medium-power radio service to enable instructions to be broadcast by the commands to the lower units. The transmission of the code words 'Beetle' or 'Stand-By Beetle' by either of these means indicated that enemy action was under way.

In addition to Beetle, several other warning systems were developed. The General Post Office installed special alarm circuits that connected their local and main telephone exchanges in the vulnerable areas of the South, with the aim of preventing the enemy sending bogus messages. In similar fashion, the Admiralty gave new instructions to naval ships for sending coded messages about the invasion, either by wireless or by pyrotechnic signal. On top of all these sophisticated systems there remained the ancient method of ringing the church bells as a warning to the public and the LDVs that the invasion had started. Although simple, the move into campanology was ultimately to cause deep confusion in September.

The overall mood in the government and the armed forces was one of resolution rather than fear or panic. The Information Minister Harold Nicolson wrote in his diary, 'We half know that the odds are against us, yet there is a sort of exhilaration in the air.'[23] It was this widespread opti-mism that impressed several American observers, like the journalist Virginia Cowles, who wrote in the *Sunday Times* on 21 July: 'No one could fail to admire the deep gallantry with which the English people wait, almost hour by hour, for the mass air raids which may signal Nazi Germany's final bid for European domination. But as an American what has struck me most has been that since the fall of France, the people seem to reflect an even deeper confidence than before.'

Cowles explained that this confidence had been emboldened by the success of the RAF, faith in the Royal Navy and Britain's long history of resisting invasion. But as an American she might have mentioned another, more immediate factor: the arrival of large quantities of arms and equipment from the USA, strengthening the army and transforming the capability of the Local Defence Volunteers. Organised by President Roosevelt's government with heroic cunning to circumvent the USA's neutrality laws, the first large consignments of rifles, machine guns, field guns and mortars started to reach Britain on 8 July. Most of this matériel was destined for the LDVs, although the 900 75-mm field guns and mortars went to the regular army. 'There was no need to worry. The equipment will soon be here and then you will have guns galore,' Churchill told General Bernard Freyberg, the New Zealander in charge of the army on Salisbury Plain.[24] In fact, the USA was even more accommodating than the original deal had outlined: instead of the agreed 500,000 rifles, the Americans sent 615,000, each with 250 rounds of ammunition.

It has often been suggested that this act was not nearly as helpful as it seemed, since the M1917 rifles were supposedly antiquated and ill matched to British needs. 'The ancient rifles,' wrote the historian Norman Longmate, 'arrived caked in heavy grease, like congealed Vaseline, which had protected them during their long years of disuse.'[25] Cleaning them up with paraffin was a laborious task.

The negative image of these American M1917s, sometimes called just M17s, was in fact unjustified. On joining up, volunteers had expected to be handed the much loved, standard-issue British infantry weapon, the Short Magazine Lee Enfield (SMLE), so they were disappointed when instead they were supplied with an alien one using American .300 rounds. Nor did the tough work of removing the congealed grease initially endear the M1917s to their users in Home Guard. Moreover, the American shipments tended to be associated with the 75,000 Ross rifles that had arrived from Canada in June. But the Ross, cumbersome and prone to jamming, was an unsatisfactory weapon and had been rejected by the British army for service before the First World War; the M1917 was far superior. The idea that it was badly outdated or ineffective is one of the more persistent myths about the summer of 1940. It was no more antique than the Short Magazine Lee Enfield, whose original concept dated back to 1907, whereas the M1917, as its name suggests, had been designed in the penultimate year of the First World War and it went on to be used during both the Korean and the Vietnam Wars. Clifford Shore, a Home Guardsman who later became a sniper instructor, said that the M1917 'was probably the most accurate rifle I have ever used'.[26] To distinguish the M1917s from British rifles, a red band two inches wide was placed round the barrel so guardsmen would not attempt to load them with British .303 bullets.

It is another myth that in the summer of 1940 the LDVs were desperately short of ammunition. Thanks to the American shipments, each guardsman on duty could be issued with fifty rounds, the same as the standard issue for the regular army.

The influence of folk memories, allied to the enduring appeal of the TV show *Dad's Army*, have obscured the truth about the equipment for the LDV. Not only was the M1917 an excellent rifle, but other American weapons supplied in 1940 to the LDVs were also highly efficient. These included a total of 25,000 Browning automatic rifles, which had a rate of fire of 500 rounds a minute, and 22,000 Browning water-cooled machine guns, which, like the M1917, used .300 bullets and were fitted with red bands to differentiate them from British weapons. Again, as with the M1917, some volunteers preferred the American Browning machine gun to its British counterpart, the .303 Vickers machine gun.

By the end of July 1940, with more than 600,000 well-armed men in uniform, backed by machine guns and improvised bombs, the LDVs were nothing like the hapless, clowning rabble of legend. Altogether, by the beginning of July, 1.166 million men had registered to serve in this force. Churchill was not indulging in fantasy when, in his inspiring radio broadcast on 14 July, he proclaimed that the Local Defence Volunteers, 'a large proportion of whom have been through the last War, have the strongest desire to attack and come to close quarters with the enemy wherever he may appear. Should the invader come to Britain, there will be no placid lying down of the people in submission before him as we have seen, alas, in other countries.'[27]

That spirit was recalled by Jimmy Taylor, who served in his village LDV unit in Hampshire as a bicycle dispatch rider: 'I think the Germans would never have had such resistance as they would have had in England. Every village and hamlet, every corner, every ditch, every river would have been defended, even with obsolete guns. They would never have had an inch that they wouldn't have had to fight over. The scenes we knew in France and Belgium during the blitzkrieg would not have been repeated in Britain, in my estimation.'[28]

Serving in the Bristol LDV in his spare time from his job as a clerk at the local Corporation's Electricity Department, Jack Yeatman recalled: 'We were under no illusions as to what would happen if the invasion did take place, but the invasion forces would not have the rapid and easy dash across country which they had enjoyed in Belgium and Northern France. We wouldn't have been able to stop them but their progress would have been slow and their casualties high. The LDV were a very real part of the defence of the realm.'[29]

The novelist and poet Cecil Day Lewis, who joined the LDV in Devon, thought that a powerful sense of local pride helped to galvanise the force: 'One thing we did have – and that's the thing that made the LDV such a roaring success in the country districts: we had the familiarity and pride of the village, the moral strength – that is the only word for it – of men used to working and living together in a small community. We were to defend our own little patch of England. As one recruit said to me, "That's all right, I'll join. But us don't have to go and fight for those bastards at Axford, do us?", naming the next village.'[30]

Churchill may have been impressed by the resolve of the LDVs, but he loathed the name. With his historical romanticism and lyrical gift for language, he found the title Local Defence Volunteers far too utilitarian, bureaucratic and mundane. The Minister for Supply, Herbert Morrison, sharing this dislike of the acronym LDV, had already put forward two alternatives, the Town Guard or the Civil Guard. Churchill, in whose view both of those names were 'too similar to the wild men of the French Revolution',[31] offered another. 'Home Guard would be better. Don't hesitate to change on account of already having made armlets etc, if it is thought the title of "Home Guard" would be more compulsive.'[32]

War Secretary Anthony Eden, partly on practical grounds, rejected the suggestion. Not only had the term LDV 'passed into military jargon', he told the prime minister, but more than 1 million armbands with LDV on them had been manufactured. 'On the whole I should prefer to hold on to the existing name.'[33] In an attempt to bypass Eden, Churchill approached Duff Cooper to ask whether the Ministry of Information would encourage newspapers to use the term and make it part of popular currency, telling him on 6 July, 'I am going to have the name "Home Guard" adopted, and I hope you will, when notified, get the press to put it across.'[34] Through the simple tactic of repeatedly referring to the Home Guard rather than the LDV in his correspondence, broadcasts and Parliamentary speeches, the prime minister ensured that the phrase became increasingly popular with the public. Towards the end of July he got his way, the force of Churchillian pressure having broken the resistance of the opposition.

By September, the Home Guard was moving towards something more like the volunteer wing of the regular army, complete with army-style ranks, stripes, appointments and discipline. Even with their improvements in equipment, arms, uniforms and training, the essential tasks of the Home Guard remained largely the same during the summer months of 1940: protecting vulnerable points, manning roadblocks, dealing with sightings of paratroopers, carrying out defensive patrols and passing on information to the regular armed forces.

An atmospheric insight into the experience of one Home Guardsman comes from the memoir of Eric Hart, who served in the Folkestone Battalion and was regularly out on patrol at night by bicycle.

> The prime evil at this time threatened us from 25 miles across the Channel, in the form of the German Panzer divisions assembling there. The modest size of our platoon meant that each member was called upon to carry out a tour of duty at least two nights per week, on the basis of two hours on duty and an hour rest period. The cycle patrol took us along the restricted [no-go zone] undercliff road. Before the outbreak of war this had been a local beauty spot, with . . . a wide variety of trees, shrubs and flowered borders, but all this had to pay the price of being in the front line. It was replaced with borders of barbed-wire barricades and awesome skull-and-crossbones 'Danger Mines' signs. Sometimes the night patrols were quite rewarding – clear skies and quiet calm as we made our almost silent progress along the deserted coast road.[35]

Ironside saw the Home Guard as crucial for the continued implementation of his plan. Indeed, as the volunteer force grew in strength, he wanted to have more of them operating the stop lines, thereby freeing increasing numbers of the regular troops for other duties. But at the very moment he was pondering his future strategy, his authority within the military establishment and the government was crumbling. As the invasion threat deepened, so disillusion with the Home Forces commander grew, the high hopes of success when he had succeeded Kirke in May having been dashed by mid-July.

The entire basis of the Ironside plan, with its vast national network of stop lines, had come to be regarded as inherently flawed, just as Sir Walter Kirke had always argued. Its conception, said critics, could lead to a dangerous, defensive mentality, just as had happened with the Maginot Line in France. Many inside the military establishment felt that stronger reserves to the rear of the most vulnerable areas would be more useful than more static defences on the beaches and far inland, yet Ironside had stubbornly held out against such an approach and continued to strengthen the fixed defences. To his critics, that was the fundamental error at the heart of his plan. Not only were the barriers seen as too weak to stop the onslaught of the Reich's war machine, but they were also viewed as a potential hindrance to the movement of British forces. At Southern Command, Alan Brooke, who believed that the 'whole policy for defence' should be 'based on mobility', feared that the network of roadblocks would 'retard the movement of military motor transport.'[36] Just as hostile was Montgomery, then the commander of the 3rd Division. With typical intractability, he simply opted out of the Ironside plan, as he recorded in his memoirs:

I found myself in disagreement with the general approach to the problem of the defence of Britain and refused to apply it . . . The accepted doctrine was that every inch of the coastline must be defended strongly, the defence being based on concrete pill-boxes and entrenchments on a linear basis all along the coastline. My approach was different. I pulled the troops back from the beaches and held them ready in compact bodies in the rear, poised for counter attack and for offensive action against the invaders. After a sea crossing troops would not feel too well and would be suffering from reaction; that is the time to attack and throw the invader back.[37]

On 2 July, Winston Churchill conducted a tour of inspection along the 3rd Division's area on the south coast, after which he had a meal with Montgomery at the Royal Albion Hotel. Montgomery later left this account: 'He asked me what I would drink at dinner and I replied – water. This astonished him. I added that I neither drank nor smoked and was 100 per cent fit. To which Churchill replied with some resentment that he both drank and smoked and was "200 per cent fit".'[38] After this awkward moment, the two men turned to the invasion threat, with Montgomery setting out his ideas on mobility. He complained to Churchill that his division was the only one able 'to fight any enemy anywhere. And here we were in a static role, ordered to dig in on the south coast. Some other troops should take on my task; my division should be given buses and be held in mobile reserve in a counter-attack role. Why was I left immobile?'[39]

Churchill, who was deeply struck by this conversation, came away from his tour of the south coast with a sense of unease about Ironside's strategy, in which men were spread thinly across miles of defences. On 8 July, in a letter addressed directly to Ironside, he argued that two divisions should be withdrawn from the beaches and added to the mobile reserve. 'A division in the reserve is worth six divisions on the beaches since only one in seven of these will in all probability be present at the points of impact.'[40] In his reply, Ironside disputed this, pleaded for more well-equipped and well-trained men, and reiterated his belief that the Germans would attack with large numbers of small craft all along the coast.

Even in the front line many soldiers felt that the focus on static defences was badly misguided, as Royal Artillery officer Shelford 'Ginger' Bidwell recalled: 'Those half-witted "dug-out" brigadiers would flit through Kent, dig new gun-pits and then start all over again in another area. Maurice Ley, a cynical old boy, on returning from an official visit to London, said to me at the time, "Ginger, there is absolutely nothing to stop the Germans reaching London within 24 hours if they land, unless they try to get there by train."'[41]

But it was not just the Ironside plan that was causing disquiet. There was also a widespread feeling that, for all his bullish physical appearance, the man himself was simply incapable of shouldering the enormous responsibility he had been given. Some said he lacked resolution, others judgement. Sir John Slessor, the head of RAF strategy, wrote that he had 'an apparent confidence in himself' that 'turned out to be unjustified'.[42] Nor was he a figure to inspire trust, as Lord Reith, the minister and former head of the BBC, recorded in his diaries after dining on 3 July with Sir John Dill, the Chief of the Imperial General Staff. 'We spoke of the distrust of Ironside – universal he said and asked why. Character, I replied.'[43] Even more damningly, there were mutterings about Ironside's commitment to fighting the war, a notion that was partly fuelled by his association with the fascist 'Boney' Fuller, as well as his name cropping up in the Kent–Wolkoff affair.

Ironside's fate was sealed when the prime minister made another of his inspection tours to the south coast, this time in the company of Brooke. Churchill had long admired the incisive clear-thinking Ulsterman, one of the few army officers to emerge from the French campaign with his reputation enhanced. Now, on 17 July, there was a meeting of minds about counter-invasion strategy, involving a complete rejection of Ironside's defensive stance. Churchill's account of the tour of Southern Command was effusive.

> All the afternoon I drove with General Brooke, who commanded this front. His record stood high. Not only had he fought the decisive flank battle near Ypres during the retirement to Dunkirk, but he had acquitted himself with singular firmness and dexterity, in circumstances of unimaginable difficulty and confusion, when in command of the new forces we had sent to France during the first three weeks of June . . . We were four hours together in the motor-car on this July afternoon and we seemed to be in agreement on the methods of Home Defence.[44]

It was obvious to Churchill that Ironside should be replaced by Brooke. On 19 July, the War Cabinet's Defence Committee decided that Ironside had to go.

Brooke was soon developing his alternative vision on counter-invasion strategy, which was very much in line with Churchill's:

> Much work and energy was being expended on an extensive system of rear defence, comprising anti-tank ditches and pill boxes, running roughly parallel to the coast and situated well inland. This static rear defence did not fall in with my conception of the defence of the country. To my mind our defence should be of a far more mobile and offensive nature. I visualized a light defence along the beaches, to hamper and delay landings to the maximum and in the rear highly mobile foes, trained to immediate aggressive action intended to concentrate and attack any landings before they had become too well established.[45]

As Brooke set to work, he was conscious of the 'almost unbearable' load of responsibility in grappling with the invasion threat:

> To find yourself daily surrounded by your countrymen, who may at any moment find themselves entirely dependent for their security on your ability to defend them, to come into continuous contact with all the weakness of the defensive material at your disposal, to be periodically wracked with doubts as to the soundness of one's dispositions and with it all to maintain a calm and confident exterior is a test of one's character, the bitterness of which must be experienced to be believed![46]

As for Ironside, though his departure was sweetened with a peerage, he felt he had been made a scapegoat for the wider failings of the British army in 1940. He complained privately that Eden had not given him a proper explanation for his sacking, and saw himself as the victim of political conspiracy. 'I was labelled as belonging to the old Chamberlain gang and over 60 or too old,' he mused in early 1941. Increasingly bitter at the way he had been treated, he never accepted any kind of public office again, never spoke in the House of Lords and hardly ever visited London. He died in 1959.

15

'A menace to the security of the country'

THE SACKING OF Ironside was an unsparing act, but in the pit of the invasion crisis there was no room for sentimentality. The same ruthlessness was applied in civilian life. Never before in British history had a government so controlled the civic sphere. Almost every aspect of society, from food supplies to entertainment, from travel to employment, was dictated by the state. In the name of protecting democracy and freedom, officialdom had taken over the nation. Clothes, petrol, meat and sugar were all rationed. Blackouts, curfews and no-go areas predominated. The routine of everyday existence involved a constant round of obedience to authority, whether it be showing identity papers or carrying gas masks. 'Don't you know there's a war on' became the slogan of the guardians of this new realm, eager to enforce their myriad of regulations. The authorities could decide where citizens lived and worked, what they were paid and how much tea they could drink.

The normal free market ceased to function. Under the Limitation of Supplies order, the production of seventeen classes of goods for the home market, ranging from cutlery to jewellery, was deliberately reduced to two-thirds of 1939 levels in order to retain raw materials for the war effort. The Restriction of Engagement order, introduced in June 1940, gave the government the ability to prevent certain categories of skilled men, particularly engineers, from moving jobs.

An insight into the dominant influence of bureaucracy is shown by an article in the *Sunday Times* of 25 July, headed 'War Rules of the Week'. Among the regulations passed were the following: the introduction of new maximum prices for barley, oats and rye; a requirement for farmers to sell all wool clipped in the United Kingdom to the Ministry of Supply at fixed prices; a complete ban on holidaymakers in the coastal defence area, which was now extended to Dorchester, Weymouth, Swanage and Portland; a new power for the Ministry of Labour to direct doctors to perform any specified service; the extension of compulsory registration with the Ministry of Labour to chemists, physicians and quantity surveyors; a ban on anyone buying a new car without a special licence from the Ministry of Transport;

Hitler will send no warning –

so always carry your gas mask

ISSUED BY THE MINISTRY OF HOME SECURITY

The government thought that the Germans were likely to use gas in any assault on Britain. By the summer of 1940, more than 38 million gas masks had been distributed

and the establishment of a new National Arbitration tribunal to settle trade disputes, prohibiting strikes and lockouts where collective bargaining existed.

As the summer progressed, officialdom increasingly took on the appearance of autocracy. On 20 August 1940, *The Times* announced that 'the whole of Great Britain has been brought within the scope of the Defence Regulations. Regional Commissioners can, subject to appropriate control, issue directions or orders for defence purposes within their areas.' Yet, far from showing anger at this unprecedented expansion in the role of the state, most of the public, especially the working class, welcomed it.

This was the moment when the concept of 'the people's war' grew in popularity as the old social order was swept away. Even those in the highest rank of government had to bear the burden, as Jean Shipton, the daughter of Clement Attlee, recalled of life in their suburban Stanmore home in 1940:

> It was a bit of a struggle for Mother, looking after the house without any help and having to go down to the shops every day – just hoping that you might get some sausages, which were mainly bread – and then walk back. There were no privileges at all for the family of the deputy prime minister. On the contrary, Mother was mad because Father knew there was going to be clothes rationing and he did not tell her. We had to make do with old linen sheets from my grandmother, which we had to turn sides to middle. No, we did not have any privileges at all. The only thing we had was that in my father's study was the green telephone, a secret telephone. That was all. My mother was just an ordinary person.[1]

The theme of everyone doing their bit in the great national cause was a constant feature of official propaganda in the summer of 1940. Ken Holland, who was an auxiliary fireman in the early part of the war, directly experienced the popular sense of resolution. 'There was never any shortage of manpower. The overall spirit throughout the country was also reflected in the fire service. There was a tremendous spirit of comradeship and a willingness to do whatever was required.'[2]

The mood of watchful readiness and diligence in the armed and support services was mirrored in the factories during the summer of 1940. When the Minister of Supply Herbert Morrison used the phrase 'Go to it' in an attempt to drive up production levels, the response was heroic rather than dismissive. Output significantly accelerated, especially of aircraft, small arms and radar equipment. At a small factory in Birmingham that made carburettors for Spitfires and Hurricanes, weekly output was doubled in less than a fortnight.

As Alf Pack, a foreman at the engineering firm of Coventry Grinders, recalled, 'I often worked eighty hours a week and sometimes went home at 10.30 p.m. At the weekend, I usually worked Saturdays until five and Sundays until one.'[3] One weekend in July, the government found that there was a shortage of fabric used for barrage balloons. On Beaverbrook's instructions, police called at the homes of the employees of the textile factories, asking them to return to work, while notices were also flashed on cinema screens. More than 90 per cent of the cotton workers, most of them women, obeyed the instructions.

At the height of the invasion threat, the War Secretary Anthony Eden had an interview with the Soviet ambassador Ivan Maisky. 'I was pretty frank with him about our position. There was no point in hiding anything from him. When the interview was over, Maisky thanked me and said, "Now I shall tell you what I have told my Government. I have told them that you will not be defeated because the spirit of your people is different from the spirit of the French people."'[4]

Yet amidst all the acceptance of sacrifice and curtailments of liberty, there was one government initiative that aroused such anger from the public that it eventually had to be abandoned. This was an attempt in July to impose a further crackdown on freedom of speech, in the name of preventing both defeatist talk and the potential leakage of information to the enemy. The press, broadcasting, films and public gatherings were all highly restricted and censored in 1940. The Postmaster General even had the power to monitor the mail of any individual or organisation deemed to be suspect by the security services; in 1940 the government employed 10,000 workers just to censor the mail. There had also been regular warnings against indulging in noisy speculation and chat about the war effort, epitomised in the famous posters designed in late 1939 by the artist Cyril Bird on the theme 'Careless Talk Costs Lives'.

But now, in the summer of 1940, the authorities decided that even tougher action was needed. Effectively, the government wanted private conversations to be scrutinised by the state, with the ordinary public acting as monitoring agents. There were two strands to this initiative, which was dubbed the 'Silent Column' campaign: one was based on propaganda from the Ministry of Information; the other on criminal sanctions through the courts. The campaign was formally approved, on 8 July, by the Ministry of Information's Planning Committee, headed by the art historian Kenneth Clark, and began on 11 July with a barrage of publicity.

In contrast to Cyril Bird's light-heartedness, the 'Silent Column' had a condescending, admonitory tone. The visual propaganda used a series of civilian stereotypes who supposedly represented a danger to national safety and therefore should be shunned by the public. Among these characters, all of whom had puerile nicknames, were Mr Secrecy Hush-Hush ('He's always got exclusive news, very private, very confidential'); and Miss Leaky-Mouth ('She goes on like a leaky tap about the war').[5] In another patronising move that smacked of treating the public like children, the Ministry

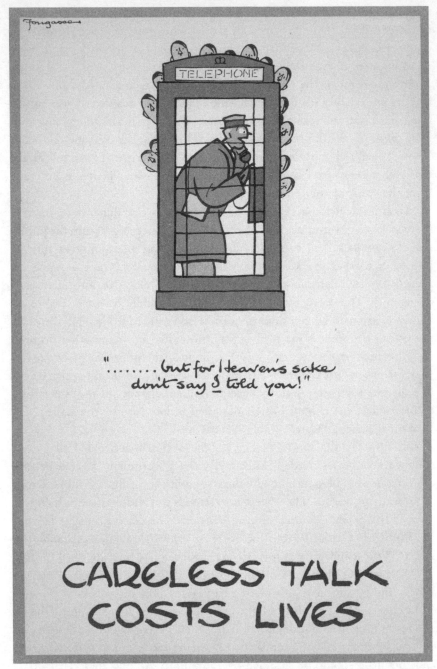

One of the official wartime notices designed by Cyril Bird, warning the public to be discreet. Bird's humorous posters which first appeared on the London Underground in late 1939 were popular, but a later government initiative against gossip and rumour-mongering, known as the 'Silent Column', aroused ferocious hostility announced that it wanted to see 'chatterboxes' installed in clubs, hotels, shops and even homes; 'into them people who offend will be invited to put contributions to charity'.[6]

The Silent Column quickly developed into something far more bellicose. The police and the courts, with the collusion of a few meddlesome members of the public, took the Ministry of Information's campaign as a cue to embark on a stream of aggressive prosecutions against individuals who were accused, under Defence Regulations, of spreading 'alarm and despondency'.[7] One woman received a month in prison after a night of passion with her boyfriend in a hotel, during which she declared ecstatically: 'Who cares if Hitler does come, so long as we can have fun like this?'[8] Unfortunately her remark was overheard by a chambermaid who reported her to the police. Perhaps the most ridiculous case was that of a vicar who, after giving an address to a large group of boys about air-raid precautions, was taken to court for communicating 'air raid information which might be useful to the enemy'.[9]

The 'Silent Column' backfired disastrously, being seen as malicious, disproportionate and demeaning of the public's sacrifices for the war effort. In its heavy-handed lack of respect for the concept of privacy, it seemed curiously un-British. As the Ipswich engineer Richard Brown wrote in his diary on 24 July: 'In this free country, we ought to have what opinions we pleased.'[10] The Ministry of Information's own opinion surveyors found that, far from raising morale, the Silent Column 'is bringing depression and suspicion', noting in London on 22 July that 'strong resentment is still felt among all classes at the Silent Column campaign. Indignation is expressed at what people say is "a policy which is turning us into a nation of spies".'[11]

What really grated with the public was the fact that the campaign, with its air of authoritarian menace, appeared to be exactly the kind of action that the Nazi regime might use. In a brilliantly coruscating article in the *Spectator*, the novelist Dorothy L. Sayers wrote: 'We have been shown a very faint glimpse of the thing that we are fighting against, and now that we have seen it, we know for certain that we hate it beyond all imagination. To distrust our fellows, to become spies for them, to betray them to the law, to go on in continual dumb fear that they should spy on us – that is the thing the Nazi government means, and it is a thing we will not endure.'[12]

The irony was that some officials in Whitehall wanted to go even further than the Silent Column. In early July the Home Defence Executive, headed by the abrasive Lord Swinton, put forward a proposal for a comprehensive defence regulation that would have made it an offence to attempt 'to subvert duly constituted authority',[13] a potentially dictatorial measure that could be used to crush any dissent or criticism of the government. But the planned regulation ran into the fierce opposition of the Home Office, whose Permanent Under-Secretary Sir Alexander Maxwell described the measure as 'inconsistent with the historic notions of English liberty'. It was, therefore, quietly dropped.

More successful was a Bill introduced into Parliament by the Home Secretary, Sir John Anderson, to allow the government to set up special courts, similar to courts martial, in the event of an invasion. Like the Silent Column, the Bill provoked widespread opposition in the press. With a few amendments, however, Anderson's Bill was passed on 1 August, although its powers were to be reserved purely for a civil emergency caused by invasion.

By then the Silent Column had been dropped, broken by the ferocity of the public reaction. The ill-judged initiative had partly been inspired by fears about the enemy within, its very name meant to be a counterpoise to the so-called fifth column, made up of traitors and German agents. But, since the early days of May, concern about the fifth column had significantly diminished. There was a widespread recognition in political and military circles that such fears had been exaggerated, that there was no clandestine army ready to pounce in the event of an invasion.

Nevertheless, this did not mean that the vigilance had been unjustified. There had undoubtedly been dangerous or defeatist elements within Britain who were at the very least hostile to the war effort and, at worst, were actively pro-Nazi. Lord Swinton, who headed the Home Defence Executive in a briskly efficient manner, was not the sort of man to be complacent. The tough approach to potential subversion continued. At the end of July, the number of enemy aliens interned in Britain reached its peak, at 27,000. In the same month chief constables were given new powers to search and arrest suspects, while the right to detain 'any individuals believed to be of hostile origin or association' was extended to regional commissioners, who were also given powers, previously held only by the Home Office, to impose bans on movement and other restrictions on individuals.[14]

The most graphic indicator of this continuing vigour was the establishment by MI5 of a new interrogation centre at Latchmere House in Twickenham for detainees who might yield useful information about the enemy. Authorised by Swinton, Latchmere took in its first prisoners at the end of July: twenty-seven British subjects and eighteen enemy aliens. The regime was cold and austere, designed to create a culture of intimidation. Guards wore tennis shoes to muffle the sound of their steps. Inmates were kept isolated in separate cells. 'No chivalry, no gossip, no cigarettes,' was one of the guiding principles of Latchmere.[15] As the war progressed, Latchmere became ever more important in acquiring intelligence and turning German spies, but in its limited first operations in the summer 1940, its chief achievement was to confirm that there was no organised network of fifth columnists in England.

By the end of July, 747 fascists and other right-wing extremists were being held in detention, most of them either in Brixton or Liverpool. But the Government remained so anxious about their influence that there were plans to expel them from Britain altogether. Swinton's Defence Executive was the guiding force behind the proposal, which has never received much attention from historians despite its radical nature. What makes the scheme all the more intriguing is the deep irony behind it, in that the weapon of deportation was threatened against racially fixated leaders of a party keen themselves on the concept of deporting non-British stock from the British Isles. Through their disloyalty to Britain's cause, the fascists could have been the targets of a policy they eagerly advocated for others.

On 10 July, Desmond Morton unveiled to the prime minister a proposal for the expulsion of political prisoners: 'Lord Swinton and his executive are very anxious, if possible, to deport overseas certain leaders of the British Union of Fascists, including Mosley and his wife. The chief reason is that it has come to their certain knowledge that Mosley and their leaders fear deportation to a quite inexplicable degree, unless they believe there to be some plot in hand to liberate them from jail for the purpose of starting serious trouble.' Morton explained that the prison warders and police guarding the fascists were unarmed. 'It has already been represented to the Home Office that this seems an undue risk to be run. These people are just nasty gangsters who will stick at nothing.' Morton therefore suggested that it would be 'better to remove them from the country, especially if this is clearly the last thing they want to happen.' But the big obstacle was the law of the land for, as Morton admitted, it was illegal to carry out 'the forcible deportation of any British subject'.[16] Churchill, enthusiastic, told his Downing Street secretariat that 'this should be put in train for Cabinet sanction.'[17] The War Office was equally supportive, holding that the presence of the fascist prisoners 'in this country, even if they are well guarded, is a dangerous liability, especially in time of invasion.' There followed an intense debate about the possible implementation of the scheme. Apart from the legal question, which would have required contentious legislation to resolve, other objections were raised.

One problem was that once the prisoners were overseas, the Home Office would have far less real control over the conditions of their detention, their treatment or even their release. More importantly, there was the difficulty of finding a suitable destination, for none of the Dominions showed much eagerness to accept the burden. A number of island colonies were considered, including Jamaica and St Lucia in the Caribbean, Mauritius and Ceylon in the Indian Ocean, and the Seychelles in the Pacific, but all involved security problems or heavy expenses. The most opportune place seemed to be the remote St Helena in the middle of the Atlantic, renowned as the final home of the exiled Napoleon Bonaparte, but there, too, the creation of a new secure camp would have required the importation of skilled labour and raw materials.

Sir John Anderson, the Home Secretary, grew increasingly sceptical about the whole idea, arguing that nowhere suitable for the detainees could be found and that the necessary legislation would be 'controversial'. On 22 July the War Cabinet accepted his view and 'decided not to proceed further' with the proposal.[18]

The Home Office admitted that the deportation plan would have been popular with ordinary people, the most common grievance being not that right-wing extremists had been treated too harshly, but that too few of them had been locked up. Within the mainstream public, there were whispers that some leading pro-Nazi figures had escaped detention because of their social status or connections to the government.

One of the most egregious cases was that of the military strategist Major General John 'Boney' Fuller, who was a close ally of Mosley and a key propagandist for the BUF. An authoritarian, he loathed democracy and was instinctively drawn to extremism, whether spiritual or political. Fascinated with the occult, he was an early disciple of Aleister Crowley, the notorious practitioner of the black arts once dubbed 'the most evil man in England'. His articles and speeches were full of praise for Hitler, whom he described as 'that realistic idealist who has awakened the common sense of the British people by setting out to create a new Germany'.[19] Hitler was so pleased with these compliments that he invited Fuller as 'an honoured guest'[20] to his fiftieth birthday celebrations in Germany. Once war broke out, Fuller preached the language of defeatism, urging negotiations with the Reich.

Yet in spite of this record, he was allowed to remain free, albeit under surveillance. Fuller himself expected to be arrested during the summer of 1940, while Mosley confessed to 'a little puzzlement' as to why his ally had not joined him in Brixton.[21] Although there is no explanation on his Home Office file, his connections to Ironside and the War Office must have served as some kind of shield.

There were other strange omissions, such as the case of the unashamed fascist Dorothy, Lady Downe, whose society connections were impeccable. The god-daughter of the late King George V and a protégée of Queen

Mary, she was the only daughter of the former Liberal MP Sir William ffolkes and the widow of Viscount John Downe. But this exalted background had not prevented her from gravitating towards the outer fringes of British politics, where she became an official in the BUF and even, in 1939, the movement's prospective candidate for King's Lynn.

When the arrests of BUF members started in May 1940, Lady Downe's reaction was one of outrage, partly because she had been excluded from the roll-call of detainees, partly because she felt that the fascists had done nothing wrong. A Home Office report of 22 September made the frank admission that her aristocratic status had protected her: 'We considered that the internment of a person of Lady Downe's social standing might give the public the wrong impression of the importance of the British Union. This consideration would of course have carried no weight if Lady Downe had really occupied a vital position in the British Union organisation.'[22]

Just as serious a case of an aristocrat escaping detention was that of Hastings Russell, the Marquess of Tavistock, who campaigned relentlessly against the war and, through his pro-German sympathies, was linked to a number of extremist groups. The heir to the Dukedom of Bedford, a position he inherited on the death of his father in August 1940, Tavistock used his vast wealth to indulge his wide range of passions, which included naturalism, pacifism, financial reform and ornithology. At his home of Woburn Abbey, he kept no fewer than 400 parrots, as well as a pet spider which he regularly fed with roast beef and Yorkshire pudding.

In the late 1930s, his erratic quest to prevent war between Britain and Germany led to his involvement with John Beckett's far-right British People's Party and the ultra-appeasement group the British Council for a Christian Settlement in Europe. Not content with the mere advocacy of a negotiated deal, he travelled in February 1940 to Dublin, where he visited the German legation to discuss potential terms. His amateur diplomacy, combined with his increasing criticism of the war effort, made him a prime target for the security services, who described his peace propaganda as 'blatantly stupid and malicious'.[23] As the war progressed, official contempt for him increased.

One official report claimed that his governess had previously worked for the Kaiser's family, which had 'inculcated in him a love of Germany'. Having failed to serve in the First World War, he 'fell into the hands of every crank and eccentric', as well as coming under 'the influence of his valet Norman Broad, who still robs him and rules his life'. As for his peace campaigns, 'wittingly or unwittingly, wickedly or in child-like innocence of purpose, the Duke has become an instrument of Nazi propaganda'.[24]

But even in the face of such a verdict, the government never moved to detain him under the Defence Regulations and he was merely kept under surveillance. That remained the position throughout the war, even though, in 1941, the Home Office admitted that 'in the event of the Duke falling into the hands of the enemy he would be likely to set up as a gauleiter or the head of a puppet British Government.'[25]

Whilst the likes of Tavistock, Downe and Fuller were never detained, their names were kept on the voluminous secret lists of British suspects deemed likely to be of potential assistance to the enemy, all of them would have been immediately arrested in the event of a German invasion. The catalogues, which were compiled from June 1940 up to 1944, were put together by the police, MI5 and the local military authorities. Each of the twelve Regional Commissioners of Great Britain was required to maintain one of these suspects lists, with all the information also reported centrally to the Home Office. The register of alleged treachery was extensive, eventually running to hundreds of names. In mid-July, for example, there were seventy-two people on the suspects' list for the southern region, and another sixty-nine for the eastern region.

The suspects were remarkably wide-ranging, from manual workers and housewives to businessmen and members of the upper class. Neither age nor religiosity was a barrier to inclusion. An elderly couple from Great Wymondley in Hertfordshire, the Reverend Charles Thomas and his wife Agnes, came under suspicion because of their pacifist tendencies and pro-Italian views. 'They have invariably spent their holidays in Italy. In 1936 they flew the Italian flag to celebrate the victory of the Italians in Abyssinia and as a result were rebuked by the Bishop of St. Albans.' A search of the Thomases' property, which was carried out in early July, 'confirmed their Italian obsession – a picture of Mussolini was hanging on the wall'.[26]

Those with German connections were invariably distrusted by officialdom. One was Else Varicopulos, a thirty-year-old woman from Leigh-on-Sea, who was born in Latvia to German parents and became a naturalised British citizen through marriage. According to the eastern regional commissioner, 'her sentiments are definitely pro-German' and she was reported to have told a neighbour, 'It will be a good thing when Hitler does arrive here.'[27]

Katherine Rouse from Burton Bradstock in Dorset expressed unpatriotic sympathies in terms of her veneration of Teutonic males, which she took so far as to get engaged to one of them. 'German men are honourable, trustworthy and of fine physique,' she told a shopkeeper in May 1940. In the climate of war, such views made the regional commissioner fear that Miss Rouse might be unbalanced. 'The mother of this woman is believed to have died in a home for mental defectives and it may be that Miss Rouse has inherited some mental aberration. At the same time, it appears that she might conceivably be an extremely dangerous person to be at large in the event of an invasion.'[28]

Political activity could also lead to inclusion on the list, as in the case of Professor J.E. Daniel of Bangor University, because he was seen as an extreme anti-English, anti-war Welsh nationalist 'who would rather assist than hinder the Germans'. One of his university colleagues told the police that 'if the Germans landed in the Bangor district he would himself shoot Daniel as he regarded him as a menace to the security of the country.'[29]

Hardline pacifists also came under scrutiny. Paul Durrell of Moor Top in Sussex was listed because of his involvement with the Forward Group of the Peace Pledge Union, 'which is said to be the most militant section of the organisation and to be carrying on its activities in secret. He has been heard to express anti-British views and has adopted a defeatist attitude.'[30]

Inevitably, however, the bulk of those on the suspects list were British Union members or fascist sympathisers who were not so dangerous as to be locked up immediately, but whose loyalty was not felt to be reliable. Again, such suspects went right across the social range. Edward Baker, 'a man of good education and social standing', who owned a yacht and worked at his father's flour mill in Maldon, Essex, was included because he had 'played a very active part in the fascist movement' in his home town. When police raided his home in August 1940 they found 'a fascist uniform', a large quantity of fascist literature and 'a Nazi dagger bearing a Swastika emblem'.[31] At the other end of the scale, William Emerson, an unemployed forty-year-old BUF member from Lowestoft, was put on the eastern region list, having been described as 'very erratic and a man with very extreme views'.[32]

One bizarre case in the Isle of Wight appeared to take pro-German treason to an entirely different, far more dangerous level. The unlikely central figure in this episode was Dorothy O'Grady, aged forty: short, plump and bespectacled, the owner of a bed and breakfast in the resort of Sandown. She had bought the boarding house with her husband Vincent O'Grady, a retired London fireman, but by the summer of 1940 she was leading a profoundly solitary existence. On the outbreak of war, Vincent had returned to London, answering a call from the government for retired firemen to re-enlist. Moreover, there were no guests at her bed and break-fast, since the Isle of Wight was in the heart of the southern coastal defence zone and severe restrictions had been placed on the movements of all holidaymakers.

Dorothy O'Grady was intensely shy, with hardly any friends; most of her neighbours in Sandown did not know her name. Apparently to compensate for her loneliness, she made long walks around the eastern coast of the island with her beloved dog Rob, a cross-bred black retriever, a habit that soon brought her into conflict with the military authorities, who increasingly regarded her as a nuisance for venturing into prohibited areas. At this time the Isle of Wight was bristling with fixed defences, coastal gun batteries, anti-aircraft installations and military camps because of its strategic position. Indeed, the island had been specifically mentioned by Hitler in his famous Directive No. 16, authorising the preparations for Operation Sea Lion.

She was reprimanded on several occasions by troops for going onto the beaches, but for all her diffidence she had a stubborn streak. On 9 August Dorothy O'Grady was out again with Rob, this time on the beach at Yaverland, just north of Sandown, taking her past several barbed-wire fences and 'keep out' signs. Having tiptoed her way round the mines, she sat down on the sand to eat an apple while Rob splashed about in the water. As she contemplated the view across the English Channel, she was suddenly surrounded by a unit from the Royal Northumberland Fusiliers, who recognised her from previous encounters. This time they decided a mere warning was not sufficient and told her she would be reported to the police. Having tried unsuccessfully to bribe the soldiers into releasing her, she was escorted, along with Rob, to the police station 3 miles away at Bembridge, where she was given a summons to appear at a magistrates' court on 27 August on charges of violating the Defence Regulations.

Mrs O'Grady's case at this stage was still a trivial one, for which the only consequence of her court appearance would probably be a fine and a caution for trespass. But then the saga took a dramatic turn. On the date she was due in the magistrates' court, there was no sign of her. While the court officials waited, the police went to boarding house in Sandown, to find a handwritten sign pinned to the door: 'No milk till I return.'[33] Mrs O'Grady had obviously fled, along with Rob. A door-to-door search in Sandown revealed nothing of her whereabouts.

The police stepped up the search for her, eventually tracking her down a fortnight later. Unable to leave the Isle of Wight because she had no travel permit, she had been staying under an assumed name, Pamela Arland, in a guest house in the village of Totland on the western coast. At the very moment that the police reached her room, she was attempting to flush a document down the toilet. She clearly seemed no minor offender. More incriminatingly, in her room were astonishingly accurate hand-drawn maps and sketches of defences to the east of the island, complete with detailed notes, even about troop numbers and lorry movements.

Other evidence against her was equally damning. A swastika badge was discovered on the underside of her jacket lapel. Military telephone wires had recently been cut near Totland, for which she was the obvious culprit. She was arrested and, in the car on the way to the Yarmouth police station, tried to swallow twenty tablets of the drug ephedrine hydrochloride, a decongestant, taken from a bottle in her handbag. She was prevented from swallowing them only by the quick action of the policeman sitting beside her.

This suicide attempt appeared to be a recognition that she was in deep trouble. Spying for the enemy and hindering Britain's security were treasonable offences, punishable by death. As she was held in Holloway prison awaiting trial, other soldiers came forward to the police to say that she had tried to bribe them with chocolates, cigarettes or cash for information about defences.

On 16 December she went on trial, charged on nine counts of breaches of the Defence Regulations, the 1911 Official Secrets Act and the 1940 Treachery Act. The landlady pleaded not guilty to all of the nine charges, but after just two days the jury convicted her on seven of them. The judge Sir Malcolm Macnaghten swiftly donned the black cap and told her she would go to the gallows, the first woman in the history of twentieth-century Britain to be sentenced to death for treason. Rob the retriever had already suffered his death sentence, having been put to sleep when Mrs O'Grady went to prison.

Her lawyer appealed against the verdict on the grounds that the judge had misdirected the jury. The appeal was accepted, and a retrial was held in February 1941, during the course of which the most serious capital charges against were dropped, although her convictions were upheld for breaking the Official Secrets Act and the Defence Regulations. The death sentence was commuted into one of fourteen years. After serving nine of them, she was released early on compassionate grounds in February 1950 because her husband Vincent, who had remained remarkably loyal to her, was gravely ill.

Mrs O'Grady's first act on coming out of prison was not to visit her sick husband but to call at the offices of the *Sunday Express*, where she gave the paper a lengthy, purportedly confessional interview. She claimed that she had never been a German spy at all, but merely a lonely, bored housewife trying to bring some excitement into her dull existence. Against the backdrop of the war drawing closer, she explained, she had begun to fantasise about playing the role of an enemy agent, soon acting it out with her research on defences, her creation of swastika badges and her disobedience to authority. The sense of danger was a thrill, she said, driving her on to ever more daring behaviour. 'All my life I had never been anything. I had always been insignificant. I never had a close friend, even at school. I felt tremendously bucked when I saw that they thought me clever enough to be a spy. It made me feel somebody instead of being an ordinary seaside landlady. Yet I was astonished when they believed it all. I never imagined they would.'[34]

Soon after this, she moved back to the Isle of Wight to be with the ailing Vincent, who died in 1953. She was shunned by local residents and often refused service in shops, but for the rest of her life she continued to maintain that she had never been a spy or a traitor. In one of her last interviews, she said, 'It was the greatest adventure of my life. Some people write books. I lived mine.'[35]

After her death in 1985, the image of Dorothy O'Grady as nothing more than a dotty fantasist became so powerful that the then Conservative MP for the Isle of Wight, Barry Field, launched a campaign to clear her name altogether, but what he and his fellow campaigners found in her file shocked them. The records appeared to show that O'Grady was indeed the sinister, deceitful figure that the original verdict in 1940 had suggested. The pose as a batty loner was, it seemed, just a cover. The file contained all the background papers to the evidence that was presented in closed-court proceedings, including a conclusion from the senior intelligence officer, Lieutenant Colonel Edward Hinchley Cooke, that her information 'would be of very great importance to the enemy and is therefore of vital importance as far as the defence of that part of the country is concerned'.[36]

It also turned out that O'Grady was not the innocent landlady she pretended to be. In reality, she had acquired a long criminal record before her marriage to Vincent. She had been sent to borstal for forging banknotes, served two years' hard labour for stealing clothes from an employer in Brighton, and been given four convictions for prostitution, the last of which had led to a spell inside Holloway jail. It appeared that she had harboured a grudge against the British authorities because of her criminal convictions in the early 1920s, and this antagonism, long suppressed, had come to the surface during the war in her treachery on behalf of Germany.

But this was not the end of the story. The author Adrian Searle remained unconvinced. Crucially, the authorities had never explained how O'Grady was meant to have sent her information to Germany. Nor was the creation of swastika badges or bribery of soldiers the kind of behaviour in which a serious spy would indulge. Searle dug deeper and unearthed a wealth of new material that confirmed his belief that the former landlady was mentally disturbed rather than a genuine agent. From her prison records, he found that she was in the grip of a psycho-sexual dysfunction, in which she was obsessed with inflicting discomfort and even extreme pain on herself. According to one of her prison doctors, Violet Minster, she suffered from regular attacks 'in which she had to "obey people" inside her who encourage her to do harmful acts to herself'.

In the context of the spying allegations, the doctor made this revealing comment: 'She also indulges in . . . masochistic practices, such as tying herself up, and all her life she has enjoyed punishment, and has often sought it unnecessarily.' Even more tellingly, Dr Minster recorded how O'Grady 'says she has sometimes placed a chair on her bed so that she can pretend she is being executed'. This matches what O'Grady publicly stated about her own experience in court. 'The excitement of being tried for my life was intense. The supreme moment came when an official stood behind the judge and put on his black cap . . . I found it disappointing that I was to be hanged instead of shot. My next disappointment was to learn that they would put a hood over my head and tie my hands behind my back before taking me to the scaffold. This upset me. I protested, "What is the good of being hanged if I can't see what's happening?"'[37]

So O'Grady's tales of wanting to entertain herself were true, without her spelling out the more explicit angle. One of the twentieth century's strangest criminal cases may have had its roots in the desire of its protagonist to experience the ultimate masochist thrill.

'Hide them in caves and cellars'

—

B EFORE WAR BROKE out, ministers had drawn up elaborate plans to evacuate the Cabinet, the civil service and other civic institutions from London in the event of a German attack. These detailed precautions had two code names. First there was 'Yellow Move', by which 44,000 civil servants in less vital roles would be sent to Wales and the North of England. Second, under the more important 'Black Move' scheme, the Cabinet, service departments, Parliament and 16,000 civil servants would be transferred to the Midlands.

The arrangements had all been made with a thoroughness that the government did not always demonstrate in its military planning. The Houses of Parliament, with their attendant staff, would have taken up residence at Stratford-upon-Avon, with the auditorium of the Shakespeare Memorial Theatre serving as the chamber of the Commons. Hindlip Hall in Worcestershire, an impressive nineteenth-century mansion in the Greek-revival style, would have been the base of the Cabinet and its secretariat, while the prime minister, his family and his private office would have gone to nearby Spetchley Court, a Palladian house built in 1811.

On coming to power, Churchill, typically, had no time for such plans. To him they smacked of defeatism and were an insult to the vast majority of London's population who would have to remain behind to face the Germans in the event of an invasion or heavy bombardment. If the worst happened, he intended to stay at his post rather than retreating to Worcestershire. The assistant secretary to the War Cabinet, Lawrence Burgis, later wrote that, had the Germans reached the capital, 'the Prime Minister would have mustered his Cabinet and died with them in the pillbox disguised as a W.H. Smith bookstall in Parliament Square'.[1]

Another scheme was developed to move the offices of the prime minister and the Cabinet into a underground bombproof bunker, code-named 'The Paddock', at Dollis Hill in suburban, north-west London, with other vital parts of the administration based in nearby schools and college. This secure military headquarters, begun in late 1938 and taking over eighteen months to construct, comprised twenty-two rooms, lay almost 40 feet underground and had a concrete roof more than 5 feet thick. Its entrance, inside a Post Office research station, was well hidden from the public. Unimpressed by all these advantages, Churchill hated the place, saying it would force him to lead a 'troglodyte' existence far from the centre of action.[2]

Fortunately there was a realistic alternative in the heart of the capital, in the network of reinforced chambers that had been created under Whitehall and later became known as the Cabinet War Rooms. This was where the prime minister would largely conduct his business for the remainder of the year.

King George VI and Queen Elizabeth shared the government's determination not to flee for sanctuary, despite the risks. Although nervous, diffident and intellectually limited, the King possessed a powerful sense of duty as well as personal courage, as befitted a former Royal Navy officer who had seen action in the First World War. He and the Queen never contemplated sending the two Princesses overseas during the war, unlike many other aristocratic families. Within the government, however, there had certainly been discussions in 1940 about sending the royal family abroad.

Churchill's aide Desmond Morton took up the matter with the prime minister, who was indignant that the proposal had even been considered. Professing confidence in victory over the Germans, Churchill told Morton in a handwritten note, 'I believe we shall make them rue the day they try to invade our island. No such discussion can be permitted.'[3] Nevertheless, even if their departure from the United Kingdom was never envisaged, there were contingency plans to remove the royals from London or Windsor Castle in the event of an emergency.

As part of 'Black Move', four country houses were designated for the purpose of safeguarding the royal family. The preferred location was Madresfield Court near Malvern, which had been in the Lygon family since the twelfth century. If, as a result of German operations, it were to become unsuitable, the three alternatives were: Newby Hall near Ripon in Yorkshire; Pitchford Hall near Shrewsbury; and Croome Court, the home of the Earl of Coventry, in Worcestershire. All four were fitted with interior signalling equipment and slit trenches were dug in their grounds, although it was decided not to install barbed-wire fences or other conspicuous fixed defences for fear of drawing unnecessary attention. The plans remained highly secret, with Madresfield featuring in them under the code name 'Harbour'.[4]

Initially the Metropolitan Police were to be in charge of the royal family's evacuation. In May 1940, a single police officer, one Sergeant Goodwill, was given the responsibility, in the event of invasion, of taking Princess Elizabeth, then aged thirteen, and her nine-year-old sister Princess Margaret, by car from Windsor Castle, where they had been living since the start of the war, to Madresfield. Soon afterwards, it was hoped, they would be joined by George VI and the Queen, who would be escorted from Buckingham Palace by a team of two inspectors and five police constables. Towards the end of June, the government decided that these arrangements were woefully inadequate, given the importance of the royals to Britain's wartime morale.

This inadequacy was graphically demonstrated by an incident in June, when King Haakon of Norway, having escaped from Scandinavia, was staying in the Palace. One day, on being asked by King Haakon whether he was satisfied with the security arrangements, as a test George VI pressed an alarm bell, supposedly to alert the Brigade of Guards and the Household Cavalry. When nothing happened, he sent an equerry to investigate. The equerry returned with a guards officer, who had assumed the alarm bell had been pushed by 'accident' but had phoned the duty police sergeant at the Palace, to be told that there was no attack, as if there had been, the sergeant 'would have been informed'.[5] Soon afterwards, a party of guardsmen were sent out and proceeded 'to thrash the shrubbery in the manner of beaters at a shoot rather than men engaged in the pursuit of a dangerous enemy'.[6]

Incidents like this persuaded the Government to strengthen drastically the royal family's escort and to hand over the planning of the possible evacuation to the War Office. On 27 June, Major James Coats, a distinguished officer in the Coldstream Guards who had won the Military Cross, was summoned to the GHQ of Home Forces, where he was given instructions to form a new unit to protect the royals if a serious threat arose. Entitled the 'Coats Mission' and based at Elstree School, this body comprised at first three officers and seventy-five other ranks.

Within the Coats Mission, there was also a separate elite group from the 12th Lancers cavalry regiment who were to be the personal bodyguards of the King, the Queen and the two Princesses. Led by Lieutenant W.A. Morris, this detachment was stationed at Wellington Barracks when George VI was at Buckingham Palace, and at Combermere Barracks in Windsor if he was at the Castle. Equipped with two powerful Daimler saloons and four armoured cars, Morris's group was ready to move quickly towards the chosen destination. When the order arrived, Lieutenant Morris would drive the King and Queen in one car as fast as possible, with the Princesses in the second car right behind and the armoured vehicles acting as escorts, while the rest of the Coats Mission troops would make their own way in a bus convoy.

According to Malcolm Hancock, who served in the Coats Mission, the standards were extremely high because of the mission's reputation. 'It was a marvellous thing. All my company were absolutely handpicked and there was tremendous competition among the guardsmen to get into the Coats Mission, as a result of which we had practically no trouble of any kind.'[7] The royal household itself, however, was another kettle of fish. Major Coats was exasperated to find that, when members of Palace staff went down to Madresfield, 'The first thing they had done was to put the Royal letterbox in the front entrance so everyone could see it', which one of Coats's colleagues described as 'the last thing in the world we should be doing'.[8]

Although the Coats Mission never had to go into real action, it was understandable that the defence authorities were in a state of constant vigilance about the potential German threat to the royal family, leading to regular alarms during the summer. On 6 July the King carried out a visit to inspect troops at Aldershot and two German aircraft dropped fifteen high-explosive bombs in the area. A military intelligence report described the location of the raid as 'significant', since Aldershot had not been targeted before and 'His Majesty's car passed' within less than 2 miles of the bomb-sites as he was driven back to London.[9] The Joint Intelligence Committee dismissed such fears as excessive. 'If the Germans really wanted to bomb the King, would they not have sent more than two machines and have dropped more than 15 bombs?' Furthermore, the monarch had been at Aldershot for more than four hours, so the best time 'to try and bomb him would probably not be while he was on his way home'.[10]

Yet, according to one German account, concerns about a direct threat to the King were fully justified, for the Nazi High Command had apparently hatched a daring plot to kidnap the leading members of the royal family during the early hours of an invasion.

The man chosen to lead this audacious conspiracy was Dr Otto Begus, a hard-bitten military police officer and committed Nazi. In 1959, he was tracked down by the British journalist Comer Clarke and agreed to be interviewed about the plot. Neither bombastic nor defensive, Dr Begus was candid about his involvement, telling Clarke, 'Well, we were enemies once. But what does it matter now? I might as well speak about it.'[11]

Begus opened by explaining that he had been 'a natural choice to lead the capture of the British Royal Family. A few weeks earlier, when the invasion of the Low Countries and France began, I had led a similar attempt to kidnap Queen Wilhelmina of Holland.' But he had been unable to capture the Dutch sovereign, who had fled to the coast half an hour before the German landing.

Four weeks after the fall of France, Begus received a written order to report within three days to a unit in Boulogne on the Channel coast.

'When I arrived, I was told by the Commanding Officer of the unit that his instructions were to put a special villa at my disposal for a secret operation. He told me, too, that I was to receive a security-protected telephone call from Münster, the secret headquarters of the Abwehr [the Nazi intelligence service] the next day.'

In his interview with Clarke, Begus did not reveal who was speaking at the other end, but it was likely to have been Admiral Canaris, the head of the Abwehr, or one of his staff. According to Begus, the voice said, 'The Führer does not regard the attempt to capture Queen Wilhelmina as a failure. Rather he regards it as an excellent rehearsal for the mission with which you are now entrusted. It is this: to capture the British Royal Family the moment the invasion begins. The Führer believes that the capture of the British Royal Family can be the most decisive single factor in the progress of the war.'

The caller then turned to the logistics of the plot, telling Begus that the plans for Operation Sea Lion were currently being drawn up. 'You will fly among the first waves of carrier planes with a strong fighter escort to deal with air and land defences. As our forces go in, several hundred men will be dropped in the vicinity of Buckingham Palace. At a pre-arranged signal, which you will be given in your sealed orders, the entire group will storm towards the Palace, stopping at nothing and shooting on sight. You will then rush the Palace and immediately hold the first member of the Royal Family who can be secured as a hostage. As soon as one Royal personage is secured, the capture of the others will be more easy, since the defenders may be induced to cease fire for fear of harming the King, the Queen or the young princesses.'

At his base in Boulogne, Begus put together a force of twenty-three men, made up of the commando unit that he had led in Holland, along with several SS officers 'picked for their fitness and courage'. His scheme had a number of stages. First, an intensive dive-bombing attack by the Luftwaffe would knock out the defences around Hyde Park. Then 400 paratroopers, armed with machine guns, mortars and automatic weapons, would drop from low-flying aircraft onto open ground or streets around Buckingham Palace. At the same time, a further 100 paratroopers, including Begus's own commando unit, would drop directly into the Palace grounds, 'then rush the royal apartments and secure the members of the Royal Family present. I told headquarters that I could see no reason why this capture might not be achieved within ten minutes of the first parachute descent.'

Abwehr headquarters sent him recent photographs of the King, the Queen, Princess Margaret, Princess Elizabeth and Queen Mary, a set of which were issued to every officer. 'We must have been the only unit – we jokingly called ourselves the Royal Unit – in the entire German army to pin pictures of the Royal Family in our rooms.'

It was now almost September and, with the invasion now seeming more imminent than ever, Begus received a further phone call, explaining the exact protocol that his unit had to adopt during the kidnap:

> On entering the presence of Their Majesties, you are to salute in the manner of the German Armed Forces. Whoever first secures a member of the Royal Family is to say, 'The German High Command presents its respectful compliments. My duty, on the instructions of the Führer, is to inform you that you are under the protection of the German Armed Forces' . . . Members of the Royal Family are not to be subjected to physical search without the most pressing reason. At all times they are to be treated with courtesy and respect . . . Immediately the capture of the Royal Family is achieved, you will get in touch by short-wave radio with the nearest Army headquarters, so that the utmost use may be made of this victory.

Begus reckoned, once the Palace had been captured, that the British would not counter-attack, for fear of harming the royals. But he never had the chance to put his theory to the test. Within three weeks of the postponement of Sea Lion, he and his men were ordered to stand down.[12]

For all Begus's aggressive outlook, the chances of his plan succeeding would have been slim. If the worst had happened and he had reached Buckingham Palace without warning, he would have found neither the Princesses, who were at Windsor Castle for most of 1940, nor Queen Mary, who based herself at Badminton, the Gloucestershire home of her niece the Duchess of Beaufort. Renowned for her regal manner, she took with her on her removal there fifty-seven servants and seventy pieces of luggage. After the war, when asked which part of Badminton the Queen Mother had lived in, the Duchess of Beaufort replied rather bitterly, 'All of it.'[13]

However, Queen Mary also had plenty of that indefatigability that infused her family, as Claude Auchinleck discovered in his role as head of Southern Command. 'She was grand, asked to be shown what we were doing, wanted to see something which would kill Germans! So we took her to a Sapper demonstration where they showed flame-throwers and grenades and blew up mines. One mine threw up a lot of lumps of earth which very nearly descended on her head. She never batted an eyelid and apparently went off pleased and grateful.'[14]

Apart from personal protection, another issue that concerned the government and the royal family was the safety of the Crown Jewels. Sir Owen Morshead, the King's long-serving librarian, later recalled a conversation that illustrated the King's chief anxiety.

In the event of the Germans landing at Kent, the King asked, 'What should we safeguard as a matter of priority?'

'Your person, your Majesty,' replied Sir Owen.

'No, I must share the fate of my subjects and the Crown Jewels should not be seized by the Germans. They alone can continue to represent England even if all else disappears in this ordeal. We must at all costs place them in hiding.'[15]

The firm of Garrards, the royal jewellers, used an unmarked car to take the precious cargo, packed into specially padded boxes, from the Tower to Windsor Castle, where the vehicle was met by Sir Owen and the King himself, both of whom personally took the boxes inside. To continue Sir Owen's account: 'He and I used pliers and other tools supplied by one of the Royal chauffeurs to wrench the major gems out of their settings in the crowns. The gems, including the Koh-i-noor diamond, were then wrapped in cotton wool and kept in hatboxes.'[16] These were placed in one of the underground vaults of Windsor Castle.

The King's decision to hide the jewels beneath the castle was confirmed by the memoir written by Marion Crawford, the governess to the two Princesses:

> One rainy day, the King's librarian Sir Owen Morshead let us explore the vaults at Windsor Castle. 'Would you like to see something interesting?' he asked us. We said we would. He took us to a stack of rather ordinary-looking leather hatboxes, which seemed at first sight just to contain old newspapers. But when we examined them more closely, we were soon unwrapping the Crown Jewels – hidden there for the duration.[17]

Apart from the Crown Jewels, in the first year of the war there was a vast exodus of valuable material from the capital's museums to distant places of safety. The Victoria and Albert Museum initially sent their collection to Montacute House, an Elizabeth mansion in Somerset that had been bequeathed to the National Trust, but by the summer of 1940 it had developed a host of conservational problems. Fortunately, the following year the collection was able to make use of an underground network of chambers at the huge disused stone quarry in Westwood, Wiltshire, which offered better conditions.

For its most important documents, the Public Record Office found a quartet of contrasting venues, made up of the women's wing of a disused prison in Shepton Mallet, the casual ward of the old workhouse in Market Harborough, and the splendours of Belvoir Castle in Leicestershire and Haddon Hall in Derbyshire. More than 1,000 tons of material were sent to these four places, with the most precious records, such as the Domesday Book and the collection of royal decrees, going to Belvoir.

Other stately homes across England were turned into cultural refuges. Mentmore Towers, the enormous nineteenth-century palace in Buckinghamshire owned by the Rosebery family, housed part of the National Portrait Gallery's collection. The Tate Gallery's works were divided between Eastington Hall in Worcestershire, Hellens at Much Marcle in Hereford and Muncaster Castle in the Lake District. Many of the British Museum's most valuable objects went to a pair of great houses in Northamptonshire: Drayton, belonging to the Sackville family, and Boughton, home of the Duke of Buccleuch, although some of the Museum's sculptures, such as the Elgin marbles from ancient Greece, were kept in a tunnel near Aldwych tube station, which was closed during the war.

The owners of country houses were not entirely altruistic in their actions, usually being paid for storage, although antiquated lighting and heating conditions in their properties often fell short of what was needed for priceless objects. Cynically, some of the owners were grateful that, having given refuge to inanimate objects, they would no longer have to open their doors to evacuees, as Sir John Ramsden of Muncaster House wrote to the Tate's assistant keeper David Fincham: 'I welcome the prospect of housing here pictures from the Tate Gallery . . . Their presence here might help preserve us from, or reduce the number of threatened hordes of small children.'[18]

The National Gallery, whose paintings formed Britain's most valuable arts collection in public hands, experienced the most difficulties. On the eve of war in 1939, the Gallery's Director Sir Kenneth Clark oversaw the transfer of the majority of its works to a number of locations in North Wales. Problems soon emerged. At one stately home, the pictures were affected by an antiquated heating system; at another the owner complained that his heating bills had risen dramatically because of the need 'to maintain a proper and even temperature in my galleries'.[19] At Penrhyn Castle, some of the largest paintings went into garages whose ill-fitting doors let in draughts, rain and rats, so, with characteristic wartime improvisation, all the openings were blocked up with old rags, while electric heaters and fans were installed to keep an even level of humidity. Less could be done about the owner, Lord Penrhyn. 'For your most secret ear,' Martin Davies, the National Gallery's assistant keeper, told his superior, keeper William Gibson, on 5 June, 'one of our troubles at Penrhyn Castle is that the owner is celebrating the war by being fairly constantly drunk . . . Yesterday he smashed up his car and, I believe, himself a little – so perhaps the problem has solved itself for the moment.'[20]

The Office of Works recognised that these arrangements were unsuitable, so a further significant dispersal of paintings was made in the early summer of 1940 to three additional, more remote, locations in North Wales. But once more, all did not go smoothly, with the maintenance of correct humidity for sensitive artwork a continuing issue. At one venue, the owner proved almost as awkward as his heating system. Complaining about extra staff and heating costs, he threatened to let his house as a girls' boarding school to generate extra revenue, as a result of which the National Gallery agreed to pay him an annual £80 fee.

A more effective, long-term solution was needed, not only because of all these individual difficulties but because even these remote parts of North Wales were no longer completely safe from Luftwaffe attack. At the end of May 1940, as the Battle of France reached crisis point, Sir Kenneth Clark and the Trustees of the National Gallery, headed by the industrialist and connoisseur Samuel Courtauld, had considered the drastic step of shipping the most valuable paintings overseas, as Gibson told Davies: 'Courtauld and Clark have decided to send the most important and not too large pictures to Canada, if they can get the Prime Minister's permission.'[21]

The question was put and the answer came on 1 June. Later Clark told a colleague, 'The Prime Minister's actual words were, "Hide them in caves and cellars, but not one picture shall leave this island."'[22] Accordingly, the search began for a large, bombproof, underground shelter. It was no easy task.

Finally, in September 1940, a disused slate quarry was found in the mountains of Manod near Blaenau Ffestiniog in North Wales. The site was exactly what the National Gallery needed. It had a winding road to its entrance and was not too far from a railway, yet it was also remote, at 1,700 feet above sea level. Above all, it had a series of six huge chambers, some of them more than 100 feet high, with exactly the right environmental conditions.

The pictures, however, could not be moved in immediately. It took another nine months to prepare the quarry for their arrival. A self-contained brick shed, with its own independent heating, ventilation and lighting system, was built in each of the six chambers to protect the paintings from periodic falls of material from the roof, parts of which needed to be reinforced with iron clamps. Power lines and emergency generators were fitted. A narrow-gauge railway, with custom-built wagons, was installed to move the artworks round the quarry. To accommodate the larger paintings, the narrow tunnel entrance was widened, with 5,000 tons of rock blasted away. Outside the quarry, the road up the mountain was improved. Altogether the works, which were carried out by the major contractor Sir William Mowlem, cost over £15,000. Finally, in the spring of 1941, everything was ready and the entire National Gallery collection was moved into the Manod.

The scheme was such a success that over the next four years the quarry housed a multitude of artworks from other collections, such as the Fitzwilliam in Cambridge, the Walker Art Gallery in Liverpool and even Windsor Castle.

In the case of another form of treasure, namely the country's gold and securities, the government moved in exactly the opposite direction. Far from trying to retain these valuables within the country, Churchill wanted all of them shipped across the Atlantic, not least because Britain needed large quantities of gold in North America to pay for military equipment and raw materials. It was a policy that led to one of the most daring British operations of 1940, capturing the essence of the national resistance to the German plans for invasion. The initiative, carried out in June and July, was a tremendous gamble that, in the words of the Bank of England, involved 'taking fearful risks which we would not contemplate for a moment in normal times'.[23] What resulted was the biggest movement of national wealth in the world's history.

Even before Churchill came to power, the British government had been secretly sending some of its precious metal across the Atlantic to pay for arms. When King George VI and Queen Elizabeth made a state visit to Canada in May 1939, two of the cruisers in the official convoy crossing the ocean carried 50 tons of gold ingots in 890 boxes. Remarkably, the news of this shipment never leaked out. Once the war began and the needs of British economy increased, Chamberlain's government began to make regular shipments of gold, from the Dominion of South Africa and from London.

By January 1940, gold worth £49 million had been shipped by battleships and cruisers of the Royal Navy. In an attempt to increase capacity further, from February the Bank of England started to use fast liners as well, although these did not prove as reliable as the Royal Navy's operations, since they were subject to 'sudden requisitions and cancellations'.[24] By mid-May, the Admiralty reported that a total of gold worth £88 million had gone to Canada by Royal Navy ships, and another £20 million by liners or merchant vessels.

In addition to the gold, the government was deeply concerned about all the securities held by individuals and institutions, representing a sizeable portion of the country's wealth. These assets, made up of bonds, deposits, stocks, debentures and shares, took tangible form in the paper certificates issued to their owners. In September 1939, in an act of absolutism that would have been unthinkable before the war, the government ordered that all securities had to be registered with the Treasury.

Now, in a highly secret operation code-named Operation Fish, Churchill's government ordered that all marketable securities be removed from the country to prevent them falling into German hands, a colossal task that was to be carried out in conjunction with a major increase in the transfer of gold. In the words of the former naval officer and journalist Alfred Draper, this was 'one of the most sweeping and far-reaching decisions of the war, for what was being proposed was that the Government should take over the investments of every private citizen without even obtaining their consent, and ship them across the Atlantic without their knowledge'.[25]

The massive task of collecting all the marketable securities was soon under way, with staff at all Britain's national and local banks putting in long hours to categorise, record and store huge numbers of certificates. Once that job had been completed, the securities were taken to special regional collecting centres, from where they were transported to the Bank of England before the final move to Scotland for the journey to Canada. In another sign of this operation's secrecy, the government decided not to publish the Parliamentary Order-in-Council, giving official authorisation to the move, until after all the marketable securities had been shifted out of Britain.

From early June, gold began to be shipped to Canada in vast amounts. By the end of the month, France had fallen and the menace of the U-boats was increasing, yet by September all the 'consignments of fish' had been safely delivered. When on one occasion Bank of Canada officials found to their dismay that three boxes of bullion appeared to be missing, these were eventually found after a search on the transport battleship, having inadvertently been piled up with some crates of Scotch whisky near the wardroom bar.

That characterised the story of Operation Fish. Despite the enormous risks, barely a single coin, ingot or box of securities was lost. Even the most serious incidents had little impact on the exodus of Britain's wealth. On 19 June 1940, the merchant ship *Niagara* sank after hitting a mine off the coast of New Zealand while carrying £2.5 million of British bullion from the Bank of Australia to North America. Yet in an extraordinary salvage operation, every single bar of gold was recovered from the muddy seabed.

It is estimated that Operation Fish saw almost £1,900 million transported out of Britain before the end of August 1940, this huge total made up of £637 million in gold and £1,250 million in securities. There were a few more sporadic sailings in the autumn and early winter, leaving gold worth just £3.75 million in the Treasury at the end of the year and no securities at all. The nation's treasure was not only safe but it had helped to pay for national survival.

17

'The sea itself began to boil'

IN HER AUTOBIOGRAPHY *Testament of Youth*, the author Vera Brittain wrote of her experience as a nurse on the western front during the First World War: 'I wish those people who talk about going on with this war whatever it costs could see the soldiers suffering from mustard gas poisoning. Great mustard-coloured blisters, blind eyes, all sticky and stuck together, always fighting for breath, with voices a mere whisper, saying that their throats are closing and they know they will choke.'[1] Those words encapsulate the horror that has always been inspired by chemical warfare. It was precisely the sense of revulsion that in 1925 led the League of Nations to draw up a treaty, known as the Geneva Protocol, which prohibited the use of 'asphyxiating, poisonous or other gases and of all analogous liquids, liquids, materials or devices' and bacteriological methods of warfare.[2]

Yet despite the Geneva Protocol, in the summer of 1940 Churchill's government would have had few doubts about using mustard gas if a German invading force had tried to land on British shores. Churchill himself, always unwavering in Britain's cause, was a wholehearted advocate of such a policy, telling the War Cabinet on 30 May 1940 that 'We should not hesitate to contaminate our beaches with gas if this would be to our advantage. We have the right to do what we like with our own territory.'[3] Nor did Alan Brooke, as commander of Home Forces, have any reservations about such a step in the event of a national emergency. 'I have every intention of using sprayed mustard gas on the beaches,' he wrote in his diaries just after he had assumed office in late July.[4]

These declarations of aggressive intent were not mere bombast. During 1940, the defence authorities not only worked out detailed plans for the use of gas but also built up a considerable stockpile of chemical weapons, most of them containing mustard gas. By September the government had amassed at its storage sites 840 tons of mustard gas, plus significant amounts of other gases. In addition, at their bases both the army and the RAF had large stores of chemical shells, bombs, canisters and drums. The No. 2 Group in Bomber Command alone possessed 264,000 pounds of chemical bombs, stored across five of its aerodromes.

One War Office paper from early July noted with confidence: 'We shall be able to develop gas attack from the air on a considerable scale for a limited period. Low spray would be the most effective method for dealing with troops on beaches. Provided the containers can be refilled without delay our existing stocks would be sufficient to spray a strip 60 yards wide and 4000 miles long. Bombs would be useful for contaminating specific points, such as piers, and so interfering with the landing of guns and equipment.'[5] Furthermore, throughout most of the latter half of 1940, Britain accelerated the production of chemical weapons, as well as expanding plant and storage facilities.[6]

The government and defence chiefs recognised that using gas against the enemy would be a drastic step, beyond the bounds of international law and the traditional morality of conventional warfare. But they felt that such ruthlessness could be justified by the nature of Britain's enemy. In its contempt for all international obligations, in its totalitarian excesses, relentless aggression towards its neighbours and brutal methods of warfare, the Nazi regime was a far darker force than anything that had been contemplated in Europe when the Geneva Protocol had been negotiated less than two decades earlier.

In December 1939, a report to the Ministry of Home Security stated that 'the Germans are known to be developing principally two types of gas: mustard and arsines [a highly toxic gas, more potent than mustard gas but less easy to control because of its high flammability].' Arsines, it was feared, might be used 'against the civil population in this country' because the German authorities 'consider that the British civilian respirator offers inadequate protection against them'. Just as disturbingly, the ministry was informed that 'Germany has consistently studied the possibility of bacterial warfare and the germs of foot-and-mouth disease are reputed to have been sprayed, experimentally, from aircraft. Great attention has also been paid to anthrax and tests are said to have been carried out with shells infected with anthrax spores conditioned to resist a heat of 200 degrees centigrade or more. They are said to result in a 95 per cent mortality, death occurring in 10 to 12 days.'[7]

In the week that Operation Sea Lion was approved by Hitler, British military intelligence officer F.L. Fraser warned: 'There is evidence that gas bombs have been distributed to German aerodromes around the Frisian coast and in western Germany, while another report mentions the unloading at Oslo of gas bombs sent by rail from Bergen. Other large bombs believed to contain gas, said to have been seen last week in Oslo, are about 10 feet long and 4 feet 6 inches in diameter with a thin steel shell.'[8] Further reports followed: of poison-gas factories in Germany; of a Polish factory manufacturing bombs with sleeping gas; and another of air-bursting bombs charged with mustard gas, all to be used against Britain.

The logistics of a potential German gas attack were an increasing concern of the defence authorities during the summer of 1940. British Intelligence estimated that by this stage the Germans had accumulated over 10,000 tons of poison gas. In a memo in early June, the military intelligence branch of the War Office warned that evidence accumulated 'in the last few months' pointed to 'the existence of gas spray equipment for fitting to German aircraft with a view to low altitude attack'. What was so sinister, in their opinion, was that such a weapon might be used to spread terror through civilian population at the moment of invasion and thereby hinder British defence operations.[9]

At the end of July, the War Office circulated an eight-point outline of how a German gas attack delivered from the sea might unfold against the English coast. First, it would take place across a wide front, perhaps 10 miles. Second, the gas would be emitted 'from ships and floats lying well off-shore, say 5 miles'. Third, the Germans would use 'arsine for choice, as being new and less easy to detect'. Fourth, the attack would take place 'just before dawn' and 'emission would be very rapid so as to obtain a high concentration. The object would be to get the defenders confused and wearing gas masks as the invading troops were landing in the half light of dawn.' Fifth, and on a more imaginative level, the War Office suggested that 'the tail end' of the gas cloud might be 'tinted with some colouring matter – or composed of some visible gas. This would make the defenders imagine some new horror.' Sixth, the 'forward localities' might be drenched by around 200 aircraft 'using medium spray mixed up with a few HE [high-explosive] bombs. The Germans would not mind spraying their own forward troops by mistake.' Then another 200 aircraft could attack 'likely railheads and debussing points with bombs or spray some two or three hours later to interfere with the arrival of reserves'. Seventh, submarines could be used 'either as a diversion or in conjunction with the main attack'. Finally, the paper argued that the Germans might lay down a smokescreen during the attack to deepen the confusion and fear.[10]

Amidst all this apprehension, the Admiralty was doubtful about the Germans' ability to mount a gas attack from the sea, pointing to the transport problems of moving large quantities of gas, the need for perfect weather conditions to blow the spray towards the shore, and the burden that the requirement to wear respirators would impose on invading troops.

Nevertheless, even in the face of the Admiralty's scepticism, the government felt that preparations had to be made to deal with the risk of gas, both for troops and civilians. Indeed, such precautions had already featured heavily in national defence planning, as reflected in the mass issue of gas masks. By September 1940, 50 million of these respirators had been issued to the population, with a further 13 million held in reserve. In addition, 45 million special attachments giving protection against toxic smoke had been issued. At one stage the government had considered a law to make it compulsory to carry a gas mask, but eventually decided it 'would be difficult and tiresome to enforce'.[11]

Apart from gas masks, a series of other steps had been taken to protect the public. About 8,000 tons of bleaching powder had been distributed to the local authorities for decontamination purposes, with another 7,000 tons held in reserve. Hand rattles were issued to air-raid wardens to act as an additional alarm system in the event of a gas attack. Cleansing stations, with supplies of spare clothing, were established at hospitals and first-aid posts for people who had been contaminated by gas spray.

The British armed forces were even more intensively prepared, having more sophisticated respirators than those issued to the public, with more advanced filters and thicker rubber headpieces. They were also given oilskins against gas spray, pots of decontamination ointment and eye shields. From September, this equipment was issued to the Home Guard based in the vulnerable areas of the South-East and East Anglia.

All these measures, in the civilian as well as the military sphere, were essentially defensive. Churchill's government had to grapple with the huge moral issue of whether or not to go on the offensive with their own gas attacks. The argument for this course was set out in a powerful memorandum of 15 June by the Chief of the Imperial General Staff, Sir John Dill. In some respects, Dill had proved a disappointment since his taking charge of the army in May, partly because of a decline in his health through the gradual onset of aplastic anaemia. But on the question of chemical warfare, Dill was purposeful and firm, displaying a clear view about Britain's national interest.

In his paper to the War Cabinet, he wrote that there were 'strong military arguments' for the first use of chemical weapons against a German invading force. 'Enemy forces crowded on the beaches, with the confusion inevitable on first landing, would present a splendid target. Gas spray by aircraft under such conditions would be likely to have a more widespread and wholesale effect than high explosive. It can, moreover, be applied very rapidly and so is particularly suitable in an operation where we may get very little warning.' Besides gas spray, he went on, 'contamination of beaches, obstacles and defiles by liquid mustard would have a great delaying effect.'

Dill admitted that there were two 'grave objections' to the first use of gas. One was that it would undermine Britain's moral standing, thereby alienating sympathy for the war effort in the USA. The other was that it would 'invite retaliation against our industry and civil population'. However, despite his acknowledgement of these two difficulties, Dill considered 'that the military advantages to be gained are sufficient to justify us in taking this step'.[12]

His opinion did not command unanimous support. Vociferous opposition came from Major General Desmond Anderson, Dill's own assistant chief of the Imperial General Staff. He claimed that, through the first use of chemical weapons, Britain would 'throw away the incalculable moral strength we derive from keeping our pledged word for a tactical surprise, which may well produce immediate gains, but will in the long run redound to our disadvantage. Germany would gain great propaganda value from the fact that we had used gas first, not only in America and other neutral states, but in her own country and dependencies as well.' With growing moral outrage, Anderson said that Dill's 'most dangerous' proposal was 'a departure from our principles and traditions', with the result 'that some of us would begin to wonder whether it really mattered which side won'.[13]

In contrast, Jack Collins, the commandant of the Army Staff College at Camberley, was infuriated by these moral doubts, imploring Dill on 27 June 'to do your utmost to get Cabinet authority to use blister gas spray on any seaborne German force attempting to land on our shores'. In such a scenario, he argued, German invading troops 'will be casualties before they can become dangerous. Those not blinded can be "written off" for the next four months, which look like being critical for us.' The use of gas would 'give the Bosche a setback and he will realize that, at long last, we have taken the gloves off and mean business'.[14]

With these arguments raging, Churchill made a decisive intervention at the end of the month. In a minute to the Chiefs of Staff, he urged a rapid increase in the production of chemical weapons, as well the development of further plans for their deployment. 'Supposing lodgements were affected on our coast, there could be no better points for application of mustard than those beaches and lodgements,' he told the Chiefs. Like Dill, the Prime Minister did not shrink from the concept of first use of gas. 'In my view there would be no need to wait for the enemy to adopt such methods. He will certainly adopt them if he thinks it will pay. Home Defence should be consulted as to whether the prompt drenching of lodgements would not be a great help. Everything should be brought to the highest pitch of readiness, but the question of actual deployment must be settled by the Cabinet.'[15] This was to be the government position for the rest of 1940: preparations for chemical warfare were to continue, with the final decision on the use of gas resting with the War Cabinet if the emergency arose.

Churchill's move meant that misgivings among parts of the military had been rendered an irrelevance. Approval for the use of gas now lay with the War Cabinet, and Churchill, backed by Dill, would almost certainly have got his way.

In the summer of 1940 the army had ten companies, gathered in three infantry groups, that were trained to handle chemical weapons. Their substantial stores were made up of 12,000 4.5-inch shells filled with mustard gas, 13,000 6-inch shells, 15,000 6-pound ground bombs and 1,000 chemical mines, each of which carried 4 gallons of mustard gas. In addition, the army had ten 'Bulk Contamination Vehicles': lorries that each carried a 130-gallon tank filled with gas. Their job would have been to contaminate the ground during a rearguard action or withdrawal. There were also 950 vintage Livens Projectors, which were simple mortars that could fire a chemical or oil-filled drum to a maximum range of 1,800 yards.[16]

Despite the army's chemical arsenal, it was the RAF that would have the prime responsibility for any gas assault on the Wehrmacht. In 1940, the air force essentially had two alternatives in using chemical weapons against the invader. One was to drop 30-pound or 250-pound bombs at the landing points with the aim of contaminating the ground and equipment, as well as reducing the efficiency of German troops by forcing them to wear respirators and protective clothing. It was estimated that one 30-pound bomb could heavily contaminate about 50 square yards, with lighter contamination spreading across about 300 square yards. The other, preferred method was to douse the enemy with gas spray released from 250-pound, 500-pound or 1,000-pound containers. The lower the altitude, the more deadly the strike would be, although low flying also increased the plane's vulnerability to ground fire.

Throughout the summer and the early autumn, all the RAF's chemical bombs and containers were filled with mustard gas, which was persistent and whose impact created large blisters not only on exposed skin but also in the lungs.[17] The government also had limited stores of phosgene, which was described by the RAF as 'lethal in reasonable concentrations' but had the drawback that it was 'non-persistent'. In addition, there were some supplies of tear-gas, whose physical effects were said by the RAF to be 'not particularly serious' but, 'by making its victims sick, makes them loath to don their gas masks and therefore more vulnerable to subsequent doses of phosgene'.[18]

The seriousness of RAF planning for gas attack against the invader was reflected in its establishment, in September 1940, of a specific committee to deal with chemical warfare, which displayed the ruthlessness that galvanised Britain at this time. At the first meeting, the use of phosgene was discussed, which one officer described as 'a very suitable weapon against the German civilian population', particularly because so few German citizens, in contrast to the British, had gas masks.[19] By this stage, as the committee was told, the RAF had worked out a thorough anti-invasion scheme, known as the 'Gas Plan'. This involved sixteen squadrons of aircraft in Bomber Command that, in an emergency, were designated for duty in spraying gas or dropping bombs on the invader. The force was made up of five squadrons of Westland Lysander utility aircraft, four of Fairey Battle light bombers, five of Bristol Blenheim twin-engined light bombers and two of Vickers Wellington medium bombers, the only planes in the group that were to be equipped with 1,000-pound spray containers. Until an emergency arrived the sixteen squadrons, based in different parts of the country, were expected to carry out their normal Bomber Command duties. As Air Commodore John Slessor, the Director of RAF Plans, stated in a memo to Brooke: 'It is not the present policy that squadrons should stand by to use gas against initial enemy landings. If the use of gas is authorised after invasion has taken place, an interval of 24 hours will be required to change over from bombing to gas spray.'[20] In practice, however, the Lysanders would not need twenty-four hours to switch their equipment. When the order came, spray containers could actually be fitted in under six hours. In other passages in his memo to Brooke, Slessor explained that 'training had been completed in respect of sufficient pilots' for the squadrons in the Gas Plan and that 'full instructions have been issued to RAF Station Commanders concerned on the operation of gas spray aircraft.' Furthermore, he told Brooke that it was 'certainly feasible for orders for gas spray to be given in the same manner as for the bombing of targets. It is not considered necessary to introduce a special code word for the use of gas, since we are operating in our country and such orders will have been issued before the aircraft takes off.'[21]

Implementation of the Gas Plan required sufficient stores of chemical weapons. In late June there was a shortage of them, with just 450 tons of mustard gas and 40 tons of phosgene in stock, as well as 1,000 charged containers and 39,000 mustard-filled bombs at the RAF bases, barely enough to mount one or two days' intensive aerial attack on the invader. This angered Churchill, particularly because the Cabinet of Neville Chamberlain in September 1939 had instructed the War Office to develop a productive capacity of 300 tons a week and a reserve of 2,000 tons. The prime minister applied pressure for this to be fulfilled, which, as in so many other areas, had the desired effect. In another indicator of Britain's earnestness of intent, production began to increase significantly. By September, the stock of mustard gas had almost doubled. On 27 September, a meeting of the Chiefs of Staff was informed that the production rate for mustard gas had reached 350 tons per week, and 45 tons per week for phosgene, while storage capacity was undergoing expansion to hold a reserve of 4,000 tons.[22] Indeed, by the autumn of that year Britain's stock of chemical gas had risen to 13,000 tons.

Complaints about shortages of supplies and equipment were a perennial theme of 1940, but there was one vital product of which Britain enjoyed a remarkable abundance: petrol. Amidst the relentless crisis over other resources, the British government had more than enough fuel for its immediate military and industrial needs. This was because, once the war had started, supplies that would have gone to continental Europe remained in Britain's storage facilities, while supplies from the USA and Asia continued to arrive. The growth of these reserves was also helped by the introduction of petrol rationing and the closure of 17,000 filling stations in southern and eastern England.

Several public figures saw the large petrol reserves as a potential boon for Britain's defences. With the same kind of ingenuity and perseverance that had characterised so many other operations, they felt that the profuse supplies could be turned to Britain's military advantage and utilised for unorthodox counter-invasion weapons. One of these advocates of unconventional petrol-fuelled warfare was the highly experienced politician, civil servant and military expert Maurice Hankey.

He and Churchill never warmed to each other, Hankey describing Winston as 'the most difficult man I ever had to work with'.[23] But then Hankey, a meticulous puritan who had a cold bath every morning and struck to a rigid diet dominated by raw vegetables and wholemeal bread, was unlikely to appeal to the epicurean prime minister.

It was early in the First World War that Hankey – then Secretary of the Committee of Imperial Defence, a crucial body charged with military planning – put forward the idea of using oil as a weapon against the Germans, primarily by burning it on the surface of water to defend the entrances to harbours, rivers or canals. He had gone so far as to conduct experiments in December 1914 but the military authorities failed to take up his suggestion, partly because oil was then far less important in the commercial life of the nation, and partly because of their preoccupation with the western front. Now, with the threat of invasion looming, Hankey decided it was time to revive his concept of setting the surface of water alight.

As a result of Hankey's pressure, the military establishment began to take the issue seriously. He was invited to a meeting of the Home Defence Executive on 27 June to outline his theories, to which Ironside responded

'No one could fail to admire the deep gallantry with which the British people wait, almost hour by hour,' wrote an American journalist in the summer of 1940. Soldiers guard a beach on the south coast.

An anti-tank crew looks out to sea on the east coast.

'There is growing confidence in our island fortress,'
claimed the government at the height of the invasion threat.
An anti-aircraft gun in front of Eastbourne pier.

Scaffolding on the beach at Eastbourne to prevent seaborne landings.

Derelict cars placed in a field form an even more primitive defence against aerial landings.

A signpost is removed in a Surrey village, May 1940, part of a nationwide effort to deny any geographical information to the German invasion force.

A typical anti-invasion measure in the early summer of 1940. Large metallic hoops are placed over a road to stop it being used for German landings.

British territory under occupation, June 1940. German troops marching through St Peter Port, Guernsey.

The sinking of the French fleet at Oran. The decision was an agonising one for Churchill, but it showed Britain's determination to continue the struggle against Nazi Germany.

Troops from the Somerset Light Infantry man an armoured train near the Kent coast.

British improvisation at its most extreme, July 1940. A fleet of Standard Beaverette reconnaissance cars, named after their eccentric creator Lord Beaverbrook.

As part of Britain's defences, 18,000 pillboxes were built. Many of them were imaginatively disguised, like this one in Felixstowe masquerading as a car.

Enemy aliens of Austrian and German origin being rounded up in May 1940. 'The most ruthless action should be taken to eliminate any chance of Fifth Column activities,' argued the Chiefs of Staff.

Returning soldiers from Dunkirk were astonished at the warmth with which they were greeted on their arrival in England, following defeat in the Battle of France.

Troops of the Home Guard manning a barricade in Sussex.

Concrete blocks at a road junction in Cheriton, Kent, July 1940. A bus shelter converted into a pillbox can be seen in the background.

United in treachery. The anti-democratic conspirators Anna Wolkoff, a pro-Nazi White Russian (*left*), and Tyler Kent (*right*), a louche American embassy clerk who wanted to destroy Roosevelt and Churchill.

In semi-exile from England since the abdication of 1936, the Duke and Duchess of Windsor were at the centre of one of the most bizarre German plots of the war.

'An undeniable fiasco,' said one German admiral of a rehearsal for Operation Sea Lion. The lack of proper landing craft was a constant source of anxiety to the invasion planners.

'A last appeal to reason.' Hitler addressing the Reichstag at the Kroll Opera House, 19 July 1940. The British rejection of his demand for negotiations gave new impetus to the Sea Lion preparations.

Early Local Defence Volunteers gathering outside a pub. 'That pack of yokels' was one Home Guardsman's description of his unit in Norfolk.

Training and better equipment had turned the Home Guard into a powerful force by the late summer of 1940, when more than a million volunteers were in uniform. Here a proud detachment marches down Whitehall.

Bren gun carriers of the 53rd Striking Force, Royal Armoured Corps,
passing through a southern town.

'Our beach and forward defences have become much stronger,' wrote Alan Brooke,
the commander of Britain's Home Forces. A 4-inch gun being fired at Fort Crosby
in Liverpool, August 1940.

The Luftwaffe's Commander Herman Goering and its Inspector General Erhard Milch. The German Air Force remained detached from the planning for Sea Lion throughout the summer of 1940, with disastrous consequences.

The sinister Gestapo officer Franz Six, who would have been in charge of security in the event of a successful invasion. Nazi rule in Britain would have been more oppressive than in other occupied territories in 1940.

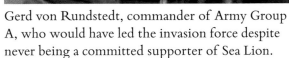

Gerd von Rundstedt, commander of Army Group A, who would have led the invasion force despite never being a committed supporter of Sea Lion.

Hitler with his naval commander Erich Raeder, another sceptic about Sea Lion.

Innovation was a central characteristic of Britain's anti-invasion preparations. A flame barrage, to be used against enemy vehicles and tanks, is demonstrated in Scotland.

British troops in decontamination suits during a training exercise in Kent, August 1940. The War Cabinet planned to use poison gas against the invader.

Women factory workers turn out batches of the 'sticky bomb', a primitive form of anti-tank grenade made with nitroglycerine. During the war, 2.5 million sticky bombs were produced.

First Sea Lord Sir Dudley
Pound. Cautious,
unoriginal but reliable.

Churchill both embodied
and inspired Britain's
fighting spirit in 1940.

The dynamic, resourceful Ulsterman
General Alan Brooke.

Edmund Ironside, Brooke's predecessor,
whose authority diminished during the
summer of 1940. Some of his subordinates
privately described him as 'gaga'.

One of the elderly, battered vessels supplied to Britain by the US government under the bases-for-destroyers deal agreed in September 1940. Churchill admitted that America had the better of the bargain.

Experiments by Churchill's Petroleum Warfare Department which involved setting the sea ablaze with burning oil, were brilliantly exploited by British propaganda to undermine German confidence in Sea Lion.

RAF reconnaissance photograph of German barges gathered in Boulogne as part of the Sea Lion invasion fleet. By September there were almost 2,000 such barges in the Channel ports.

'A scene of appalling devastation,' said one of Churchill's aides. The East End of London after the first night of the Blitz. The capital was hit for fifty-seven consecutive nights by the Luftwaffe.

'Unwearying vigilance' in the face of the enemy. A gunner at a 9.2-inch gun battery at Tynemouth, autumn 1940.

with enthusiasm. The commander of Home Forces declared that, thankfully, Britain had 'vast supplies' of petrol and he was now interested in 'a number of possible uses' such as fire ships, flamethrowers against fighting vehicles, 'petrol in submerged barrels near beaches', and 'gutters leading to the sea by which massive quantities could be released on to the water and ignited'. The executive agreed to Ironside's recommendation that a 'quick investigation' should be conducted into whether any of these ideas were practicable.[24] In his eagerness to press forward with his petrol experiments, Hankey acquired two other crucial allies. One was Brigadier Sir Donald Banks, a distinguished soldier and public servant. The other was Geoffrey Lloyd, a vigorous, wealthy Tory who was the MP for Birmingham Ladywood and the former secretary for mines. When the Petroleum Department, previously an adjunct of the Mines Department, was turned into a separate ministry in May 1940, Lloyd was appointed its secretary.

On 1 July, Hankey wrote to Churchill, explaining that, through his discussions with military officers and petroleum experts, he was certain 'that something substantial can be done to develop a weapon to supplement the means of defence at present available. You will remember that we have available at the present time enormous quantities of petroleum products in this country – actually more than we can store . . . Give us the word, we believe that something can be done to help.' With this letter, Hankey enclosed a six-page memorandum setting out the case for burning oil. It could be used, he said, as a 'valuable supplement to anti-tank guns, mines, obstacles and barbed wire' in 'natural defiles leading from the coasts, eg ravines, roads up cliffs and through woods'. In suitable conditions, 'it can be turned on by tap as a surprise from reservoirs concealed in adjacent high ground. It can take the form either of a burning oil or it can be sprayed as liquid fire. Or it can be piled up in barrels or other containers with a bursting charge.' Fire could also be used 'in artificial defiles such as streets, especially narrow streets such as those leading from beaches and harbours in many of our coast towns. This should be most effective in holding up an invader for a time.'

Static flame traps, Hankey argued, would not be enough. He also wanted to see the weapon in mobile form.

> We should at once, without a moment's delay, prepare columns of motor oil tanks. They should assume various forms – the usual pattern of oil transport lorry mounting a tank for road transport purposes; brewers vans or ordinary lorries carrying oil in casks fitted with a small bursting charge and a simple ignition – electrical or otherwise; galvanised or other tanks of oil mounted on lorries; old cars filled with 4-gallon petrol tins and tip lorries which can rapidly deposit their contents of barrels on the road.

He concluded by urging the government to drive forward this scheme by setting up a 'Petroleum Warfare Executive' under Lloyd's chairmanship.[25] To give extra support to his case, Hankey sent these papers to Churchill's aide Pug Ismay, with a covering note stressing that 'Geoffrey Lloyd is prepared to drive this thing with volcanic energy and I am behind him 100 per cent.'[26]

Churchill, with his boyish delight in military innovation, might have been expected to respond eagerly but, because of his personal antipathy to Hankey, he was somewhat lukewarm. He explained, through his personal assistant Desmond Morton, that he was opposed to the creation of another 'formal Executive Body', but was happy for Lloyd to 'press on, in collaboration with the military authorities, with the various devices described'.[27]

Long the master of administrative manoeuvring, Hankey put the most narrow, linguistic interpretation on the prime minister's rejection of his organisational proposal. Instead of a 'Petroleum Warfare Executive', he set up a 'Petroleum Warfare Department' within Lloyd's existing ministry, with Brigadier Sir Donald Banks as its chief. On 9 July the new organisation, without Churchill's approval, came into existence, based in three small rooms at the ministry.

Even before the creation of the Petroleum Warfare Department, advanced experiments with burning oil were under way. The first were held at Dumpton Gap, on the Kent coast near Broadstairs, on 3 July. Several tests were conducted, including the explosion of a 50-gallon steel barrel on the beach and the igniting of eight 4-gallon tins in a row to form a fire barrier across a road. 'The effect was striking,' wrote Hankey of the latter.[28] Of the former, Banks noted the reaction of a group of 'high-ranking officers' at the scene. 'The flaming oil shot up to such a height that there was an instantaneous and precipitate movement to the rear.'[29]

Another experiment featured a car filled with 4-gallon tins of petrol and rolled into an old lorry chassis, which was meant to represent a tank. Hankey recorded that 'there was dense black smoke and flames which burnt furiously for about 25 minutes. If this device was adopted, derelict cars containing petrol in their tanks could be used as effective road blocks and fire barriers.' Equally impressive was the discharge of burning oil through controllable nozzles on a pipe connected to a large 600-gallon tank. 'There was a fierce flame and considerable smoke,' he noted happily. The one conspicuous failure was 'an attempt to flood the sea with a mixture and set fire to it'. This had to be aborted because of a heavy thunderstorm and the receding tide.

Three days later, a similar set of tests were carried out at Dungeness on the south Kent coast, this time involving Colonel William Livens, whose flair for combining practicality with originality was reflected in his invention of the Livens Projector during the First World War, a simple device for firing oil- or gas-filled drums. Again Hankey and Lloyd pronounced the experiment largely a success, although they felt that the most effective, simplest device was the pipe with a number of holes, laid along the roadside and linked to a concealed reservoir of oil. Soon after this, Lloyd began to make the arrangements for the supply of oil, pipes, nozzles, tanks and transport for this appliance.

In his report, Hankey understandably failed to mention that the experiment at Dungeness nearly turned into a disaster. As Banks later recalled, Livens had installed a battery of 5-gallon drums in the shingle

> when, while he was explaining how it was intended to deposit these like flaming comets upon the beach 200 yards away, something established contact between two bare wires and the most remarkable display of projection fireworks took place. By a stroke of luck there was a faulty connection to the particular battery of drums in the middle of which we were standing and the consensus of opinion was that it was safer to stand on the drums themselves than anywhere else in the neighbourhood.[30]

Hankey was determined to present a relentlessly positive picture because he sensed there would be hostility in some quarters to the whole idea of petroleum warfare, but his fears proved unwarranted. The military embraced Hankey's theories, especially the creation of static flame traps; as one commander commented, 'the only difficulty will be to find sites for the installation where the blaze of explosion will not set fire to the whole of the surrounding countryside.'[31]

Work on these devices proceeded quickly. By 20 July, the first nine sets of perforated pipes, with their accompanying oil tanks, had been installed, with another twenty-five delivered to the army. More than 200 flame traps were eventually installed, most of them in the South-East and East Anglia, and remained largely the same unsophisticated but intimidating weapon that had first been tested in early July.

Each installation generally consisted of a large oil tank, with a capacity of 500 gallons or more, situated about 200 feet from the road and connected to a number of steel pipes perforated with holes with a diameter of one-eighth of an inch spaced 2 feet apart. In most cases the pipes were hidden in trenches by the roadside or disguised as handrails, although occasionally the plumbing was left exposed. Since the oil tank was usually placed on higher ground than the road, simple gravity was enough to produce sufficient pressure for a series of powerful jets from the holes, but where the pipes were laid on flat ground, pumps were needed. The jets were turned on by a valve operated by a soldier or Home Guardsman lying in a nearby pit and waiting for the enemy to arrive. The method of ignition was even simpler: the soldier or Home Guardsman just threw a burning Molotov cocktail at the fountain of oil, immediately turning it into an inferno.

As Lieutenant General Charles King observed on 10 August: 'It is unlikely that we shall have enough anti-tank weapons to cover all our road blocks for many months, if ever. These flame traps do at least give the Home Guard a sporting chance of frying a few Germans.'[32]

The ambitions of the Petroleum Warfare Department went far beyond the static flame trap. Encouraged by that perceived success, Lloyd, Hankey and Banks also developed two mobile versions, the more common of which featured a 200-gallon cylindrical tank mounted on the back of a Bedford 30-hundredweight lorry. A pair of long rubber hoses were connected to this tank, capable of firing 28 gallons of a petrol-oil mixture to a distance of about 70 feet. Pressure was provided by ARP trailer pumps normally used by the fire brigades. The valve-operated nozzles of each pipe were fitted with prongs so they could be stuck into the ground and their jets directed more accurately.

According to a War Office report on this weapon: 'It is highly mobile and it can be used to cover road blocks, sunken roads, defiles, cross-roads etc. It will be particularly useful for street fighting, where the nozzles can be projected from an upper window or round the corner of a building. It is essentially a weapon of surprise because of its comparatively short range.'[33] In another, even simpler version of the device, the lorry carried five cylindrical drums, each filled with 43 gallons of a petrol mixture and fitted with short lengths of hose. In an emergency, these drums could be placed at short intervals along a road, ready for an ambush.

A more important creation was the development of the 'flame fougasse'. This innovation took its name from a weapon of late medieval times, where a barrel of gunpowder was placed in a pit and covered with rocks that were hurled through the air when the explosive was detonated. The modern version of the flame fougasse owed its design to Colonel Livens, creator of the Livens Projector, who in 1940 came up with the idea of placing a large 40-gallon barrel of oil at an angle in the ground, with a propellant charge at its rear. When the oil was ignited, a violent jet of flame shot out from the barrel with a range of about 30 yards. Through patient experimentation, Livens found that the best mixture was one comprising 40 per cent petrol and 60 per cent gas oil.

Like the static flame trap, the design of the most widely used flame fougasse was remarkably straightforward, a central part of its appeal. A barrel with the combustible liquid was placed horizontally at an appropriate spot, such as on the approach to a roadblock or at a bend where a vehicle would have to slow down. A section of drainpipe was inserted at the rear, into which were put the explosive charge and a simple electrical wire for detonation. The whole device was then covered with soil, apart from the top of the drainpipe and the round front face of the barrel, which was hidden by camouflage netting.

The flame fougasses were usually set in batteries of four and, for the most part, were protected by the Home Guard. Those who witnessed the device in operation were certain it could have been lethal against the Germans, as Fred Hilton, a Lancastrian who served in the 260th Field Company of the Wessex Division, later recalled: 'At the demonstration we did, the flame covered an area of about 50 square yards and nothing could have lived in it. I think this would have stopped some of the tanks. Of course, this was the whole point of the exercise.'[34]

There were several variants on this main type. One was the demi-gasse, in which a barrel of oil was openly left on side by the road, ready for firing. It was largely a psychological weapon, its lack of disguise aimed at inspiring fear in the German troops who, in theory, would come to see all roadside tar barrels as potential threats.[35] Another variant was the 'hedgehopper', in which the barrel of oil was placed upright and buried in a pit hidden behind a wall or hedge, with an explosive charge attached to its bottom. Once detonated, the barrel was meant to leap over the obstacle and right into the enemy column. The problem with the hedgehopper was that it could be hard to get the quantity of explosive exactly right, so it came to be frowned upon by the War Office. Some other types were improvised, like the use in Middlesborough of simple wooden ramps to roll flaming barrels onto a roadway. With all these different versions, the fougasse concept could be described as the Petroleum Warfare Department's biggest success. In all, 50,000 barrels were issued for 7,000 sites, most of them in southern England.

On a smaller scale, the idea of using petrol as a weapon was also seen in the development of early flamethrowers in 1940. The first to arrive was the Harvey flamethrower, officially known as the Transportable Mark I: a cumbersome wheeled device with limited fuel capacity that needed two men for its operation. Despite its limitations, the War Office in July ordered 2,000 and the weapon first went into service in August 1940. Lloyd's Petroleum Warfare Department came up with an even more primitive armament, a sort of portable flame trap that could be moved around on a handcart made from a car axle and planks of wood. With a crew of five, it comprised a 50- to 65-gallon barrel, a 100-foot-long hose and a pump operated by hand. Not surprisingly, given its makeshift nature, it went into service only with the Home Guard rather than the regular army, although more than 300 units were soon equipped with it.

Some experiments carried out by Banks's department were too eccentric or impracticable to be put into action. One involved using burning cars to defend an aerodrome by deterring enemy landings. The test, held at RAF Hendon, was not a success: 'The drivers revved up, set the cars going and cut off the petrol, locked the steering and baled out of the open doors. One or two who had gathered too much momentum rolled over and over on the grass like shot rabbits,' recorded Banks.[36] Another almost hit a plane and then narrowly missed the main hangar before crashing into a wire fence.

No further application was found for a catapult that could hurl a Molotov cocktail more than a hundred yards. Because its action resembled that of a fast bowler, it was nicknamed 'Larwood' after the great England cricketer. Equally unwanted was the prototype for a lawn sprinkler that sprayed petrol instead of water. Always innovating, Colonel Livens came up with a new projector, dubbed the Toucan, made of a 12-inch tube that could fire an ordinary, commercial 5-gallon drum. Even more creatively, he devised a large rifle for firing milk bottles filled with phosphorus, although neither of these armaments was taken up by the government.

After July 1940, the Petroleum Warfare Department was engaged in a much bigger project, one that ultimately would come to have an impact on German planning for Operation Sea Lion.

The British had been contemplating the use of burning oil on the sea well before the war, and in May 1939, in an Admiralty experiment at Shoeburyness, 17 tons of petrol, spread over an area of 1,100 square yards, burnt for five minutes. Hankey himself had long been gripped by the idea of deterring the invader by creating a vast flame barrage on the surface of the water, having been inspired by his reading of ancient Roman and Greek history. He wrote in 1940: 'It is described in Gibbon's "Rise and Fall of the Roman Empire" and Greek Fire, which was only an application of the same principle, was used by the Byzantine Emperors for years and years to maintain their sea power and defend Constantinople itself against their enemies.'[37]

His notion was to use the burning oil chiefly as an offensive weapon on the German coast and waterways, but because of the difficulty of transporting huge quantities of oil across the sea, the Admiralty did not pursue the proposal. Nor had Hankey's early offshore experiments in July 1940 with burning oil at Dumpton and Dungeness been too promising. For the remainder of the month, his efforts were largely concentrated on the development and delivery of the static flame trap.

However, neither he nor Lloyd's Petroleum Warfare Department completely abandoned the idea, and their enthusiasm was renewed at the end of July when Arthur 'Bert' Harris, the head of No. 5 Group in Bomber

Command, showed an interest in this technique. Harris had an almost visceral loathing for Germans, and his entire strategy as head of Bomber Command was focused on killing as many as possible.

Harris set out his views in a memo to the army's Western Command, which was passed on to Hankey: 'One always likes to try and put oneself in the other fellow's place when thinking over these problems. It has struck me that the Boche, with his urge for innovation, whatever methods he decides to employ, will certainly employ something out of the ordinary if he ever attempts a landing.' He went on to argue that the British should respond with their own unorthodoxy.

> We should investigate the possibility of releasing quantities of petrol in the sea and setting it alight as the tows come in. It is obviously impracticable when considering the length of the coastline that we have to protect in this country. At the same time, however, the human inability to face flame being what it is, I think that there may be something in the idea and I have suggested to my own Commander-in-Chief an experiment of dropping light containers of petrol (such as the ordinary four-gallon petrol tin) in quantity to see if we can put up a concentration on the surface of the water which would present an effective barrier to small craft coming in to beach.[38]

The experiment never went ahead in the RAF, unsurprisingly, given the force's other duties, but Hankey, Lloyd and Banks were now determined to press on with their own trials.

On 24 August, the biggest test yet with burning oil at sea was conducted on the northern shore of the Solent estuary near Titchfield, in front of a large gathering of spectators and experts. Ten Scammel petrol tankers gathered at the top of a cliff 30 feet high and then 160-foot-long pipes from each of them were taken down into the water, well below the high-water mark. The ten valves on the tankers were turned on, immediately delivering oil into the sea at a rate of about 12 tons per hour.

What happened next impressed all who saw it, according to the account by Banks: 'Admiralty flares and a system of sodium and petrol pellets were used for ignition and within a few seconds of the pumps being started a wall of flame of such intensity raged up from the sea surface that it was impossible to remain on the edge of the cliff and the sea itself began to boil.'[39] At that moment, as smoke began to billow thousands of feet in the air, some Luftwaffe aircraft appeared in the sky over the Solent on their way back from a raid. The next day, said Banks, German communications 'stated that South Coast towns had been attacked with excellent results, very large scale fires having been observed in the vicinity of Portsmouth'.[40]

A breakthrough seemed to have been reached and the cynics had apparently been proved wrong. Harold Simpson, the commanding officer of the

Admiralty's Fuel Experimental Station at Haslar, wrote that 'with all the waggons discharging, the fire produced was definitely man and boat-stopping, being a continuous bank of smoke and flame fully 30 yards in width.'[41] However, in some respects the success at the Solent was deceptive, since the conditions were so favourable, with calm seas, blue skies and a sheltered setting. None of this was likely to apply in the autumn along the more exposed parts of the coast in Kent, Sussex or East Anglia, when the winds might be stronger and the waves rougher. Nevertheless further trials, while failing to match the spectacular conflagration at the Solent, certainly indicated that the idea of a burning sea was not fanciful.

Bernard Kimpton, an electrical engineer at the Petroleum Warfare Department, was heavily involved with this work throughout this period. 'The psychological effect of a flame barrage was tremendous. The smoke was the thing you saw from the sea, with flames shooting out from underneath it. I occasionally had to go out in a boat and check for gaps during tests, and I can tell you it was a horrible thing to watch. The combination of fire and water instilled an instantaneous fear.'[42]

From September, all the Petroleum Warfare Department's trials on the burning sea barrage were held at Studland Bay in Dorset, where the right mixture for the oil and petrol was perfected and where different types of pipes were trialled. But it was not until February 1941 that the Chiefs of Staff approved the installation of 50 miles of piping, made up of 25 miles in South-Eastern Command, 15 in Eastern and 10 in Southern. In the end, however, as the invasion threat lifted and Hitler turned his gaze eastwards, only a small fraction of the barrage was installed, most of it in east Kent. Yet all the work had not been in vain. In the countdown to Operation Sea Lion, the German commanders grew aware that Britain was experimenting with a new weapon. As Field Marshal Montgomery later wrote, 'They were now threatened by the unknown horrors of the Fourth Element: fire on the cliffs and fire even in the very sea.'[43]

18

'Foul methods help you kill quickly'

———

Tom Andrew, a garage mechanic from Elsham in Lincolnshire, left school in 1939, yet by the following year he was involved in a secretive, potentially suicidal mission in response to the invasion threat. 'We were told that if the Germans caught us, there would be no chance. If they found our dugout and did not want to question us, they would throw a grenade in. If they wanted to interrogate you, that was the worst as you would be tortured and killed anyway.' But Andrew felt equipped to deal with the invader. 'We trained pretty hard, every available moment practically. The regular army came to train us in unarmed combat and how to handle explosives. I remember one instruction in how to use a commando knife. We were told that if we tackled a German from behind, if you got your fingers around the front of his helmet and pulled it back, the chin strap would choke him and then you could put the knife in from behind.'[1]

His experience highlighted one of the most clandestine aspects of counter-invasion planning in 1940, an initiative that was both deadly in its intent and coldly realistic about the possibility of a German occupation of Britain. For Andrew was part of a well-armed, quasi-official organisation called 'the Auxiliaries', which would have sprung into action in the event of the Wehrmacht making successful landings. The vague name was deliberately deceptive. In essence, the Auxiliaries were an underground guerrilla army, their members recruited to carry out acts of sabotage, assassination and insurgency against a German invading force. They were effectively Europe's first anti-Nazi resistance force, brought into existence long before the French Resistance began to operate.

As Don Handscombe of Essex recalled: 'We would have killed without compunction. Our patrol might have made that decision about local people, Quislings or collaborators for example, without having orders from above.'[2] Added to this ferocity was an air of fatalism, as shown by George Pellet, an auxiliary from Kent. 'They told us our expected lifetime after the invasion started would be seven days. They reckoned that after seven days, either Jerry would be back out of it or we'd all be finished up. Because once we started blowing their equipment about, Jerry would go really mad.

209

It didn't worry me much because I thought at least I was doing something a bit more than standing guard on a railway bridge.'³

In his 1957 book on Operation Sea Lion, the writer, army officer and adventurer Peter Fleming, elder brother of novelist Ian Fleming, claimed that the man responsible for the creation of the Auxiliaries was General Andrew Thorne, the Commander of XII Corps in the south-east of England. According to Fleming, soon after Dunkirk, when Thorne saw how thin the defences were on the south coast, he told the War Office that 'if the enemy's attack on this position could be delayed or interfered with by irregulars operating against the German supply-routes and concentration areas, the Home Forces' chances of repelling it would be, however negligibly, improved.' What Thorne therefore wanted was 'a network of "stay-behind parties" (or, as it would have later been called, a *maquis* or resistance movement) whose object would be to harass the enemy's preparations for the second phase of his advance on London'.⁴ Fleming had a deep personal interest in emphasising Thorne's role, since he was the officer chosen by the War Office to organise the network under Thorne's command.

It was as a military intelligence officer that Fleming saw action during the Norwegian campaign. Indeed, when he arrived at Namsos, heading an advanced reconnaissance party, he was the first British soldier to land in Norway. That operation was doomed to failure, but he emerged with his reputation enhanced.

Following instructions from Thorne, he set up the misleadingly named 'Observation Unit' and began recruiting for this irregular force. Those with a strong knowledge of the countryside, such as farmers, labourers, even poachers, were particularly valued. Fleming was assisted in this task by Mike Calvert, an Indian-born, Sandhurst-educated captain in the Royal Engineers who had also served in Norway, where he had carried out a number of daring sabotage operations during the organised retreat against the advancing Germans.

The Observation Unit that Fleming and Calvert set up in mid-1940 under General Thorne could be described as the first guerrilla detachment in Britain's defences. But it was only part of the wider story about the Auxiliaries, whose genesis can be found in a separate development. This was the creation in 1938 of Section D as part of the Foreign Office's Secret Intelligence Service, with the aim of investigating 'every possibility of attacking potential enemies by means other than the operation of military forces'.⁵ Known as 'the dirty tricks department' and headed by Lawrence Grand, a major in the Royal Engineers, Section D liaised closely with the War Office's Military Intelligence Research branch, whose staff included a small, balding, terrier-like brigadier by the name of Colin Gubbins. The possessor of a quick brain and a natural air of authority, after distinguished service in the First World War he joined the staff of Edmund Ironside at Archangel to fight against the Bolshevik revolution, an experience that sparked his lifelong fascination with irregular warfare. A later transfer to Ireland to take part in the British army's campaign against the IRA provided intriguing lessons about how an outnumbered but determined resistance movement could wage war against a larger, occupying power.

This thinking bore fruit in his work at the Military Intelligence Research branch in 1939, producing training manuals on irregular warfare and advising Lawrence Grand of Section D on sabotage techniques. One of Gubbins's manuals contained a list that was to have a significant influence on the activities of the Auxiliaries. Called 'the nine points of the guerrilla's creed', it explained that the aim of insurrection forces 'must be to develop their inherent advantages so as to nullify those of the enemy'. Among the nine principles were the advice to 'confine all movements as much as possible to the hours of darkness' and to avoid undertaking 'an operation unless certain of success owing to careful planning and good information'. Above all, wrote Gubbins, with words that embodied his own character, 'when the time for action comes, act with the greatest boldness and audacity'.[6]

In the spring of 1940, as the war intensified, it was Major Lawrence Grand's Section D, not Gubbins's intelligence branch, that had the main responsibility for drawing up plans for guerrilla warfare as part of home defence. In fact, an internal report by Section D in August 1940, setting out the section's achievements, boasted that 'at our most forlorn moment when our army was pouring back from Dunkirk through gates which we could never have shut against an invading enemy, Major Grand conceived the plan of organising through Great Britain a closely co-ordinated sabotage and intelligence network among the civilian population who could be left behind in any territories which the German armies might occupy.'[7]

In reality there was no secret force built up by Section D. No 'stay-at-home parties' had been formed, nor had any training been given to any volunteers in the techniques of insurgency. A few dumps of explosives and stores of equipment were created, but without a network to use them they were largely pointless.

One story told by the historian David Lampe illustrates the disastrously naive management of Grand's Section D. 'No one seems even to have thought of co-ordinating the activities of this embryonic resistance organisation with the police or with the armed services – or with anyone else. One Section D emissary in pin-striped trousers and dark coat turned up in a Scottish village and asked the bewildered postmaster, whom he had never seen before, to hold a store of explosives for him. Not surprisingly the man from Section D was immediately arrested by the village constable.'[8]

Little further progress had been made by Grand on his home defence organisation by the time Gubbins returned from Norway. Disturbed by the potential imminence of invasion, the Chiefs of Staff and Ironside decided that a new, more vigorous approach was needed. Given his previous experience in serving Ironside in Russia and his pioneering research on irregular warfare, Gubbins was seen by the general staff as the ideal man to head this initiative. So swiftly did the government want to act that before the end of June 1940 they had not only found a leader for the force, but also a name. As Gubbins later put it, the title of 'auxiliary units' covered 'a multitude of possible lines of action and wouldn't create too much suspicion'.[9] In a memo to Pug Ismay of 22 June, the military secretary to the Cabinet Ian Jacob set out the latest thinking from the top of the army. 'Regarding the question of paramilitary activities in this country in the event of the enemy gaining a footing, the CIGS has decided that an organisation is to be set up under Brigadier Gubbins to undertake this task. The organisation will be directly under the Commander-in-Chief.' As he told Ismay, he was troubled by potential duplication with Grand's ineffectual Section D outfit, which, for all its inadequacy, was still in existence. 'There is obviously great danger not only of overlapping but, more important, of considerable confusion as both organisations will be working in the same areas and also seeking recruits.' One solution, he said, would simply be 'to close down' Section D, but his preferred alternative was to bring the section under Gubbins's charge. 'It is most important that there should be proper military control from the outset, as obviously these auxiliary units, whether uniformed or not, must be prepared to co-operate with and possibly even work under the local military commander. Further, it is very necessary that the selected men should receive training in the various weapons and devices with which they will be armed.' As a result, 'whatever organisation' Grand had 'got going' should 'definitely be placed under Gubbins and work under his orders.' To start the auxiliary units, Jacob suggested an initial fund of £1,000 a month for expenses.[10] With the aim of keeping the enemy 'continually on the jump',[11] it was suggested their key roles be intelligence, sabotage and assassination.

In practice, most of Grand's Section D was fully absorbed within the Auxiliary Units by mid-July. At the end of the month, in a memo to the Cabinet Office, Sir Bernard Paget of Brooke's Home Forces admitted that the 'military value' of Section D was 'insufficient' to warrant its continuation, especially since its members had been guilty of 'several indiscretions', showing 'the impossibility of maintaining the necessary degree of secrecy'.[12]

Interviewed in 1959, Gubbins recalled being summoned to the War Office on his return from Norway.

The briefing was brisk and to the point. I was told, 'We must expect the German invasion at any time. The enemy will be attacked from the air and at sea as they cross the Channel. Their supply lines will be hammered all the time. As soon as they land, our main force, held at strategic points inland, will be flung into battle. But they may achieve some success before the main part of our forces can get to grips with them. There may also be parachute drops which could put areas behind the lines in German hands for a while. For this reason you are instructed to form an organisation to fight the Germans behind their lines. You will report directly to General Ironside and to the Prime Minister.' As I left the room, I realized it wasn't going to be a particularly easy task. There were precious few arms and the main priority was going to the regular armed forces.[13]

Not a man to be daunted, Gubbins quickly set about building up the new organisation, ably supported by his assistant Peter Wilkinson. Operating from his office at Whitehall Place in the heart of London, Gubbins divided the coastal area around Britain into twelve sectors, and then embarked on recruiting field commanders for each of them. These commanders were known by the bland title of 'intelligence officers', although that was another linguistic deception for in reality they had little to do with the official intelligence services. Gubbins's immediate geographical priority was to focus on Kent, justifiably seen as the greatest danger area. It was inevitable that Peter Fleming should become the intelligence officer there, with his Observation Unit in XII Corps now becoming subsumed within Gubbins's new organisation.

The initial job of 'intelligence officers', liaising with Gubbins and Wilkinson, was to recruit the members of the Auxiliary cells in their own territories. Gubbins had a very clear idea of the personnel he wanted. 'My secret army had to be composed of men who knew the areas in which they would operate as well as their own homes. Men who could move about from coppice to coppice in darkness and daylight, making use of every bush and ditch. Men who could appear from "nowhere", hit hard and then vanish as mysteriously as they came.' He found that First World War veterans were often the best candidates, although young men who had not yet been called up or were in reserved occupations also found their place. In Lincolnshire, Gubbins 'sought out fenmen who knew every foot of their marshes and tricky fens', while in Hampshire he looked for forest rangers who moved across the land 'as silently and swiftly as their own red deer'.[14] Farmers and gamekeepers were also valued; one Auxiliary member in Norfolk was King George VI's own gamekeeper at Sandringham. In Northumberland, a place was found for a one-armed molecatcher who happened to be an excellent shot.

All this recruitment had to be carried out in great secrecy. Peter Boulden, a young farmworker from Sussex, recalled how clandestine the process was: 'I was approached to join a special unit, but was not told what I would be doing. Once we had volunteered, we had to sign the Official Secrets Act so we would not reveal anything. None of us were supposed to know about other groups. If we did not know, we could not tell the Germans anything.'[15]

George Pellet of Bekesbourne in Kent was serving in the Home Guard when he was contacted by an army captain to join a unit.

> He couldn't tell me much about it but he said that it would more interesting.
> 'Do you like a bit of adventure?' he asked.
> 'Yeah.'
> 'Then perhaps you're the chap for this.'
> I was told not to say anything to the wife. She used to ask a lot of questions and I used to make up the answers. The idea was that Jerry would torture her to find out what I was doing so I wasn't allowed to tell her anything. It was a funny business. I think it broke up marriages.[16]

Like Pellet, many of the recruits were from the Home Guard and indeed, as Ismay had suggested, the Auxiliary Units officially formed part of the LDV organisation, which itself was under the command of Home Forces. Although they did not perform routine Home Guard duties, the Auxiliary recruits were all given Home Guard uniforms and were allocated to one of three nominal Home Guard 'battalions': 201 for Scotland, 202 for the North of England and 203 for southern England. All these trappings helped to serve as a cover for the Auxiliaries' hidden activities.

At first the Auxiliaries were seen by the government as a temporary expedient in the event of the imminent German invasion, their role being limited in both time and scope. The emphasis was simply on the rapid development in the number of cells, not on the formulation of sophisticated plans or the comprehensive supply of matériel.

There was a darkly realistic tone to the advice Gubbins gave the twelve intelligence officers on 17 July. 'If we assume that the enemy has been successful in concentrating his main force, it is evident that the village cells, outnumbered and overrun, cannot achieve anything more than a very occasional act of sabotage, and that discovery will lead to a clean sweep of saboteurs in their area.'[17] Those acts of sabotage would rely largely on access to dumps of explosives distributed in the coastal areas, some of them by Grand's discredited Section D.

For all their limitations, Gubbins and his team made significant progress in their first three weeks. By late July, in his Eastern Command, which covered four vital areas from the Wash to Portsmouth, 150 explosives dumps had been created and 250 men enrolled. In the three areas of Southern Command, 115 dumps had been established and 200 men recruited.[18]

But after the initial burst of activity, Gubbins and the War Office recognised that something more permanent was needed beyond creating some cells and gathering sticks of gelignite. On this point, they were heavily influenced by Peter Fleming, who told them that 'a guerrilla without a base is no better than a desperate straggler'. What Fleming proposed was that the units should have well-stocked underground hideouts, complete with rations, cooking and toilet facilities, explosives, weapons and wireless sets. Such retreats, he contended, would give the guerrillas 'a sporting chance, not merely of inflicting one suicidal pinprick, but of remaining a thorn in the enemy's flesh for weeks or perhaps even in some cases for months'.[19]

Fleming's proposal was enacted and, over the following months, each sector developed its own network of hideouts, called operational bases (OBs), varying in size and layout. Some were in disused mineshafts, some in smugglers' caves. One was constructed in an airfield bunker, another in the cellars of an abandoned farmhouse.

Many of the early shelters were little more than makeshift dugouts, but a more sophisticated standard design was quickly developed, which consisted of an arched central chamber of corrugated steel, lying about 10 feet underground and reached by a tunnel or shaft that lay behind a concealed entrance. Here there would be bunk beds, as well as weapons, explosives and other sabotage equipment. Off this main chamber was a smaller brick compartment fitted with a stove, a chemical Elsan toilet, washing facilities and the entrance to an escape tunnel. On average, they were about 20 feet long, 10 feet wide and high enough to accommodate most Auxiliaries without stooping.

Usually built by the Royal Engineers, who were told that the chambers were to be secret food stores for an emergency, these bases were well concealed in woodlands or hedgerows, although in open, low-lying areas they might be dug into the sides of ditches or drains. Adding to their covertness, their entrances, water tanks and exits were concealed by foliage or ingenious man-made camouflage. George Pellet gave this description of the hidden entrance to his base in a wood near Bekesbourne in Kent: 'You had to know the tree you stopped at and at the base of the tree, you put your finger underneath and lifted a catch and the entrance came up, weighted like a clock. It was damn well built.'[20] In another hideout used by Peter Fleming's force in Kent, the entrance was even more elaborate. The Auxiliary had to drop a marble down what seemed to be a mousehole. The marble would then roll along a pipe 12 feet long and fall into a tin can, the sudden metallic noise serving as a signal to the men inside to open the trapdoor, which itself was concealed in the roots of a tree.

As well as bunk beds, furniture, sodium lamps, food rations, paraffin cookers, washbasins and toilets, the operational bases usually contained significant arsenals for the units. Indeed, the members of the Auxiliary Units were far better armed than any other part of the Home Guard or even the regular army. From the earliest days of the force, each cell was equipped with a wide variety of arms: hand grenades, phosphorus bombs, ammunition, dynamite, gelignite, RDX (an explosive more powerful than TNT) and ammonal, a high-explosive powder consisting of ammonium nitrate and aluminium.

The Auxiliary cells had a large supply of sabotage devices, such as the 'time pencil fuse', which operated on the basis of the time taken for a certain amount of acid in a glass container to eat through a copper wire. When the wire had been sufficiently corroded by the acid, it would break and thereby release a spring that activated a detonator attached to an explosive. The thicker the wire, the longer the delay. Although it had many potential uses in sabotage, this device had a particular appeal as an improvised weapon for hampering German movements in the event of an invasion. Combined with a slab of RDX and a strong magnet, it could be placed on a railway line or the driving wheel of an enemy tank with destructive results.

Another innovation was the Anti-Personnel (AP) Switch, known descriptively to the Auxiliary Units as 'the Castrator'. Effectively a miniature anti-personnel mine, this was a thin cylindrical device, the size and shape of a pen, that would be placed vertically in the ground so that only its head protruded. A man's foot stepping on this head would cause an internal spring to release a firing pin, immediately sending a bullet upwards as if shot from a rifle. The Auxiliary Units also received special tyre-bursting mines, which were hollow bronze castings filled with 2 ounces of high explosive and disguised as pieces of coal or lumps of horse dung.

An illustration of how well equipped the operational bases were can be seen from the ordnance left behind by the cell at Dengie on the Essex coast when, long after the war had ended, the regular army was asked to clear the hideout. There the soldiers found 14,738 rounds of ammunition, 1,205 pounds of explosives, 3,742 feet of delayed-action fusing, 1,271 detonators, 719 booby-trap switches, 314 paraffin bombs and 131 fog signals.

Geoff Devereux from Worcestershire recalled that in his OB his cell had enough explosive to demolish the main bridge in Worcester over the Severn or 100 German tanks. One surprising item in his stores, which was not intended for use against the Germans, was a gallon cask of army run. 'It was labelled with a very strict warning of penalties if used before an invasion.'[21]

On Churchill's direct instructions, every member of the Auxiliary force was given a revolver to carry. At first American .32 Colt automatics were distributed, some of them originally the property of the New York Police Department. Then from August 1940 the Colt was superseded by another famous US import, the .38 Smith and Wesson, although other types were also used. In keeping with the clandestine, paramilitary nature of the Auxiliaries, their revolvers were often provided with ammunition that, because of the large flesh wounds it inflicted, was illegal under the Hague Conventions on the conduct of war.

Apart from their individual revolvers, the Auxiliaries had access to a range of other arms. In 1940, each cell was given at least one Thompson sub-machine, the famous 'Tommy Gun' that, in the British public's imagination, was indelibly associated with Chicago gang warfare. Tom Andrew from Lincolnshire recalled his excitement at the arrival of weapon in his unit: 'It was like a sporting gun in beautiful blue steel in a beautiful case. It had a 50-round magazine drum and a straight 20-round drum, so 70 rounds of ammunition, already loaded in two containers.'[22] Auxiliary cells also had the Browning automatic rifle, a heavy weapon not entirely suited to guerrilla warfare, and the lighter .22 rifle, usually fitted with a telescopic sight and a silencer.

The toughness of the Auxiliaries was further highlighted by their fondness for carrying combat knives, the most common in the summer of 1940 being the RBD hunting knife. Despite its popularity, it was gradually replaced from November by a short, double-edged dagger, known as the Fairbairn-Sykes fighting knife. It quickly became a classic of British weaponry, carried by most British troops on D-Day and cherished for its lethal effectiveness.

In addition to knives, the Auxiliary cells had access to other more primitive hand-to-hand combat weapons, including garrotte wires, coshes and clubs. Peter Fleming's first unit in Kent even had a dozen crossbows in its stores, Fleming having been convinced of the deadly accuracy of this weapon by his pre-war travels to remote parts of the world. One of his typically innovative ideas was that, in an invasion, flaming arrows could be used to blow up petrol dumps, thereby preventing the fuel from falling into German hands.

With the same spirit of enterprise, Fleming had set up the first Auxiliary training centre, initially focused on the members of his force in Kent. The centre was based in 'The Garth' at Bilting, a remote, half-timbered farmhouse whose interior doubled up as an ammunitions store. Here, Fleming and Calvert taught the early Auxiliary recruits the dark arts of guerrilla warfare. He showed them how to blend into the landscape, and how to make booby-traps from milk churns and sewage pipes. He tested their ability to remain motionless on the ground and instructed them on positions to adopt as a sniper. Another of his techniques was to have his men wear specially darkened goggles to simulate the experience of night-time.

As with the wider structure of the units, Brigadier Gubbins felt that the training of the Auxiliary Units needed to be put on a more formal, systematic basis. He managed to commandeer the beautiful seventeenth-century house of Coleshill in Wiltshire, belonging to the Pleydell-Bouverie family, another of those majestic stately homes that proved so useful to the anti-invasion effort. The attraction of Coleshill was its sprawling parkland and woods, which Gubbins saw as highly suitable for guerrilla training. Soon the extensive grounds were equipped with a rifle range, dummy tanks and aircraft damaged beyond repair, enabling the first intensive courses to be provided to the Auxiliaries from late August 1940.

Like all aspects of Auxiliary operations, the role of Coleshill was shrouded in secrecy, involving subterfuge even in the centre's transport arrangements. Most Auxiliary trainees did not travel directly to Coleshill but were instructed to report to the post office in the tiny nearby village of Highworth, where they had to give the discreet, long-serving postmistress Mabel Stranks a password and proof of identity. Mrs Stranks would then disappear behind the counter to phone the Coleshill staff who would send an official car to collect the trainee, provided his credentials proved satisfactory. Sometimes the process could last more than an hour; she allegedly once kept General Montgomery waiting in his car while she carried out a thorough identity check on him.

Most of the Coleshill courses took place over a weekend, with instruction in August 1940 being provided by a handful of regular army officers from the 3rd Division of Claude Auchinleck's Southern Command. As Coleshill moved to a more secure footing, its courses expanded and more instructors were brought in, including commando leaders and specialised combat experts like William Fairbairn and Eric Sykes, the former Shanghai policemen after whom the knife they invented was named and whose uncompromising motto was 'Foul methods help you kill quickly'.

One Coleshill graduate, Henry Hall, gave this vivid description of the guidance from this pair: 'They taught the vulnerable parts of the body – mouth slitting, ear-trapping to break ear drums, eye-gouging, the grallock (or disembowelling), rib-lifting, "lifting the gates" – temporary dislocation of the jaw, ear-tearing, nose chopping, shin-scraping with the edge of a boot, shoulder jerking – a sharp pull downwards to dislocate the shoulder and releases to get away from any hold.' According to Hall, Fairbairn would always conclude every piece of advice with the injunction, 'Then kick him in the testicles.'[23]

Apart from such combat training, the Auxiliaries were given lectures and demonstrations in a host of other guerrilla techniques. A War Office memorandum in early September 1940 set out how the weekend courses were run: 'The course comprises 24 Home Guards and some six Intelligence and Attached Army Officers. The course assembles at 1800 hours on Friday and disperses at 1700 on Sunday. The importance of secrecy is stressed. Warning is given against undue complacency as to the impossibility of invasion during the coming winter.'

Over the two days of the weekend, the syllabus included instructions on revolvers, grenades, demolitions, hideouts, communications and 'German army methods', as well as exercises in night patrols, fieldcraft and the use of explosives.[24] Copies of the 'Partisan Leader's Handbook', a pamphlet produced in 1939 by Gubbins setting out 'the principles of Guerrilla Warfare and Sabotage', were also used as part of the course. Written in Gubbins's characteristically forceful style, this document mixed practical advice with moral encouragement. 'Remember that guerrilla warfare is what a regular army has always most to dread. When this warfare is conducted by leaders of determination and courage, an effective campaign by your enemies becomes almost impossible,' read one uplifting passage. Other parts of the forty-page booklet examined road and rail ambushes, the destruction of sentry posts, the concealment of arsenals, the creation of information systems and acts of sabotage.[25] Presiding over this lexicon of destruction, the Auxiliary staff grew so enamoured of Coleshill that before the end of the year they had moved their entire administration there from Whitehall. However, not everyone was so keen on the military takeover of the mansion. The two elderly Pleydell-Bouverie sisters, who stayed at Coleshill throughout the war, had a number of nervous dogs that became hysterical at the sounds of all the explosions in the parkland and could be calmed only by cocktails of aspirin and brandy.

Away from Coleshill, the Auxiliaries carried out their regular patrols and further training in their own areas. The basic procedure during the first two years of the units' existence was that one man would act as an observer from a concealed position during the day, while the rest of the cell remained in the operational base. Then at night, the patrol would stealthily move out from the base towards the chosen target, acting on the information that the observer had gathered.

Observers were told to avoid 'sudden movements' or 'smoking' so as not to reveal themselves, and those on patrol had to 'keep to the low ground' and 'be ready to freeze when meeting the enemy unexpectedly'. The darker the night, 'the closer together must the patrol keep'. In all their movements, Auxiliaries were urged to 'proceed deliberately, as haste merely leads to excitement and confusion'. To communicate with each other, 'natural sounds should be made rather than whistles, hunting horns and rattles. A password is advisable.'

Every man, according to the guidance, should be equipped with a revolver, a Mills bomb (the standard issue hand grenade), a wire cutter, a box of matches, a detonator, a fuse, a cosh and a first-aid dressing, while one patrol member should also carry a rifle 'to cover a withdrawal'. As to clothing, the official guidance stated that

> boots with nails should never be worn. Gym shoes are best, except in wet weather. Avoid squeaking shoes, rattling coins or ammunition, sneezes, coughs, oaths, the carrying of letters or documents. Steel helmets are not the ideal headgear for patrol work. Balaclavas are best. It is advisable to blacken the face, as its whiteness at night becomes almost luminous. For purposes of recognition a patch of cloth, or coloured scarf may be useful.[26]

Those instructions were closely followed. Charlie Mason, a Home Guardsman from Yorkshire, gave up washing the denim Home Guard uniform that he wore at night on patrol, since he felt that the mud and grease that caked his garments served as a form of camouflage.

In addition to patrols, intensive training was continued in the Auxiliaries' own areas, as John Thornton from Shropshire recalled:

> Some of our training was at Holmer where there was a big lake. We had to run across a pontoon bridge there carrying all our equipment. One part of the bridge was 'mined' and if you stepped there the bridge collapsed and you went in! If you didn't fall in, the instructors – a severe and bloodthirsty lot – pushed you in and you were wet all day. We also practised killing on a stuffed dummy mounted on a doorway with elastic bands. We were always trained to cut upwards with our knives, never downwards. This was to prevent the enemy grabbing your wrist and disarming you. After killing the enemy, we were told to cut off their 'knackers' to demoralise the rest.[27]

This training was deadly serious and occasionally had lethal results. One Auxiliary with George Pellet's unit in Kent was shot during an exercise, when he was caught by gunfire from troops playing the role of German snipers with live ammunition. Pellet and his comrades were crawling along the ground beneath a bank to avoid the bullets, when 'one bloke got scared and he got up and ran. Silly bugger. They killed him stone dead.'[28]

For all the isolation that accompanied their development, the Auxiliary Units were not the only element of Britain's secret resistance force. As a response to the government's recognition that they would need some sort of communications system, the War Office set up what became known as the Special Duties Section, headed by Major Maurice Petherick, with its headquarters and training centre in Hannington Hall in Wiltshire. The section was made up of wireless operators, couriers and messengers who would provide vital intelligence on enemy movements in the event of an invasion. This Special Duties network, which eventually had a personnel establishment of 3,250, included civilian staff as well as skilled technicians from the Royal Corps of Signals and female volunteers from the Auxiliary Territorial Service, effectively the women's army. The network was even more secret than Gubbins's force, and indeed most Auxiliaries were unaware of its existence.

There were several elements to the chain of information that ran through the section, which would have gone into action the moment the Germans landed in Britain. The first comprised the 'runners', civilians who would look out for any signs of enemy activity, including espionage or troop movements. In keeping with the character of the Auxiliary movement, these runners would deposit any written messages in a variety of dead drops, such as drainpipes, hollow tree trunks, or birds' nests. These urgent reports would then be picked up by other couriers or 'cut-outs' who would pass them on to their nearest wireless units or 'out-stations'. Altogether almost 200 of these 'out-stations' were created around the southern and eastern coasts, most of them manned by civilian operators, usually female and on that account sometimes dubbed the 'secret sweeties'.

Once the messages had been put into code, they were transmitted at a prearranged time to teams of Royal Signals or ATS operators at bigger 'in-stations' further inland, also known as 'control' or 'zero' stations, from where the information would be sent to the Auxiliary Unit's intelligence officer based at the nearest army HQ. The codes, which were never in Morse, were written on special digestible paper but no other instructions were put in writing.

Gathering intelligence across the airwaves from between five and ten coastal 'out-stations', each 'in-station' served an area about the size of the county and, in the early days of the Special Duties Section, was designed to look like a meteorological hut, complete with weather charts and equipment, to disguise its real purpose.

One ATS member, Maria Bloxham, had painful memories of serving in a 'zero' station: 'We were always in strange places. We were always hidden. We were always in a wood or a copse. Difficult to get to, beastly to get to, usually involving tramping over muddy fields. No cars, no bicycles allowed because of the terrain. And we had a hut there, enclosed by barbed wire, guarded by the Home Guard . . . We had never more than two hours' sleep at a time. That was difficult, but you got accustomed to it.'[29] Like the Auxiliaries, the wireless operators knew that their prospects could be grim, as Yolande Aston, serving in the ATS on the south coast, recalled: 'It was understood that we were expected to stay behind to work our radio stations after invasion, even if the army had to retire. We were clear about the "do-or-die" expectations. I was persuaded against even telling my family about my work.'[30]

Apart from the Special Duties Section, two other semi-official organisations lent support to the Auxiliaries. One was the Scouts Section, comprising small numbers of regular army troops that helped with training in the Auxiliary areas, as well the creation of dugouts and assistance to patrols. The other, a much smaller, more secretive force, was known simply known as 'The Other Side'. Active only in northern Kent, this was a network of double agents who would pretend to be collaborators with the Nazi regime if the Germans mounted a successful landing in the area. Through their closeness to the enemy occupiers, agents of 'The Other Side' hoped they would be able to send intelligence to the embattled regular army and the Auxiliaries.

According to the historian Norman Longmate, their chosen methods for transmitting messages would have been highly primitive because it would have been too dangerous for them to use conventional technology like the wireless or telegraph. 'The few vital lines which carried a secret message' were to be revealed through clothes hung out on a washing line, various items spelling out words in Morse code, 'with a large article like a sheet or a table cloth signifying a dash and a smaller item, such as a towel or a tea-cloth, a dot'.[31] For all such daring improvisation, it is unlikely that 'The Other Side' would have had anything more than a minimal impact in the immediate aftermath of invasion.

Indeed, some felt that this was true of the Auxiliary organisation as a whole. Gubbins's own personal assistant Peter Wilkinson said later that he believed its influence was 'grossly exaggerated'. At the very best, he said, 'they would have been a flea bite behind enemy lines. They might have sown a certain amount of confusion and insecurity but they were never on a scale that would have been of any decisive importance.'[32] Some officers went further, regarding the entire resistance initiative as disreputable and counter-productive.

A previously unpublished letter of 23 July 1940 to Winston Churchill from Gordon MacLeod, a Home Guard commander in Wareham, Dorset, illustrated such concerns. Having expressed his alarm over the development of 'a system of sabotage which could be brought into operation within the enemy lines in the event of his establishing a foothold in this country', MacLeod then told the prime minister in stark terms:

> Quite apart from its questionable aspect under International Law, in view of the brutal retaliatory measures which action of the kind has already evoked from the enemy in occupied territory both in this war and in that of 1914–18 and the certainty that it will similarly bring death and untold suffering to

innocent non-combatant members of the community if embarked upon in this country, I cannot think that the ill-considered proposal has been made without your knowledge or approval.[33]

MacLeod could not have been more wrong. Like so much else in the summer of 1940, from the incarceration of aliens to plans for the use of gas, the creation of Auxiliary Units was entirely in keeping with Churchill's dynamic, unorthodox approach. No matter what its potential effectiveness, Gubbins's force was another symbol of Britain's willingness to fight. When Churchill was fully appraised of the scheme, he was all in favour of it.

On 25 August he wrote to the War Secretary, Anthony Eden, 'I have been following with much interest the growth and development of the new guerrilla formations of the Home Guard, known as "Auxiliary Units". From what I hear these units are being organised with thoroughness and imagination and should in the event of invasion prove a useful addition to the regular forces.'[34] At Churchill's request, the War Office provided him with regular updates on the work of the Auxiliaries throughout the autumn.

In the first such report, dated 4 September, the War Office explained that 'the number of Home Guard enrolled is approximately 2,300 men, comprising 350 patrols', adding that two weekend courses had already been held at Coleshill 'attended by 52 patrol leaders of the Home Guard'. The abundance of weaponry for the units was also highlighted in the report. 'In the course of the next 10 days, 500 Browning Automatic Rifles, 250,000 rounds of ammunition, 400 pistols and ammunition, 10,000 grenades, 5000 AW bombs and various other items will be distributed.' The War Office concluded on an upbeat note: 'Progress has been far better than expected and, as before, the limiting factor is the smallness of the establishment. The addition of the Scout Sections . . . will have a considerable effect on the efficiency of these units.'[35]

The expansion, training and equipping continued for the rest of the year. Eventually more than 600 patrols were formed, with total recruitment reaching 3,500 by late 1941. The force was not finally disbanded until the autumn of 1944, when the possibility of a German invasion ended. Gubbins himself, having so successfully established the organisation, left in November 1940 to become head of the Special Operations Executive (SOE), whose task was to promote sabotage and resistance to the Reich overseas.

Shortly before this, Peter Fleming had handed over the leadership of his unit to Norman Field, an officer in the Royal Fusiliers who had been badly wounded at Dunkirk. Concerning the threat from the Reich, it was Field's view that 'the Auxiliary Units would not have arrested invasion, but they would have made life difficult for the invader.'[36]

19

'The Führer orders an abduction to be organised at once'

━━

THE NAZIS' IGNORANCE about Britain extended to the constitution. Contemptuous of democracy, driven by their totalitarian impulse, they had no understanding of the British traditions of Parliamentary governance and a constitutional monarchy, and therefore overrated the political power of the Crown. It was an outlook that led them to attach undue weight to the insubstantial, unreliable figure of the Duke of Windsor, who had been forced to abdicate the throne in 1936 because of his desire to marry the American divorcee Wallis Simpson. In the excitable minds of the leading Germans, particularly Hitler's Foreign Minister and former German ambassador to Britain, Joachim von Ribbentrop, the Duke could be a pivotal figure in bringing about an end to British resistance, by creating pressure for peace negotiations and serving as the focus for opposition to Churchill.

Like many other figures in the British political establishment during the 1930s, the Duke was pro-appeasement and sympathetic to the German cause. In the wake of the Abdication crisis, Ribbentrop believed that it was Edward VIII's pro-Nazi stance rather than his determination to marry Wallis Simpson that had sealed his fate, since 'dark forces hostile to Anglo-German understanding' had been driven from the throne.[1] The couple's link with Nazism may have been personal as well as political. According to a report given to the FBI by Father Odo, a Benedictine monk, Ribbentrop had been the Duchess's lover and 'while in England, he had sent Wallis Simpson 17 carnations every day', the size of the floral gift supposedly signifying 'the number of times they had slept together.'[2]

After handing over to his younger brother George VI, the Duke's enthusiasm for Hitlerism appeared to grow even stronger, as did his links to fascism. Sir Ronald Lindsay, the British ambassador to the USA, told the State Department in late 1937 that the Duke's supporters had 'inclinations towards Fascist dictatorships' and that 'his friends and advisers are semi-Nazis.'[3] These suspicions were compounded when in October that year the Duke and his new wife made a highly publicised visit to Hitler's retreat at

Berchtesgaden, where they were received with the kind of flattery that was at the time denied to them in England.

When war broke out in 1939, the Duke was given a semi-honorific post as a major general on the British military mission to France, a role that only exacerbated doubts about him and Wallis. There were even suggestions that they were leaking military and political secrets to their pro-German contacts. The intermediary who may have been passing on this information was Charles Bedaux, a wealthy Franco-American businessman whose sixty-room, sixteenth-century chateau in the Loire Valley had been used for the Windsors' wedding in 1937. Close to the Nazis, Bedaux even worked undercover for the Abwehr and in 1944 was arrested for treason by the American military, killing himself in a Miami prison before he could be put on trial.

Despite his military status in wartime, the Duke was all too keen to express his resentment of the British government and its policies. In one extraordinary episode in January 1940, he even appeared willing to contemplate open treachery. On a visit to the London home of his friend and lawyer Sir Walter Monckton, he encountered Lord Beaverbrook, the press tycoon who was not then in political office and was flirting with all kinds of anti-war groupings. According to Monckton's account of this 'frightful' meeting, both Beaverbrook and the Duke 'found themselves in agreement that the war should be ended at once by a peace offer from Germany. The Beaver suggested that the Duke should get out of uniform, come home and after enlisting powerful City support stump the country in which case he predicted the Duke would have a tremendous success.' Afterwards, Monckton pointed out to the Duke privately that such action against the Coalition would represent 'high treason'.[4]

Given the web of intrigue that had long existed around the Duke, it was all too predictable that Anna Wolkoff, arch plotter, Nazi sympathiser and dressmaker to Wallis Simpson, should be linked to an alleged plot involving him and Ribbentrop. The episode, never revealed before, featured bold claims that may have been more a reflection of Wolkoff's conspiratorial, self-aggrandising imagination than any historical reality.

On 16 July 1936, soon after he had ascended to the throne, Edward VIII was on horseback in an official procession going along Constitution Hill in central London when suddenly a stocky man in a brown suit moved forward from the crowd, brandishing a pistol. The potential assailant, who was quickly disarmed, was identified as George Andrew McMahon, an embittered right-wing Irish journalist and petty fraudster who, as a result of his nationalist outlook, harboured a neurotic sense of grievance against the British government. In his defence, McMahon asserted that he had been paid £150 by representatives 'of a foreign power'[5] to kill the King but had only pretended to cooperate with them in order to expose their machinations.

It was almost five years later that Wolkoff, by then behind bars, declared her role in this strange affair. Interviewed by Maxwell Knight at Aylesbury prison in April 1941, she said that in early July 1936 she had dined with Arthur Kitson, a Scots-American inventor, economist and passionate anti-Semite. Kitson had apparently confided during their meal 'that he had received information from the USA that there was to be an attempt on the life of Edward VIII'. He then asked her to use her society connections to get a warning to the King, which she claimed to have done.

Shortly afterwards, having fulfilled her promise, Anna went on a trip to Austria with a society friend. In Knight's narrative, when the pair arrived at their appointed inn near the Austro-German border, the innkeeper 'asked them if they had heard that an attempt had been made on the life of the King. Anna says that she remarked – "So soon!" The innkeeper appeared interested in this remark and [seems] to have reported it to the local Nazi authorities.' As a result, claimed Anna, she was visited that evening by Rudolf Hess and some other Nazi officials, who invited her to dinner after discovering 'that she was very Jew-wise'. Over dinner, they explained that Franz von Papen, the former German Chancellor, was about to be appointed German ambassador to Britain. 'She then lectured the officials on the short-comings of Von Papen,' information that they promised to pass on to the Führer. A few weeks later, it was announced that Ribbentrop would be the new ambassador to Britain. As Knight commented, Wolkoff gave 'the impression that she considered herself to be responsible for the fact that von Papen did not come to London as Ambassador, his place being taken by Ribbentrop'.[6]

When he became Foreign Minister, Ribbentrop wanted to bring the Duke and Duchess under Nazi control, thereby using them as an ally in the Reich's attempt to force Britain out of the war. The German attack on France in May ended the Duke's ineffectual role at the British military mission and prompted his plan to move across the border into neutral Spain, with the idea of eventually returning to England. Ribbentrop saw the immediate appeal of the Windsors' stay in Madrid, where General Franco's pro-German authoritarian regime would allow the Nazis to exercise their influence on the couple. 'We must get hold of him. We must get Franco to detain him,' Ribbentrop told the German embassy in the Spanish capital on 23 June, as soon as he learnt that the Windsors' entourage was about to arrive there.[7]

The British government, on the other hand, were keen to ensure that the Duke came back to Britain as soon as possible. Churchill's sense of urgency was all the greater since this was the very moment at which Butler and Halifax had put out feelers for peace negotiations through the Swedish ambassador, Björn Prytz, precisely the sort of initiative that the Germans hoped that the Windsors could promote.

Once installed with his wife and retinue in the Ritz Hotel in Madrid, the Duke was in no hurry to depart for neutral Lisbon. His resentment towards the British government was stronger than ever, particularly because Churchill, who had been an ally of his during the Abdication crisis, had not offered him any significant position in Britain, nor had the royal family given any indication that he would be welcomed back.

The British ambassador in Spain at this time was Samuel Hoare, a former Cabinet minister who had been one of the leading appeasers of the late 1930s and had a reputation for deviousness, hence his nickname of 'Slippery Sam'. His awkward long-term goal was to uphold British interests in the Mediterranean and Gibraltar while trying to ensuring that Spain was not drawn fully into the embrace of the Axis powers. In the immediate term, his aim was to see that the Duke and Duchess did not openly undermine Churchill's government. Although outwardly affable to Hoare, in private the Duke, still seething about his status, was unreliable, giving hope to the Germans that he could be manipulated if kept in Spain.

The US ambassador to Madrid, Alexander Wendell, was disturbed by some of the Duke and Duchess's opinions of German military strength, which, as Wendell told Washington, might give succour to the anti-war party in England. This kind of alarming talk reached London as well; Sir Alexander Cadogan, the head of the Foreign Office, received a disturbing intelligence report from a source in Prague:

> Germans expect assistance from Duke and Duchess of Windsor, latter desiring at any price to become Queen. Germans have been negotiating with her since June 27th. Status quo in England except undertaking to form anti-Russian alliance. Germans to propose to form Opposition Government under Duke of Windsor, having first changed public opinion by propaganda. Germans think King George will abdicate during attack on London.[8]

Despite his colossal political and military burdens at this time, the prime minister had to focus his mind on how to deal with the Duke, who was now trying to set conditions on his return to England, particularly regarding his royal status. Churchill, infuriated by this continuing prevarication, decided that the Duke, despite his royal pedigree, had to be threatened. 'Your Royal Highness has taken active military rank and refusal to obey direct orders of competent military authority would create a serious situation. I hope it will not be necessary for such orders to be sent.'[9] The prime minister was strongly supported in this uncompromising approach by King

George VI, who expressed the hope that the telegram would have 'a salutary effect'.[10] The Duke reluctantly backed down in the face of the threat of a court martial, agreeing that he and the Duchess would quickly return to Britain without insisting on conditions.

By this time, 3 July, they had left Madrid and arrived in Portugal, where they were accommodated in a luxurious villa at the coastal town of Cascais. Apparently the British embassy in Lisbon had been instructed not to provide them with official hospitality and the grandest hotel in the area, the Palacio at Estoril, said it had neither the space nor the security. The seaside villa and its estate, near the Boca do Inferno (literally, the Jaws of Hell) rock formation at Europe's westernmost point, was owned by Ricardo Espírito do Santo Silva, a rich banker whose wealth, self-confidence, charm and good looks had helped earn him a reputation as a dazzling host and ladykiller. Exploiting his social graces, he cultivated strong connections in both British and German diplomatic circles, although MI6 increasingly regarded him as pro-Nazi.

The Windsors planned to leave Lisbon by flying boat on the evening of 4 July and reach Poole harbour the following day. Then came startling news that dramatically altered their plans. That morning the Duke drove to the British embassy in Lisbon to sort out the final travel arrangements. There he was given a telegram by David Eccles, the British government's senior economic adviser in Spain and Portugal, who also did some undercover intelligence work for the Foreign Office. From the prime minister, it read:

> I am authorised by the King and Cabinet to offer the appointment of Governor and Commander-in-Chief of the Bahamas. If you accept, it may be possible to take you and the Duchess direct from Lisbon dependent on the military situation. Please let me know without delay whether this proposal is satisfactory to your Royal Highness. Personally I feel sure it is the best [offer] open in the grievous situation in which we all stand. At any rate I have done my best.[11]

This offer was remarkable, having neither historical precedent nor constitutional grandeur. If the Duke was to take on such a role, he might at least have expected to serve in one of the great Dominions like Canada or New Zealand, rather than a tiny Crown colony off the coast of Florida, a set of islands whose economy was increasingly dependent on American tourism.

The Duke was initially astonished when he received the Bahamas offer, which appeared to contradict the entire thrust of the government's policy towards him. Only days earlier, Churchill had seemed desperate to have him back in England; now the prime minister was apparently desperate to keep him away.

In his perplexed state, he turned to Eccles. 'What would you advise me to do?'

'I'd take it, sir,' Eccles replied. 'You'll be safe there. You'd get blown up here.'[12]

The offer was accepted on 4 July but the sense of relief in London was only temporary, with the Bahamas appointment soon becoming the cue for a renewed bout of prevarication by the Windsors. Instead of agreeing to a swift departure across the Atlantic, the couple engaged in intense haggling over their travel arrangements, their retinue and their future plans. At one stage, amidst growing exasperation within Churchill's government, the Duke threatened to change his mind and refuse the governorship.

The troubles over the logistics of the Windsors' departure for the Bahamas, which were to waste an inordinate amount of Churchill's time during July and early August, boiled down to two main points: first, the route of the journey itself, and, second, the staff that the Duke wanted to take with him. In keeping with official coldness towards the Windsors, they were told to make their own travel arrangements to the islands. The Duke therefore made reservations for the voyage on an American shipping line via the USA, telegraphing his secretary Major Gray Phillips, 'It is essential we go via New York for Duchess to see specialist.'[13] The government strongly objected to this proposal, fearing the reaction in the USA and concerned not only that the Duke might be indiscreet about the Churchill government, but that he might also be used as a vehicle for anti-British, anti-war propaganda.

At the suggestion of the Colonial Office, the government decided to pay for the Windsors to travel to Bermuda, where they could pick up another steamship on the way to the Bahamas. This scheme merely prompted the Duke to fury, seeing it as further evidence of official hostility towards him and declaring to Churchill on 18 July: 'Strongly urge you to support arrangements I have made otherwise will have to reconsider my position.'[14]

Neither Churchill nor his ministers were in any mood to retreat in the face of such bluster, but now the impasse was compounded by the second difficulty, sparked by the Duke's determination to take to the Bahamas two soldier servants, both of whom were of military age. The Duke wanted the two men, Corporal Webster and Piper Fletcher, to be his chauffeur and valet, but once more the government objected. As the Colonial Secretary, Lord Lloyd, explained to the Duke, 'to take fit and efficient soldiers out of the Army at this juncture would set an unfortunate precedent,' although he promised that he would 'try and send you for this purpose men over military age or otherwise unsuitable for military service.'[15] The Duke remained insistent. Privately, Lloyd told Churchill's office that the Duke 'had to be treated as a petulant baby'[16] and urged him to relent, but the prime minister was adamant, telling the Duke: 'I regret that there can be no question of releasing men from the Army to act as servants to Your Royal Highness. Such a step would be viewed with general disapprobation in times like these, and I should ill serve Your Royal Highness by countenancing it.'[17]

As it dragged on for day after day, the row fuelled the Duke's bitterness towards both the government and the Bahamas posting. What irritated the Windsors even more was the contrast between the hostility of the British and the apparently considerate attitude of the Germans in arranging for all the Windsors' personal belongings and furniture to be sent from their Paris home to the Portuguese villa, using special vehicles, with some of the more valuable items being transported in limousines.

This ostentatious show of concern had, of course, an ulterior motive: to exploit the differences between the Duke and Churchill's government, luring the former king more deeply into the German embrace and drawing him back to Spain rather than allowing him to sail to the Bahamas. The Windsors' departure for Lisbon at the beginning of July had infuriated Ribbentrop, who blamed both Franco and the German embassy in Madrid for failing to keep them in Spain.

However, having calmed down, Ribbentrop sought more subtle methods of trying to entice the Windsors into his web. He began to realise that the intensive wrangling over the Bahamas appointment could actually help the German cause, partly because the Windsors' departure from continental Europe was now significantly delayed, and partly because the couple were still usefully ensconced in the lair of Santo Silva, whose pro-Nazi connections might help to facilitate any anti-British intrigue. The fact that his rambling coastal estate was hard to protect appealed to Ribbentrop as he plotted to bring the Duke and Duchess under the Reich's control, perhaps through persuasion, if necessary by force.

Soon after the announcement of the Bahamas posting, Ribbentrop's eagerness to develop a plot against the Windsors was boosted when, on 11 July, he received a report from the German ambassador in Lisbon, the sophisticated, cosmopolitan Oswald, Baron von Hoyningen-Huene. The Baron told Ribbentrop, with some truth, that the British government had made the appointment with 'the purpose of keeping him away from England since his return would greatly strengthen the position of the English friends of peace'. But according to the Baron, 'the Duke intends to postpone his journey to the Bahamas for as long as possible, and at least until the beginning of August, in the hope of an early change in his favour.'[18]

Ribbentrop's imagination was immediately gripped by this report; here was a real chance to push for a peace settlement. The timing could hardly have been better, with Hitler barely a week away from making his much vaunted Reichstag speech, where he would present Britain with his peace offer.

That same night, Ribbentrop sent an urgent dispatch to the German ambassador in Spain, Eberhard von Stohrer, stating that his central goal was to secure the Duke's return to Spain 'as quickly as possible' and then compel him 'to remain on Spanish soil'. Once there, the Duke 'is to be informed that Germany wants peace with the English people, that the Churchill clique stands in the way of that peace, and that it would be a good thing if the Duke were to hold himself in readiness for further developments', including potentially the assumption of the English throne.

Ribbentrop also raised the possibility that the Duke, given his official status, could be arrested as a British officer under neutrality regulations. A less coercive alternative, he added, might be for the Spanish to suggest to the Duke that his life would be in danger if he took up the Bahamas appointment, perhaps hinting that the 'English secret service' planned 'to do away with him at the first opportunity'.[19]

The German plot, which had Hitler's full approval, now developed quickly. Having received Ribbentrop's instructions, von Stohrer called on the Spanish Interior Minister Ramón Serrano Súñer, a diehard Anglophobe. During their discussion on 12 July, von Stohrer and Don Ramón hatched a scheme whereby a Spanish emissary would visit the Windsors and invite them to return to Spain for a hunting expedition. Once the Windsors had been enticed onto Spanish soil, they would be persuaded to remain by a range of expedients, such as the need for talks with Franco's government about the future of Gibraltar, or supposed intelligence revelations about a lethal threat from the British secret service, or even pure financial bribery.

Despite his anti-British outlook, Don Ramón was not as pro-Nazi as some post-war histories suggested. He regarded the entire plot as 'puerile'[20] and went along with it only because he felt that he could help to maintain Spain's neutrality, his most cherished goal during the war. His lack of faith in the conspiracy was reflected in his acceptance of von Stohrer's choice as emissary: one Miguel Primo de Rivera, an aristocrat whose illustrious pedigree and ambition were matched by neither personal accomplishments nor brains.

Don Miguel took a leisurely approach to his mission, leaving for Portugal on 14 July and not returning until more than a week later, although during this time he also had two long interviews with the Duke, the second in the presence of the Duchess, telling von Stohrer and Don Ramón that both were highly revealing. According to the reports of these conversations that von Stohrer sent to Berlin, the Duke 'had moved further and further away from the King and from the present English Government', with the result that he was 'toying with the idea of disassociating himself from the present tendency of British policy' by 'breaking with his brother', whom he regarded as 'utterly stupid'. The Duke, said Don Miguel, also 'very much desired' to return to Spain and express 'thanks for the offer of hospitality', although as to the idea that he might regain the English Crown 'he seemed astonished', arguing that such an outcome had been made impossible by the Abdication.[21]

For all the positive emphasis he had tried to put on his two conversations, the reality was that Don Miguel's mission had yet to achieve much, for the Windsors had given no absolute commitment to return to Spain. Understandably, however, Churchill's government was deeply concerned about the rumours of a plot that had been picked up by intelligence sources, due partly to Don Miguel's indiscreet tongue. Worryingly, it appeared that 'pressure is building from Berlin for the Duke of Windsor to return to Spain and remain there, pending a decision by Hitler on how to use him after a successful invasion of Britain.'[22]

It was partly in response to such intelligence that Churchill decided that more pressure was urgently needed to get the Windsors out of Europe. On 24 July, he telegraphed the Duke, explaining that 'arrangements have now been made for Your Royal Highness to leave by American Export vessel on 1 August for Bermuda' and to travel from there to Nassau, the capital of the Bahamas. Again Churchill stressed that it would be impossible for the Duke to land 'in the United States at this juncture. This decision must be accepted.' More importantly, the prime minister dropped his objections to the Duke keeping one of his trusted members of staff. 'Sir, I have now succeeded in overcoming the War Office objection to the departure of Fletcher, who will be sent forthwith to join you.'[23]

In reply, the Duke expressed his appreciation to Churchill of 'your successful efforts regarding my soldier servant' but worried that the bar on any visit to the USA might remain in place even after the November presidential elections. 'May I therefore have confirmed that it is not to be the policy of His Majesty's Government that I should not set foot on American soil during my term of office in the Bahamas? Otherwise I could not feel justified in representing the King in a British colony so geographically close to the United States.'[24]

The Duke further showed his reluctance to comply with the British government by suggesting that he might delay his departure from Lisbon by another week. Alarmed that any such delay might widen the potential scope for German intrigue, Churchill again insisted that the Duke leave Lisbon on 1 August, but, anxious to avoid worsening the rift, he promised that there would be no permanent injunction against visits to the USA and that his government was keen 'to fall in with Your Royal Highness's wishes' in future.[25]

Churchill felt that more practical action was needed to hasten the departure of the Duke. On the evening of 26 July, he summoned to Downing Street the Duke's long-serving legal adviser, Sir Walter Monckton KC, a suave, tactful, sharp-witted barrister who was at that time working as a senior official at the Ministry of Information, where one of his many responsibilities was the interrogation of internees held under the Defence Regulations. Because Sir Walter was trusted by both the Duke and the government, the prime minister felt he was the ideal man to carry out a delicate, vital task.

Monckton's mission, as Churchill explained at their meeting, would be to fly urgently to Lisbon, warn the Duke of possible German machinations and ensure that the Windsors sailed as arranged on 1 August. In order to reinforce the importance of their imminent departure, Churchill handed Monckton a letter to be personally delivered to the Duke. Although full of reassuring words, its central point was a frank warning to the Duke about the risks of expressing defeatist sentiments or becoming a pawn of German schemers. In the Bahamas,

> many sharp and unfriendly ears will be pricked up to catch any suggestion that your Royal Highness takes a different view about the war, or about the Germans, or about Hitlerism, which is different from that adopted by the British nation and Parliament. Many malicious tongues will carry tales in every direction. Even while you have been staying in Lisbon, conversations have been reported by telegraph through various channels which might be used to your Royal Highness' disadvantage.

In conclusion, he said, 'we are all passing through times of immense stress and dire peril, and every step must be watched with care.'[26]

The German plot was indeed gathering momentum. Ribbentrop had decided to send a German agent to Portugal with dual aims: of ensuring that the Windsors were brought over the border to Spain; and of countering any attempts by the British secret service to protect the couple. The man he selected for this operation was Walter Schellenberg, a ruthless, young major general in the SS whose astuteness and self-proclaimed understanding of foreign affairs had impressed senior Nazis.

In his memoirs, Schellenberg recalled his interview with Ribbentrop on 24 July in which the Foreign Minister explained the vital importance of the plot. 'We've had word that he has even spoken about living in Spain and that if he did go there he'd be ready to be friends with Germany again as he was before. The Führer thinks this attitude is extremely important and we thought that you, with your Western outlook, might be the most suitable person to make some sort of exploratory contact with the Duke.' Ribbentrop then said that a financial inducement could be offered, perhaps as much as 50 million Swiss francs deposited in a bank account in Switzerland. Alternatively, intimidation could be used against him. 'The Führer attaches the greatest importance to this operation and he has come to the conclusion after serious consideration that if the Duke should prove hesitant, he himself would have no objection to your helping the Duke to reach the right decision by coercion – even by threats or force if the circumstances make it advisable.'

He explained that an ideal opportunity to carry out the plot would shortly arise when the Duke and Duchess were to be persuaded to travel with Spanish friends towards the Portuguese border with Spain for the purposes of a holiday. The Reich Foreign Minister added: 'From that point he can immediately be brought into another country [Spain].'[27]

The next morning, 25 July, Schellenberg left for Madrid by plane on the first leg of what had been code-named Operation Willi.

As soon as he arrived, he went into action. In accordance with Ribbentrop's instructions, his first task was to persuade the Windsors to leave their villa at Boca do Inferno and make the trip towards the Spanish frontier. The chosen method of persuasion was a letter, written by Don Miguel, the Duke's old friend, who decided to use the fiction that the Windsors' lives would be in danger from the British government if they remained in Portugal or travelled to the Bahamas. In his elaborate plan he proposed that 'in a short time' they should travel to the Portuguese village of Guarda on the pretext of undertaking a hunting expedition. 'Guns or fishing apparel' would add authenticity to the deceit. Once in Guarda, their party would be met by the Portuguese captain of the Border Guards, 'who is a man in our complete confidence', and by Don Miguel himself, before being taken across the border to stay at a nearby castle owned by one of his aristocratic friends.[28]

The missive, on which so much depended, was clumsy in tone, crude in its threats and awkward in its English: in fact, more likely to alarm than persuade the Duke. Its delivery was entrusted to a second emissary, a former bullfighter and diehard Falangista turned Abwehr agent, Don Angel Alcazar de Velasco.

As de Velasco headed for the villa at Boca do Inferno, Schellenberg flew to Lisbon to strengthen the web of conspiracy with the help of the Portuguese police. He wanted to ensure that there would be no obstacles placed in the way of the Windsors once they departed for Spain, and also to create a climate of fear around the villa that would add substance to Don Miguel's warnings about the couple's safety. Agents placed on the staff kept the couple under permanent surveillance while spreading dark rumours about the threat from the British secret service. Schellenberg arranged to have stones thrown at the couple's bedroom window one night, after which the Portuguese guard diligently searched the entire villa.

In fact, Schellenberg's efforts to whip up anxiety were almost too successful. Perturbed by these strange occurrences and hints of conspiracies, the Duke and Duchess began to feel like threatened prisoners. On 26 July, they made bookings at the elegant Hotel Aviz in Lisbon, where they planned to spend the remainder of their stay in Portugal. Such a move would have returned them to the hands of the Churchill government, since the hotel was a favoured establishment of the British secret service. Through his contacts, Schellenberg quickly organised a visit to the couple at the villa by a senior Portuguese police officer, who told them that the Hotel Aviz was too dangerous. More apprehensive than ever, they agreed to remain where they were. The plot, it seemed, remained on track.

However, from 28 July, Operation Willi began to unravel. For all the Duke's sense of grievance, he was by no means ready to engage in open defiance or treachery, as was made clear by his reaction when he read Don Miguel's badly constructed letter. Instead of embracing the chance of finding Spanish sanctuary, he seemed merely perplexed, re-reading the letter three times. Even when Alcazar, the Abwehr agent, tried to reinforce the point about the invented threat from the British secret service, the Duke looked thoughtful, even puzzled. Refusing to give any immediate answer, he told Alcazar to come back in forty-eight hours for his reply.

The next blow came that evening, when Sir Walter Monckton reached the villa after his flight from London. He arrived at a highly opportune moment, for his warnings about a German plot against the couple, backed up by Churchill's letter with its language about a time of 'dire peril', appeared to be substantiated by Alcazar's visit and other recent incidents at the villa. That night at dinner, Sir Walter expanded on this theme, as the Duchess recorded in her memoirs, telling them, 'Winston is convinced that Hitler is crazy enough to be tempted, in the event of a successful invasion of Britain, to try to put the Duke back on the throne in the belief that this would divide and confuse people and weaken their will to resist further.'[29] With that, any last objections and prevarications from the Windsors evaporated. Shaken by this advice, they agreed to travel to the Bahamas as arranged on 1 August.

Schellenberg, through his spy network at the villa, could sense that

Operation Willi was suddenly collapsing. The situation was now desperate for the Germans, particularly as the Duke confirmed the next day, 30 July, to the emissary Alcazar that he and his wife would be travelling to the Bahamas by sea rather than to Guarda by land. As he explained to Alcazar, abandoning all his defeatism of previous months, 'the situation in England was still by no means hopeless' and 'no prospect of peace existed at the moment.'[30] Schellenberg soon conveyed this grim news to Berlin. The astonishing reply that Schellenberg claimed to have received that night from Ribbentrop revealed how frantic the Nazis had become in their determination to entrap the Duke: 'The Führer orders that an abduction is to be organised at once.'[31]

To Schellenberg, such a step seemed ridiculous. For a start, it would be difficult to carry out, particularly as he had no idea how powerful the British secret services were in Portugal. Just as importantly, it would be counter-productive, since the Duke would be unlikely to cooperate with the Germans if he were held against his will. However, Schellenberg could not simply give up or disobey Berlin's orders, so he organised a number of scare measures designed to intimidate the Windsors into delaying or abandoning their voyage. These included: sending flowers to the Duchess with an anonymous note warning that she and her husband were in danger; giving the Duke a list of Jews and emigrants sailing on the ship, with the implication that he might be targeted by troublemakers; spreading a rumour that a bomb had been placed on board; and sabotaging a motor car that was to carry some of their luggage. But it was all too late. Emboldened by Monckton, the Windsors had made up their minds to leave.

At the eleventh hour, Ribbentrop abandoned any attempt to conceal Germany's central role in the plot, deciding instead to make an indirect plea to the Duke through Santo Silva, the pro-Nazi banker and owner of the Boca do Inferno villa. Santo Silva was instructed to tell the Duke that 'following the rejection of the Führer's final appeal to reason, Germany is determined to compete with England by every means in her power. It would be a good thing if the Duke were to hold himself in readiness for further developments.'[32]

According to the report of the German ambassador in Portugal, Baron von Hoyningen-Huene, when Santo Silva gave him this message the Duke again displayed some of his pro-German instincts, declaring that if he had been king 'it would never have come to war' and concluding with 'an expression of admiration' for the Führer, a disturbing remark if true, given that the Battle of Britain was about to begin and the invasion barges were being assembled on the French coast.[33] Nonetheless, such reported warmth towards the Germans did not prevent the Duke from rejecting their overtures.

Warm words were of no use to Ribbentrop. Operation Willi had ended in failure. At 6.40 p.m. on 1 August, the American liner left the port of Lisbon with the Windsors on board. As Sir Walford Selby, the British ambassador in Portugal, told London on 2 August, with obvious relief: 'Duke and Duchess sailed last night.'[34] They arrived in the Bahamas unscathed on 15 August, with the Duke officially taking up the governorship two days later, remaining there for the duration of the war.

For Churchill, the hero of the hour was Sir Walter Monckton, whose influence had been crucial at the darkest moment. 'It was very lucky you were on the spot to dissipate strange suspicions,' he wrote to Sir Walter once the Duke was halfway across the Atlantic.[35] Those suspicions had been all too real.

20

'The days are numbered for those bums over in England'

—

Like the sinking of the French fleet at Oran and the dismissal of Hitler's Reichstag speech, the failure of Operation Willi represented another setback to the Reich's hopes of persuading the British government to abandon the war. Furthermore, many leading Nazis seemed half-hearted about Operation Sea Lion. 'Can it be that the Germans are bluffing about their invasion of Britain?' asked the American journalist William Shirer, soon after the Reichstag speech. Having visited the Channel area, he found plenty of defensive measures, like dugouts and machine-gun nests, but he 'did not see any evidence at any place along the coast of German preparations for an invasion'.[1]

From the end of July, the attitude of the German High Command became much more serious, cohesive and determined. In August 1940, the Luftwaffe began its full onslaught against the RAF in the epic struggle that became known to history as the Battle of Britain. Goering had promised that, within just four weeks, Fighter Command would be finished.

He had ostentatiously remained aloof from Sea Lion, feeling that the enterprise was unnecessary since the swift destruction of Britain's air defences would force the British government to surrender without any landings. At one point, as the invasion planning approached its peak, the Wehrmacht's staff war diary spelt out Goering's detachment explicitly: 'The Reichsmarschall is not interested in the preparations for Operation Sea Lion as he does not believe the operation will ever take place.'[2] The Luftwaffe leading officer Albert Kesselring experienced this indifference at first hand during the Battle of Britain, as he recalled in his memoirs:

> In contrast to our preparations for previous campaigns, there was not one conference within the Luftwaffe at which details were discussed with group commanders and other services, let alone with the High Command or Hitler himself . . . I was left in the dark about the relation of the current air raids on England and the invasion plan; no orders were issued to the Chiefs of Air Commands; no definitive instructions were given about what my air

fleet had to expect in the way of tactical assignments or what provision had been made for co-operation with the army or navy.[3]

Yet this was not as big a hindrance as might have been supposed, for the negation of the RAF's defensive shield around southern England had always been one of the perquisites of Sea Lion. Almost every directive or planning document since June had stressed that the achievement of air superiority was a necessary condition before an invasion could be launched. Indeed, Hitler's own famous Directive No. 16, issued in mid-July, ordering the start of detailed planning for Sea Lion, stated as its first priority that 'the English Air Force must be beaten physically and morally to a point that they cannot put up any show of attacking force worth mentioning.'[4]

He went on to stipulate that the preparations for 'the entire operation must be completed by the middle of August'.[5] Given Germany's lack of invasion vessels and the Kriegsmarine's overall inferiority compared to the Royal Navy, that was an absurdly unrealistic target. In comparison, Operation Overlord, the Allied invasion of northern France, took two years of comprehensive planning, rehearsal and organisation. The Kriegsmarine made clear its opposition to what it perceived as a fantastic timetable, the pressure only adding to its hostility to the whole invasion scheme.

In its response to Directive No. 16, the army had on 25 July set out its detailed requirement for transport across the English Channel if it were to successfully mount the invasion. This consisted of 90,000 men in the first wave, supported by 650 tanks and 4,500 horses, and 170,000 men with equipment in the second wave, backed up by no fewer than 57,500 horses and 34,200 vehicles. According to the army's analysis, the transport of these two large waves of men and equipment, making up thirteen landing divisions, would entail the use of 1,722 barges, 471 tugs, 1,161 motorboats and 155 ships, with the attack to take place along the English coast between Ramsgate in Kent and Lyme Bay in Dorset.

In a gloomy response, the operations division of Raeder's naval staff set out a litany of objections, starting with the key point that, given the state of the naval preparations and the current rate of progress, Sea Lion 'could not be carried out before the 15th September'. The navy further pointed out that, because the army High Command wanted the landing to take place at dawn, two hours before high water, the crossing would be carried out 'mainly during darkness' when it would be 'difficult to move and manoeuvre' unless there were at least a half-moon. Practically, that limited the options to only a few days in late September, a time of year when favourable weather 'cannot be guaranteed'.

In addition, there was the severe threat from the Royal Navy. 'In view of the weakness of our naval forces, the enemy's penetration into the area of transports cannot be effectively prevented, because of the size of the crossing area and in spite of flanking minefields and our own air superiority.' The Kriegsmarine also warned that the crossing would take far longer than the army envisaged: 'With the available shipping space, the minimum interval between the first and second waves will be 48 hours. The transportation of the second wave will finish 8 to 10 days later at the earliest.' Accordingly, the operational staff concluded, 'it must recommend the postponement of the operation until next year.'[6]

Flushed with triumph at their string of victories across continental Europe, the German army was at this stage eager for the assault, challenging the very idea of postponement. On 30 July, Halder sent Colonel Hans von Greiffenberg, the chief of the army's operations branch, to meet the senior naval staff, but the negative message was only reinforced. The navy told Greiffenberg that the preparations for Sea Lion 'cannot under any circumstances be ready before 15 September', while 'speedier construction of landing craft is impossible'. Further adding to the catalogue of woe, the navy said that the 'towing vessel situation is bad'; the 'operation cannot be protected against the British navy'; tide mines were 'not yet available in sufficient quantities'; and that the front for the proposed crossing was too wide, especially because the Isle of Wight, Portsmouth and Ramsgate were all considered 'unsuited' or 'unpromising' for landings.[7]

That night, on Greiffenberg's return to headquarters, Halder ruminated despondently in his diary:

> The navy in all probability will not provide us this fall with the means of a successful invasion of Britain. If the navy holds that it cannot, before mid-September, give us these ships which it believed to be able to get together, there remain only two possibilities for us: postpone the invasion to the bad weather period, which might bring us some local advantages for our landings, but on the whole would be detrimental to our effort; or else wait until the spring of 1941.

However, with a greater grasp of the long-term military reality than Raeder had shown, Halder saw that a postponement to 1941 might work against Germany's interests. 'Our position in relation to Britain would not be improved by the delay. The British could strengthen their defences, augment their armaments, and increase their air strength. America might become effective.'[8]

Despite Halder's moment of despair, all hope had not been lost that the invasion would be mounted. The Kriegsmarine's negativity could be overcome. Raeder's voice was just one among several at the top of the German armed forces. With Goering so detached, the grand admiral was outnumbered by the OKH (the German army's High Command) and the OKW (the Supreme Command of the Armed Forces). Furthermore Hitler, for all his hesitations about Sea Lion, was not opposed to the assault and, with his distrust of the sea, was always more likely to favour the army over the navy. Even more importantly, the plan to invade Britain had been given greater urgency by his growing conviction that he would soon have to direct his forces to another theatre entirely.

It was during a visit to see Wagner's apocalyptic opera *Götterdämmerung* at Bayreuth that the Führer came to the conclusion that Russia must be subjugated, soon afterwards telling the army to draw up plans for an attack in the spring of 1941. The decision had heavy implications for Sea Lion. It could have meant that Hitler, in his focus on the East, would lose interest in the British invasion, while there was also the long-term strategic argument that the defeat of Russia would make Churchill's position untenable and finally bring about a British surrender, thereby rendering Sea Lion an irrelevance. On the other hand, the looming attack on Russia strengthened the imperative to finish off British resistance as quickly as possible, certainly before the end of the year, since the Reich would not want to fight on two fronts and divide its military resources.

A key step towards the implementation of Operation Sea Lion was taken at a crucial conference held on 31 July. Chaired by the Führer and attended by most of the armed forces chiefs, except, inevitably, Goering, this meeting was dominated by a discussion of the Reich's strategy concerning Britain. Raeder told his fellow commanders that the naval preparations were now under way, particularly on the programme for converting barges into troop transports, but once more he urged a postponement in the invasion until at least May or June 1941, again referring to the limited size of his force, the risk of poor weather and the difficulty in providing protection across a broad coastal front against the might of the Royal Navy.

Hitler and the other commanders refused to accept Raeder's case, maintaining that the dangers of a long postponement into the following year were too great. 'The British army is now weak, but in eight months it could be reconstituted,' warned the Führer.[9] The one concession he made to Raeder was his acceptance that the invasion could not be launched until 15 September at the very earliest, since the preparations would not have been completed until then. This date was to hang over all discussions about Sea Lion, not only in Germany but even in Britain, once it was picked up by Bletchley Park and other forms of intelligence.

The meeting ended with Hitler setting out the strategy towards Britain over the coming weeks in the build-up to Sea Lion. The all-out air war against the RAF would begin shortly, while the development of the transport fleet would continue. If the outcome of the Luftwaffe's offensive were unsatisfactory, then the invasion preparations would be halted. However, if the British were beaten in the air, Hitler said, 'we shall attack.'[10] This approach was clearly spelt out in two documents issued immediately after the conference, one from Hitler, the other from Keitel.

The former was the Führer's Directive No. 17, dated 1 August 1940, which stated: 'For the prosecution of the air and sea war against England, I have decided to carry on and intensify air and naval warfare against England to bring about her final defeat.' For this purpose, the Luftwaffe 'with all available forces will destroy the English air force as soon as possible. The attacks will be directed first against airborne aircraft, their ground and supply organisation and then against industry, including the manufacture of anti-aircraft equipment.' The intensification of the air war was to start from 5 August, but it was for Goering to choose the exact time. Because of the requirements of Sea Lion, the southern ports of England were largely to be spared. 'In view of our own intended operations, attacks on harbours on the south coast will be kept to a minimum.'[11]

In his instructions, issued the same day, Keitel wrote that 'preparations for Seelöwe [Sea Lion] will be continued and will cease on 15 September for the Army as well as the Air Force. Eight or at the most fourteen days after the launch of the air offensive against Britain, scheduled to begin on approximately 5 August, the Führer will decide whether the invasion will take place this year or not. His decision will largely depend on the outcome of the air offensive.'[12]

Although Sea Lion had been approved, one vital issue still had not been resolved at the Führer's conference: the question of whether the invasion would take place along a narrow or a broad front. The navy, understandably, wanted as thin a corridor as possible to maximise the protection they could provide on either flank. The army took the opposite view, believing that a narrow front would enable Britain to concentrate her firepower, whereas a number of landings across a wide area would force the British to dissipate their naval and land defences. Hitler and the Wehrmacht High Command largely took the army's side, although the navy still fiercely objected, saying that this policy would lead to a massacre of the assault troops before they even reached land.

In an attempt to reach a settlement, Halder met Schniewind of the naval staff on 7 August. Far from promoting a compromise, their encounter only degenerated into a slanging match. At one stage Halder exploded with rage at the idea of a narrow front. 'I might just as well put the troops that have landed through the meat grinder straight away,' he yelled, though this was a rather melodramatic statement.[13] The front that the navy proposed between Folkestone and Beachy Head was roughly 45 miles wide, much the same width as the landing area used by the Allies in Normandy during Operation Overlord. No agreement could be reached, and both sides left it for the Führer to decide. That night, Halder wrote in his diary that the conference had succeeded only 'in confirming the existence of irreconcilable differences between us. Navy maintains that landing is possible only on the narrowest frontage . . . and feels confident of being able to assure a continuous shuttle service to the lodgement. However, this would be too narrow a front for us, all the more so as it leads into a terrain that offers unacceptable obstacles to any swift advance.' Halder further expressed his frustration at the elongated timetable proposed by the navy. 'In view of the limited transport resources, completion of the cross-Channel operation on a broader frontage would take 42 days, which is utterly prohibitive for us. Our views are diametrically opposed on that point.'[14]

Despite the impasse over geography and timetables, the Kriegsmarine proved highly cooperative in other ways. Although weighed down by his concerns and his scepticism, Raeder was determined to fulfil his orders by having the invasion fleet ready for the assault by 15 September. Indeed, the energy that the German army and navy showed during these weeks destroys the myth that the Reich was never serious about the invasion. The creation of a large amphibious assault force at the Channel ports was a mammoth feat of logistics, construction and organisation.

Given that at least 260,000 troops would be involved in the opening waves of Operation Sea Lion, the preparations entailed a large range of tasks along the coast. Billets and camps had to be set up for the soldiers and sailors. Administrative headquarters, communications bases, supply depots and liaison units had to be established in every port from Rotterdam to Le Havre. Harbours that would be used for embarkation had to be cleared of all obstructions; in Dunkirk this was a major job, since 177 vessels, including some large steamers, had sunk there during the Battle of France. Considerable salvage work also had to be done at Dieppe further to the west. In addition, loading bridges had to be installed, mines cleared and lock gates repaired at all the places.

The Kriegsmarine was also responsible for laying minefields around the southern English coast to hamper the Royal Navy's counter-attacks. It was a task for which Raeder's force already had massive experience, having laid a series of minefields off the east coast in the early months of the war, inflicting heavy losses on the British. In connection with Operation Sea Lion there were four principal German minefields: one, code-named Dora, off the south-western coast, aimed at impeding Royal Navy vessels operating from Plymouth; another, named Anton, was laid roughly between Brighton and Dieppe; and two others, called Bruno and Caesar, lay further east across the Dover Straits.

They were by no means impregnable. For a start, magnetic mines, in which the Germans had placed great hopes at the start of the war, were increasingly ineffective because of degaussing techniques, while there was only a small supply of acoustic mines, which were triggered by the sound of the ship's propellers. The Kriegsmarine therefore had largely to rely on the moored contact mine, which detonated when a ship bumped into it. Such mines were easy to lay, but they were also vulnerable to the vagaries of strong tidal movements: at high tide they tended to lie too deep in the water, and at low tide they were easily visible on the surface. Moreover, they could easily be ripped away in strong currents, while the very act of laying them gave the British an indication of the planned invasion route.

Just as importantly, the Royal Navy, after suffering severe damage in the early months of the war, had developed a highly efficient minesweeping force. In September 1940, the British had no fewer than 698 minesweepers. One telling indicator of the ineffectiveness of the German mine barriers was the fact that, even after they had been laid, more than 1 million tons of Allied shipping was passing through the Channel every week.

By far the most onerous burden on the Kriegsmarine was the assembly of the invasion fleet, which the navy estimated would have to comprise more than 3,700 vessels. Around 24,000 men, in addition to the sailors of the Kriegsmarine, would be required to operate this fleet. Because of the urgency of Sea Lion, not all of these recruits were suitable for the operation, lacking the necessary background or training.

These limitations lent a makeshift nature to much of the invasion fleet. Apart from the 2,300 barges and around 1,200 motorboats, the bulk of the transports for troops, supplies, heavy equipment and horses was made up of 170 large ships, most of them former freighters, steamers or passenger liners. On average each large steamer could carry about 900 men, 60 horses, 90 motorbikes, 35 lorries and 5 anti-tank guns.

The transport of the bulk of the troops was a daunting problem. The huge number of barges was needed because, unlike the Allies at D-Day in 1944, the Germans had no proper, custom-built landing craft, nor did they have time to make any by the deadline of 15 September. Before Sea Lion was initially agreed, the Kriegsmarine had been working on the development of the Pionierlandungsboot 39, a self-propelled assault boat with a simple wooden hull that could carry forty-five troops and run up a beach at speed. Although 1,500 had been ordered, the first two prototypes were not delivered until late September, far too late to play any role in Sea Lion.

The navy therefore had to turn to the commercial fleet that carried freight on the waterways of Germany and some of the occupied nations. These flat-bottomed craft, known by the Czech term of *prahme*, were integral to the economies of northern Europe, shifting everything from timber to coal. Now, in the Kriegsmarine's hour of need, they were to be used for naval purposes, despite having never been designed for travel across the sea.

Altogether 2,318 barges or *prahme* were requisitioned for Sea Lion and they fell into two main types. First, there was the smaller Peniche, 38.5 metres long and capable of lifting a maximum of 360 tonnes. Known to the Kriegsmarine as Type A1, the Peniches were the most common barge in the fleet, with 1,336 of them pressed into service. Type A2 was made up of the larger Kampine, which had a capacity of up to 620 tons and a length of 50 metres. By mid-September, 982 Kampinen had been commandeered by the navy.

Even before the Peniches and Kampinen could go into action, they required significant conversion work, especially to carry tanks. So diagonal braces were fitted to strengthen the holds, the wheelhouses were cropped and a layer of concrete was laid on the floors. An exit was created by removing the pointed bow and installing a hinged wooden bulwark that could be lowered. Many were also fitted with a 7.5-cm gun, howitzers, anti-tank guns and, in some cases, even field guns.

The most difficult step turned out to be the creation of an effective external ramp for the unloading of troops, horses or tanks. Initially, the Kriegsmarine tried a simple ramp made of planks of wood laid horizontally on two beams. When that proved too awkward and time-consuming in practice, track supports were produced, which could be slotted into a U-shaped bracket in the bow, although these remained stable only if the barge were firmly aground.

The flat-bottomed design of the barges, suitable for rivers and canals rather than the open sea, meant that most of the troops would have had a physically arduous crossing, as the vessels 'had no stability in water and tossed about in a sickening motion even in the most moderate of seas,' according to Alexander Hoffer, a rifleman in a mountain regiment who was to take part in the first wave.[15]

However, the Kriegsmarine had no alternative to the *prahme*. As the conversions began, a small number of other, specialised types of barges were developed. One was the Type B, of which seventy were built by September, to be used for the unloading of submersible tanks at a significant distance from the shoreline. The Type C barge was adapted for the Panzer II or Schwimmpanzer amphibious tank, whose floats made it too wide to go down the ramps of the other *prahme*. A large hatch was cut out of its stern, enabling the Panzer IIs to drive directly into the deep water. Four Schwimmpanzers could be accommodated in the holds of these craft, of which seventeen were converted for Sea Lion.

There was also the Type AS, to be used by the advance infantry detachments. This had its sides reinforced with concrete and featured wooden slides fitted to its hull to carry ten small, fast assault boats. By the middle of August, eighteen Type AS barges had been produced. Finally there was the Type AF, pioneered by the Luftwaffe, which had two redundant BMW aircraft engines mounted on a platform at the rear of vessel, with the coolant stored in tanks mounted above deck. Despite its unorthodox twin power plants, the Type AF was inefficient and could travel at only 6 knots, although the Wehrmacht's desperation for transport meant that 128 of them had gone into service by the end of September.

Of the *prahme* that were requisitioned, only 800 were motorised, and even those that were self-propelled did not have enough power to make it across the Channel. The Kriegsmarine therefore needed a large fleet of tugs. Eventually, by mid-September, around 280 seagoing tugs were rounded up from the German coastal ports, plus another 140 from the occupied countries. It was planned that many of those in the first wave of the invasion would also carry lightly armed troops, so they were fitted with between one and four assault boats. The standard method was for each tug to pull two barges, one of which would be unpowered with a motorised one following astern. These units of three were called 'tows', and would generally have been 300 to 500 metres long. Six such tows with Type-A *prahme*, capable of carrying a reinforced infantry battalion, would form a single group under the command of a naval officer whose task was to keep the flotilla together, being issued with a high-speed boat, fitted with navigation and radio equipment, for this purpose. As they began to cross the Channel, the tow groups would come together in bigger columns, each called a *Schleppverband*, up to four abreast.

The theoretical procedure for the invasion force, on its arrival at the English coast, was for advanced troop detachments to head for the beaches in *Sturmboote* or motorboats launched from minelayers and trawlers. Then came the specialised barges with their submersible and amphibious tanks to provide close support. After this the main body of the *prahme* would arrive. Having been released from the tugs, the motorised barges would advance onto the beaches. The unpowered barges, having been taken to within 20 metres of the shore, would then have to drop anchor and wait for the water level to drop as the tide receded before they could be unloaded, another indicator of the transport fleet's makeshift nature.

Admiral Theodor Krancke, who like many Kriegsmarine officers was deeply sceptical about Sea Lion, felt that much of the planning for the operation was based on fantasy.

> Since a squadron of eight battleships with well-trained crews requires considerable training before learning to navigate in formation by night without navigation lights and to keep station, it was mere wish-fulfilment to contemplate crossing the Channel in any sort of order with this congeries of barges and small craft. Even in the most favourable weather conditions and without any enemy interference, this huge procession would have dispersed in a few minutes and lost all cohesion.[16]

An official report into the invasion fleet, written in November 1940, found that 'many of the powerful barges were faulty and the crews were not familiar with the equipment. Crew discipline aboard the large vessels such as steamers and trawlers was bad.'[17] From an army perspective, Gerd von Rundstedt, the head of Army Group A, was just as scathing, as he stated in an interview with the writer Milton Shulman in October 1945.

> The proposed invasion of England was nonsense, because adequate ships were not available. They were chiefly barges which had to be brought from Germany and the Netherlands. Then they had to be reconstructed so that tanks and other equipment could be driven out of the bows. Then the troops had to learn to embark and disembark. We looked upon the whole thing as a sort of game, because it was obvious that no invasion was possible when our Navy was not in a position to cover a crossing of the channel or carry reinforcements. Nor was the German Air Force capable of taking on these functions if the navy failed. I was always very sceptical about the whole affair.[18]

Some of these doubts were confirmed by the few rehearsals that were conducted in the build-up to Sea Lion. In mid-August, there was an exercise held off Boulogne in France with a full Schleppverband, including more than fifty tugs, barges, steamers and motorboats. Among the spectators watching from the shore were the leading generals von Brauchitsch, the supreme commander of the army, and Adolf Strauss, the head of the 9th Army in France. The spectacle can hardly have reassured them. Because of fears of collisions, the naval officers let the gaps between the vessels become far too wide, which, in a real invasion, would not only have made it impossible to provide protection to the *prahme* but would have meant the beach landings would have become too scattered. Moreover, the soldiers on the barges tended to gather at the bows, obstructing the crews operating the tow lines, while, due to misjudgements, several of the motorboats dumped their troops in the water before reaching the shore.

The whole rehearsal struck Admiral Krancke as an 'undeniable fiasco':

The barges did not come far enough up the beach, the troops had to go into the water up to their breasts, and reached the shore soaked through and in completely broken order. Guns, ammunition, and transport reached dry land only after a long struggle, if at all. The defence could have easily wiped out the entire landing force with a few machine guns. Artificial smoke, which might have shielded the attackers from observation, was used in all manner of ways, but proved useless since it simultaneously prevented any general view of the unloading and increased the confusion still more.[19]

Towards the end of September, at a trial in Ostend, a large steamer took nearly fourteen hours to offload its cargo, which included 30 trucks, 25 motor cars, 700 troops and 200 tons of supplies, all taking place in calm seas without any enemy action.

Despite all these obvious difficulties, the Germans pressed on with the preparations throughout August and early September. As the barges were brought up from Holland, Germany and the Seine, they began to fill the Channel ports. It was an impressive sight, as one harbour commander recalled: 'I walked for miles from prahm to prahm; a patch of water was hard to find.'[20]

The work of converting all these vessels was a huge burden on Germany's economy. According to a Kriegsmarine paper of 26 July, the creation of the invasion fleet required 30,000 tons of iron and steel, 40,000 cubic metres of lumber and 75,000 cubic metres of concrete. The German cable industry provided 1,000 sets of towing equipment, while 7,000 German engineers working full-time were needed for the job of cutting out the bows and installing the supports on the *prahme*. A glimpse into these industrial demands is shown by the single example of the Troop Transport Depot at Frauendorf in eastern Germany, where the list of equipment sought by the depot for Sea Lion work included 50,000 life jackets, 4,000 horse stalls, 200 washstands, 4,000 paddles, 100 cranes for loading motor vehicles, 100 toilets and 1,000 tons of straw for sacks.

It was not only *prahme* and steamers that needed to be adapted for Sea Lion. A fleet of auxiliary sailing coasters were to be used for shipping land army units across the Channel, the bulk of them made up of 200 motor fishing vessels. Because they did not have flat bottoms, they could not be run aground on the beaches like the barges, and it proved impossible to make ramps for them that were long enough to reach the shore, so special lifting equipment had to be installed.

To make up for the lack of naval firepower and cover in the landing zones, the Kriegsmarine fitted a number of coasters with 15-cm guns. It was planned to have twenty of these vessels but in fact only five went into service, partly because they were so primitive; on each of them, no less than 120 tons of sand ballast was needed to compensate for the weight of the gun on deck. In addition, there were twenty-seven light auxiliary gunboats, which had been converted in makeshift fashion in the naval yard at Wilhelmshaven, with each requiring 40 to 60 tons of ballast.

On a more defensive level, the Kriegsmarine also took a number of fire-fighting vessels from the Reich's emergency services, while fifteen medical support ships, fitted with degaussing coils and bow protection gear, were also brought into the fleet. Interestingly, when Germany tried to register these vessels with the Red Cross under the Geneva Convention, the British government objected, declaring that they were 'unable to recognise these ships as hospital ships, since due to their small size, they did not have the necessary facilities to transport and treat the wounded'.[21]

In another aspect of its unending conflict with the Kriegsmarine, the army, understandably, considered many of these arrangements inadequate. Far more transports would be needed to haul the invasion force across the Channel. In an atmosphere of controlled desperation, General Alfred Jacob, head of the army's corps of engineers, sent out instructions in July 1940 that seagoing ferries were to be constructed from 'any available auxiliary and bridging equipment'.[22] It was an order that led to some extraordinary improvisation within the army, although many of the subsequent vessels were wholly impractical. As one army officer recalled, 'anything and everything which could float was commandeered.'[23]

The flotilla of unorthodoxy was made up of rafts constructed from wooden planks, fitted with outboard engines and given buoyancy through the use of empty fuel tanks, wine barrels, petrol drums and kapok-filled floats covered in sailcloth, none of which made the vessels very suitable for crossing the Channel. However, one initiative was far more successful: the development of a solid, seaworthy ferry by the Luftwaffe's aircraft designer Fritz Siebel, who had become intrigued by the concept of transporting troops and equipment across the Channel.

Siebel's fertile mind produced a concept more ambitious than a mere raft. At this time there were two types of closed pontoon in the German military. One was the Herbert bridge, named after its designer Hans Herbert. The army's High Command came up with the idea of attaching two Herbert bridges together to form a large catamaran, powered by three Ford truck engines and spanned by a wooden deck large enough to accommodate troops, vehicles and guns. Given that there were sixty Herbert pontoons in service, this ferry could quickly be made available within the Sea Lion timescale, but it proved to be unstable, barely seaworthy and dangerous. In fact the trials of the prototype led to several fatalities.

However, the second type of closed pontoon in German service was more promising as the potential basis for a ferry, as Siebel recognised. This was the Schwere Schiffsbrücke, or Heavy Pontoon Bridge, of which the Reich had 364. Undaunted by the failure of the Herbert bridge, Colonel Siebel developed an effective design that took two Heavy Pontoons, placed them 6 metres apart and connected them with a number of steel cross-beams, on which was placed a large metal platform covered with wooden planking. Propulsion was provided by four Ford V8 truck engines, linked to marine propellers and mounted in two pairs at the rear of the ferry, with additional power coming from three BMW aircraft engines installed behind the Ford quartet.

When Siebel first demonstrated the prototype on Rangsdorf lake in eastern Germany, the response of the army was unenthusiastic. 'Nothing new, may not stand up in the surf,' wrote Halder.[24] But Siebel soon modified the design, significantly improving speed, manoeuvrability and reliability, with the vessel reaching 8 knots in subsequent tests. When equipped by the Luftwaffe with several flak weapons, the Siebel ferry turned out to be an extremely stable platform and orders were given for production to go ahead. By late September, twenty-five were in service, ready to be used in Sea Lion in two separate flotillas, one assigned to Ernst Busch's 16th Army, the other to Adolf Strauss's 9th Army, with the aim of providing flak cover and transporting equipment. The Luftwaffe was so impressed with the design that, long after 1940, it kept on producing them.

The army, like the navy, had to introduce new or improvised equipment. One army weapon that would have made its first appearance in action on the English beaches was the Pak 38 anti-tank gun, which arrived in service in mid-1940. With its 50-mm calibre, it was more powerful than the standard German anti-tank gun, the 37-mm Pak 36, and would have been the sole weapon of its type capable of consistently penetrating the armour of the British Matilda II tank, although it would have been used only by the elite units in the infantry.

Less sophisticated was the planned use of captured French armoured tractors to haul supplies off the beaches. After the fall of France, the Germans had seized about 3,000 Renault UE Chenillettes, a small but efficient carrier that had been under production since 1932 and could pull about 1,000 kilograms. Bigger but available in much smaller quantities was another French tractor, the Lorraine 37L, which could pull up to 1.5 tonnes. Only thirty of the Lorraines were in German hands, but together with the Renaults they would have significantly reduced the Wehrmacht's reliance on horses in the first wave.

The German army had to attend to a host of other details in planning, like the organisation of rations for the men in the vanguard. These rations, wrapped in waterproof packs, were to last no more than two weeks, with the invaders expected to live off the land in British territory as far as possible to minimise the pressure on supply lines. Room in the invasion fleet also had to be found for seventy-two dogs that would act as guards for the army snipers.

The Germans had pioneered the use of paratroopers in their attacks on Scandinavia and Western Europe earlier in 1940, and the Fallschirmjäger, to use their German name, had become a potent symbol of all-conquering Nazi aggression. However, the threat they posed had been greatly exaggerated. The Fallschirmjäger, who made up the 7th Air Division under the dynamic leadership of Kurt Student, had actually struggled to seize some of their designated targets in the Low Countries. The division (whose original name was later changed in 1943 to 1st Parachute Division) was also short of men and transports. With a total force of 4,500 in May 1940, it was only a third of the strength that the Luftwaffe had envisaged when the division was first established in 1938.

Nor did it have the aircraft to fly the airborne forces across the Channel. In July 1940, when Directive No. 16 was issued, the Luftwaffe had no more than 262 lumbering Junkers 52s, its fleet of transports having been mauled during the Battle of France. Given that each Ju52 could carry a total of twelve paratroopers, that meant, realistically, the planes could transport a force of just 3,000 men during the first wave of Sea Lion.

The Luftwaffe also had an assault glider, the DFS 230, which had been developed in 1933 and seen action in Holland. Its great drawbacks were that it had to be towed by a Ju52 and could carry only nine men. Nor did the Reich have the troops for a full airborne assault. Indeed, in total, Germany could muster no more than 7,000 paratroopers in September 1940, compared to the 23,000 American, British and Canadian paratroopers who landed in northern France during Operation Overlord. Despite these limitations, the final plans for Sea Lion gave the 7th Flieger Division the vital task of securing the Military Canal near the south coast of Kent, as well as Lympne airfield and the flanks to the west of Folkestone.

The paratrooper division was among the best of the German armed forces, but even its elite status was eclipsed by the Brandenburg Regiment, the highly secretive, well-trained special unit that had been founded in October 1939 by Admiral Wilhelm Canaris, the head of the Abwehr, to carry out commando and sabotage operations. The regiment bore some resemblance to the renowned British special force the SAS in its focus on daring, clandestine warfare behind enemy lines. Its members were recruited not just for their resourcefulness and physical fitness but also for their linguistic aptitude. Their ability to speak English made many of the leading Brandenburgers invaluable for Sea Lion, for which they were to don British army or Home Guard uniforms in order to heighten the confusion among the defence forces.

In one of the Brandenburg's proposed strikes, 120 men from its 11 Company, which was based in Dieppe and was given the code name of Pionierbataillon 909, were to land near Eastbourne, wearing British uniforms and equipped with light motorcycles and short-wave radio equipment capable of transmitting long distances. They were then to penetrate inland and, with an assault from the rear, take out the heavy British gun batteries at Beachy Head, in addition to a radio station to the north of this site.

In the German archives, there is an account of the recollection of Erich Roseke, who was a machine gunner with 11 Company and was due to take part in this audacious, improbable manoeuvre. 'Our platoon was to be the first to land – in British uniforms. It was not possible to train on models of the targets because nobody knew exactly what these targets would look like. We only had unclear photographs of positions, radio stations etc.'[25] Roseke also remembered the English lessons they were given in the run-up to the operation, including phrases for confrontational situations where the Brandenburgers had revealed themselves to the enemy. 'Hands up! Drop your arms! Resistance will be useless. Be quiet or I'll kill you. You will stay here as hostages. You are encircled.'[26] Roseke, who later won the Knight's Cross, Germany's highest medal for gallantry, felt that the training and intelligence were 'a totally inadequate preparation for our deployment and our hearts sank when, after an inspection by Major Kewisch, we heard him say to our commanding officer, "What a shame we will lose those boys."'[27]

Another Brandenburg Commando unit, consisting of two officers, fifteen NCOs and 114 men equipped with fifty motorbikes, was given instructions to land at Dover, then neutralise bases on the neighbouring coast and the British artillery that was suspected to lie to the north of the port. An additional unit from 4 Company, under the command of Captain Wilhelm Hollman and known as 'The Wild Dogs', was to attack Dover directly, with the aim of immobilising the coastal guns above the town and preventing the British from sinking blockships at the harbour entrances.

Detailed Sea Lion plans continued to be discussed throughout August, as the army and navy maintained their arguments over the breadth of the front, while Hitler still equivocated over the landing itself. After the stalemate of the meeting with naval staff on 7 August, Halder and other army chiefs, including von Brauchitsch, kept up their objections to the navy's insistence that landings could take place only between Folkestone and

Beachy Head, although as a compromise they were reluctantly willing to abandon the idea of the westerly assault on Lyme Bay in Dorset. In another sign of continuing friction, however, von Brauchitsch wrote to Keitel on 10 August, demanding not only the retention of the army's proposal for a landing in Brighton but also, in return for dropping Lyme Bay, the inclusion of a landing on the Kentish coast east of Dover. As it stood, von Brauchitsch warned, the navy's scheme was on 'too narrow a front, with no good prospects of surprise and with insufficient forces reinforced only in driblets'.[28]

The essence of this revised army plan, which represented a significant reduction from the first, more bullish proposals made in July, was that there should be five main landings, namely at Brighton, Beachy Head, Hastings, Folkestone and Deal, with the first wave made up of ten specially selected infantry divisions, plus advance elements from nine mobile divisions. In turn, each of these landing divisions was to be subdivided into a first and second transport echelon; the first aimed to establish a bridgehead on the coast, and the second, following closely, would try to push through towards a line running from Portsmouth to Ramsgate. The army hoped this could be achieved in three days. A second wave would follow, bringing the rest of the mobile divisions and pushing to a line between the Thames and Southampton. Two subsequent waves would land later to finish the land fight, presuming that by now the British were in full retreat. Yet even in this more limited form, this was still too big an undertaking for the navy.

The Führer would have to decide, although even now, on the eve of the Battle of Britain, he was remarkably hesitant about Sea Lion. That mood of uncertainty was evident at the Führer conference held on 13 August to decide the scope of the invasion. At this meeting, Hitler seemed more focused on the prospects of failure than any determination to smash Britain, and even seemed keen to downplay the importance of Sea Lion.

Almost as if to reassure himself, Hitler argued that Britain could be brought 'to her knees' by other means if the invasion were not mounted, such as through the conquest of Egypt or the seizure of Gibraltar. 'Our operations should not be directed against individual military objectives but towards the achievement of final victory.' In a remark that was to be confounded by history, he argued that 'we are not entering the decisive phase of the war against England.'[29] After this dispirited lecture in strategy, he refused to give a final decision on the breadth of the landing front, although in his pessimistic frame of mind he inclined towards a more narrowly based attack than the army wanted.

Confusion and indecision reigned the next day, when Raeder saw the Führer at the Reich Chancellery. In the account that he later wrote in the naval staff's war diary, he recorded that 'the Führer does not propose to carry out an operation whose risk is too great. He advocates the view that the aim of defeating Britain is not dependent on the landing alone, but can be achieved in a different way. Regardless of the final decision, the Führer wishes in any case to maintain the threat of invasion against Britain.'[30]

That evening Jodl saw Hitler, who finally spelt out his decision on the first wave, heavily influenced by Raeder. The front was to be narrower than Halder and von Brauchitsch wanted, with its focus on four key beaches from Selsey Bill to Folkestone, the 9th Army taking the western side and the 16th the eastern. Hitler confirmed that the original plan to land at Lyme Bay was now to be dropped, as was the thrust against Deal, not least because the navy had declared the east Kent coast unsuitable for navigational reasons. But as twin sops to the army, he also proposed that plans should be drawn up for a direct raid on Brighton by an advanced assault force, backed up by airborne landings on the South Downs by the 7th Flieger Division. Neither the army nor the navy was satisfied, but at least the final details of the operation's planning could now proceed.

Inevitably, further disputes arose in the final weeks of August. The army envisaged Hitler's proposal for an attack on Brighton as an opportunity to land a large force there, complete with artillery and heavy equipment, carried by seventy steamers and 200 fast motor boats operating from Le Havre. Once more the navy said this was impossible, and as a compromise agreed that fifty steamers could be loaded and dispatched from Le Havre, twenty-five of them sailing directly to Brighton behind the motor boats, while the remainder would go across the Channel with the rest of the Sea Lion invading force, turning towards Brighton on the English coast if the situation allowed. The army were deeply unhappy with this approach. But Hitler, in a directive of 27 August, declared that 'the army operations must allow for the facts regarding available shipping and security of the crossing and disembarkation.'[31]

The planning for the assault against the four key areas of the Kent and Sussex coast was more fruitful. These sectors were designated from B to E, sector A, covering Ramsgate to Deal, having been abandoned. Landing area B encompassed the 14 miles of coast from Folkestone to Dungeness and was to be attacked by two infantry divisions of the 16th Army, supported by a Luftwaffe anti-aircraft regiment and the commandos from the Brandenburg Regiment. This corps would leave from Rotterdam, Ostend and Dunkirk. The 16th Army was also to provide the two divisions that would embark from Calais and land in sector C, an 11-mile stretch of coast between Rye and Hastings, supported by three battalions of amphibious and submersible tanks. Sector D, the shoreline between Bexhill and Beachy

Head, was to be invaded by the men of the 9th Army, sailing from Boulogne under the command of Erich von Manstein, backed by the Pioneer Commando Company from the Brandenburg Regiment and another battalion of amphibious tanks. Further units from the 9th Army would sail from Le Havre to land on the beaches across a 21-mile stretch from Worthing to Selsey Bill.

Once the beachheads had been secured, von Rundstedt, who was the overall commander of the land forces, could commit the second and subsequent waves of reserves so the invaders could advance through southern England. There were now just nine infantry divisions designated for the first wave of landings, in addition to the airborne division targeting the South Downs. It was a far cry from the army's original ambitious plan for an invasion by thirteen divisions in the first wave across a front 200 miles wide.

Operation Sea Lion was to be launched on S-Day, as it was now designated. Given that the preparations would not be completed until 15 September, it was likely that S-Day would probably take place in the last ten days of that month. Due to their lack of concrete intelligence about British defences, the Germans could only guess at what sort of opposition they would encounter. However, they were under no illusions, knowing that resistance would initially be tough, not just from the navy and the RAF, but also from the increasingly reinvigorated British army, whose operational strength they estimated to be twenty divisions, although in reality it was twenty-six.

German respect for British fighting ability permeated a report from the IV Army Corps, which extolled the BEF's courage in France and Belgium. Entitled 'Lessons to be Learnt from Fighting the English', this document stated that the 'English soldier has shown to be a first class fighter. In defence the Englishman has to be killed. In the fighting, few Englishmen were taken prisoner compared to the French or Belgians. Thus the loss of blood was always high on both sides.' The report further stated that the men of the BEF were 'disciplined' in conduct, 'tough and dogged in outlook' and able to endure wounds with 'a stoic calmness'. Just as importantly, 'the English soldier's conviction that he was going to win the war is unshakeable.'[32]

Indeed, the German High Command calculated on potential losses of between 30 and 50 per cent for the troops in the advance elements that would be the first to land on the beaches from their motorboats. To lessen the concentration of British defensive forces on the south coast and dissipate the Royal Navy's resources in and around the English Channel, the Germans planned to launch a pair of diversionary feints, one across the North Sea, the other against Ireland.

The North Sea diversion, called Operation Herbstreise or 'Autumn Voyage', was designed to create the illusion that the invasion force was heading for the east coast between Newcastle and Aberdeen. Despite the Kriegsmarine's severe shortage of transport, this initiative was deemed important enough for a significant flotilla to be formed, including eleven large steamers, four liners and a gunnery training ship, all escorted by three light cruisers. The convoy, whose vessels would largely have been empty, was to be launched two days before the actual invasion started.

A more ambitious, if equally unrealistic, plan was Operation Green. Conceived by Field Marshal Fedor von Bock, this envisaged an initial assault on the Irish coastline between Waterford and Wexford by 4,000 crack troops from the 4th and 7th Army Corps, embarking from western France, backed up by waves of Dornier and Stuka bombers. Because of the length of supply lines from the continent, the initial invasion force would have to be self-sufficient, establishing martial law and commandeering supplies, as well as using forced labour.

It is testimony to the seriousness with which Bock formulated Operation Green that his planning papers included seventy pages of detailed sketches of 233 Irish cities, towns and villages; even the names and addresses of every petrol station owner were provided. Nor did Bock stint on the scope of the operation, with a total of 50,000 troops allocated for the eventual occupation of Ireland if the invasion had taken place.

The conquest of Ireland was not an objective in itself for the wider German High Command. The aim of Operation Green was largely to support Sea Lion, mainly by drawing off British troops based in Ulster, by diverting the Royal Navy from the Channel and by providing western airfields for the Luftwaffe from which to bomb Britain.

For both sides, Britain and Germany, the question of Ireland was a minor issue compared to the looming climax of Sea Lion in September. At the end of August, von Brauchitsch issued his instructions to the army, explaining that the aim of the 'forced landing' would be 'to knock out the English homeland as a basis for the continuation of the war against Germany and, if necessary, to occupy it completely'. He warned that the 'order for launching the operation depends on the political situation', although preparations were being undertaken 'in such a way that the invasion can be carried out from 15 September. The task of the army will be, while maintaining its tasks as an occupation force in France and the protection of other fronts, to land with strong units in southern England, to defeat the English army, to occupy the capital and, depending on the situation, further areas of England.'[33]

A mood of anticipation was sweeping through the troops. On 4

September, as the build-up accelerated, the shipping section of Raeder's naval staff reported that the invasion fleet was well on its way to completion. According to its latest account, '168 transports, 1,910 barges, 419 tugs, including trawlers and 1,600 motorboats had been requisitioned. Most of the remaining vessels had been already been assembled at the embarkation ports or were on their way there.'[34]

That same night, 4 September, Hitler gave his bombastic speech to a hysterically cheering crowd at the Berlin Sportpalast, promising that the attack on England was imminent. The harsh tone of his address could not have been more different to the restraint of his Reichstag speech almost two months earlier. 'The hour will come when one or the other will crumble, and that one will not be National Socialist Germany.'[35] His glorying in the idea of Britain's forthcoming destruction was shared by many of the men under his command, as shown by the words of one tank commander, Karl Fuchs, in a letter to his mother: 'The days are numbered for those bums over in England. They won't be able to attack German cities and peaceful farms any more. All of us feel that once we're over there, no one will show any mercy, no matter who's involved. All those bums are the same. If fate sends me over there, I'm going to fight until I keel over!'[36]

21

'All that for tuppence and an orange'

~

Brigadier 'Jasper' Harker, the head of MI5, was often described by his many critics as a weak leader, which is why the dynamic Lord Swinton effectively took charge of the organisation during 1940. But Harker apparently could display remarkable coolness, even insouciance, when the invasion threat was at its height. On one occasion, after MI5 had moved its headquarters out to Blenheim Palace in Oxfordshire, Harker was staying nearby at Hinton Manor, the home of his City friend Nicholas Davenport, who later recalled:

> I well remember the night in August when the Home Guard commanding officer rang me up at midnight to say that the Germans had set sail from the Dutch ports for the invasion. I went into the Brigadier's room to warn him:
>
> 'Jasper, the balloon has gone up. The Germans are on their way across the Channel.'
>
> 'Don't be a fool,' he replied, 'MI5 hasn't telephoned.' He then turned over and went back to sleep.[1]

It was inevitable that, as the Germans accelerated their preparations for Sea Lion, the number of reports reaching Britain about the imminence of an invasion increased dramatically. Rumours about Wehrmacht plans were picked up by British Intelligence, Bletchley Park and foreign embassies, while naval and RAF reconnaissance relayed sightings of German movements around the coast. The sheer volume of this information meant that no one in government could deny that Reich's war machine was gearing up for some kind of major assault, whether by sea or by air. Typically, at the beginning of August, the Combined Intelligence Committee received news from Norway of German tests being carried out on landing craft large enough to accommodate tanks, while on 7 August it was noted that there had been 'a noticeable increase in the last few days in the number of threats of early invasion emanating from German sources and passed on by neutral diplomats'.[2]

What Britain lacked, just like Germany, was high-quality intelligence that could provide dependable information about the enemy's thinking and activities. Ultra transcripts from Bletchley Park provided snapshots of Luftwaffe battle plans; in addition, MI6 had one 'very well placed and reliable German source', an Abwehr officer and a Nazi Party veteran, Paul Thümmel, who passed occasional reports to Britain via Switzerland.[3] But such material was limited in its scope.

In the absence of an extensive spy network, the British had no alternative but to continue with less reliable sources, gossip and reconnaissance, although these could often be revealing. RAF patrols over northern France in August 1940, for example, noted the construction of aerodromes, gun emplacements and the first arrivals of the *prahme*. Photographs taken on 22 August showed a 'landing and embarkation exercise' off the French coast, featuring boats that were each 'capable of holding about 50 soldiers'.[4] The British secret service also received a hint about the involvement of the Brandenburgers in the German invasion plans, when one source reported 'the assembly of an air formation of thirty English-speaking men who it is thought are probably to be dropped by parachute for espionage or sabotage purposes'.[5]

Sometimes the government received tiny snippets of information that gave a glimpse into German preparations, like this secret service message of 22 August: 'It has been reported by a reliable source that the Records Office of a German Air Force formation was much agitated over the apparent loss of a package, containing among other things – one gazetteer of small harbours on the south and south-east coast of England; one guide to Dundee and the Firth of Tay.'[6]

Even the distant British imperial realm of India was able to provide speculative news about German intentions. In the archives of the India Office there is a fascinating report to the Secretary of State for India, Leo Amery, from the British consul in Kandahar, passing on information received from 'a German Jew in Afghan employ' who had recently left Berlin. This informant claimed that

> the Germans are making preparations to invade Britain on September 15th at dawn. The invasion will be carried out by air with support from the sea and will begin with landing troops from gliders. For this purpose large towing planes and gliders, capable of carrying 50 men each, are being manufactured in Bremen, Munich and Rangsdorf. The informant stated that the planes were now being delivered to the German government and that he had himself seen some in the course of manufacture.[7]

However, this report just demonstrates that so much of the intelligence lacked any real credibility, for no German heavy glider actually took to the air until early 1941.

What is striking, however, is the confidence with which the British authorities and the general public greeted the prospect of an assault. The

The mass circulation *Daily Mirror* reports Churchill's warning that the invasion could be imminent. Several British intelligence sources estimated that the landings were likely to start on 15 September. The newspaper also covers the Luftwaffe's bombing of Buckingham Palace, which turned out to be a propaganda gift to the government

mood was now entirely different from May and June, when the invasion menace provoked widespread anxiety. Churchill's indomitability had exerted a remarkable influence on the country's spirit, as had the expansion of the army, the creation of the Home Guard, the import of weapons from

America, the growth in aircraft and armament production, the incarceration of aliens and the organisation of national defences. It was a myth that in August 1940 the RAF was all that stood between Britain and conquest. This was no beleaguered nation, nervously awaiting its fate.

This growing confidence was highlighted by the testimony of US military attaché Raymond Lee, who developed a profound admiration for the United Kingdom over her response to the invasion crisis. In a letter to a fellow US officer in early August 1940, he wrote of the British: 'the more time they have, the stronger this fortress becomes. As for myself, I forecast that they would have their principal defences pretty well completed by the middle of August, so far as ground operations are concerned. I think the Germans will run up against something pretty rough.'[8]

A positive mentality in the populace was captured by the opinion surveyors for the Ministry of Information, who found morale remarkably high, noting on 3 August, 'There is growing confidence in "our island fortress".'[9] Extraordinarily, the ministry's surveyors in London recorded that 'streamers are already being made privately in the East End to celebrate victory and remarks are made that "it will only be a matter of months."'[10] In another sign of the public's growing self-assurance, the radio audience for Lord Haw-Haw's sneering broadcasts from Germany dramatically decreased. Listeners now found him as boring as he was unconvincing.

These attitudes were mirrored by the press, whose regular speculation about German invasion plans was accompanied by patriotic dismissiveness of the Reich's chances of success. Typical was a report from the *East Anglian Daily Times* of 10 August, which told of 'a heavy concentration along the French and Belgian coast of an impressive collection of barges suitable for troop transport and of a formidable massing of German warplanes'. According to the paper, there was no cause for alarm because of the 'staggering hazards' that awaited the invaders, who would be 'an easy target for the highly mobile British troops in defence. It would be like pheasant shooting on an ambitious scale, with outsize birds and magazine rifles and machine guns instead of 12 bore shotguns. Between our Regulars and our Home Guards, the invading Germans would have blitzkrieg enough to last them for what would probably be a very brief lifetime.'[11]

It was coverage like that which prompted the exiled former Russian leader Alexander Kerensky, on his arrival in New York in August 1940 after emigrating from occupied France, to comment: 'The British morale is wonderful and in strong contrast to the French.'[12] The South African statesman Jan Christian Smuts pointed to the same difference in his radio broadcast from Cape Town. Claiming that the Germans' success on the western front had been achieved against weak opposition, Smuts said that

'France was a divided, sick soul before the end came', whereas 'the British people are united as never before in their history, under leadership of un-rivalled brilliance and courage.'[13]

At this point, British military and political leaders exuded far more confidence than they had done in the early summer. When Brooke's Home Forces GHQ drew up a paper examining whether the Germans were likely to mount their invasion on the east or the south coast, their analysis radiated the same optimism. The document argued that the Germans would find it difficult to make any successful landings on the east coast, since the North Sea crossing was 'comparatively long' and 'the danger of interference by our fleet is great', while at such a distance 'it would be impossible for the Germans to give their bombers fighter support.' The GHQ paper admitted that a crossing to the south coast would be much easier for the invaders, both in terms of length of crossing and air support. In addition, 'our south coast offers a longer front for landings' although even here the Germans would still have to face the might of the Royal Navy and the RAF. The paper stated with a note of reassurance, 'The Straits of Dover would be a dangerous bottle neck for any seaborne expedition.'[14]

The same belief in Britain's ability to defend herself could be found in Churchill's private utterances as much as in his public addresses. The prime minister had long been sceptical about the Reich's ability to mount a successful invasion, whilst regarding the threat as a useful vehicle for galvanising the public.

In a paper for the Cabinet in mid-August, he directly addressed the question of how the British military would cope if the Germans did actually attack. Brimming with his characteristic pugnacity, he argued that Britain's 'first line of defence against invasion' was the enemy's ports; 'resolute attacks with all our forces upon concentrations of enemy shipping' would deal a heavy blow to the Reich. The second line of defence, he said, lay in 'vigilant patrolling of the sea to intercept any invading expedition and to destroy it in transit'. But even if the Germans did manage to land, Churchill maintained that they would still face an arduous challenge from British counter-attacks. 'Such attacks should be hurled with the utmost speed and fury upon the enemy at his weakest moment, which is not, as is sometimes suggested, when actually getting out of his boats, but when sprawled upon the shore with his communications cut and his supplies running short.'[15] The bullish atmosphere was infectious. Self-confident phraseology was now being used by the naval staff, whose assistant chief admiral Sir Harold Burrough wrote in a paper of 7 August: 'Invasion as distinct from Raid has never appeared to be a likely German operation of war. As days go by and the Army defences strengthen and the weather tends to become less settled, the idea of invasion will fade to an impossibility.'[16]

British calmness was vividly illustrated in an extraordinary episode that was orchestrated by the Germans at the start of the Battle of Britain in an attempt to induce widespread panic in the population. In line with the Führer Directive No. 17 calling for the intensification of the air war against Britain, Goering had planned to launch his great aerial offensive on 5 August, which was code-named Adlertag or 'Eagle Day'. Much to his frustration, the start of Unternehmen Adlerangriff, or 'Operation Eagle Attack', had to be delayed for several days because of poor weather, with the new date fixed for 13 August. Thanks to the Enigma code breakthrough, Bletchley Park picked up a signal on 8 August from Goering to his squadrons, proclaiming that 'within a short space of time you will wipe the British air force from the sky.'[17]

To coincide with the beginning of the planned offensive, the Luftwaffe and the Reich's propaganda machine under Josef Goebbels came up with a devious initiative that they hoped would spread fear and confusion across the country. On 20 July, British Intelligence received a report 'from a fairly reliable source' that 'considerable use will be made of dummy parachutes' in the build-up to the invasion.[18] This is indeed exactly what happened.

Adlertag was launched on 13 August with sustained attacks by the Luftwaffe over southern England, although with nothing like the destructive impact for which Goering had hoped, as the Luftwaffe lost forty-five planes compared to the RAF's thirteen. That night the Germans put their scheme of trickery into action. Around eighty unmanned parachutes were dropped from German aircraft over Staffordshire, Derbyshire, Yorkshire and south-west Scotland, plus three satchels containing maps and documents purporting to be sabotage instructions to parachutists. At the same time the New British Broadcasting Station, which featured Lord Haw-Haw and was Goebbels' propaganda outlet aimed at listeners in enemy territory, carried solemn, regularly repeated bulletins about the arrival of the parachutists. This was a desperate attempt at disinformation. In reality, neither the empty parachute drops nor the broadcast provoked the slightest concern in Britain.

As a scare tactic, it failed miserably, for the operation was quickly exposed as a hoax. The parachutes were sent to London by special messenger, where Air Ministry and MI5 experts examined them and immediately detected the subterfuge. For a start, the parachutes were not of the standard German type, while the harnesses and packs 'were found attached in an improvised manner'. Even more revealing were the locations of their discovery, which showed that no parachutists had been involved. One was found 'in the centre of a cornfield and there were no tracks leading away from it'. Another appeared on the rooftop of a house, and six in Scotland had evidently been dropped 'from a very low altitude' as the shrouds had not unfurled.[19] The ham-fisted attempt by the Germans to spread despondency again showed the hurried, improvised nature of much of the planning for Sea Lion, as well as the Reich's fundamental failure to understand Britain's mood or the national psychology.

The Germans were now facing a far bigger problem than the minimal impact of their deception. The farce of the parachute drop was symptomatic of the greater early failure of the Luftwaffe to take control of English skies, as the RAF put up much greater resistance than Goering had expected. The first day of the aerial dogfights set the pattern for the opening phase of the Battle of Britain, as German losses significantly exceeded those of Fighter Command.

On the following day, the Luftwaffe was again badly mauled, losing nineteen aircraft, compared to the RAF's seven. Worse was to follow on 15 August, when Goering mounted his biggest attack yet. All three of his air fleets went into action, including Luftflotte 5, which tried to attack northern England from its bases in Norway. Altogether, the Luftwaffe made 1,786 sorties that day but lost seventy-five aircraft, a rate of attrition so high that Luftflotte 5 never again went into action in the battle. Less than a week later, Churchill made the resounding speech in the House of Commons that extolled the heroism of the fighter pilots through the memorable line: 'Never in the field of human conflict has so much been owed by so many to so few.'[20] Goering's dreams of annihilation were turning to ashes. The goal of air superiority over southern England was more distant than ever.

The early success of Fighter Command in the battle could not be attributed just to the courage of the pilots, vital though that was. In the Supermarine Spitfire and Hawker Hurricane, the RAF had two fast monoplanes that were highly manoeuvrable and capable of speeds of over 300 mph. A deadly adversary for the German bombers, they were a match even for the advanced fighter the Me109. They were also available in substantial numbers; at the start of the battle Fighter Command could deploy 328 Spitfires in nineteen squadrons, and 568 Hurricanes in twenty-eight squadrons.

The RAF had the further advantage of a highly sophisticated control organisation, developed by the austere, technocratic Fighter Command chief Hugh Dowding. This constantly fed information about the Luftwaffe's movements from the radar stations and the Observer Corps into his headquarters at Stanmore, where it was analysed and then passed on to the fighter group and sector stations. Reports from radar operators could reach Dowding's control room in less than twenty seconds. With this comprehensive but remarkably simple system, fighters did not have to waste time and fuel on patrols, but instead could target raiders directly. One of the Luftwaffe's many shortcomings in the Battle of Britain was failing to recognise the crucial importance of the Dowding system to Fighter Command's operations and making no sustained attempt to knock out the radar stations.

Additional factors contributed to the RAF's ability to challenge the Luftwaffe so effectively. One was the inspirational leadership of the tough, charismatic New Zealander Keith Park, who was in charge No. 11 Fighter Group based in the South-East of England, the front line of the battle. Another was the Civilian Repair Organisation, which ensured that many of the fighter planes shot down over British soil could soon be returned to the squadrons. Amazingly, due to the work of the CRO, no less than 60 per cent of all Hurricanes downed in the Battle of Britain went back into operational service. There was also the fact that the pilots were fighting over their own territory, so if they successfully bailed out, they could go back on duty, whereas downed Luftwaffe pilots became prisoners of war.

The idea that RAF airmen were mostly dashing young products of the public schools is another myth. In fact, the majority were hardened professionals who had joined up before the war and had already seen action in France and over the Channel.

One Air Ministry stratagem that served the RAF well in 1940 but has often been overlooked was the creation of decoy airfields to draw Luftwaffe fire away from the genuine bases. They fell into two types. The first, K daytime airfields, came complete with dummy aircraft, hangars, shelters, gun pits and food stores. These were generally built by set-design experts from Shepperton Film Studios and were sited on large fields, heaths or, occasionally, disused First World War aerodromes. The second type were the Q night-time airfields, which were much easier to construct since they needed nothing more than a set of lights laid out to look like a flight path in the dark. To avoid accidents with the RAF's own crews trying to land on the Q airfields, subtle differences were incorporated into the lighting systems to distinguish them from real airstrips. Crude though it was, the decoy method was reasonably effective. According to *Flight* magazine, at least 322 Luftwaffe attacks were directed at dummy satellites during the Battle of Britain and the Blitz.[21]

The Luftwaffe High Command had started Adlerangriff with strong expectations of an easy victory. As a Messerschmitt pilot told the American journalist William Shirer just after the start of the air offensive, 'It is a matter of a couple of weeks, you know, until we finish off the RAF. In a fortnight the British won't have any more planes.'[22]

The initial attitude of the German pilots was highlighted by an incident recalled by Kenneth Webb, at the time a boy of thirteen working on the family farm in Berkshire during the Battle of Britain. To his excitement, on 15 August he witnessed a Hurricane shooting down a Ju88 bomber. As the German plane descended, two of the aircrew leapt out. 'My father ran back to the farm, grabbed his Home Guard rifle, put on his armband and drove to find the two airmen.' Along with some of his Home Guard colleagues, Webb's father found the men and then escorted them to the farm to await the arrival of the regular army.

One of the Germans, who spoke fluent English, was surprised when Webb's mother offered him a cup of tea. 'But you have still tea?' he asked, having been taken in by Goebbels' propaganda that broken Britain was on the brink of starvation. After finishing his cup, the German then became defiant. 'Looking around the room at the onlookers, he firmly said, "The war will soon be over for you and the German army will soon be here." At this my father took three quick paces across the room and brandishing his fist in the German's face shouted, "Any more talk like that and I'll knock your bloody head off!" This effectively stopped all further conversation.'[23]

As the losses mounted, German self-assurance began to evaporate. In the first phase of the battle, 290 German planes were shot down, almost three times the number of RAF aircraft lost. In the second phase, which lasted from 24 August to 6 September, the Germans focused more narrowly on Fighter Command's airfields, a change of strategy that produced better results, but the Luftwaffe's losses still remained significantly higher than the RAF's: 297 to 226.

Noting this British aerial success, Admiral Cunningham, the Royal Navy's shrewd commander in the eastern Mediterranean, wrote: 'How splendidly the RAF lads are doing at home. I am sure their wonderful bags of enemy planes are keeping everyone's tail up. I may be wrong but I cannot see an invasion as a practicable proposition.'[24] The success of the RAF boosted the public's morale even further towards the end of August. According to one opinion survey for the Ministry of Information, 'Confidence and cheerfulness are noticeable everywhere, and the punishment inflicted on the raiders appears more than to counteract the damage that they do.'[25]

Fighter Command was not the only part of the RAF engaged in undermining German invasion plans. Throughout the months of the Battle of Britain, Bomber Command took the fight to the Reich and its occupied territories, attacking its manufacturing plants, aircraft factories, ports and aerodromes. In July and August alone, RAF bombers dropped 1,454 tons of explosives on German industrial targets and communications, and flew 1,097 sorties against airfields in occupied countries. All this activity came at a heavy price. Bomber Command lost 718 men during the Battle of Britain, which was actually a higher death toll than the 544 men in Fighter Command. Despite this catalogue of heroic sacrifice, the British bombing campaign did not cause nearly as much devastation in 1940 as it did later in the war, partly because in the summer of 1940 the RAF had no heavy four-engined bombers, having to rely on twin-engined medium bombers with an inadequate payload that were highly vulnerable to enemy fighters and anti-aircraft fire. Moreover, before the development of effective navigation aids, precision bombing was almost impossible.

Nevertheless the force had some dramatic successes, most notably on the night of 12/13 August when ten Hampdens from 49 and 83 Squadrons attacked an aqueduct on the Dortmund–Ems canal, a vital waterway for the transport of invasion barges from Germany to the Channel ports. What made the mission so dangerous was that the planes had to fly at low altitude through twin barrages of anti-aircraft fire on either side of the canal. Despite the risks, the mission's leader Acting Flight Lieutenant Roderick Learoyd was undaunted as his craft sped towards the target at an altitude of just 150 feet. Even when he was almost blinded by German searchlights, lost two of his bombers and had his own plane so badly hit that he had to fly solely on instruments, he carried on towards the aqueduct, dropping his delayed-action bomb at exactly the right point. The subsequent explosion tore the bridge apart. Learoyd then somehow managed to nurse his stricken plane back to his base at RAF Scampton in Lincolnshire where he made a smooth landing even though his landing flaps were inoperable. For his astonishing bravery, he was awarded the Victoria Cross. His audacity was not just a morale booster at home, but also inflicted real damage on the enemy. The canal was unusable for ten days, another reason why the Kriegsmarine's preparations could not be completed until mid-September.

It was the British army, not the RAF, that had always been of greatest concern to Churchill's government in the early summer months of 1940, especially after Dunkirk. Yet by August the picture had been transformed. Arms had arrived, troops had been recruited, leadership had been galvanised. The change had been symbolised by the replacement of the pessimistic, compromised, sometimes shambolic Ironside, as the commander of Home Forces, with the dynamic Ulsterman Brooke, who was a master of strategic planning. He was also fortunate in that he had far more resources at his command than Ironside had enjoyed in the dark days of mid-June. As he himself put it to the Chiefs of Staff at the end of July, during the last six weeks 'a material change has taken place in that our beach and forward defences have become much stronger. Consequently there is every probability of being able to prevent a seaborne attack getting a footing on land.'[26]

Even the Soviets, nominally in favour of the Nazi cause, were impressed by British preparations against attack. The decrypts of secret Russian intelligence traffic, later released after the fall of the Berlin Wall, revealed that in late August the Soviet ambassador Ivan Maisky conducted a two-day tour of defences on the south coast and reported back to Moscow that the coastal belt, running 20 miles inland, is 'one continuous military camp. It is forbidden to go there. The whole zone is divided into army, corps and division areas.'[27]

This belief in Britain's growing ability to resist invasion was linked to the substantial increase in the equipment and personnel of the Home Forces. Following previous shipments of armaments from the USA, on 31 July a further 200,000 rifles and more field guns arrived, followed by further convoys in August. In addition, 820 field guns of 75-mm calibre had been imported from America, along with 2,600 tank machine guns and 60,000 Thompson sub-machine guns.

Equipment was also pouring out of British factories. As the historian David Newbold recorded, 'the number of field guns in the hands of British troops had increased from about 600 at the beginning of June to over 1600. By the end of August, Home Defence formations were expected to reach 80 per cent of their establishment. There were also over 250 mobile medium and heavy guns with the troops, compared to just 140 in June.'[28] The supply of two-pounder anti-tank guns had increased fourfold since June, while the army also had twice the number of Boys anti-tank rifles and Bren light machine guns. Just as the Home Guard was now well equipped by its American rifles, so the regular army had more than 1 million .303 rifles in the service of front-line troops, plus another 75,000 in depots and a further 65,000 under repair. The Birmingham Small Arms (BSA) company, whose Small Heath factory was the only one in the United Kingdom producing rifles, was turning out at least 2,000 new weapons a week. Nor did the shortages of ammunition continue. By the end of August, the army had around 400 million rounds for their troops, enough, it was estimated, to last six weeks.

It was the same story with British-made tanks, whose number had doubled between June and mid-August from 404 to over 800. By early September, there were a total of 1,200, of which 720 were in front-line service, this figure including 360 infantry and Cruiser tanks, and 300 light tanks. Similarly the mobility of the army was significantly enhanced by the arrival of customised transports in place of the municipal buses. Brooke told the Chiefs of Staff, 'Formations are now well supplied with troop-carrying vehicles of the charabanc type.'[29]

This was a vital point, for his arrival heralded a new approach to home defence. The entire apparatus of stop lines, pillboxes, entrenchments and roadblocks were an anathema to Brooke who felt that they bred a timorous, Maginot Line mentality, a view that was entirely in line with Churchill's own thinking. The prime minister had always wanted more emphasis upon 'mobile columns trained and equipped to take vigorous action against any enemy who may succeed in setting foot in this country'.[30] The resort to fixed defences begun in June, epitomised by Ironside's stop lines, partly compensated for the lack of well-equipped troops, but that moment had now passed. According to Pug Ismay, the total strength of the entire army in Britain, including those in training units, the reserves and air defence, as well as men from the Dominions, stood at 75,945 officers and 1,758,122 soldiers, figures that make a mockery of the belief that Britain was pathetically weak at the time of invasion threat.[31] Brooke in his own front line could muster twenty-six divisions, two of them armoured.

In addition, by mid-August 1.3 million men had volunteered for the Home Guard, almost 1 million of whom were now well armed, well trained and provided with proper uniforms. A month later, the total number of volunteers had risen to 1.5 million. Colonel William Watson of the Durham Light Infantry recalled that the troops in the Home Guard in the West Country, where he was based in 1940, were 'extremely good. They all wanted to co-operate with us and we got them on a very high footing. My view was that we should not turn them into Grenadier Guardsman, but instead should exploit their own ingenuity and individuality.'[32]

Of Brooke's twenty-six divisions, fifteen were deployed in early August between the Wash and Cornwall, reflecting his correct belief that the south coast was the most likely landing point for the Germans. To meet the demands of the new stress on mobility, he moved significant numbers of units nearer the coast, as well as strengthening his reserves around London. So the 2nd Armoured Division was shifted from the East Midlands to East Anglia on 16 August, while Freyberg's 2nd New Zealand Division was brought forward to the Maidstone—Ashford area in Kent. In addition, two brigades from the Australian forces were added to Southern Command, and the 3rd Regular Division was sent to strengthen the South-West.

Because the emphasis was now on mobility, Brooke's headquarters regarded many of the static defences not as a bulwark but as a potential hindrance to the movement of Home Forces. Work on the inland stop lines ceased, roadblocks were removed, trenches were no longer dug, and preparations were halted for demolishing the main lines of communications, like bridges and railways. Construction of fixed fortifications continued only on the beaches and the surrounding areas, again highlighting Brooke's determination to tackle the Germans where they landed rather than allowing them to gain a foothold. Even some of the signposts that had been taken away with such feverishness in May and June were put back, because, as a memorandum by Southern Command noted, their universal removal from all roads was 'likely to prove more of a handicap to ourselves than to the enemy', not least because 'drivers cannot drive and map-read at the same time.'[33]

Naval power in British home waters was vital to national survival. Here again, the picture was one of growing self-confidence, despite the huge demands on the Royal Navy. The fierce arguments of the early summer within the Admiralty about the distribution of the capital ships were now over.

Although much of the fleet was stationed in the far North, there were still substantial forces around the eastern and southern coasts, including two cruisers and nine destroyers based on the Humber, four cruisers and seventy destroyers in the Channel force, and the battleship HMS *Revenge* at Plymouth. In addition to the destroyers, cruisers and capital ships, the Royal Navy had access to a host of other craft that could be used for defensive purposes, from minesweepers and motorboats to drifters and auxiliary trawlers. It has been estimated that there were in total almost 1,000 vessels along the 2,000-mile perimeter of the Home Fleet at this time. As the historian Duncan Grinnell-Milne wrote:

> All things considered, it can be asserted that the Royal Navy at this time was ready and able to defeat any practicable invasion from the sea. Its ships were well distributed to meet all probable and some improbable threats, well dispersed to lessen the expected damage from air attack . . . Its lines of concentration were short enough to allow any threatened area to be covered by light forces, at worst within ten hours, at best within two or three hours' steaming.[34]

Even so, there were still deep concerns within the Admiralty about a shortage of destroyers, given the calls for convoy and escort duties on top of the anti-invasion measures. It was precisely this unease that had led Churchill to exert such sustained diplomatic pressure on President Roosevelt throughout the summer to release a number of redundant American destroyers.

In his very first telegram to the White House as prime minister, Churchill had asked for 'the loan of 40 or 50 of your older destroyers to bridge the gap between what we have now and the large new construction we put in hand at the beginning of the war'.[35] Although sympathetic, Roosevelt was inhibited from agreeing to the request, partly because of America's strict neutrality laws, partly because, less nobly, there was a widely held view in Washington that Britain could not long survive, so the dispatch of ships could be counter-productive if they fell into German hands. Nevertheless, Churchill kept up the barrage of calls for support, writing on 31 July, 'I know you will do all in your power but I feel entitled and bound to put the gravity and urgency of the position before you.' He went on to add that he was 'beginning to feel hopeful about this war if we can get round the next three or four months. The air is holding well . . . But the loss of destroyers by air attacks may well be so serious as to break down our defence of the food and trade routes across the Atlantic.'[36]

By this stage, there had been a fundamental shift in the position of the United States, with the result that Churchill's entreaties now fell on more fertile ground. American public opinion was warming to Britain's cause, as were many in the US military, a process fuelled by Churchill's inspiring rhetoric, supported by the heroic performance of the Royal Navy and the RAF.

On 22 July, Raymond Lee sent back to the USA a dispatch, based on consultations with other senior American officers in London: 'The consensus was that: a) the Germans cannot subdue Britain without landing; b) cannot land without controlling the air; c) cannot control the air without wrecking the RAF on the ground. Finally I posed the question: "Do you think there is an even chance that Britain will remain unsubdued on September 30th?" The unanimous verdict was "Yes".'[37]

More privately, Britain's cause in Washington was significantly boosted by a fact-finding mission in late July 1940 led by Colonel Bill Donovan, a highly decorated soldier and former Attorney General of the United States. During his visit to England, he saw a host of leading politicians and military leaders, as well as Sir Stewart Menzies, the head of MI6. Donovan was deeply impressed by Britain's resolution. In his report to the president on his return to the USA at the beginning of August, he stressed that 'the British would fight on and would not surrender their fleet; their morale was high but their equipment was deficient.'[38]

Nevertheless, the legal obstacles remained, so creative minds on both sides of the Atlantic went to work. One ingenious proposal was put forward by lawyers supportive of the president, whereby he could avoid the neutrality laws by using legislation passed by Thomas Jefferson during the Barbary Wars against North African pirates in the early nineteenth century, allowing the president to take naval action without the approval of Congress.

Roosevelt, finding the idea too legalistic, too sly, was drawn to an alternative proposal, which was initially conceived by the prestigious Century Club, a group of influential figures who feared that their country would be in serious danger if Britain fell. The club's idea was that the destroyers could be supplied to the United Kingdom in return for the use of naval and air bases in British imperial territories near America, including Bermuda, British Guiana, Jamaica and Newfoundland. This appealed to Roosevelt, since he could present the destroyers-for-bases arrangement as a measure that enhanced American security. Lord Lothian, the British ambassador, was also an enthusiast for the scheme. Indeed, as early as June, he had argued that Britain should offer the USA the lease of facilities in the Caribbean and Newfoundland to 'promote American goodwill'.[39]

The idea did not initially find favour with the War Cabinet, the Colonial Office or the Admiralty, largely because of concerns about the loss of British territorial sovereignty. But the escalation in the invasion threat and the Royal Navy's losses in the Atlantic brought a change in attitude towards the end of July, when the War Cabinet expressed its willingness to negotiate a deal over the bases in return for the destroyers.

The proposal was put to the US Cabinet on 2 August, where it was adopted on the condition that the bases be sold rather than leased by Britain. Immediately, Lothian informed Downing Street by telegram of the decision, requesting a swift response. This was, however, easier said than done. It was now Saturday 3 August and Churchill had gone down to Chequers for the weekend. When an attempt was made by an Admiralty commander to speak to him in the afternoon, an official at Chequers explained, 'Sorry, the Prime Minister is asleep until 5.45 pm and left word that he cannot be disturbed.' On hearing this, the First Lord of the Admiralty and Labour politician A.V. Alexander threw up his arms in mock despair and said, 'The British Empire rocks and the Prime Minister sleeps.'[40]

Once he had woken, Churchill gave his full attention to the issue and that night sent off a telegram to Lothian, which stated that the bases-for-destroyers scheme 'was agreeable, but we prefer that it should be on lease indefinitely and not sale. It is understood that this will enable us to secure destroyers and flying boats at once.' He told Lothian that it was vital to settle the negotiations 'quickly' for 'now is the time when we want the destroyers.'[41]

The president now raised a new condition, in that he wanted a firm commitment from Churchill that, in the event of a successful German invasion, the British would sail its ships across the Atlantic. In fact, this was much in line with what Churchill had told the House of Commons on 4 June in his famous 'Never Surrender' speech, in which he declared that if 'this island or a large part of it were subjugated and starving, then our Empire beyond the seas, armed and guarded by the British fleet, would carry on the struggle'.[42] However, two months later, the prime minister had deep reservations about making the kind of declaration that Roosevelt wanted, fearing it might smack of defeatism regarding Germany as well as subservience towards America.

A fascinating account of how Churchill and his government drew up their reply to Roosevelt was left by John Balfour, a Foreign Office diplomat who was intimately involved in the discussions. Previously unpublished, Balfour's document is compelling for the insight it provides into Churchill's behaviour and views at the moment he was under the most intense pressure.

Balfour had produced a draft telegram for Churchill on the advice of the Foreign Office and other ministers, and on the night of 6 August he was summoned to take this to the prime minister, along with a copy of the 'Never Surrender' speech of 4 June. On his arrival, Balfour was shown into the Cabinet Room, where

> the Prime Minister, in smoking jacket with a soft shirt, was hunched in an attitude of tense anger like a wild beast about to spring. 'Come in, come in, sit down!', he snapped, and then, clawing furiously at the ill-fated draft before him, he burst out, 'Why do you fellows write such long telegrams? Can't you make them shorter? And where's my speech to which you refer?' I hurried to help him, like a whipped cur, only to discover to my horror that his secretaries who had promised to annex the relevant papers had let me down. 'Get it!', he bellowed. Out I shot from the room with my self-confidence in tatters.

After a fruitless hunt for the speech with the Downing Street secretaries, Balfour decided he had no alternative but to go back to his room at the Foreign Office to fetch the file.

> Away I ran across the darkened street and into the Office – disregarding the Local Defence Volunteers at the door – one of whom ran after me, crying, 'Just a minute, just a minute, where's your pass?' Cursing breathlessly and muttering that I was on my way to get papers for the Prime Minister, I produced the pass and careered on down the passage. Sweat was pouring from me as I re-entered the Cabinet room, there to find the Prime Minister in the full flood of dictating to an impassive lady stenographer . . . He paced up and down like an unleashed tiger, pausing every now and then to find the appropriate word, or halting for a moment to take a sip from a long whisky glass. 'Pray make it clear at onesh,' he lisped with his thick, menacing intonation, 'that we could never agree to the slightesht compromising of our full liberty of action nor (after a dramatic pause to hit the right phrase) to tolerate any such defeatisht pronouncement.'

Churchill glowered around the room before continuing with his rewording of the telegram to Lothian. '"The situation," he ejaculated, "is very different to what it was in June, very different! We are showing that man (ie Hitler) that we are resolute. The Americans are asking us to go too far, much too far. We can't agree to a proposal of this kind for the sake of a number of old destroyers – very serviceable no doubt – but not vital."' At this point the prime minister became more mellow and apologised to Balfour for being so abrupt earlier, before ordering that the new draft be sent to Lord Halifax for his approval.[43]

In the end, Churchill's fierce rejection of the demand for reassurance about the fleet was toned down and a more emollient telegram was sent to Washington, which paved the way for the final agreement.

In a further missive of 14 August, Roosevelt stressed again that he was willing to provide the destroyers in return for the use of bases, as long as he could be certain that if 'the waters of Great Britain became untenable for British ships of war, the latter would not be turned over to the Germans but would be sent to other parts of the Empire for the defence of the Empire.'[44] In his reply, Churchill said with a melodramatic flourish that 'the worth of every destroyer you can spare us is measured in rubies', before adding that he was

> ready to reiterate to you what I told Parliament on June 4th. We intend to fight this out here to the end and none of us would ever buy peace by surrendering or scuttling the fleet. But in any use you make of this repeated assurance you will please bear in mind the disastrous effect from our point of view and perhaps also from yours of allowing any impression to grow that we regard the conquest of the British Islands and its naval bases as any other than an impossible contingency. The spirit of our people is splendid. Never have they been so determined. Their confidence in the issue has been enormously and legitimately strengthened by the severe air fighting of the past week.[45]

The final, detailed negotiations over the British facilities and the US supplies were conducted mainly in Washington by Frank Knox, the US Secretary of the Navy, the US Secretary of State Cordell Hull and Lord Lothian. At times, according to Balfour, Churchill became indignant at the whole transaction, feeling that Britain had by far the worst of the bargain. 'Those bloody destroyers' became a phrase of his at the time. Similarly, one Foreign Office lawyer was prompted by the outline of the deal to recall 'the story of the girl who remarked to a magistrate, "And all that for tuppence and an orange."'[46]

Roosevelt and the members of his Cabinet were adamant that, under US law, they could not give away the ships unless they could show to Congress and the American public that significant concessions had been won that enhanced their nation's security. Meanwhile, Britain's need was becoming more urgent because of the invasion threat and the toll from U-boat warfare. As Balfour recalled, 'The Prime Minister was impatient to clinch matters without insisting further.'[47] Finally, on 2 September, the agreement was signed between Cordell Hull and Lord Lothian, its terms being made public three days later.

Under the deal, Britain provided America with land on ninety-nine-year, rent-free leases for the establishment of air or naval bases on Newfoundland, Jamaica, the Bahamas, St Lucia, Bermuda, Trinidad, Antigua and British Guiana. In return, the American government handed over fifty destroyers of First World War vintage, forty-three of them going to the Royal Navy and the other seven to the Royal Canadian Navy. Britain additionally received twenty torpedo boats, five bombers and 250,000 more rifles.

Churchill's instincts had been right: the USA had the better of the deal. All the destroyers required extensive refitting before they could be accepted into service by Royal Navy. Even as late as May 1941 only thirty of them were operational. But on another level, the Anglo-American agreement was enormously important, boosting morale on both sides of the Atlantic and heralding the beginning of the partnership that was eventually to see the destruction of the Reich in the West. It was a tangible expression of US support for Churchill's government, reinforcing the will of the British people to continue the fight, while demonstrating that Britain would give absolutely no consideration to peace talks.

The need to reinforce the Royal Navy's destroyer force was emphasised by a deadly incident that took place at the end of August, illustrating the dramatic rise in tensions over a possible German invasion that kept the navy at that time in a constant state of vigilance.

The Admiralty received a report on the evening of 31 August that an enemy fleet had been sighted by RAF reconnaissance emerging from the Zuider Zee on the Dutch coast and heading towards England. Immediately the Admiralty ordered the 5th Destroyer Flotilla from the Humber and the 19th Destroyer Flotilla from Harwich to attack the invader. At the same time five destroyers from the 20th Flotilla, which had been sent from Immingham in Lincolnshire to carry out mine-laying duties in Dutch coastal waters, were told to ditch their loads and join the hunt for the enemy.

As it turned out, the German formation was not an invasion force at all, but a minor convoy moving from the Elbe to the River Meuse, supported by a defensive mine-laying operation by the Kriegsmarine off the Netherlands. The Immingham unit sailed straight into this area with disastrous results. Three of the five destroyers hit mines and were sunk or badly damaged in subsequent explosions. The HMS *Esk* sank quickly with the loss of all but one of her 150-strong crew. The *Express* had most of her bow blown away, leading to the deaths of ninety men on board, including her captain J.G. Bickford. The third vessel to go down was the *Ivanhoe*, which detonated a mine as she tried to pick up survivors from the sea. She lost fifty-three of her crew.

The final death toll from this single naval disaster was over 300, which puts into perspective the air-crew losses in Fighter Command during the Battle of Britain.

'The supposed invasion turned out to be nothing,' wrote Colville in his diary on 1 September.[48] But like the rest of the country, he knew the climax was fast approaching. Hitler would have to mount the assault in the next few weeks or postpone it into 1941. In late August the Italian Foreign Minister Ciano saw Hans Mollier, the press attaché at the German Embassy in Rome. 'He says that the landing is now imminent and that thousands of landing craft are ready in the Channel ports; that the operation, which is a very bold one, will be hard and bloody, but its outcome is certain. Mollier spoke of peace terms by the end of September.'[49]

22

'A new aristocracy of German masters will have slaves'

―

S INCE THE END of the Second World War, there has been a stream of speculation as to where Hitler might have established his headquarters in England had the invasion been successful. One persistent legend holds that, as an enthusiast of monumental architecture, he had selected as his base the vast art deco edifice of London University's Senate House in Bloomsbury. Similar gossip has long surrounded another art deco building, Du Cane Court in Balham, south London, a fashionable late 1930s residential block. Outside London, there have been parallel claims made for Apley Hall in Shropshire and Blenheim Palace in Oxfordshire, the birthplace of Winston Churchill. Even Blackpool has put forward its credentials, the local tourist board asserting that Hitler wanted to use the Lancashire resort as his 'personal playground'.[1]

There is little real credibility to such theorising. For a start, it is fanciful to suggest that German bombers in 1940–1 could hit or avoid any target at will, particularly in built-up areas. Even with sophisticated navigational aids, true precision bombing was never achieved by either side in the war – except at low level. Nor is there any evidence that Hitler actually wanted to move to Britain in the event of conquest. A ferociously insular figure, he much preferred his German homeland to foreign territory. Despite the fact that his sister-in-law Bridget, an Irishwoman who married his half-brother Alois in 1910, maintained that Adolf came to stay with them at their home in Liverpool before the First World War, it seems highly unlikely that he ever set foot in Britain. He was living as a destitute artist in Vienna at the time and throughout most of his life showed scant interest in his relatives.

Given that their leader had still not decided whether or not to launch Operation Sea Lion, the idea that the Nazis had already chosen their English headquarters is fanciful, although that does not mean that they had given no thought to the occupation of Britain. In fact, while the armed forces were still working out the details of the assault, the SS and the army developed a blueprint for the implementation of Nazi rule.

It had two striking features, one of which was its limited scope: there was certainly no comprehensive plan for German governance, with most of the practical details deferred until after conquest. The other was that Britain, initially at least, was to be treated much more harshly than the other occupied nations of Western Europe or even the Channel Islands.

Nothing symbolised this brutality more graphically than the directive from the German High Command for the 'Military Administration of England', issued on 9 September 1940, which called for the mass deportation of most of Britain's young and middle-aged men. 'Unless local conditions necessitate an exception, the able bodied male population between 17 and 45 is to be interned and, as far as possible, removed to the mainland.'² If fully enacted, it would have effectively meant long-term genocide for the British population, since the means of reproduction would have been drastically reduced. Eleven million men, one quarter of all British people in 1940, would have been exiled to the continent to face incarceration and slavery.

Walther Darré, a leading Nazi who was the Reich's Food Minister and head of the SS's Resettlement Office, pledged that the SS 'will finish this work of destruction without any sentimentality' so that from the wreckage would emerge 'a new aristocracy of German masters who will have slaves assigned to it, these slaves to be their property'.³

The directive for mass deportations was part of a series of twelve orders issued by the German military less than a week before Operation Sea Lion preparations were due to be completed. In essence the vanquished country would lie under the grip of tough military rule, with the commanders of the invading army having complete control over conquered territory. There was to be no Vichy-style, semi-independent regime. This was reflected in the first of these orders, signed by Franz Halder, the chief of the army's general staff, which related to the running of the economy under occupation. Once more, Britain's absolute subservience to the Reich was clear. 'It is the task of the Military Administration of England to secure the country's resources for the benefit of the Army and the German war economy.'⁴

The second order, signed by the army's commander-in-chief von Brauchitsch, included the clause outlining the deportation of all able-bodied men aged between seventeen and forty-five. Other clauses emphasised the ruthless nature of the occupation regime. One warned that 'armed partisans of either sex will be treated with the utmost severity. Civilians in a captured locality or behind enemy lines who take part in fighting are to be considered partisans. Hostages should be taken from among those people who support the active enemy elements.' Another clause stated that English authorities could continue to function 'if they maintain a correct attitude', while

Appeal
to the population of England.

§ 1.

English territory occupied by the German Armed Forces will be placed under German Military Administration.

§ 2.

The military Commanders will take all necessary steps to ensure the security of the Armed Forces and for the maintenance of public order and security.

§ 3.

Provided that the population behaves in an orderly manner, the Armed Forces will respect person and property.

§ 4.

Provided that they maintain an honourable attitude, the local authorities will be allowed to continue to function.

§ 5.

Any ill-considered act, any form of sabotage, any resistance, active or passive, against the German Armed Forces, will be met with the sharpest possible reprisals.

§ 6.

I hereby warn all civilians against the commitment of any hostile acts against the German Armed Forces. Such acts will be remorselessly punished by sentence of death.

§ 7.

The Orders of the German Military Authorities are to be obeyed. Disobedience will be severely punished.

The Commander-in-Chief of the Army.

This notice, signed by the Commander-in-Chief of the German Army, would have been posted all over Britain in the event of a successful Nazi conquest. The most ruthless part of the German occupation plan would have been the deportation of all able-bodied men aged between seventeen and forty-five stringent security would be imposed so that 'law and order will prevail'. Under German subjugation, the interests of the British people would count for nothing. The 'welfare of the inhabitants' was to be considered only 'in so far as they contribute directly or indirectly towards the maintenance of law and order and the securing of the country's labour force for the requirements of the troops and the German war economy'.[5]

The third order reinforced the way in which the Germans would act as state-sanctioned plunderers in occupied Britain. A 'Chief Supply Officer for England' was to be appointed after the invasion, who would 'be responsible for seizing such stocks of food, petrol, motor transport, horse-drawn vehicles, etc, in the country as have not already been taken over by the armies'.[6] All private property would therefore be at risk. This creation of a climate of plunder and sequestration would also have resulted in the systematic looting of Britain's great art treasures. Indeed, in August 1940, Department III of the Reich's security service drew up a list of artworks and artefacts in Britain that were to be targeted after conquest.

One icon of British cultural life that might have been taken to Germany as a further act of humiliation directed at the British was Nelson's Column in Trafalgar Square. According to Department III's document of 26 August, 'Ever since the Battle of Trafalgar, the Nelson column [sic] represents for England a symbol of British might and world domination. It would be an impressive way of underlining the German victory if the Nelson column were to be transferred to Berlin.'[7]

The army's fourth order was 'A Guide on How Troops are to Behave in England', which opened by stressing that 'a firm and cautious attitude towards the civilian population is to be adopted; correct soldierly behaviour is a self-evident duty.' The guide went on to warn that 'strict reticence will be observed when conversing with the local population', while 'acts of violence against orderly members of the population' would 'incur the severest penalties under military law'.[8]

Such restraint had nothing to do with leniency, as was highlighted by the draft 'Proclamation to the People of England', which von Brauchitsch would have issued after a successful invasion, explaining to the beaten people the depths of their subjugation. 'All thoughtless actions, sabotage of any kind, and any passive or active act in opposition to the German armed forces will incur the most severe retaliatory measures. I warn all civilians that if they undertake active operations against the German forces, they will be condemned to death inexorably. The decrees of the German military authorities must be observed. Any disobedience will be severely punished.'[9] A separate proclamation followed, giving more details of how various types of resistance would be crushed: 'Acts of sabotage will meet with the most severe punishment. The destruction of crops and military stores or damage to official notices will be treated as sabotage. Gas, water and electricity installations, the railways, docks and fuel tanks are specifically under the protection of the armed forces.'

This instruction went on to list a number of practices that would be treated as crimes by the Germany military courts, including: encouragement of strike action; verbal insults of the Wehrmacht or its commanders; support for escapees into unoccupied territory; any attempt to disseminate anti-German information to 'persons or authorities' outside Britain; and 'assembling in the street, circulating pamphlets or holding public meetings or processions without previous authorisation from a German commander'.[10]

According to the seventh order, again signed by von Brauchitsch, German criminal law was to be applied in any case brought before the military courts. In keeping with the Reich's approach to occupation, the punishments to be exacted by these courts were harsh: 'Anyone in the occupied territory attempting to commit acts of violence or sabotage of any kind against the German armed forces, its personnel or installations will be condemned to death.' A mix of paranoia and brutality was revealed in the catalogue of other punishable offences named under this order, such as 'listening to non-German wireless transmissions publicly', having any unauthorised association with prisoners of war, or making 'anti-German utterances of any kind, especially contemptuous or defamatory statements'.[11]

Beyond the military courts, local German army and police commanders would have been empowered to dish out summary justice. The terms of the eighth order, on police jurisdiction, were specific, stating that the commanders could impose summary sentences of up to six weeks' imprisonment or fines up to 30,000 Reichsmarks [the equivalent of £3,125 – about £150,000 in today's money].

Under the ninth order, British citizens had to surrender 'all firearms, including sporting guns, ammunition, hand grenades, and other war material' within twenty-four hours of the establishment of German martial law. Anyone failing to do so would 'be condemned to death or in less serious cases to penal servitude or imprisonment'.[12]

The next regulation covered a ban on the use of all wireless-transmitting equipment, even by amateur enthusiasts, with the death penalty as the ultimate sanction for the most serious transgressors.

The final two orders in the twelve were: first, a notice enforcing a strict blackout, complete with details such as a requirement that street lighting 'should not be visible from the height of 500 metres, either vertically or obliquely';[13] and second, a list of all the goods that were to be requisitioned by the German authorities, ranging from 'metal goods of all kinds' to 'industrial oils and fats', with the stipulation that such goods 'must not be sold, altered or removed'.[14] The text, like that of the other proclamations, would have been printed on notices to be pasted on walls across the streets of occupied Britain.

So draconian was the planned regime that, once the conquest was over, the Germans felt they would be able to occupy the country with only 250,000 men, compared to the 300,000 needed in France. The decision as to who would be the ruler or Reichskommissar of occupied Britain had not been decided by September 1940, but Hitler's choice probably came down to two candidates. One was the Foreign Minister Joachim von Ribbentrop, whose spell as ambassador to London had given him experience of English society and a capricious affection for the country, especially the seaside. During his time in England, he rented a bungalow at Minnis Bay on the Thanet Coast,[15] and was reputed to have had plans to make himself a holiday retreat at St Michael's Mount in Cornwall in the event of conquest. The other contender was Ernst Bohle, the head of the Nazi Party's foreign organisation, a confidant of Rudolf Hess and a lieutenant general in the SS. Bohle had actually been born in Bradford, the son of a German teacher and engineer who had emigrated to England.

What was certain was the identity of the man chosen to be the chief of the German Security Police in occupied Britain: the thirty-year-old Professor Franz Six, a sinister figure who combined a devotion to Hitlerian racial dogma with methods of pitiless efficiency. He would later become an SS commander on the eastern front, where his unit was said to have been responsible for the cold-blooded liquidation of perhaps as many as 2,000 people, including at least thirty-eight Jewish intellectuals. Balding and bespectacled, with low, prominent ears, he was almost the physical representation of the famous phrase coined by Hannah Arendt to describe the Nazis: 'the banality of evil'.[16] It was Hermann Goering, then at the peak of his powers in Nazi Germany, who formally appointed Six to the position of British Gestapo chief in September 1940.

In a brief interview in 1960 with the journalist Comer Clarke, Six confirmed that he would have become the chief of the Security Police if the invasion had succeeded. He admitted that 'all Britons would have been eventually interrogated about their beliefs and background', for which purpose there would have been 'internment camps and interrogation centres outside every city and big town'. Resorting to the exculpatory language that had so notoriously featured at the Nuremburg war crimes trial, he declared: 'My job would have been to see that the orders of the German Government were carried out quickly and efficiently.'[17]

During his research in 1960, Clarke talked to another senior, unnamed former Nazi, who told him of an even more baleful aspect to the German occupation plans. Reflecting the regime's fixation with racial purity, Clarke's informant claimed that there was a proposal to create a network of reproductive centres, where young British women would have been forced to participate in an Aryan breeding programme by becoming the 'sex slaves' of virile Germans:

> I know there were plans for 12 farms. Two were to have been in Wales and two in Scotland. It was hoped that Scotland would have a particularly high percentage of Nordic-type girls. Girls would have been set up in quarters in large country mansions and kept until they conceived. Individual German males would have mated with scores of girls. The mansions would have been furnished congenially and there would have been no reason to complain that the scheme was not made pleasant to both parties. As soon as it was obvious that a girl was going to have a baby, she would have been moved to hospital. If the resulting infant proved to be a satisfactory type, the girl would be sent back to conceive again.[18]

Understandably, none of this was set out in writing in 1940.

By far Six's biggest and most urgent task would have been to preside over the round-up of thousands of prominent Britons who were seen as unremittingly hostile to Germany, from leading politicians like Churchill to Jewish refugees and European exiles such as the former Czechoslovakian president Eduard Beneš. In total, 2,820 British suspects faced immediate arrest if the British armed forces had been defeated. Their names were noted down in a SS handbook, variously known as the Sonderfahndungsliste GB (Special Wanted List GB), the Nazi Black Book, or the Gestapo Black Book. It was compiled from May 1940 by Heydrich's Reich Security Office under the supervision of its deputy chief Walter Schellenberg, who later that summer headed the unsuccessful operation to kidnap the Duke of Windsor, although one of Schellenberg's subordinates, Walter zu Christian, claimed in a post-war interview with Comer Clarke that he was its real author.

A former major in the SS, Christian had been working as a spy for the Reich Security Office since 1936; his activities were focused on Britain largely because he spoke good English, having attended a school in Sussex. According to Christian, Heydrich 'wanted Churchill as his personal prisoner. Definite orders were given to a Kommando unit that Churchill should be arrested and brought immediately to Berlin.' Interestingly, Christian endorsed Franz Six's chilling assertion that ordinary Britons would also have been subjected to heavy interrogation in internment camps across the country. 'Every man and woman would have been sent to the camps in turn and methodically screened, as to their background, job, sympathies and so on.'[19]

For all Christian's boasts about his expertise, there were glaring errors in the Black Book, such as the inclusion of Sigmund Freud, who had actually died in September 1939; of Lytton Strachey, who had been dead since 1932; and of Paul Robeson, the black singer and civil rights activist, who had returned to America. Clement Attlee was listed twice, first as a retired major living in Stanmore, then as the 'Führer of the Labour Party'.[20] There were also some unlikely names, such as that of Lord Halifax, hardly a stalwart opponent of Nazi Germany, and the actress Dame Sybil Thorndike, a pacifist and member of the Peace Pledge Union, an organisation regarded by some in 1940 as barely distinguishable from the British Union of Fascists because of its ideological hostility to the war effort.

Many of those who suspected they would be targeted by the Gestapo preferred the idea of suicide to interrogation. The publisher Victor Gollancz, who featured on the list, carried a lethal opium pill given to him by his doctor because, as he put it, 'I didn't think I could stand torture.'[21] The writer and National Labour MP Harold Nicolson, also on Schellenberg's list, felt the same way, telling his wife Vita Sackville-West that he would kill himself if the Germans invaded rather than be 'tortured and humiliated'.[22] Inclusion was, understandably, seen as a badge of honour by many. 'I had them on my list too,' said David Low, whose cartoons in the *Evening Standard* had so superbly satirised the excesses of the Axis powers.[23] Others saw the humorous side, such as the author and liberal campaigner Rebecca West, writing to her fellow suspect Noël Coward, 'My dear, the people we should have been seen dead with.'[24]

The Blacklist was accompanied by another extraordinary Gestapo document, a handbook titled 'Informationsheft GB', which provided a highly detailed analysis of society in Britain, covering everything from the public-school system and the press to the climate and the role of the Anglican Church. As with the Blacklist, it contained a host of misunderstandings and errors, like the description of Sir Robert Vansittart, the Foreign Office diplomatic adviser, as the 'Speaker of the Commons', or the wild claim that the Boy Scout movement was 'a disguised instrument of power for British cultural propaganda'.[25] A number of minor trade unions, such as the Society of Packing Makers and the Amalgamated Society of Journeymen Felt Hatters, were portrayed as dangerous Marxist organisations.

Unsurprisingly, the text featured the characteristic Nazi obsession with the Jewish influence, which led to a completely distorted view of Britain in 1940. The book claimed that 'to a large extent the British food industry is supposed to be in Jewish hands', going on to assert that there were 'numerous Jewish-owned film companies' promoting 'an anti-German attitude'. Similarly, it declared that in all Britain's press corporations, 'the Jews either hold leading posts or finance these enterprises'.[26] Yet, for all its mistakes and distortions, Informationsheft GB gave an insight into how the Germans viewed British society. One passage read: 'The English national character has a flaw of putting tradition above all, retaining for as long as possible what might have been right some decades ago'; many critics of conservatism would have echoed those sentiments.

The handbook also carried remarkable details about the structure and even the personnel of MI6, information of which even the most senior figures in British public life would have been ignorant. This was because this section was largely compiled from material provided by two British spies, Sigismund Payne Best and Major Richard Stevens, who were captured by the Sicherheitsdienst in November 1939 after they were lured into a trap at Venlo on the Dutch-German border in a clever plot orchestrated by Schellenberg.

Best and Stevens may not have been the only British Intelligence officers who assisted with the compilation of Informationsheft GB. After the war, Schellenberg revealed under Allied interrogation that there had been a spy in MI6 by the name of 'Ellis'. This was almost certainly a reference to Colonel C.H. 'Dick' Ellis, who had worked for the secret services since 1923, spending much of the inter-war period in Berlin. According to the renowned espionage experts Chapman Pincher and Nigel West, Dick Ellis privately confessed after his official retirement that he 'had sold vast quantities of information about his employers' to the Germans.[27] Given his long experience and seniority, Ellis's involvement would help explain why the Informationsheft GB could be so specific about parts of the bureaucracy of British Intelligence.

Whatever minor contribution Ellis could have made, fifth columnists were generally short on the ground. As zu Christian admitted after the war, 'My knowledge of the British people told me that we weren't likely to find many traitors.'[28] The absence of Nazi insider support was graphically revealed in the so-called Gestapo 'Whitelist', prepared by the Munich branch of the Reich Security Office in September 1940. This was a catalogue of people who might be expected to be enthusiastic collaborators in the event of occupation, but from the German viewpoint it was pathetically short, containing just thirty-nine names, not one of them a person of stature or influence. Among those listed were a lecturer living in the Midlands with his sister, a woman who had taught English in a girls school in Heidelberg, and an academic from Edinburgh.

This was hardly an impressive vanguard for the potential invaders, its dismal calibre and minuscule size evidence that the Reich had gained absolutely no foothold in Britain. This problem was perhaps most acute for the Abwehr. At the outbreak of war, most of its few active agents in England were immediately classified as Category A enemy aliens and interned under the Defence Regulations, with several more rounded up over the following months. One exception was the Welsh electrical engineer Arthur Owens, known to the Abwehr as 'Johnny', who had used his trade since 1936 as a cover to supply sensitive information to the Germans, particularly about defence installations and military technology. Owens had a number of motivations for his treachery. One was personal indulgence, as the Germans not only paid him well but also supplied him with attractive women. Another was that, as a Welsh nationalist, he felt no real loyalty to Britain. He also bore a grudge against the British government because he felt his family had never been properly rewarded for a new type of naval ordnance that his father had invented in the First World War.

His clandestine relationship with the Abwehr had been noted by watchers of MI5, so to stay out of prison and protect his lifestyle he agreed to become a double agent. Operating under the code name 'Snow', Owens fed the Germans information that had been approved by his British handlers while reporting back to the MI5 on Abwehr developments. Understandably, neither the British nor the Germans really trusted him and even his own son candidly admitted, 'I would say the only side he was on was his own side. It looked like he changed sides with the prevailing wind. He was very much for himself.'[29] For all such doubts, 'Snow' was to prove invaluable to the British in the build-up to the invasion; indeed, it was partly through his duplicity that MI5 was to gain control of every spy that landed in mainland Britain from mid-1940.

After the French armistice in late June 1940, the Abwehr's need for a spy network in Britain became ever more urgent, not least because Owens was providing little useful information at the time. His own Abwehr handler Nikolaus Ritter, who had an interest in talking up his asset, had to admit, 'Johnny was unable to gather all the intelligence required on landing grounds, and some of it was stale by the time it was filtered through.'[30]

Admiral Canaris, the head of the Abwehr, therefore decided in July to launch a new initiative, code-named Operation Hummer Nord (Lobster North), to get spies into Britain who would act as scouts for the invasion force that would follow. Like Operation Sea Lion itself, there was a whiff of desperation about Hummer Nord because of the extremely tight timetable. Effectively, the Abwehr had scarcely more than thirty days to recruit, train and brief their new agents before sending them into Britain in advance of the invasion. The officer that Canaris put in charge of Hummer Nord was Generalleutnant Erwin von Lahousen, one of his closest allies and later a key figure in the internal resistance to Hitler.

In recruiting the new phalanx of spies, the Abwehr tried to focus on young men who were physically fit, daring and had some technical experience, which was vital for using radio transmitters. That was the ideal; the reality was very different. The Abwehr struggled to find the right recruits or to equip them properly for their jobs. Such failings were graphically illustrated in the first mission, when a disastrous attempt was made to land four spies on the coast of Kent at the beginning of September 1940. In the ill-fated quartet were: Karl Meier, a naturalised Dutch subject who had been born in Germany and was a member of the Dutch Nazi Party; Jose Rudolf Waldberg, an Abwehr agent since 1937; and two other Dutchmen, a hotel receptionist called Charles van den Kieboom, and a commercial traveller by the name of Sjoerd Pons.

Their task, once they had landed in England, was to report on the strength of British defences, the siting of aerodromes, infantry units and anti-aircraft guns, damage to ports and the morale of the civilian population. They were to pose as refugees fleeing the continent and were provided with revolvers, maps, two radio transmitters, food rations to last ten days and £120 in sterling. In another indicator of the mission's shambolic organisation, Meier was the only member of the party who actually spoke English fluently. Having completed a brief training course, in which they were taught the rudiments of Morse code, cryptology and radio transmission, the four men were transported to the port of Boulogne in north-eastern France, from where they were taken across the Channel in a fishing trawler escorted by two minesweepers.

Early on the morning of Tuesday 3 September, still under the cover of darkness, the little convoy arrived 7 miles off the southern Kent coast. At this point, Meier and Waldberg disembarked from the trawler and climbed into a dinghy, taking their equipment with them. Almost immediately they had a scare when a Royal Navy patrol vessel passed nearby. In their panic, they threw some of their belongings overboard, including their maps and false identity papers. Once the patrol had gone, they resumed their paddling until they reached the beach at Dungeness.

After leaving their dinghy in the water to float out with the receding tide, the two spies walked up the beach, put their wireless set under an overturned hoarding, hid their other equipment beneath a disused lifeboat that had been washed ashore after Dunkirk, and, in their nervous, exhausted state, settled down for a few hours' sleep. When they woke, just after nine o'clock, they moved the transmitter to a safer place under a tree.

By now both men were extremely thirsty and desperate for a smoke, so Meier decided to go into the nearby village of Lydd to buy some drink and cigarettes. It proved to be a fatal error. Attracted by an advertisement for 'champagne cider' outside the Rising Sun in the high street, Meier knocked on the door of the pub and when the landlady, Mabel Cole, answered, he asked for a glass, betraying his ignorance of British licensing laws. Mrs Cole's suspicions were further raised by his foreign accent and his odd request for a bath, a service not usually provided by public houses. She explained that, if he wanted a drink, he would have to come back later.

At opening time Meier duly turned up and, instead of champagne cider, ordered a half-pint of mild. As he stood at the bar, he and Mrs Cole briefly chatted. When she made a remark about the Germans starving because of the Royal Navy's blockade, Meier replied with rather too much asperity, 'How do you know they are?'[31] Confirmed in her doubts, at an opportune moment Mrs Cole slipped into another part of the pub to speak to Horace Mansfield, aged twenty-four, an Air Ministry examiner and another of her customers. As soon as Mansfield came up to the bar, Meier sensed he was in trouble, put down half a crown to pay for his beer and hurried out.

Having followed him outside into the street, Mansfield produced his own Air Ministry pass and demanded to see Meier's identity card or permit to enter a defence zone. In a flustered state, Meier said he did not have any such documents because he was a refugee. Incriminatingly, he blurted out, 'We arrived last night,'[32] thereby revealing that he was not alone. Meier was hauled off to the police station, where, after several hours of interrogation, he confessed that he had been sent from France in league with Waldberg to spy for Germany. A search now started for his colleague and their equipment, Meier being driven through the Dungeness area in a police car with Mansfield and a number of officers to show them where the pair had landed and initially hidden.

While Meier continued to be held by the police, Waldberg had throughout the day remained in hiding by the shore. He managed to get the radio working and that night, at 8.30 p.m., sent a slightly incoherent message to his handlers: 'Arrived safely document destroyed English patrol two hundred metres from coast beach with brown nets and railway sleepers at a distance of fifty metres no mines few soldiers unfinished block house Waldberg'.[33] As the hours passed without his comrade's return, Waldberg realised how grim his prospects were.

Then, to his alarm, from his hideout he glimpsed the police conducting their manhunt and now sent another, far more anxious, message: 'Meier prisoner English police searching for me am cornered I can resist thirst until Saturday if I am to resist send aeroplanes Wednesday evening three kilometres north of arrival long live Germany Waldberg.'[34] Having made this transmission, he packed up the set and moved to another hiding place near a water-pumping station. It was to no avail. Early on the morning of 4

September he was transcribing a third message when he was discovered by the police and arrested.

The other two members of the party, Pons and Kieboom, were apprehended even more quickly. After dropping off Waldberg and Meier, the fishing trawler had sailed eastwards for about twenty minutes before releasing another dinghy, in which Pons and Kieboom paddled to the beach at Dymchurch. But they never made it beyond there. As they walked towards a field, where they planned to hide their gear, they were challenged by a patrol from the Somerset Light Infantry. Unable to provide any explanation for their presence at Dymchurch, beyond the unconvincing claim that they were refugees, they were taken into custody.

All four spies had been captured within less than twenty-four hours of their arrival on British soil without a shot being fired. That outcome was not only a reflection of woeful German planning but also of British vigilance, fuelled by hyper-awareness of the invasion threat.

The four men went on trial at the Old Bailey in November 1940 before a jury. Three of them were found guilty and executed, but, much to the government's fury, Pons escaped the hangman's noose because the jury seems to have felt that he acted only under extreme duress. His courtroom defence was based on his claim that he had been coerced into the operation by the threat that, if he did not cooperate, he would be sent to a concentration camp for currency offences.

According to a Special Branch report after the trial, 'Although there is no doubt that Pons was as guilty as his three confederates, the Jury unfortunately believed his evidence, given on oath, that he had been blackmailed by the Gestapo and that he had come to England with the intention of giving himself up immediately on landing.' It went on to note that 'he is a dangerous man and obviously should be kept in custody until the cessation of hostilities.'[35] Accordingly, Pons was imprisoned under the Defence Regulations until 1945, then deported to his native Holland.

During the Old Bailey trial Meier was asked why he did not try to save himself once he had landed by just going straight to the police 'to make a clean breast of it'. His answer showed a deep confidence in the imminence and the inevitable triumph of Operation Sea Lion. According to one report of the court proceedings,

> Meier replied that, having seen the downfall of Holland, Belgium and France, he was convinced that Germany would successfully invade this country and overrun it just as easily as she had conquered the other European countries. He was certain that at the end of their ten days' rations, he and his companions would be out in the open again attached to a victorious army. If he ratted on the Germans and fell into their hands when they invaded us his last state would be worse than his first.[36]

Other German spies sent to Britain under Operation Hummer Nord proved much more malleable, as events in the coming days showed, with Arthur Owens, or 'Snow', playing a central role. For months, Owens had been out of favour with the Abwehr, due to his limited supply of information, as well as with MI5, due to his perceived unreliability. All that changed when the first German spy was due to be parachuted into England in early September 1940. His Abwehr handlers informed Snow about this mission because they required his assistance. He in turn informed MI5 because he needed to re-establish his credibility. Guy Liddell, the head of MI5 counterespionage, wrote on 27 August: 'Snow is in daily communication with the Germans and arrangements are being made [by them] to land an agent [in Britain] by parachute. A suitable spot is being found, the location of which will be communicated to the Germans.'[37]

The parachutist was Gosta Caroli, a Swedish journalist who had moved to Hamburg in the mid-1930s, becoming a fanatical supporter of the Nazi Party as well as an agent for the Abwehr. Shortly before the war, Caroli combined both roles by posing as a travel journalist in England while gathering intelligence for the Germans.

On the night of 5 September, just as the last of the Kent spies was arrested, Caroli leapt from a matt black He111 and descended on rural Northamptonshire. Against the advice of the Heinkel pilot who had urged the use of a secondary parachute for his equipment, Caroli jumped with his heavy wireless transmitter strapped tightly to his chest. Due to its weight, he descended much more quickly than he expected. Even worse, when he landed, the wireless smashed into his chin and knocked him unconscious. When he came round, he managed to drag himself, his parachute and his equipment to an overgrown ditch on farmland near the remote village of Denton, where he passed out again. Eventually his prone body was spotted by a labourer, who summoned Cliff Beechener, a tenant farmer and member of the local Home Guard.

As Beechener later recalled, he grabbed his twelve-bore shotgun and marched towards the spot. 'When I came to the ditch all I could see was a pair of shoes sticking out from under some ash plants. The shoes were orange-coloured leather − and it occurred to me that I would not think much of a chap with shoes like that.' Caroli then woke up. 'He saw my gun and said, "Kamerad, kamerad, I surrender." He spoke good English.'[38] The police were called and Caroli was taken into custody. Apart from his wireless, the other items found on him were £200, a revolver, a bottle of brandy, a list of cipher codes, writing materials and a false identity card with a number provided by Snow.

Since it was obvious, even to the local police and the Home Guard, that

Caroli was a spy, he was handed over for interrogation by MI5, whose officers instantly recognised the potential opportunity to use him as a double agent if he could be broken. Crucially, unlike the Kent spies, he had not yet communicated with the Abwehr, so his handlers would not know that he had been captured. Caroli was given a simple choice: death or working undercover for the British.

One piece of leverage that MI5 had on Caroli was that, during his lengthy interrogation, he had revealed that another parachutist would soon land in Britain. This other spy, he admitted without stating his name, was a close friend, their bond forged during their Abwehr training together. MI5 expertly exploited this knowledge. In return for his cooperation, Caroli was promised that his friend would be spared the gallows once he was caught. He accepted the deal.

It was a vital breakthrough. Caroli became the first block on which the whole edifice of Britain's double-cross system was built. Within a fortnight, MI5's new ability to deceive Germany was proven in dramatic fashion. Provided with the code name Summer by his handlers, Caroli used his transmitter to contact the Abwehr, explaining that he had sustained injuries on landing somewhere between Oxford and Buckingham, was now posing as a refugee but urgently needed assistance. At once the Abwehr contacted Snow. The message read: 'Swedish friend in fields near Oxford. How can we contact you at once? Standing by for your answer.'[39]

This was a key moment for MI5. If the Germans could be misled into thinking that Caroli had been rescued by his fellow agent, then not only would Snow's credibility as a German asset be hugely enhanced, but also the Abwehr would believe that they had the beginnings of a real spy network in Britain. In turn, that would lead to more German agents being drawn into MI5's elaborate web of deceit. As one of MI5's senior officers, Tommy Robertson, put it at the time: 'There is a strong possibility that this single spy Caroli may be the forerunner of a whole battalion. Upon the action now taken really depends all the months of work spent on Snow.'[40]

Robertson proposed that MI5, pretending to be Snow, should send back a reply to the Abwehr, telling Caroli to meet Owens at High Wycombe railway station. To add convincing details, the ersatz Snow told the Abwehr that he would be wearing a white buttonhole and the password would be: 'Have you seen the stationmaster?' To add a degree of authenticity in case some Germans were watching, Caroli really was taken to High Wycombe station. There he met not Owens, but a shadowy figure called Sam McCarthy, whom the Germans regarded as an underworld associate of Owens, although in reality, despite his background as a petty criminal and near-alcoholic, he was an MI5 agent, code-named Biscuit, whose main job was to keep an eye on the errant Welshman.

The plan worked to perfection. McCarthy, for once refraining from drink, played his part without a false move, right down to the white buttonhole. He and Caroli left the station together, strolled some of the way along the verge of the A40 to make sure no Germans were following, and then Caroli was picked up by MI5 again. That night, MI5, still posing over the wireless as Snow, told the Abwehr that 'the Swedish friend' had been safely entrusted to the care of his confidant McCarthy.

The Abwehr fell for it. 'Thanks for help to friend. Won't forget. Expecting reports of his trip. Please try to give daily reports. Paramount importance constant observation of airports, planes etc.'[41] Guy Liddell wrote with satisfaction in his diary the following evening: 'The meeting between Biscuit and Summer took place. There was no-one else there. The Germans have expressed their warm thanks to Snow for his services.'[42]

The double-cross system had been born. From that moment on High Wycombe station, when Biscuit acknowledged Summer's password, not a single spy arrived in Britain without MI5's knowledge. In fact, Guy Liddell soon set up a committee to handle the cases that Snow increasingly generated. Known as the Twenty Committee, because that figure is represented in Roman numerals by two Xs, this body was headed by the brilliant Oxford academic John Masterman who later commented, 'By means of the double agent system, we actively ran and controlled the German espionage system in this country. This is at first blush a staggering claim, and in the first place we could not bring ourselves to believe that we did so. Nevertheless it is true, and was true for the greater part of the war.'[43]

The efficacy of this system was proved within days when Caroli's training partner Wulf Schmidt, the man for whom he had traded his loyalty, arrived in Britain. A Danish national who had worked all over the world, Schmidt was another zealous Nazi supporter who ended up backing the British cause. Like Caroli, he was injured when he landed, near the Cambridgeshire village of Willingham. Again like Caroli, he fell asleep lying on his parachute and awoke to find himself under arrest. Driven through London on his way to be interrogated by MI5, he was amazed to see how resilient British society really was, having been subjected to Goebbels' taunting propaganda. 'I had been told that England was on the brink of collapse, that there was no food in the shops and that London was in ruins. None of it was true. I realized that the picture I had been given of a totally defeated Britain, with the people on the run and the resistance to Germany nil, was entirely misleading.'[44]

Through a mixture of threats and persuasion from MI5, including claims that he had been betrayed by Caroli and let down by the Abwehr, Schmidt agreed to become a double agent. Under the alias of Harry Williamson and the code name Tate, he was one of MI5's most successful operatives, not least because his handlers regularly allowed him to transmit accurate information in order to maintain his credibility. After the war he remained in England, working as a photographer for the *Watford Observer*.

Lahousen's final attempt in September 1940 to land spies in Britain, an episode with elements of glamour, daring, confusion and, ultimately, death, was also symbolic of the hazardous futility of his previous initiatives. The glamour came from the leader of the mission, an exotic secret agent and former professional dancer called Vera Schalburg, whose dark, beguiling looks led to her soubriquet of 'the beautiful spy'.[45]

As the protégée, mistress, or possibly even wife of Hilmar Dierks, a German spymaster who ran Abwehr agents in Western Europe, she was reportedly sent on her first mission to Britain in 1938 or 1939, when she was instructed to use her charms on London society in order to gather political and military gossip. Her feminine allure may have been too captivating for one admirer. According to her MI5 file released in 2000, in the summer of 1939 while in England, Vera gave birth to an infant who was quickly sent to an orphanage in Essex. There was no indication of the father's identity, but subsequent rumour held that he was a senior figure in the British establishment, speculation that later would play its part in the outcome of this strange saga.

Vera appears to have left London hurriedly before the outbreak of war. Her next visit to Britain was to take place under far more dangerous circumstances. Lahousen had decided that, as well as trying to land spies on the Kent coast, he would simultaneously land a group of German agents at the opposite end of the country, in northern Scotland. The four-strong party chosen to undertake this Caledonian mission was Vera, Dierks himself and two highly regarded operatives: Robert Petter, a skilled wireless operator from Zurich; and Karl Drucke from Hessen, an experienced agent who posed as a German businessman.

The extraordinary plan devised by the Abwehr was for the party to be flown by seaplane from Norway to the Scottish coast, where they would launch their rubber dingy, accompanied by their equipment and a set of bicycles, on which they were to travel the entire 600 miles to London. The scheme, already fanciful enough, was almost immediately overtaken by tragedy.

On the night before their departure from Hamburg to Norway, the quartet went out for a farewell meal, during which large quantities of beer and schnapps were consumed. Having left the restaurant, they began the journey back to their hotel by car, with Dierks at the wheel. Within moments, he had lost control of the vehicle, which skidded, overturned and came to a grinding halt in the street. Dierks was killed, but surprisingly the other three escaped with only minor injuries.

Initially, Lahousen wanted to cancel the mission but soon changed his mind, not least because the Abwehr, which still urgently needed more trained spies in Britain, was emboldened by the apparently successful parachute landings of Caroli and Schmidt. On 21 September, the remaining three agents set off again for Stavanger in Norway. There they practised transferring from a landed seaplane into a rubber dingy, as well as unloading their equipment and bicycles. They also were given some English currency and false identities that had been manufactured by Agent Snow's network. Schalburg was to be Vera Erikson, the Danish niece of an Italian countess living in Kensington; Petter took on the alias of Werner Walti, a Swiss subject living in Sussex Gardens; and Drucke became François de Deeker, a French refugee.

As the trio made their final preparations, their dismal luck, resulting from poor planning and recklessness, continued. When finally, on the night of 30 September, the skies were clear enough for the seaplane to land Vera and the two men in their boat near the shoreline, the conditions were so rough that the bicycles fell in the sea before the three even reached the dinghy. Cold, wet and disorientated, they made it to dry land in the early morning, but now without any means of transport. So they decided that they would try to travel to London by train. To increase their safety, they agreed to split up and journey from the first railway stations they came across, Petter heading eastwards, Drucke and Schalburg going westwards.

At 7.30 a.m., the pair arrived at the small station of Portgordon, where they instantly aroused the suspicion of the stationmaster, John Donald, particularly when Vera asked where they were, all public transport signs at that time having been removed as an anti-invasion measure. Donald later explained: 'It is very unusual for anyone to call at 7.30 am and ask for the name of the station and this coupled with the fact that the man appeared to be endeavouring to prevent me getting a full face view of him made me suspicious.' Just as incriminating were their clothes. 'I noticed that the bottom of the man's trousers and shoes were wet, also the bottom of his overcoat. The woman's shoes were wet and there was a slight deposit of hoar frost on the shoulders of her coat.'[46]

Donald telephoned the police while a station porter kept the couple occupied and soon Constable John Grieve arrived on the scene. He asked to see Drucke's identity card, which immediately struck him as fake because, despite his claimed status as a refugee, there was no immigration officer's stamp. When he questioned Vera about their movements, her vague answers were just as damning, as PC Grieve recalled.

> I asked them where they had stayed the previous night. The woman said, 'We stayed in a hotel at Banff.' The man did not answer. I asked them the name of the hotel in Banff in which they had stayed. The woman shrugged her shoulders. I said to the woman, 'How did you get to Portgordon from Banff?' She replied, 'We hired a taxi to within a mile of Portgordon and then we walked.' I told them I was unsatisfied with their explanations and told them I was to take them to the Police station.[47]

The game was almost up. At Buckie police station, they were questioned by Inspector John Simpson, who was already convinced that they were enemy agents because of their implausible stories. His belief was confirmed when he opened the suitcase that Drucke had lugged the whole way from the beach. In it, Simpson found 'a small Mauser pistol loaded with six rounds of ammunition in the magazine', as well as 'a wireless transmitting set, three small and two large batteries, a voltmeter, a Morse tapping key, headphones, a three-way plug and wire'.[48] Apart from all this material, one other telling piece of evidence against the two was the discovery on Drucke of a half-eaten German sausage of a type that was not sold in England.

With commendable acuity, the police recognised that the pair in custody might not have been alone. Making enquiries, they were soon on the tail of Petter, alias Werner Walti. He had been more successful than his colleagues, having made it to the town of Buckie where he caught a train to Edinburgh with one change at Aberdeen, due to arrive at Waverley station in the Scottish capital at 4.30 p.m. He may have thought that he had managed to evade the authorities, having gone through an identity check at Dundee without any incident, but the net was tightening. The police had managed to get a description of Petter from railway staff at the beginning of his journey, whom he had asked about train times to the South. In the afternoon this was flashed through to the Edinburgh police, who hurried to Waverley, but just too late to meet passengers off the 4.30.

At this point Petter made a serious mistake. On being told that the next train to London did not depart until 10 p.m., he decided to deposit his heavy case, which, like Drucke's, contained his espionage equipment, at the left luggage office and then went out into the streets in search of a meal. By now the Edinburgh police, led by their diminutive chief constable William 'Wee Willie' Merrilees, were conducting a full search of the station. Soon they came across Petter's suitcase in the left luggage office, easily recognisable from the whitish marks around the bottom, an indication that it had been standing in salt water. Merrilees ordered the case to be opened. Inside was Petter's wireless transmitting set.

A trap was now laid, with Merrilees placing himself and several plain-clothes officers near the office to await the spy's return. He duly came back at about 9 p.m., handing his left-luggage ticket to a porter as Merrilees prepared to move. In his memoirs, the chief constable left this vivid account of what happened next:

> The suspect was standing with his left hand hidden in his trouser pocket, arm apparently rigid. Clearly he was armed. I sauntered up to him. As he watched, I gestured with my hands as if to someone behind him – an old trick. When he half-turned to see who was there, I sprang forward and grabbed his wrist. I can assure you it was no light grip. I wrenched, and his hand was jerked out of the pocket, grasping a Mauser automatic pistol, fully loaded. I hung on to him until my assistant arrived, and we bundled him into the left-luggage office, and bolted the door.

Even then Petter did not give up. Surrounded by officers, he suddenly produced a flick knife. As Merrilees recalled, 'We were just in time to prevent him using the gleaming blade.'[49] Petter was taken to police head-quarters in Edinburgh, along with Drucke and Vera, and then south for interrogation by MI5.

There is no doubt that MI5 attempted to turn the three, adding them to the double-cross network, but Drucke and Petter, hardened officers of the Reich, refused to crack. As a result, they were put on trial at the Old Bailey in June 1941, found guilty and executed on 6 August. Vera Schalburg was never placed in the dock despite the overwhelming evidence against her, which may have been an indicator that she agreed to cooperate with the British. Certainly there is an interesting note in Guy Liddell's diaries for 3 October, soon after her arrest: 'Vera is begin-ning to crack.'[50] Similarly, Vera stated during one of her long sessions of questioning by MI5 that she had been promised some clemency by Dr Harold Dearden, an expert in psychological techniques for breaking prisoners. 'I do not wish to say anything more because I have been inter-rogated on several occasions by Dr Dearden and other persons. Dr Dearden said it was all finished and that I should not be "on trial" and would not be shot or hanged.'[51]

Lord Jowitt, who prosecuted Drucke and Petter, later wrote cryptically that 'it may be she was able to be of some use to our authorities.'[52] The reality is that, given the publicity about her case, it would have been almost impossible for her to work as a double agent, certainly not in an active role. Alternatively her alleged past relationship with a senior public figure may have served as a form of protection, particularly if she threatened to expose his identity in court. At the very least, the recognition that she was the mother of a child in England may have inhibited the authorities from a terminal step.

Like the rest of her story, her life after her release from prison in 1945 is full of mystery. It is usually said that she was deported to Germany, but in an article for *After the Battle* magazine in 1976, the resourceful writer Winston G. Ramsay recounted an intriguing incident he had uncovered in an Allied internment camp after the war, when Lahousen asked an unnamed senior British Intelligence officer about her. 'You're wondering what happened to Vera, "the Beautiful Spy" as we called her. Well, you're absolutely right. She came over to us. If you ever want to see her again, well, I should have a look around the Isle of Wight. I think you might find her there – with another name, of course, and nobody there has the slightest idea about her background.'[53]

The story of the German spies was a resounding triumph for the British authorities. The counter-invasion measures and the national mood of alertness had proved their worth. Contrary to the fashionable view, it was the British who were ruthless and well organised, the Germans who were incompetent. In his diary Guy Liddell noted an exchange he had on 8 September 1940 with Major General Kenneth Strong, the head of the German section of military intelligence who had just been interviewing the Kent spies. 'Strong has great regard for German efficiency and cannot bring himself to believe that they could have been so stupid as to send these men over here without having schooled them properly and worked out plans by which they could be really effective.'[54]

23

'One gigantic conflagration'

~

THE ACHIEVEMENT OF German air superiority was central to the plans for Operation Sea Lion. By the beginning of September 1940, there were signs that the Luftwaffe's strategy was beginning to yield results. Despite the heroism of RAF pilots and the efficiency of the Dowding system, the weeks of hard pounding had taken their toll. Heavy casualties meant that less experienced pilots had to be moved into the front line after inadequate training. The output from the aircraft factories struggled to make up the losses of planes. No. 11 Group in the South-East of England was under tremendous pressure. The base at RAF Manston near Ramsgate was so badly hit that it had to be abandoned, while Biggin Hill and Kenley were severely damaged.

To preserve its resources, Fighter Command started to send up units of five to seven planes to meet the German formations instead of the usual full squadrons. During the first weeks of fighting in the Battle of Britain, the Germans had generally been losing twice as many planes as the British. But, from 31 August to 6 September, the balance was much more even: 161 RAF losses to the Luftwaffe's 189.[1] At a strategy meeting on 7 September, Dowding, a naturally cautious, pessimistic figure, told his staff that they would now have to confront the reality that Fighter Command might start 'to go downhill'.[2]

However, that very day brought a dramatic change in the RAF's fortunes. Instead of maintaining its destruction of Fighter Command's bases, the Luftwaffe switched the focus to London. Throughout the summer the Germans had been carrying out bombing raids, both day and night, against industrial targets further north. Hull, for instance, had been bombed regularly since 19 June, while at the end of August 455 tons of high explosives were dropped on Liverpool over four successive nights.

The onslaught on London on 7 September was on a far bigger scale, as the Luftwaffe hit the docklands and the heart of the capital in two huge assaults. In the first wave almost 350 bombers, escorted by over 600 fighters, flew to the target, creating a fleet that stretched 20 miles across the sky. The colossal raid, involving the most concentrated enemy force launched against

Britain since the Spanish Armada in 1588, began at 4.15 p.m. and lasted for two hours. The arrival of darkness brought no respite for Londoners. A second giant wave of 250 bombers arrived to assail the city in the early hours of the morning, the first heavy night raid of the war.

The devastation caused by the 625 tons of explosive and more than 900 incendiary canisters was immense. The death toll reached 448 and another 1,600 people were injured. On the Peabody Estate in Whitechapel, 78 residents were killed when the basement of the building where they had taken shelter received a direct hit. Nine miles of warehousing and buildings along the Thames were destroyed, while over 100,000 tons of shipping were lost. At the Surrey docks, the fires were so intense that more than 300 pumps were needed to tackle them. A.P. Herbert, a petty officer in the Thames Auxiliary Patrol, was on duty that night in his motor boat. 'The scene was like a lake in Hell. Burning barges were drifting everywhere. We could hear the hiss and roar of the conflagration, a formidable noise, but we could not see it, so dense was the smoke. Nor could we see the western shore.'[3]

The experience of trying to douse the flames while the Luftwaffe flew over the capital was graphically described by auxiliary fireman Frank Hurd, whose crew was sent to tackle a blaze at Beckton gasworks:

> Chaos met our eyes. Gasometers were punctured and were blazing away, a power house had been struck rendering useless the hydraulic hydrant supply (the only sources of water there). An overhead gantry bearing lines of trucks communicating with the railway siding was well alight. And then overhead, we heard 'Jerry'. The searchlights were searching the sky in a vain effort to locate him. Guns started firing, and then I had my first experience of a bomb explosion. A weird whistling sound and I ducked beside the pump together with two more of the crew. The others, as scared as we were, had thrown themselves down wherever they happened to be. Then a vivid flash of flame, a column of earth and debris flying into the air and the ground heaved. I was thrown violently against the side of the appliances.[4]

That night signalled the start of the Blitz, the long aerial terror campaign that aimed to pulverise capital into submission. Following the attacks of 7/8 September, London was hit for fifty-seven consecutive nights by the German bombers. In the first month of the Blitz alone, 5,730 Londoners were killed and 9,000 seriously injured. From November 1940, the heavy nocturnal raids were extended to provincial cities, a move that was to result in the notorious raid on Coventry.

Yet for all the suffering and damage caused by the Blitz, the Luftwaffe's new strategy was a blessing for Fighter Command. The indiscriminate targeting of the urban population meant that the airfields were no longer under attack. At the very moment when the RAF was under its greatest strain, the Luftwaffe gave it some breathing space. Pilots could be rested, planes repaired, communication lines restored.

The Germans would soon pay heavily for this error. Wrongly thinking that the job had almost been finished, Goering had turned the Luftwaffe's attention to mass destruction. But there were other factors at work. One was the vengeful impulse for retaliation. Goering and Hitler had both been outraged when the RAF, on Churchill's orders, had sent ninety-five Hampdens, Wellingtons and Whitleys to bomb Berlin on the night of 24/25 August as a reprisal for a Luftwaffe attack on London the day before. That German attack had been unintentional. In fact the targets had been Thameshaven and Rochester, but the Luftwaffe's planes had flown off course. The British raid caused little real physical damage to the German capital, but the psychological impact was enormous, since Hitler's regime had boasted that Berlin was invulnerable to British air attack.

Sensing insult, Hitler worked himself into a fury against the British, particularly as in the subsequent two weeks Bomber Command carried out five further raids on Berlin. It was this explosive indignation that infused his ranting speech at the Sportpalast in Berlin on 4 September, when he told his hysterical audience that he would 'raze' Britain's cities 'to the ground' and was on the verge of launching the invasion.[5]

Goering explicitly spelt out the motive for retaliation when he launched the start of the Blitz: 'This moment is a historic one. As a result of provocative attacks on Berlin in recent nights, the Führer has decided to order a mighty blow to be struck in revenge against the British capital of the British empire.'[6] Yet the motivation went deeper than mere revenge. For the top Nazis, the bombardment of London was not a radical alteration in strategy but another aspect of the wider objective of forcing a surrender. Always detached about Operation Sea Lion, Goering saw this as a golden chance to prove that on its own the Luftwaffe could bring the United Kingdom to her knees.

Hitler saw the adoption of the new urban target as a means of coercing Britain to capitulate. Under Directive No. 17, issued on 1 August, he had reserved for himself the right to order terror attacks. Now was the moment to strike, as the preparations for Sea Lion reached their climax. In his mind, the bombing could serve as a possible substitute for invasion. Even if the Blitz did not compel Britain to surrender quickly, it would still make the task of the seaborne expedition easier. In advance of the landings, the heavy raids on London would alarm the government, draw resources away from the defences, terrorise the public, undermine supply lines and cause a stream of refugees to flee the capital, hindering the mobility of the British army and leading to labour shortages. Moreover, the city's flaming destruction matched his apocalyptic outlook. During the summer of 1940, Hitler had asked Albert Speer,

> Have you ever looked at a map of London? It is so closely built up that one source of fire alone would destroy the whole city, as happened once before, 200 years ago. [Although he was in error about the date, he was undoubtedly referring to the Great Fire of London, in 1666.] Goering wants to use innumerable incendiary bombs of an altogether new type to create sources of fire in all parts of London. Fires everywhere, thousands of them. Then they'll unite in one gigantic area of conflagration.[7]

At the time that the Blitz was launched, the German High Command had become more united and optimistic about the prospects for Operation Sea Lion, buoyed up not only by the Luftwaffe's reports of Fighter Command's supposed imminent demise but also by the growing assembly of the invasion fleet in the Channel ports. At the end of August, the Kriegsmarine staff had told Hitler that they would have to extend the deadline for the completion of all the naval preparations beyond the original one of 15 September. This was partly because of the need to organise the diversion across the North Sea, Operation Herbstreise – a feint with large transports across the North Sea targeted at the east coast, while the true invasion took place in the south. However, they also had to finish laying mine barriers along the flanks of the proposed crossing, for which 6,800 mines were required.

The new timetable, taking this into account, was issued on Hitler's behalf by Keitel, the commander-in-chief of the Wehrmacht, on 3 September: 'The earliest date for the departure of the transport fleets will be 20.9.40. S Day (invasion day) will be 21.9.40. The order for the start of the operation will be given on S minus 10 days, that is probably on 11.9.40. The final decision on S Day and S Time [the beginning of the first landing] will follow at the latest on S-3 day at noon. All measures will be taken so that the operation can be held in check 24 hours before S time.'[8] The moment of destiny had almost arrived. Effectively, Hitler had told his commanders that he would give his final decision on Sea Lion within just eight days, on 11 September.

On 5 September, all leave in the German army in Western Europe was cancelled. On the following day, the eve of the bomber assault, Hitler met his chiefs again to discuss progress. Even Raeder, the perennial sceptic, sounded a little more enthusiastic but he could detect that Hitler was still deeply uncertain about whether to proceed or not, as he told his naval staff at a meeting the next day. 'The Führer's decision to land is still by no means settled, as he is firmly convinced that Britain's defeat will be achieved even without a landing. As before, the landing is regarded by the Führer as the means by which the end of the war can in all probability be achieved at one stroke. The Führer, however, is not thinking of carrying out this operation if the risk it involves is too great.'⁹ Again, this statement reinforces the fact that Hitler and Goering believed that, at the eleventh hour, Britain could still be conquered by the air war alone.

Across the water, Britain was braced for the invasion that appeared to be imminent. All the evidence pointed in that direction, from Hitler's speech to the RAF reconnaissance of the enemy barges. The tension was further cranked up by a stream of reports from the Combined Intelligence Committee. On 1 September, the committee was told that 'the attack on England should be expected in September, possibly in the first half of the month. The signal for the attack will be a wholesale air attack with all available aircraft,' which would be followed by 'airborne landings' and the main expedition 'over the Channel, where mines, submarines, e-boats, [fast attack craft], parts of the fleet and aircraft on both flanks will prevent the British Fleet intervening'. According to this report, the Germans were also planning to use a 'colourless gas inducing exhaustion and insensibility'.¹⁰ Two days later, the committee noted an increase in 'concentrations of barges' in the Channel ports and in waterways leading to the coast.¹¹

Responding to the mounting tension, Brooke, the commander of Home Forces, recorded in his diary for 4 September that he had met Dill, the Chief of the Imperial General Staff, to discuss 'how we are to meet the German invasion if it comes within the next few days'.¹²

The following day, his headquarters produced a summary on the German threat, warning 'that Hitler may intend in the near future to carry out a direct attack on Great Britain. To achieve success, the objective must be one giving decisive results and the maximum mutual support of the three services. This will mean the greatest possible use of force in the minimum time, with the shortest possible sea voyage. The objective will probably be London and the attack will be carried out ruthlessly and with every means available.' The note concluded:

> It is evident that the Germans are now engaged in trying to gain air superiority over our fighter force. On the result of this attempt will depend their future action. If Hitler thinks that he has achieved a fair measure of superiority during the next few days, a full scale invasion in small craft may be attempted within an area between Southwold and Shoreham and for some distance on either flank . . . Conditions are most favourable about 12 or 13 September but there is a possibility of change, ie the present fair period may decide action any time after 6 September. After 13 September conditions start to deteriorate and any postponement beyond 20 September would be risking a definite break in the weather.¹³

The idea of a German assault across the sea over the shortest possible route generated some alarm in Sir Dudley Pound, the chief of the naval staff, who was concerned about the inadequacy of the defences at Dover. Partly in response, Brooke moved the New Zealand division to east Kent to strengthen the land defences there.

But the American military attaché General Raymond Lee, looking at the wider picture, felt privately that Britain would rise to the challenge. In a perceptive diary note for 5 September he wrote, 'On a cold-blooded appraisal, one might say that the betting on Britain beating off an invasion in this fall is about 3 to 1, with the odds lengthening every week. There is still a little time for an attempt and I really believe that Hitler will have to try to admit what he can hardly afford to admit: first that invasion is hopeless and second that he is in for a long war. The first means a defeat in this year's campaign and the second, an ultimate defeat. The results of this month's intensive air attack are remarkably slender. All the railroads are running, road circulation is normal, telephone and telegraph services are in order, industrial production undamaged.'

The indications of an impending strike continued to accumulate. On 5 September decoders at Bletchley Park picked up a Luftwaffe Enigma signal indicating that a major attack on London was about to be launched. The next day, the Royal Navy's Operations Division reported that 'a large collection of self-propelled barges has been located moving westward along the Belgian coast. In all these craft amount to not less than 500 . . . An attempt at invasion may be expected in the very near future.'[14] A report to the meeting of the Combined Intelligence Committee, also on 6 September, gave more detailed findings from the latest reconnaissance operations over northern France and the Low Countries. One RAF plane had recently taken a set of photographs that showed 61 barges in Boulogne; 14 steamers and 53 barges in Calais; 134 barges in Dunkirk; and 273 barges, 46 small craft and 3 merchant ships at Ostend.

Against this backdrop, it was hardly a surprise that the German aerial bombardment of London in September should have been interpreted by the military authorities as the possible start of the invasion. Goebbels' propaganda machine had tried to ratchet up such anxiety, the New British Broadcasting Station telling its listeners that 'Hitler may at any hour give the orders for the invasion to begin.'[15]

Late on the afternoon of 7 September, the Chiefs of Staff held yet another meeting, with Pound in the chair, to examine the very latest intelligence on the threat. As the senior officers gathered, they could hear bombs falling and exploding across the capital, a sound that gave a powerful sense of urgency to their discussions. Major General 'Paddy' Beaumont-Nesbitt outlined the evidence for the expected assault, including the move of the bomber groups to northern France, the collection of gun emplacements in the Calais area, the attempt to gain air superiority over southern England and, above all, 'the concentration of barges totalling some 500 in ports from Le Havre to Ostend inclusive. It is estimated that these barges could carry 50,000 troops with a fair proportion of equipment and material.' As a result of this information, the Chiefs of Staff Committee 'agreed that the possibility of invasion had become imminent and that the defence forces should stand by on immediate notice'.[16]

For most of the services, this instruction was little more than an expression of current practice but the situation was different for the Home Forces and the Home Guard. The Chiefs of Staff now decided to 'place troops in Southern and Eastern Commands at immediate notice and warn troops in other commands that this action had been taken'.[17] The code word within the Home Forces for immediate notice was 'Cromwell'. There were, however, two problems with Cromwell: one was that its implementation was not always explained properly to the units in the front line, particularly those from the Home Guard; the second was the absence of any intermediate stage between eight hours' and immediate notice, so, for many local officers, the implication of Cromwell was that the invasion was actually under way.

Once it had been dispatched, the order inevitably had an enormous impact throughout the defence forces. Telegraph services and telephone exchanges were taken over by the military. Messages were flashed up in cinemas, telling all service personnel to return to their bases. Partly because of the German bombing, partly because the term 'immediate notice' was widely misunderstood, and partly because it was issued on a Saturday night when many inexperienced officers were on duty, there was a widespread belief that enemy landings had started.

The misinterpreted report did lead to some confusion, nervousness, even excitement, but, given that so many troops in southern and eastern England genuinely believed that the major German offensive had begun, it produced no evidence of cowardice or loss of nerve. In fact, Patrick Barrass of the Essex Regiment was impressed at how calmly his unit reacted to receiving the signal for 'Cromwell': 'When the signal arrived, the Commanding Officer said, "We'll have early teas", as if it were a cricket match. We were concentrated and fully kitted, ready to move off in a few minutes. There was no tension. It was just taken as a job.'[18] There were also some overzealous responses. The stationmaster at Lincoln was visited by two officers who told him to put into action the local plan for disrupting the railway network by immobilising trains and destroying the main yard. Unconvinced by the officers' demand, the stationmaster rang the HQ of Southern Command, who told him to carry on as normal.

For some soldiers, the night was a thrilling one. Major R.F. 'Henry' Hall of the Dorset Regiment, which was in the 43rd Division and was to be part of Brooke's GHQ reserve in Hertfordshire, recalled: 'The whole of the 43rd division moved by road with a police escort to Hatfield Forest, north of London. It was a wonderful experience, travelling as fast as we could through deserted streets, particularly through London, rushing up to a position where we had the task of GHQ Reserve, which meant that had the Germans landed in Kent, which was defended by XII Corps, we would counterattack on London if they got as far as that.'[19]

The commotion was much greater in the Home Guard, where there was little awareness of what 'Cromwell' actually meant. 'Gentlemen, I have grave news for you; it has begun,' a Luton commander told his battalion shortly after they had assembled for drill practice.[20] Presuming the worst, local Home Guard leaders took it upon themselves to order that the church bells in their neighbourhoods, silenced since June, should now be rung to indicate that the invasion had started. That night the peals sounded from one belfry to another across Britain, creating a sacerdotal crescendo that fuelled the climatic national mood of crisis.

Here again, public reaction was generally characterised by resolution rather than hysteria, as exemplified by the experience of Molly Smith, a mother living in Farnborough. She admitted that she found the noise of the bells 'the most hair-raising experience' but when her father banged on her door to declare, 'the beggars are dropping', her husband 'grabbed his rifle and I always had the leg of a chair handy'.[21] One ten-year-old boy, who had been evacuated to live with his grandmother in the Cotswolds, recalled that, 'when the church bells rang out in the night', the wife of the local chimney sweep could be seen 'sharpening her carving knife on the stone sill of her cottage'.[22]

For most of the volunteers in the Home Guard, this was the decisive moment for which they had joined the force. They loaded their rifles, set up their roadblocks, embarked on their patrols, manned their checkpoints. A flavour of the tense atmosphere in the Home Guard that night was provided by the history of D Company, based in Cannock Chase in Staffordshire.

> All platoons turned out well, live ammunition was fetched in a handcart from Chasetown Police Station, where it was stored at that time, and amidst subdued excitement, five rounds were handed to each man to be loaded in the magazine, bolt closed over, the safety catches on. This was the first time many of the men had carried live ammunition and, as they marched off from

company HQ to their respective road blocks, the company commander waited with outward unconcern but with inward trepidation for the sound of the opening shot, not being able to feel at all sure whether the first victim would be an innocent civilian, a policeman or a genuine Hun.[23]

Inevitably, under this intense pressure, rumours and sightings abounded of German invaders. In Epping Forest, half a dozen Home Guardsmen were sent out to investigate a report that fifty German paratroopers had landed in the area. The information was false, the supposed white canopies of the descending Germans turning out to be puffs of smoke from British anti-aircraft shells. On the other side of the country, there was a report that three German parachutists had been seen leaping from a Luftwaffe plane that passed over the Conway valley. The local Home Guard made a search but found nothing. At St Ives on the Cornish coast, the local Anglican vicar mistook a local fishing fleet for a Kriegsmarine formation and ordered the bells of his church to be rung, bringing out the Home Guard.

But the darkest fears did not materialise. The Cromwell signal turned out to have triggered the biggest false alarm in British history. Churchill himself thought the consequences were generally positive, writing later that 'the episode served as a useful tonic and rehearsal for all concerned.'[24]

One lesson learnt was that there had to be better communications for the front-line troops. So on Brooke's instructions, Cromwell was significantly refined: a temporary, intermediate stage between eight hours' and immediate notice was introduced so that vigilance could remain heightened in his Home Forces without a declaration that invasion was imminent. Additionally, church bells were to be rung only if a Home Guard commander had seen at least twenty-five parachutists descending. Although there had been no landings, the British armed forces remained on heightened alert, based on the understandable belief that the Germans were still planning an invasion. In fact, the Cromwell signal was not officially withdrawn until noon on 19 September, almost twelve days later, when it was replaced by a new, more flexible system.

Far from feeling relief that the Germans had not landed, Brooke was consumed by the sense that Britain was still in profound danger. On the morning of Monday 9 September, the Chiefs of Staff reiterated that they considered the next four days to be 'the most dangerous period for invasion',[25] a position reinforced the following day by a report of the continuing build-up of barges in the Channel ports. In Ostend alone, it was estimated, there were now over 300 of them. The Combined Intelligence Committee noted that this assembly had been accompanied not only with 'the movement of German dive bombing units to forward aerodromes in the Pas de

Calais area' but also with the 'preparation of craft fitted to carry 8.8cm anti-aircraft and anti-tank guns'.[26]

Even Churchill, who had been so sceptical of the invasion threat throughout the summer months, now admitted that the evidence of a potential assault was now irrefutable. At a meeting of the War Cabinet on 11 September, the prime minister pressed for the area around Dover to be urgently further reinforced with men and guns. 'The enemy is continuing to pass convoys of ships westwards along the French coasts,' he told his colleagues, with the result that 'a powerful armada is thus being deployed against the coasts of France opposite this country.' If, he warned, the enemy 'should succeed in getting lodgements of troops ashore on this coast and could capture the guns deployed there, they would have not only a bridge-head but a sheltered passageway commanded by the coast defence guns from both sides of the Channel'. Churchill finished the meeting on an optimistic note. 'He thought it was by no means impossible that the Germans could in the end decide not to launch an attack on this country because they were unable to obtain domination over our fighter force.'[27]

That evening, he made another of his renowned broadcasts to the British public, this time with the invasion threat as his central theme. 'We cannot tell when they will try to come; we cannot be sure that in fact they will try at all; but no one should blind himself to the fact that a heavy, full-scale invasion of this Island is being prepared with all the usual German thoroughness and method.' If this invasion is going 'to be tried at all', he continued, 'it does not seem that it can be long delayed. The weather may break at any time.' Therefore 'we must regard the next week or so as a very important week for us in our history,' for 'what is happening now is on a far greater scale' than the threat from the Spanish Armada or Napoleon's fleet.[28] Churchill was in his element, viewing the deeds of his government through the prism of his romanticised version of history.

When he accompanied Churchill on a visit the next day to inspect the defences in Kent, Brooke was impressed with his leader's ebullience: 'His popularity is astounding, everywhere crowds rush up and cheer him wildly, encouraging him with shouts of "Stick it."'[29]

In Churchill's uniquely long career in politics, September 1940 undoubtedly represented his own finest hour. Never before or since has a British prime minister been in such absolute accord with the public. Opinion polls showed his approval rating stood at 88 per cent. He embodied the will of the nation at the moment of its greatest peril, inspiring the British people while also taking inspiration from their fortitude.

On the Sunday afternoon after the first heavy Luftwaffe raid, the prime minister travelled to the bombed areas of the East End, where, astonishingly, he was greeted by a large cheering throng. Pug Ismay, who accompanied him, later recalled the visit.

> We found a scene of appalling devastation. Whole streets and houses were reduced to so many mounds of rubble and on top of many of these pathetic heaps there already floated proudly toy Union Jacks. Wasn't that a superb and spontaneous gesture of defiance? One of the first places we visited was an air raid shelter that had taken a direct hit. Forty people had been killed and over 200 wounded. It was crowded with poor people of both sexes and all ages, perhaps searching for some possession that had been torn from them by the blast. And when Mr Churchill arrived, they surged upon him. 'It was good of you to come, Winnie,' they cried, 'Give it 'em back, we can take it.'

Ismay concluded, 'It was difficult to be dry-eyed, too difficult.'[30] Public defiance could also be shown in the most eccentric ways. He remembered one elderly woman coming up to Churchill and telling him, 'There's one thing about these 'ere air raids: they do take your mind off the bloody war.'[31]

This spirit of determination helped the civil defence system to function successfully in London as well as in the vulnerable areas during these fateful days. In a report to a meeting of the Chiefs of Staff on 10 September, Sir Hugh Elles, the chief of Civil Defence, stated that 'the liaison between the military and civilian services had shown a general improvement', while 'the curfew restrictions that had been imposed on certain areas near the coast seemed to be working reasonably well.' The proportion of the population that had left these areas, he explained, varied from 40 per cent in East Anglia to 30 to 50 per cent in East Kent. Yet 'half the population still remained in Dover and refused to be frightened out.'

Continuing with the positive theme, he reported that 'the police were satisfied that arrangements for immobilising transport in an emergency and for keeping the specified roads clear of traffic would work satisfactorily.' Similarly, 'the arrangements for destroying dock facilities seemed to be well co-ordinated'. In all, Elles concluded, the nation had come strongly through the start of the Blitz. 'Everyone was outspoken in their praise of the ARP and the Fire Fighting services. The work of the hospitals deserved high praise,' as did the altruistic attitude of the public: 'The people as a whole were more worried about damage and distress caused in other parts of the country than over their own sufferings.'[32]

It was precisely this early show of British resilience that so disturbed the Germans. The aerial offensive was not progressing as Goering had promised, nor had the morale of the British public cracked.

Further private doubts were expressed by the Kriegsmarine staff following Churchill's broadcast of 11 September from the Cabinet War

Rooms. 'The speech leaves no doubt about the extraordinary gravity of Britain's present situation, but on the other hand, it is sustained by remarkably strong confidence in victory.'[33] According to the timetable agreed by the German High Command, Hitler had been due to give his final decision on Operation Sea Lion by 11 September but, showing how concerned he was about failure, he announced that day that he would postpone his decision until 14 September, claiming that he wanted to allow more time to see whether the bombardment of London might yield decisive results. The earliest date at which the invasion could now take place would be 24 September. Those around him could see his commitment to Sea Lion, always fragile, now evaporating. The risks were becoming greater with each passing day. Postponement would enable him at least to avoid the catastrophe of defeat on English beaches. His own Commander-in-Chief Keitel was all too aware of the profound hesitation of his master. 'I could not help gaining the impression that when it came to the question of actually executing the operation, he was in the grip of doubts and inhibitions.'[34]

In the absence of any decision, preparations continued. More mines were laid in the Dover straits, barges arrived at the ports, more rehearsals were held for the troops. In its final incarnation, Operation Sea Lion called for nine divisions to be landed on the southern English coast in the initial main assault. Under the overall command of von Rundstedt, the leader of Army Group A, four divisions of Busch's 16th Army would embark from Rotterdam, Antwerp, Ostend, Dunkirk and Calais, landing between Folkestone and St Leonards. Two divisions from Strauss's 9th Army would leave from Boulogne and the Canche estuary to disembark between Bexhill and Eastbourne. Finally, elements of three further divisions from the 9th Army would land between Beachy Head and Brighton. These landings would be supported by 250 amphibious tanks and the 7th Flieger Division, which would seize the grounds and airfields north of Folkestone.

As the British government recognised, the Germans regarded the investment of Dover as crucial so that their supply lines could be quickly established. In theory, the Luftwaffe was to use part of its bomber and dive-bomber forces to protect the 16th and 9th Armies, in addition to bombing the British coastal defences and transport infrastructure in the run-up to invasion. In practice, the Luftwaffe's support was always questionable because of Goering's uncooperative attitude, as in his cool pronouncement: 'Sea Lion must not disturb or burden the Luftwaffe operations.'[35]

Apart from providing the transport fleet and laying the minefields, the Kriegsmarine also planned to deploy ten destroyers and twenty torpedo boats to protect the west flank of the crossing, with a further thirty torpedo boats covering the east flank. Raeder's force further planned to have ten medium-sized U-boats in the English Channel west of the Isle of Wight, as well as five small U-boats.

Under the final Sea Lion plan, the assaults on the landing zones would have been spearheaded by the Vorausabteilung, or Advance Detachments, each of which contained 1,600 men. These hand-picked elite troops would have arrived at dawn, ahead of the main body of the fleet, having been taken close to the shore in minesweepers or minelayers, and then transferred to fast motorboats or *Sturmboote*. Boats with smokescreen machines would be assigned to the advance units to help conceal the invaders, although the Kriegsmarine disliked this measure as the artificial fog also hindered navigation. The main body of the fleet would have followed in the barges towed by the tugs, escorted by auxiliary patrols and Siebel ferries.

The weight and quantity of armaments would have brought their own problems. Each division in the first wave had at least two batteries of mountain or field guns, a company equipped with 2-cm flak guns and another company equipped with 4.7-cm self-propelled anti-tank guns. In addition, the 16th Army had nine batteries with a total of seventy-two rocket launchers, a deadly new weapon for the Reich that could lay down a ferocious bombardment against the enemy in a matter of seconds. On top of this, each of the first-wave armies was allocated one artillery regiment staff, a 10-cm gun detachment, a motorised heavy field howitzer detachment and a reconnaissance detachment.

Nor would this large, complex force have been able to move swiftly across the Channel, since the tugs could go no faster than 6 knots and many would have been slower. The fleet that sailed from Calais, heading for the landing zone between Hastings and Dungeness, would have been required to depart eight hours ahead of its planned arrival on the English coast; it would have comprised about 100 tows and extended around 15 kilometres from the French port. The fleet sailing from Boulogne would have been even larger, consisting of tows stretching 20 kilometres from the French shore. If it had succeeded, the Germans would have been able to land a formidable number of troops on British soil.

According to the final Sea Lion plan, 67,000 soldiers would have been operational in England within a few hours of the first landing. Within two days, that figure could have reached 138,000, rising to 260,000 within a fortnight of Sea Lion's beginning. In fact, the historian Peter Schenk, who made a detailed study of the German plans, estimated that at least 300,000 troops would have been put into the operation because the 16th Army would have been heavily reinforced. In comparison, 326,000 troops landed in France within the first six days of Operation Overlord in 1944.

But in 1940 the Reich faced enormous problems that the Allies were spared four years later, since the final assembly of the German fleet took place under increasingly aggressive attacks from the Royal Navy and the RAF. The greater the number of barges the Germans moved into Belgium, Holland and northern France, the more vulnerable the invasion fleet became to British predation. Such attacks had major implications for Sea Lion far beyond the direct physical damage they caused, in that they were evidence of a number of factors: the growing confidence of the British; the comprehensive failure of Goering's strategy; the continuing command of the sea by the Royal Navy; and British refusal to countenance any thought of peace negotiations. All of them preyed on the Führer's mounting anxiety.

The Royal Navy, in keeping with Nelsonian tradition, had long maintained a forward policy against German encroachments in home waters. One of the myths about this period is that the Royal Navy was 'kept out of the way' during the invasion crisis.[36] Nothing could be further from the truth. The offensive spirit was epitomised by Admiral Drax, the head of the Nore Command, who proclaimed on 4 September that he wanted 'to hit Germany hard by destroying the invasion force'.[37]

He lived up to those words on 8 September, when he sent a substantial contingent, comprising two cruisers, five motor torpedo boats (MTBs) and eleven destroyers, on a raid across the Channel. One part entered Ostend harbour and fired off four torpedoes, sinking two steamers and severely damaging another two. On the evening of 10/11 September, three destroyers set out from Harwich and shelled a number of vessels at Ostend, sinking a self-propelled barge and a trawler. The following evening, Royal Navy destroyers, MTBs and gunboats patrolled along the Channel coast and even entered Cherbourg harbour to shell several German vessels.

At the same time as launching these raids, the navy maximised its strength at home against invasion by moving several of its capital ships south from Scapa Flow. The two battleships, *Nelson* and *Rodney*, along with the battle-cruiser *Hood*, eight destroyers and two cruisers, were transferred to Rosyth. The Royal Navy now had a powerful force throughout home waters, far in excess of anything possessed by the Kriegsmarine. In destroyers alone, the Admiralty's list showed that there were 106 in British waters in mid-September, compared to the 10 that the Kriegsmarine planned to deploy for Sea Lion. In Portsmouth and Sheerness, both in the front line of the invasion, there were thirty-two destroyers and five cruisers. In Plymouth, there were eleven destroyers, two cruisers and the mighty 28,000-ton battleship HMS *Revenge*, which would have been able to intercept the German fleet before any landings had even taken place.

In the air, the epic struggle of the Battle of Britain had rightly captured the public's imagination. In truth, however, the period from 7 to 15 September had seen only minor fighter skirmishes as a result of a combination of poor weather and the Luftwaffe's concentration of bombing attacks on London. The lull was exactly what Dowding wanted in order to re-equip and rest his fighter squadrons.

At the same time, Bomber Command dramatically stepped up its assault on the Channel ports. From 5 September, the Germans' burgeoning invasion fleet became a prime target. On that and the following night, most of Bomber Command's force of Blenheim medium bombers carried out raids on the ports. On the night of 7 September, while London was experiencing the start of the Blitz, the Blenheim attackers were joined by twenty-six Handley Page Hampdens and eleven Fairey Battles. From then until the end of the month, the bombardment of the invasion fleet became Bomber Command's overwhelming priority, these raids accounting for three-quarters of their missions and the release of over 1,000 tons of explosive. On the night of 13 September, ninety-one sorties were flown against German shipping in the occupied ports. The number was doubled the next night. With typical imaginative and heroic insouciance, given the ferocity of German anti-aircraft defences, the bomber crews nicknamed this part of the coast 'the Blackpool Front' because of the illuminating glow cast by the fires.

One of the most successful bombing raids at this time was carried out against Antwerp on the night of 15/16 September. Beginning half an hour before midnight, the attack lasted for almost three hours, causing widespread damage. According to an Air Ministry press release the next day:

> in spite of fierce opposition by anti-aircraft batteries and numerous search-lights, the bombers repeatedly got through to their objectives and played havoc. Barges were set ablaze and exploded, flashes lighting up the whole of the docks. A goods yard caught fire, buildings were wrecked and a trail of fire, following a series of explosions, spread rapidly along the quay-side, engulfing warehouses and other buildings. By 1.30 am one of the main wharves was a mass of flames and other fires could be seen in all parts of the docks. Bombs from aircraft arriving later straddled the dock bases and burst on jetties and among the shipping. When, an hour later, the last raider left the blazing dock, the fires could be seen many miles out to sea.[38]

This was not mere propaganda. The Germans' own daily military report of the raid admitted that 'the north of Antwerp has been hit particularly hard. One bomb hit a depot which contained 450 tons of ammunition; this caused great damage to all surrounding buildings and sheds. The navy school, silos and the fire station were damaged severely.' A separate report stated that, in the harbour, three cargo ships had been sunk and another badly damaged.[39]

The Antwerp raid not only caused widespread destruction for the Germans. It also led to another act of astonishing heroism, when one RAF Hampden bomber of 83 Squadron was hit by an incendiary shell and quickly burst into flames. Displaying both raw courage and an indifference to severe pain, the plane's wireless operator/air gunner John Hannah forced his way through the fire to grab both fire extinguishers. Although ammunition was exploding all around him and the aluminium floor was melting in the extreme heat, Hannah managed to put out the flames and then, in the absence of the navigator who had bailed out of the burning aircraft, helped the pilot to bring the crippled plane home. For his valour he was awarded the Victoria Cross.

After the war Sir Arthur Harris, who in September 1940 was head of No. 5 Bomber Group, claimed that raids like this had been the prime factor in forcing Hitler to abandon Sea Lion. This is a gross exaggeration, all too typical of Harris's tunnel vision about the efficacy of bombing warfare. Even according to the most optimistic estimates, by 21 September the RAF had destroyed or severely damaged 21 transports and 214 barges, only about 12 per cent of the entire invasion fleet, losses that could easily be made up by reserves.

The more important effect was psychological and political, for the raids dramatically showed that, contrary to Goering's boasts, the Germans did not have command of the sky, not even over their own occupied territory. It was a reality that helped to undermine German morale, already weakened by their inability to win the Battle of Britain. The Luftwaffe pilot Ulrich Steinhilper admitted that 'The British are slowing getting on our nerves at night because of their persistent activity . . . But there is nothing we can do about it other than curse.'[40]

For so long supreme in Europe, the Germans had lost the initiative. Their senior commanders were divided, their leader undecided. Even events that might have caused a shudder in Britain only months earlier now back-fired on the Reich.

On 13 September, six German bombs fell on Buckingham Palace, two of them in a quadrangle only 30 yards from King George VI and Queen Elizabeth, who were currently in residence. 'A magnificent piece of bombing, Ma'am, if you'll pardon my saying so,' commented one of the policemen on duty.[41] The royal couple, although slightly shaken, were relieved that they could genuinely say that they had shared the experience of thousands on their subjects under fire. With his sharp political antennae and understanding of the British people, Churchill at once recognised that the incident could embolden rather than depress the nation. When told that night that the BBC and the Ministry of Information wanted to censor any reports about the Palace bombing, he exploded: 'Dolts! Fools! Idiots! Spread the news at once. Let it be broadcast everywhere. Let the people of London know that the King and Queen are sharing the perils with them.'[42] Instead of adopting his usual tone of derision for the British, Dr Goebbels was reduced to asserting pathetically that Buckingham Palace had been bombed because there was an ammunition dump on its premises.

The Tory MP Chips Channon was astonished at the cheerful national mood, recording on 12 September, 'This island race is extraordinary. Everyone I have seen today was in the highest spirits. They are all convinced that an English victory now lies just around the corner.'[43] In contrast, the mood within the German High Command was one of nervous despondency, not confident anticipation. Hitler's own Luftwaffe adjutant Nicolaus von Below claimed that by 14 September, 'no one believed in the operation any longer.'[44] That same day Raeder, having abandoned his brief flirtation with optimism, set out his gloomiest picture yet. 'The present position does not provide conditions for carrying out the operation, as the risk is still too great,' he wrote, adding that 'if the Sea Lion Operation fails, this will mean a great gain in prestige for the British; the powerful effect of our attacks will thus be annulled.'[45] The Führer agreed with that position, as he explained at a conference that afternoon, attended by all his top commanders. He was in a contradictory, even febrile state. Lavishing praise on the Luftwaffe for its aerial victories and the Kriegsmarine for its preparations, he argued that an invasion of England was 'essential' and would bring the war to a swift close. Germany now had 'a good chance to force Britain to her knees', he said, while 'every pause benefits the enemy.' Yet he did not follow up the logic of his words. Instead, he said there would have to be another postponement in his decision, because, 'notwithstanding all our successes, the prerequisites for Operation Sea Lion hve not yet been completely realized,' particularly 'complete air domination'.[46]

Exactly eight days earlier Hitler had told his ecstatic audience at the Sportpalast that he was on his way to England. Now to his commanders he announced another postponement in his decision on Operation Sea Lion until 17 September. As the depths of autumn beckoned, the light was beginning to fade on the Führer's dreams of conquest.

24

'The extraordinary gravity of Britain's present situation'

———

THE RUMOURS STARTED soon after the Luftwaffe launched its heavy bombardment of London. The stories, circulated by the press and by neighbourhood gossip, varied in their details but they usually had the same essential features: that during the second week or third week of September 1940 the Germans had actually tried to send an invasion force against the English coast but had been repelled by the stalwart defences.

According to the narrative that gained increasing currency during these weeks, large numbers of Wehrmacht troops had been killed in action as a result of this confrontation, their corpses washed up on England's southern shores or on the occupied coast. There were also said to be heavy German casualties filling up hospitals in Belgium, Holland, Germany and northern France. Entire trainloads of wounded and bandaged men were alleged to have been sighted at stations and harbours throughout Western Europe. One gruesome theme of many reports was that thousands of the Germans had either been killed or badly burned by fire.

There had, inevitably, been whispered speculation about failed German landings throughout the summer months. But the tale of 'the bodies on the beach' was on a different level altogether, both in its grip on the public's imagination and in its widespread coverage in the press, particularly in the USA where there were no censorship restrictions.

It was there that the story was initially aired when, on Wednesday 11 September, the popular New York tabloid the *Sun* ran an article under the headline, 'British fire halted invasion as Nazis tried to rush coast.' The *Sun* told its readers that 'an unofficial British source returned from England only a few days ago' had learnt from friends in the armed forces that the Nazis 'had made a disastrous attempt to land on the south-east coast of England', when their barges, each of which 'contained 200 men with full equipment', sank 'under a withering fire' from the British land batteries 'as soon as they appeared' near the shore.[1] Two days later the *Sun*'s report was reprinted, in expurgated form, by the *Glasgow Herald*, bringing the story to the attention of the British public for the first time.

Across the Atlantic, the credibility of the *Sun*'s journalism appeared to be reinforced on 14 September, when the internationally respected Associated Press Agency carried an interview with Dr Charles Bove, the former head of the American Hospital in Paris, who had just returned from the French capital. Dr Bove told the agency that he had heard stories of 'hundreds of German bodies in the water near Cherbourg'. The dead, he believed, must have been the participants in a failed invasion.[2] This time the *Daily Mirror*, one of Britain's best-selling papers with a circulation of over 4 million, picked up the story.

Further impetus came on 17 September when the *New York Times* reported that British sources in Lisbon had revealed that 'a small-scale German attempt at landing somewhere along the English coast last week was beaten off with heavy losses to the would-be invaders.' A severe lesson had been learnt, for the *New York Times* quoted the British informant as stating, 'British artillery and small patrol craft played havoc with the German barges and not a single German reached land alive. Scores of bodies are reported as still being washed up on our shores.'[3] The claim that the British had used burning petrol on their coastal waters was then raised by the *Sun* in another of its dramatic articles, which stated that the German barges 'ran into flames' when RAF bombers dropped incendiary bombs to ignite tanks of oil that had been strategically placed in the water. As one German soldier reportedly told a French nurse who was tending his injuries from the fire, 'We were caught like fish in a frying pan.' Putting the German death toll at 80,000, the *Sun* said that 'hospitals in occupied France are filled with Nazi soldiers, all of them suffering from severe burns.'[4]

As early as 13 September, the day that Buckingham Palace was bombed, Richard Brown, an engineer and air-raid warden based in Ipswich, recorded in his diary that he had heard from New York that 'Jerry corpses were being washed up on the Yarmouth beaches in quantities.' One of his neighbours said that there were '30,000 of them but I should have thought they'd be too weighty with equipment to do anything but sink'.[5] In Croydon, the perspicacious teenager Colin Perry had also heard the tale, writing in his diary, 'An invasion attempt has been mounted but not one Nazi returned. Their bodies are being washed up along our shores.'[6] The indefatigable opinion researchers from the Ministry of Information had also heard the stories, noting on 16 September: 'There were persistent rumours that an invasion was in progress or that an invasion had been attempted and failed, leaving hundreds of German corpses floating in the channel.'[7] Anecdotes about the German bodies were being repeated all over southern and eastern England.

Some of the most persistent rumours were focused on the remote coastal

Suffolk hamlet of Shingle Street, whose tiny population had been compulsorily evacuated in the summer of 1940 so that the area could be used for military exercises and the construction of a radar station. Local legend had it that this was one of the places where the Germans had tried to land, but were overwhelmed when the British activated their new defences by setting the sea alight with burning oil pumped from underwater pipelines. Ronald Ashford, a member of the local Home Guard, later gave this account of what happened that night in Shingle Street.

> It was a clear, dark evening. About 9 pm the heavens seemed to open up south of Orford Lighthouse in the Shingle Street area. We heard a tremendous amount of gunfire and explosions. The night sky was lit up with a red glow. Sporadic gunfire went on for several hours. We received word that a German landing had taken place. This was later confirmed by eye-witness accounts of a shoreline littered with burned bodies. It appeared that this landing had been expected . . . The seabed had been laid with piping from the shore at intervals with flammable liquid.

Ashford then recounted that, later in the war, a refugee from Belgium, who had joined the British armed forces in 1944 and was now based in this area of Suffolk, claimed to have known about the invasion attempt on that September night in 1940: 'He had been living in the Belgian port area at the time in question. He said that he had witnessed survivors landing at the port – some badly burned – and bringing many bodies with them.'[8]

Indeed, the evidence from the continent about the failed invasion often seemed to be compelling. Renée Meurisse, a Belgian Red Cross nurse, gave this vivid account of her experience in a newspaper interview.

> During September 17, we heard rumours that thousands of German soldiers were being washed ashore along the Belgian beaches. At seven o'clock that night a German Red Cross train pulled into Brussels station. We had been expecting a refugee train, so we were surprised when we saw a train-load of Germans . . . Sending a call for more nurses and ambulances, we began taking the wounded from the train. The moans and the screams were terrible. I helped to carry a young German from the train. He was horribly burned about the head and shoulders. A doctor helped me to put him in a corner and we determined to find out, if we could, what happened . . . Finally, we managed to piece together the whole story. He said they had been told that they were going to invade Britain, that nothing could stop them, that it was just a matter of getting into boats and going across the Channel. He told me it was horrible. The whole channel was in flames. The British bombed and machine-gunned us. Hell couldn't be worse. And then he died. We looked after more than 500 soldiers as best we could. Many died there in Brussels railway station.[9]

In his gripping diary for the early war years, the distinguished American journalist and historian William Shirer described the rumours and disturbing sights that fed the story of the burning sea, writing cautiously from Geneva on 16 September: 'The news coming over the near-by border of France is that the Germans have attempted a landing in Britain, but it has been repulsed with heavy German losses. Must take this report with a grain of salt.' Two days later his scepticism was a little diluted when he was at Potsdam station, watching wounded men being unloaded 'from the longest Red Cross train I've ever seen'. He wondered 'where so many wounded could have come from, as the armies in the west stopped fighting three months ago . . . The reports reaching Switzerland from France were that many German barges and ships had been destroyed and a considerable number of German troops drowned.'[10]

In his excellent history of the invasion threat in 1940, Peter Haining quoted a fascinating passage from a letter written by a French doctor, Paul Schiff, to a relative:

> I went back to Dunkirk and spoke to a friend who was the manager of the Le Seur works. He told me that the road to the beach was being guarded night and day by German soldiers with fixed bayonets who had orders to shoot anyone who tried to go any further. My friend said that there were lots of bodies that had been washed up onto the beach. They were all apparently blackened and burned. The Germans were burying them in the sand.[11]

Dr Schiff's account was backed up by a Madame Pauline Lozère, who ran a shop in Gravelines, near Dunkirk, and kept a diary throughout the German occupation. In it she recalled having been told by 'some German officers' of a failed attempt to cross the Channel: 'No one knows how many were killed. The soldiers could be seen washed ashore upright. It was like an army of the drowned. Their heavy equipment had slipped to their feet so they were kept upright.'[12]

Despite its widespread prevalence on the continent, as well as in Britain and America, the tale of the bodies on the beach has often been dismissed as mythology. That was the line the German regime tried to adopt towards the whole affair, releasing an official statement on 21 October 1940 that claimed, 'It is a typical British manoeuvre, attributing plans to an enemy which do not exist and which cannot be traced, and then claiming a success when nothing occurs.'[13] The same disdain was shown by the writer and Auxiliary pioneer Peter Fleming in his book on Operation Sea Lion, first published in 1957, in which he wrote: 'A rumour which swept first the United Kingdom, and then much of the rest of mankind, was wholly spontaneous, wholly baseless and wholly inexplicable,' adding that the claim that any German corpses had been discovered on British beaches was without foundation.[14] However, the picture was not nearly as clear cut as Fleming suggested.

There were indeed some corpses of German soldiers washed up on the British shores at this period, although their numbers were nothing like the tens of thousands mentioned in the more lurid continental rumours. The dead were almost certainly not from an abortive invasion attempt, but more likely from embarkation exercises that had gone badly wrong or had been targeted by the British.

This highly plausible scenario was spelt out after the war by Clement Attlee, who had succeeded Churchill as prime minister. In a characteristically crisp Parliamentary statement on 18 November 1946, based partly on documents captured from the Reich, he told the Commons that 'there is no evidence' that the German barges 'ever left harbour as a fleet to invade this country. Bombing raids on those harbours were carried out by Bomber Command and some barges which put to sea, probably to escape the raids, were sunk either by bombing or encountering bad weather. During the next six weeks, bodies of German soldiers were washed up at scattered points along the coast between Cornwall and Yarmouth, amounting to about 36 over a period of a month.'[15]

For the troops manning the coastal defences, the discovery and collection of the corpses was one of their more unorthodox tasks during the autumn of 1940. Gunner William Robinson was serving in the 333 Coastal Artillery Battery at Folkestone when he was asked to become part of a six-strong unit searching for German corpses. 'The first day we found two soldiers. They had no badges. We took them back in a lorry to a field at the back of New Romney. We left them there behind a canvas screen and carried on. During the course of the next few days we found seven or eight more. I was told – and I believe it – that they were caught by the RAF during a pre-invasion manoeuvre in the Channel,' Robinson recalled in a television appearance in 1957. In a subsequent interview with his local paper, the *Folkestone and Hythe Gazette*, he explained that he knew the men were German because of their field-grey uniforms. Having further revealed that the bodies were all buried in a mass grave, he said that he was given 'a special inducement' for the job of twenty cigarettes and an extra two shillings each day.[16]

In addition to the discovery of the German corpses, some of the invasion stories in East Anglia may have been inspired by the disaster near the island of Terschelling, which took place shortly before the Cromwell signal was given, when three Royal Navy destroyers on patrol were hit by German mines with the loss of over 300 lives. Most of the dead and injured were brought through ports in Suffolk and Norfolk on their way to the mortuary or the hospital, a sight that inevitably inspired curiosity in local civilians. Pat Barnes, a schoolgirl living in Norwich at the time, remembered that 'for two days a convoy of army ambulances' passed her family home. The unusual traffic was so heavy that her mother asked a soldier what had happened: 'She was told that they had contained the bodies of dead Germans washed up on the beach, as an invasion had been attempted. But that was all she had been told. This picture had remained vivid in my memory. It seemed as though there were hundreds of trucks, going from nowhere to nowhere at walking pace.'[17]

Such testimony may help to explain the rumours in England, but it cannot be applied to the stories from occupied Western Europe about burnt and badly wounded German soldiers arriving in Belgian, French and Dutch hospitals. Here again, however, the counter-offensive by the RAF and the Royal Navy may have been responsible for many of these casualties.

The British attacks on the Channel ports are usually viewed through the prism of the limited damage they inflicted on the barges, but the harbours were also full of troops engaged in loading, rehearsing and training exercises. According to one British Intelligence report, an RAF attack on barges at Calais scored a direct hit with incendiary bombs on a battalion practising disembarkation techniques, with the badly burnt survivors subsequently taken to Paris for specialised treatment.

Further support for this explanation can be found in a War Office report from a 'Senior Belgian Staff Officer' about the heavy Bomber Command raid on the Belgian city of Antwerp on the night of 15 September 1941. In a statement made in September 1942, on the second anniversary of the raid, this officer recalled that 'The whole of the dock area was alight and the city shook with explosions, with one colossal one in the middle. Next day we learned it was a boat fully laden with mountain artillery and mountain troops, which had exploded. Three thousand houses had their windows smashed and the streets nearby were littered with wreckage.' With perhaps a degree of hindsight, he continued, 'from that moment we knew that a major operation had been crushed before it had begun. What happened at Antwerp happened along the entire European coastline from St. Nazaire to the Hook of Holland.'

A few days after the raid, he travelled to Brussels to visit an injured officer friend at the Brugmann Hospital.

What I didn't know was that the Brugmann hospital was strictly a German military hospital and no civilian was allowed to enter. German sentries overhauled me as I stood talking, took me by the collar and dragged me out. But not before I had sufficient time to see in the corridor and in the gardens, hundreds and hundreds of German soldiers with bandages on their limbs and hiding their faces, which a Belgian official guaranteed to me was through having had a hot bath . . . in the sea.[18]

In line with this account about the counter-invasion damage caused by the British, there is an intriguing note in the archives of the Naval Intelligence Division (NID) of the Admiralty for November 1941. The note is attached to a report by a 'French naval officer' who gave the Royal Navy an outline of the kind of instruction that the elite German troops underwent in north-western France before the invasion. This included training 'in the technique of rapid landing operations on a steep coastline' with the help of 'alpine equipment, axes, ropes and rope ladders'. On the cover of this report, the NID had written: 'Attached is from a French Naval Officer and may account for the many stories of burnt Germans. In September 1940 the Germans were carrying out disembarkation exercises at Ouessant [an island near Brest with a vital radar station]. A shell fired by a British destroyer hit a fuel oil store and the burning liquid, fanned by the wind, burnt a large number of Germans.'[19] It is possible that some bodies from Ouessant may have ended up on the western coast of England, although far more such casualties, many of them fatal, would have been dealt with in France.

The real value of this saga to the British lay, not in the physical damage inflicted, but in the propaganda benefits. There was nothing 'spontaneous' about the way the rumour spread; indeed, the opposite was true. The combination of the whispers about corpses and the pioneering work on petroleum weaponry was cleverly exploited by the British to maximise German fear about the risks of a potential crossing, just at the time when the barge assembly in the Channel ports was at its peak. In his history of the Second World War, Churchill was frank about how his government fostered the disinformation: 'We took no steps to contradict such tales, which spread freely through the occupied countries in wildly exaggerated form and gave much encouragement to the oppressed populations.'[20]

In fact, British Intelligence played an active role in fomenting the stories. Soon after Dunkirk, a body called the 'Underground Propaganda Committee' was established to spread morale-sapping, anti-Nazi reports in occupied Europe, largely through the network of embassies in neutral countries like Spain, Portugal, Switzerland, Turkey and Sweden. The committee also planned to use the British Security Commission in New York to promulgate clandestine anti-German material. Rumours that the committee disseminated were code-named Sibs, after the Latin word *sibilare*, meaning 'to hiss'. In September 1940, sanction was given to a number of Sibs about the failed invasion. According to one proposed Sib that was approved by the government: 'Small scale attempts at invasion have been made and have been beaten off with devastating losses. Thousands of floating German corpses have been washed ashore.'[21] Another, relating to Scandinavia, was more creative: 'The fishing populations of the west coast of Denmark and the south coast of Norway are selling fish but they won't eat them. The reason is that there are large numbers of German corpses on which the fish feed. There have even been cases of shreds of clothing and buttons, etc, being found inside fish.'[22]

The author James Hayward argued convincingly that many of the reports in the American press around mid-September 1940 were based on the work of British propagandists. He pointed out, for instance, that widespread coverage was given on both sides of the Atlantic to a statement on 21 September from a certain Robert Solberg, who had just returned to New York with his family after living for twenty years in France, where 'bodies of German troops were being washed ashore daily'.[23] In reality, Solberg was intimately connected with US Intelligence and was close to 'Wild Bill' Donovan, Roosevelt's military adviser and a strong supporter of Britain's cause, having been given access to British security files during his fact-finding mission in July.

It was the experiments by the Petroleum Warfare Department that gave a real stimulus to the British effort at disinformation, building on the rumours of the failed invasion. One senior British Intelligence officer who had a leading role in the promotion of this propaganda was John Baker White. In his semi-autobiographical book published in 1955 titled *The Big Lie*, Baker White claimed that the tales of burnt corpses had been vital in forcing Hitler to hesitate in September 1940:

> I am convinced that one rumour, one deception, above all others, discouraged the Germans from launching their invasion attempt in 1940. It is true that other factors compelled Hitler's decision to abandon the attempt: the failure to destroy the RAF, the fear of his generals to embark upon the operation without complete air cover and certain fine weather. All played their part but one rumour created the psychological conditions that bred nervousness, reluctance, uncertainty and even real fear. It consisted of eight words: the British can set the sea on fire.[24]

The story of the burning sea was spread not only by Britain's intelligence network but by the broadcaster and *Daily Express* journalist Sefton Delmer, a fluent German speaker, who had so contemptuously rejected Hitler's Reichstag speech in July. Now Delmer mockingly declared in one of his transmissions to Germany, 'we English, as you know, are notoriously bad at languages, and so it will be best, meine Herren Engellandfahrer, if you learn a few English phrases before visiting us.' Among those he suggested were: 'the boat is sinking' and 'the water is cold, very cold'. Then, still adopting the tone of linguistic helpfulness, he turned to a more lethal part of the lexicon.

> Now I will give you a verb that should come in useful. Again, please repeat after me:
> Ich brenne . . . I burn
> Du brennst . . . You burn
> Er brennt . . . He burns.

In his 1962 autobiography, Delmer wrote of this broadcast, 'Crude stuff, but excellent in one important respect. The line about burning in the Channel fitted in perfectly, as of course it was intended to, with the information which our deception services had planted on Hitler's espionage service. Our rumour agencies, too, had been spreading it everywhere.'[25]

The British government were delighted with Delmer's broadcast. In fact, to ram home the message, they produced a propaganda leaflet based on his text. Entitled 'Wir Fahren Gegen Engelland', the title of the popular song that constantly blared out over German radios during the summer of 1940, this leaflet was written in German, French and Dutch, and purported to be a short phrasebook to enlighten the invaders. Among the terms listed were:

> 'We feel seasick. Where is the bucket?'
> 'The sea smells of petrol here.'
> 'See how well the captain burns.'
> 'We must turn back.'[26]

In early October, no fewer than 1 million copies of this leaflet were dropped by RAF aircraft over occupied northern Europe.

But even well before this, the propaganda had worked its way into the minds of the men in the German armed forces preparing for the invasion, as the British learnt from interrogating some Luftwaffe pilots shot down over England. Baker White recorded that one pilot who landed at Charing in Kent disclosed that in his wing 'they knew of the burning sea defences. Three days later another Luftwaffe man volunteered the same information – and he came from a different airfield. It had been our first large-scale attempt at the Big Lie, and it had proved amazingly successful.'[27]

This was not empty jingoistic boasting. A highly revealing recollection of this crucial period was provided by Alexander Hoffer, who served in one of the German mountain regiments:

> It seemed that almost from the first day that we arrived from Germany, the RAF came over. Night after night the alarm would sound and we would have to turn out in battle order. There were always fires in the docks after the bombing. The RAF tried to set fire to the barges, sometimes only hours

after they had reached the area. Then the . . . rumours began. The English could set fire to the surface of the sea and would do this just before we landed.[28]

According to the Petroleum Minister Geoffrey Lloyd, the German High Command appeared to have taken the burning sea rumours seriously enough to have carried out a major maritime experiment in the Channel in which a batch of troops were fitted with asbestos suits, placed on barges and then instructed to sail into a barrage of ignited gasoline. In Lloyd's account, 'a large number of the headpieces of the suits were defective and the men inside roasted to death,'[29] an outcome, which, if true, can have done nothing to quell Teutonic anxieties.

Although setting the sea alight could have been deemed a success in September 1940, if only in propaganda terms, there was another counter-invasion initiative with burning oil that proved a dismal failure. Following the example of Francis Drake, who had famously used fireships in pre-emptive strikes against the Spanish Armada at Gravelines in 1588, the British government came up with a plan to send a formation of lighted tankers into the heart of the German invasion fleet at the occupied ports. Again it was Geoffrey Lloyd, the energetic Petroleum Minister, who was the origi-nator of the idea.

On 27 June, Lloyd saw the Downing Street aide Desmond Morton, who wrote to Churchill that day about the suggestion 'to use the petroleum in connection with fire-ships to be sailed into ports in Germany or under German control. It should not be difficult to lay hands on some old shipping of small tonnage and shallow draught and to fix them up with explosives and a large cargo of oil. If these ships could be sailed into selected enemy ports and exploded, they would scatter burning oil all over the harbour, possibly with most pleasing results.'[30] Predictably, the suggestion appealed to the adventurous spirit of Churchill, who overrode doubts in the naval staff and instructed that preparations for the operation should begin.

The officer chosen to lead it was the heroic Captain Augustus Agar, who had won the Victoria Cross in the First World War and epitomised the Royal Navy's valorous tradition. When he saw Churchill to discuss the plan, he made the prime minister chuckle by urging that the operation be code-named 'Roasting the Nazis'. Replying in kind, Churchill said, 'It is not so much that I don't want them to come. Nobody does. I want them to be beaten before they come, Agar. I don't want a single German to set foot on British soil.'[31] Instead of adopting Agar's ferocious title for the mission, the Admiralty decided to call it 'Operation Lucid'.

Unfortunately the high priority that the government claimed to have given the mission was not matched by the quality of equipment. The only tankers that the Admiralty would spare were, in Agar's words, 'the oldest old crocks laid up on our rivers and creeks which had not been to sea for years and were useless except for scrap metal'.[32] Nevertheless, the engineers, working flat out, managed to get them ready for service, although they remained slow and unreliable.

Agar and Morgan Morgan-Giles, his staff officer, presided over some last-minute rehearsals, in which the small crews practised steering and evacuating the old hulks. In its final form, the plan was for each of the four decrepit tankers to be filled with a mixture of 50 per cent heavy oil, 25 per cent diesel and 25 per cent petrol. In each case, explosive charges were placed in the hull by demolition experts so that the ship could be scuttled. With the oil mixture and explosives on board, the tanker would be sailed across the Channel towards her designated French port. Just as she approached the harbour entrance, detonation timers would be set and most of her crew would leave by speedboats, leaving just three volunteers on board. These volunteers would then go through the boom at the harbour mouth, set the final course for the ship and then scramble into another speedboat, hopefully escaping just before the explosive charges went off. As the ship blew up, a large oil slick would run across the harbour, setting the enemy shipping on fire. According to Morgan-Giles, 'The trials showed that the flames could leap more than 100 feet in the sky. A human would last two seconds in that situation.'[33]

Chief Petty Officer Ronald Apps was also involved in the month-long preparations at the Royal Navy dockyard at Chatham:

> We practised setting the controls and evacuating the ship with two speedboats alongside us which had been commandeered from Southend. These speedboats were remarkable things. They could go at 35 or 40 knots and the idea was that, at the blowing of a whistle, we had to rush down, get in the boats and we were away. Those four weeks were a bit hairy because the tanker was full up with fuel oil when it came to us and was primed and ready to explode.[34]

By the evening of 25 September the Admiralty felt that the operation could go ahead, aimed at the two northern French ports of Boulogne and Calais. The first tanker to go into action was the *War Nizam*, which sailed from Sheerness at 6.30 p.m., followed by an escort of two destroyers, three minesweepers and several motorboats. Unfortunately, despite the urgent work carried out on her, the *War Nizam*'s poor maintenance began to tell against her, as Morgan-Giles testified: 'Instead of doing the six knots we were planning, she did about two knots because she was so old and battered.'[35] The *War Nizam* had to return to Sheerness.

The next attempt was undertaken the same evening by the *War Nawab*, which sailed from Portsmouth but soon proved herself to be completely unseaworthy, as Morgan-Giles observed: 'The mixture of petrol and oil leaked through the rivet holes from the tanks, down into the stokeholes and was sizzling on the floorplates down there. The stokers, trying to run the ship across, came up on deck and everyone thought they were drunk but it was only petrol fumes.'[36] Two further missions were tried on successive nights at the beginning of October, but both had to be aborted because of severe gales. The final attempt was on the evening of 7/8 October but again had to be abandoned because of a mix of bad weather and lack of seaworthiness. Even worse, the escort destroyer carrying Agar and Morgan-Giles hit a mine, blowing off part of the stern, although the vessel managed to limp back to England.

That marked the end of Operation Lucid. For Morgan-Giles, the entire episode, despite being a flop, proved again Britain's determination to resist invasion. 'It was never very feasible because the ships were so old and it all had to be done in a hell of a hurry. But at the time there was such a strong mood of fighting the German threat. Our backs were against the wall but there was not much doom and gloom.'[37]

It was rather the Germans who were engulfed by gloom. For them, the mere idea of the burning sea could not have come at a more inopportune time.

25

'We knew far too little of England'

———

JUST AFTER THE start of the Battle of Britain in mid-August, the historian Basil Liddell Hart had written a perceptive article in the *Sunday Pictorial* in which he argued that the performance of Fighter Command was the key to the defence of Britain. 'It is the RAF, whose actual operations have been carried out by a few thousand men, that has barred Hitler's path and baffled his purpose. Without its capacity to beat an enemy twice or thrice its own strength, there would have been no chance of saving our army from France and a very precarious chance of resisting invasion.'[1]

A month later, the Germans' failure to crush Fighter Command and gain the air superiority they needed for the seaborne assault was proved in dramatic fashion. On Sunday 15 September, the Luftwaffe embarked on its first major daylight attack on England since the beginning of the Blitz against London. Its aerial operations against Fighter Command over the previous five days had been severely disrupted, not only by the change in strategy, but also by unfavourable weather over the Channel, something that Hitler used as one of the reasons for delaying his decision on Sea Lion, announcing at his Führer's conference on 14 September, 'Four or five more days of good weather, and a decisive result will be achieved.'[2] In similar vein, on a visit to Italy Ribbentrop declared grandly: 'The landing is ready and possible. English territorial defence is non-existent. A single German division will suffice to bring about complete collapse.'[3]

That same contempt for Britain's defences prevailed in much of the Luftwaffe. Guided by Goering's dismissive boasts, many pilots thought that Fighter Command was already broken as a force and that the task of the big raids on 15 September was to deliver the final blow, but the Germans were quickly disabused of this complacency. Fighter Command had used the lull since 7 September productively, to re-equip its squadrons and bring in more pilots. The force was now stronger than it had been at any time since the start of the battle, with every radar station now fully operational. Amidst clear skies that day, Goering sent over 200 bombers against London and another 30 against the Southampton docks, with his fighters carrying out no fewer than 700 sorties. The raids turned into a major setback for

327

the Luftwaffe, as their aircraft were met by reinvigorated fighter defences, getting badly mauled over British territory. At the close of the day, Fighter Command claimed to have shot down 185 Luftwaffe planes, a gross exaggeration as German losses actually amounted to 60, but this was still more than double the Fighter Command total of 26. It was a ratio that represented a return to the first days of the air battle, when the Luftwaffe was losing twice as many planes as the RAF.

So clear-cut was the margin of the RAF's victory that 15 September later came to be officially marked as Battle of Britain Day, the historic moment when Germany lost any chance of gaining mastery of the skies over southern England. 'Greatest day for the RAF,' proclaimed the *Daily Telegraph*,[4] while for the *Daily Mirror* the RAF's effectiveness boded well for the imminent struggle against the invader: 'As each hour passes now Hitler's evil star is on the wane. Unless he destroys Britain his fate and the fate of his German rats is sealed. We are ready! Every man and woman knows what to do. The fighting Services and civil defenders are all in the front-line. If Hitler attempts this monstrous vanity we will smite him a hammer blow.'[5] Readers of the *Daily Express* were greeted with the uplifting story that a German bomb had landed on Madame Tussaud's waxwork museum, taking a lump out of Hitler's face, covering Goering in dust and broken glass, but leaving Churchill 'as firm as a rock, his glass blue eyes sternly supervising the clearing of the wreckage'.[6]

On the other side of the Channel, the Germans fell into recriminations. In a meeting held in his personal, customised train, the Reichsmarschall raged at his commanders, claiming that 'the fighters have let us down.'[7] The brilliant fighter ace Adolf Galland believed that Goering's own leadership was to blame, writing later that 'failure to achieve any notable success, constantly changing orders betraying lack of purpose and obvious misjudgement of the situation by the Command, and unjustified accusations had a most demoralising effect on us fighter pilots, who were already overtaxed by physical and mental strain.'[8]

Worse still, heavy German losses at the hands of Fighter Command that day were immediately followed on the nights of 15 and 16 September by RAF attacks on shipping and communications in the Channel ports, as illustrated by the heavy damage inflicted on Antwerp. A Wehrmacht report for the evening of 16 September showed the battering that the Germans took in other places on the coast: 'Air raid on piers at Zeebrugge and Ostend. Bombs on convoy six kilometres out of Gravelines. Damage caused by night air raids heavier than initially anticipated. Calais: Army repair centre hit. 25 lorries burnt. Bombs on water mains and different quarters of the city. Dunkirk: 5 barges sunk.'[9] Noting this heightened aggression by the British bombers, the Kriegsmarine staff diary recorded for 17 September: 'The RAF are still by no means defeated. On the contrary, they are showing signs of increasing activity in their attacks on the Channel ports.'[10]

By now Hitler had twice postponed his verdict on Sea Lion. Given that ten days' notice was required under the Kriegsmarine plan, the scheduled landing was now slipping into late September, a period when the weather was unreliable and the nights longer. Whilst the Führer could not continue to delay his decision, it was already obvious what direction he would take. He was never a keen advocate of invasion and always schizophrenic in his attitude towards the British; by this point his enthusiasm for the operation had waned dramatically. In the face of a resilient RAF, a powerful Royal Navy and a defiant Churchill, he feared he could not risk failure.

Intriguingly, it is possible that Hitler had firmly decided against the invasion more than a fortnight earlier, even before the Blitz was launched. The evidence for this lies in a fascinating post-war interview with the German paratrooper leader Kurt Student, who had a role in invasion planning. On 2 September, he recalled, he was invited to

> take tea with the Goerings at Karinhall, their house near Berlin. The Reichsmarschall received me jovially. After tea, he lit up one of his favourite Virginia cigars. I expressed concern about the way it was planned to use airborne troops. Goering listened attentively. Then he suddenly said, 'The Führer does not want to invade Britain.' I looked at him shocked, unbelieving. 'And why not?' Goering shrugged his shoulders resignedly, as if to say, 'I don't know either.' He said, 'There will be nothing doing this year, at any rate' . . . Yet this was the moment when the Luftwaffe was gaining air superiority.

In the same interview, Student said that Goering had been deeply impressed by the way in which the British had responded to the invasion crisis, telling Student, 'We have forgotten that the Englishman fights best when his back is against the wall.'[11]

The Führer's negative attitude had driven him inexorably towards the decision he formally took on 17 September. After a meeting with his senior commanders, he announced through an order from Keitel that Operation Sea Lion was to be postponed indefinitely, although 'preparations will be continued' to ensure that the British had to maintain their vigilance.[12]

This was confirmed two days later, on 19 September, by a further order from Keitel, which outlined the first practical steps in the wholesale abandonment of the enterprise. This instruction stipulated that 'movements for the strategic concentration of transport shipping, as far as have not yet been completed, will be discontinued' and that 'concentrations in assembly harbours will be dispersed so that losses of shipping tonnage owing to enemy air attack will be kept to a minimum'.[13]

A memorandum at this time from the Kriegsmarine staff again emphasised that it was the all-too-visible, continuing power of the Royal Navy and the RAF that had led to the abandonment of the invasion.

> The preparations for a landing on the Channel coast are extensively known to the enemy who is increasingly taking counter-measures. Symptoms are, for example, use of his aircraft for attacks and reconnaissance over the German operational harbours, frequent appearance of destroyers on the south coast of England, in the Straits of Dover and on the Franco-Belgian coast, stationing his patrol vessels off the north coast of France, Churchill's last speech etc.[14]

Raeder himself wrote: 'I considered it extremely fortunate that the invasion project was not carried out, as the resulting setback would have been disastrous.'[15] In the same vein, Gustav Kleikamp, the head of the navy's transport fleet based in Calais, described in late October 1940 his relief that the operation had not proceeded, believing it could have descended into a fiasco. 'In my opinion the belated beginning and insufficient preparations, as well as a complete lack of training in craft and *prahme* at steaming together, would have given the greatest trouble or might have rendered it impossible at the end of September or early October to take a transport fleet with the desired success and order to the enemy shore, especially at night.'[16] That fear of failure, which could also be viewed as realism, had been been central to the German navy's profound reluctance throughout the summer to undertake the expedition.

The Kriegsmarine's reservations were fully justified. To the German armed forces, the fundamental problem was that the British still retained command of the sea in Western Europe and no amount of planning, barge loading or Siebel innovations could overcome that. As Frederick-Karl Plehwe, the head of the German army's liaison staff at naval headquarters, observed in 1940: 'I would like to lay great emphasis on the fact that the decisive deterrent to the operation was the expected large-scale intervention by the British fleet.'[17]

Nor could the Luftwaffe have served as a protective artillery substitute for the Kriegsmarine's weakness. Even air superiority might not have been enough, given how formidable the Royal Navy remained in Channel waters. As Kurt Assmann, the German naval historian, wrote in his study of Sea Lion just after the war, 'It was believed that the lack of sea power could be replaced by air power, or, put in another way, that German air power would be able to eliminate the enemy's sea power. For this operation that was impossible.'[18]

The view that the German navy could not have protected the invading troops was shared by Admiral Dönitz, who replaced Raeder as grand admiral in 1943: 'Even if the Luftwaffe had succeeded at all in defeating the RAF in the Battle of Britain, it would still have been incapable of keeping the Royal Navy away from a seaborne landing force,' not least because 'the bombs in use at the time were of far too small a calibre.'[19] That was exactly the result when a major Sea Lion wargame was conducted at the Royal Military Academy, Sandhurst, in 1974, based on a scenario in which the Germans launched their invasion on 22 September, despite having failed to gain air superiority. Its outcome was that although some of the first-wave German troops were able to land on British soil, most of the invasion fleet was wiped out by the Royal Navy's destroyers. In the final analysis, 65 per cent of the barges were sunk and of the troops who embarked on the crossing from the Channel ports, only 15,400 made it back to France.

In 1943, Hitler expressed his regret at having failed to launch the invasion, putting the blame on the Kriegsmarine and claiming, 'I should never have allowed the Navy to talk me out of Sea Lion.'[20] However, he was the one ultimately responsible. As Kurt Student pointed out, 'One thing is certain: Hitler was dilatory in his handling of the invasion operation plan.'[21] The Führer's lukewarm, inconsistent approach not only meant that his commanders were always trying to read his mind but that the planning, especially on the army side, was insufficiently rigorous.

General Günther Blumentritt, the chief of von Rundstedt's operations staff, wrote in 1949, 'Intelligence from England was extremely meagre. No one knew whether there were any coastal defences or field fortifications on the English coast or where they were, if they existed. It was not known which beaches were mined. No one could say exactly what forces the British had available for defence.' Blumentritt added this remarkable insight into the shallowness of the army's understanding of England:

> I should state, for the record, that no member of my staff had an accurate picture of the English south coast. Our maps were inaccurate. Relief maps were sent to us from Munich! . . . It must not be forgotten that we Germans are a continental people. We knew far too little of England. We knew literally nothing of amphibious operations and had no experience. At the same time we were preparing the Sea Lion plans, accounts of the campaigns of Caesar, Britannicus and William the Conqueror were being read, and in Paris books about Napoleon's 'Camp of Boulogne' (1804) were being sought in the bookshops.[22]

This ignorance extended far beyond military planning. It also led Hitler and the Nazi rulers to misread the British public, to underestimate the resilience of the British home defences, to put unjustified faith in the Duke of Windsor, to believe a peace deal could be reached, to embark on absurd spying missions, to believe their own propaganda and, perhaps most importantly, to fail to grasp that Churchill was not some despised reactionary aristocrat but rather the embodiment and catalyst of the British will to resist.

Some German military figures felt that Hitler should have shown more courage and pressed ahead, but they were in the minority. Most were glad that caution rather than recklessness had prevailed.

The limited scope of British intelligence in September 1940 meant that the news of Hitler's decision on 17 September did not reach Churchill's government at the time. The risk of invasion appeared to remain just as great, the need for vigilance just as powerful. This was precisely the climate of alertness that the Germans wanted to maintain, despite Hitler's abandonment of the invasion plan, believing that the pressure of the threat drained military resources that could be used elsewhere as well as undermining the British public's faith in the government.

In truth there was precious little evidence to support their theory. In fact, thanks to increased production, support from America and enhanced recruitment, the armed forces were stronger than ever, while the British nation was perhaps never so united as it was in September 1940. Far from weakening Britain, the German menace continued to exert a unifying and galvanising effect. In the absence of any reliable knowledge about Hitler's policy, there was no relaxation in defence activities and counter-invasion measures. On the very day that the Führer told his commanders of Sea Lion's postponement, the Chiefs of Staff Committee discussed the risks of the Germans making an imminent landing 'in fog or weather of low visibility'.[23]

This was an issue that deeply concerned Churchill who had written the night before: 'I consider that fog is the gravest danger, as it throws both air forces out of action, baffles our artillery, prevents organised naval attack and specially favours the infiltration tactics by which the enemy will most probably seek to secure his lodgements. Should the conditions of fog prevail, the strongest possible air barrage should be put down on the invasion ports during the night and early morning.' He concluded, 'fog is our foe.'[24] In response to such concerns, General Paget from Home Forces said 'that the patrols and sentries on the beaches would be increased in number in thick weather, but the essence of the defence was depth'.[25]

As Hitler retreated, Britain continued to prepare. Again on 17 September, the sense of gravity about the threat was reflected in a comprehensive paper issued by the Joint Planning Staff of the War Cabinet, detailing how the Germans might mount the invasion. It was ironic that, just when Hitler was telling his commanders of Sea Lion's abandonment, the British planners were warning that the danger was greater than ever. They urged that RAF reconnaissance of the Channel be increased, fast naval forces be stationed 'within call of the threatened areas', and port defences strengthened. In practice, most of these steps had already been taken.[26]

Some of the planners' concerns about invasion were mirrored in a speech that Churchill gave to the Commons that afternoon. So portentous were some of his passages about the threat that he asked the House to go into secret session, unreported in the press or Hansard, in order that he could speak frankly to MPs. 'There are some things which it is better for us to talk over among ourselves than when we are overheard by the Germans,' he explained, before turning to Hitler's potential invasion.

> The assembly of his ships and barges is steadily proceeding, and at any moment a major assault may be launched upon this Island. I now say in secret that upwards of 1700 self-propelled barges and more than 200 sea-going ships, some very large ships, are already gathered at the many invasion ports in German occupation. If this is all a pretence and stratagem to pin us down here, it has been executed with surprising thoroughness and on a gigantic scale.

In all, he warned, the 'shipping available and now assembled is sufficient to carry in one voyage nearly half a million men.' But, even in the face of such a foe, he was sure that the country could meet the challenge: 'I am confident that we shall succeed in defeating and largely destroying this most tremendous onslaught with which we are now threatened.'[27]

Despite the indefinite postponement by Hitler, and the gradual dispersal of the invasion fleet from 19 September, the night attacks on London grew even more savage, as if to compensate for the failure to launch Operation Sea Lion. On three successive nights from 17 September, more than 1,000 tons of high explosive and 1,500 incendiary canisters were dropped on the capital by German bombers. On all but two of the last eight nights of September, more than 200 Luftwaffe aircraft attacked London. Unlike the daylight fights during the Battle of Britain, it was impossible for Dowding's force to counter this peril effectively since its night fighter capacity was poor and its navigation aids inadequate.

In the absence of a defensive nocturnal shield, the London public had to bear the brunt of the indiscriminate bombing. In the first two weeks of the Blitz alone, 25,000 people who had been made homeless had to be provided with temporary accommodation by the London County Council. Conditions in these emergency centres could often be appalling. In one, over 2,000 people had to sleep on the floor, using just ten buckets and coal-scuttles as lavatories. The scene at a vast warehouse in Stepney was described by Nina Masel, a researcher from Mass Observation: 'You couldn't see anything. You could just smell the fug, the overwhelming stench of thousands and thousands of people lying toe to toe.'[28]

The most common form of shelter to which London civilians resorted were the platforms of London Underground stations, regarded as the safest places from the bombs. Initially the authorities tried to stop this practice, which led to a major public outcry, particularly as the government faced criticism for having failed to build any deep underground shelters before the war for just such an eventuality. Anger was combined in some places with resentment over claims that in the West End of London private arrangements had been made for sheltering more affluent citizens. In one highly political protest against this inequality, Communist councillor Phil Piratin led a group of fifty demonstrators to the Savoy, where they occupied the hotel's well-appointed basement shelter. Piratin said, 'If it is good enough for the rich, it is good enough for Stepney workers and their families.'[29]

Indignation was widespread at the government's policy on the use of the Underground. The *Daily Mirror* thundered: 'Why allow the homeless to wait in odd holes and corners, in amateurish shelters and improvised dug-outs until somebody or something – some local pundit or fussy official – gets on with a scheme for opening every West End or comparatively safe basement to all-comers.'[30] In the face of potential civil disobedience, the government relented and agreed that the tube stations could be used as temporary dormitories. It was a highly primitive solution, for at first they lacked any sanitation, beds, or refreshments, although these amenities were later introduced. The Croydon teenager Colin Perry was horrified when he visited one such shelter on 21 September: 'Airless, stuffy, and stifling hot and I glanced at the type of people who sought refuge there. I could not understand where their courage was, for staying nightly in a living coffin was not my idea of dodging bombs.'[31] Nevertheless, during the last week of September an average of 150,000 people remained in the Underground each night, reaching a peak of 177,000 on 27 September.

The savagery of war continued on the seas as well as in the skies. One particularly tragic incident occurred on that pivotal day of 17 September, when a German U-boat sank the passenger ship the SS *City of Benares*, with the loss of 260 lives, en route to Canada. What made this sinking so poignant was that the *Benares* had on board ninety boys and girls who were being taken across the Atlantic under the official evacuation scheme run by the Children's Overseas Reception Board (CORB); indeed, she was one of the first vessels to carry CORB evacuees when she sailed from Liverpool on 12 September. Five days later, 250 miles west of Rockall, she was struck by a torpedo and started to sink immediately. There was a desperate struggle to get the children into the lifeboats that were thrown by the crew into the sea.

One of the few survivors, Colin Ryder-Richardson, recalled, 'These little kids beside me – some of them were only five years old. They were in their dressing gowns, with no life belt, clutching teddy bears. They had just woken up.'[32] Only one lifeboat managed to escape the wreckage, although many of those who managed to reach her subsequently died of exposure as it was eight days before a Royal Navy rescue ship arrived. Ryder-Richardson was among just thirteen children who came through the harrowing ordeal. On 2 October, the government announced the end of the CORB, mainly because the Royal Navy could not spare any escorts to provide improved protection for any future evacuation journeys.

Like the Blitz, that episode illustrated the cruel reality of war for Britain. With the government and intelligence services unaware of Germany's intentions, concern about the invasion actually deepened in military circles at this time. As Churchill said in his Commons speech of 17 September, 'The process of waiting, keyed up to concert pitch day after day, is apt after a while to lose its charm of novelty.'[33]

In the same vein, Brooke wrote in his diary for 18 September, 'Every indication continues to look like an invasion being staged, ready to be launched at any time.'[34] The Royal Navy shared that view, with Pound writing on 20 September, 'At the moment there is a most gigantic concentration of shipping and barges from the Scheldt to Le Havre and I firmly believe that an invasion will be attempted.'[35] That mass of invasion vessels was also highlighted in an intelligence report to the Admiralty on 21 September, which stated that 'during the month 2200 barges with a total carrying capacity of 500,000 tons have been assembled in the ports nearest to this country. They have concentrated rapidly and have moved through the open sea as well as inland waters. The south-western move and concentration of barges has persisted in spite of adverse weather conditions and RAF attack.'[36]

It was on the same day, 21 September, that the British finally learnt that the German invasion plan was called Sea Lion, or Seelöwe, more than two months after the phrase had been coined by the German High Command. Throughout this period, knowing that the Germans were plotting an assault, the British had given the operation the code name 'Smith', but four days after its postponement the real name was picked up, thanks, inevitably, to a Bletchley Park decrypt of Luftwaffe traffic. A subsequent report by the War Office on 10 October 1940 stated that 'the name of this operation was first mentioned' by a reliable source

on the 21st September 1940 when the German Admiralty asked Luftflotten 2, 3 and 5 [the airfleets that fought in the Battle of Britain] to provide 'Flugsicherungsschiffe' (Aircraft Security Vessels) at Brest, Borkum,

Trondheim, and Schellingwoude in connection with 'the Seelöwe undertaking.' Reference was made to an order issued in this connection by Air
Staff in the Luftwaffe and to the possible notification of S-1 date [the eve
of the invasion].[37]

But knowledge of the invasion plan's true nomenclature did nothing to
ease the pressure on the British.

The burden of response was especially great on the home defence forces,
which would have to tackle any landing on the beaches. Intensive manoeu-
vres were held, equipment checked, patrols organised, the front line
strengthened. At noon on 19 September, the Cromwell alert was finally
withdrawn, but this did not mean any reduction in vigilance.

The War Office explained that a new, more sophisticated system would
operate in place of Cromwell: 'The following states of readiness will be
maintained by all troops of the Field Army. Beaches will be patrolled during
the hours of darkness and troops will stand to at dawn. In foggy weather
very active patrolling will be carried out and sentry posts will be increased
as necessary.' After the Cromwell episode, however, the War Office decided
that 'the Home Guard will not be called out except in special purposes as
ordered by the Commander-in-Chief.' Apart from the intensification of
beach defences, there were to be two further stages in the hierarchy of
alertness in an emergency. First, 'the message Stand To may be sent out
indicating conditions particularly favourable for an invasion. On receipt of
this message, troops will come to a complete state of readiness.' Second,
'for a full scale state of readiness including the calling out of the Home
Guard, Action Stations will be sent indicating the immediate threat of
invasion.'[38]

For the Admiralty, too, the enervating state of being on permanent alert
throughout these days seemed counter-productive, so new instructions were
issued on 22 September:

> In order to take full advantage of adverse weather conditions and enable
> naval and other forces to obtain some relaxation from the first degree of
> readiness, it has been decided to promulgate by signal twice daily at 0200
> and 1400 the suitability of the weather conditions for the employment of
> small craft in the various areas. This information will be issued by the
> Admiralty by means of the codeword Deluge, which has the following
> signification – 'the suitability of the weather conditions for the employment
> of small craft in the area is as indicated: i) suitable; ii) possible; iii)
> unsuitable'.[39]

One of the army's concerns at this time was that some of the advance
German troops in the invasion might use British uniforms, making them
impossible to identify as the enemy. 'Many thousands of battle-dress suits

fell into enemy hands on the evacuation of France,' warned Lieutenant General Bernard Montgomery, who was now in command of V Corps on the south coast. True to his unorthodox character, he came up with an ingenious, if unintentionally hilarious, solution so that British patrols could expose any German soldier in disguise. Under his proposal, predicated on a scenario where the British were holding an individual or a small unit at gunpoint, the suspects would be required to utter a sentence in English, 'the words of which every German finds difficulty in saying'. Helpfully, he paraded his phonological credentials by asserting: 'I am told that no German can say "North Sea" properly.' If phonology did not work, then the British patrolmen could try phrenology: 'They should make the party remove their headgear to expose their heads. The very marked characteristic square-head of the Teuton can easily be recognised.'[40]

Claude Auchinleck, his immediate superior as head of Southern Command, disliked this suggestion, diplomatically telling Montgomery that he thought it both dangerous and overly complex. Sir Bernard Paget told Auchinleck, 'The real safeguard against "incidents" is vigilance and care by sentries and patrols, and common sense and cool heads on the part of all troops.'[41]

Nor was the Home Guard ignored in this stream of anti-invasion guidance. In late September, Southern Command issue a booklet to all its Home Guard units with advice on tackling 'the Hun, who always prefers tricking his enemy to fight him', entitled 'What would you do, chum?' Referring to a situation in a pub where 'a chatterbug' was talking about military movements, for example, the pamphlet said that the only action was

> to report him. Remember, Adolf has his ear to every wall. Here is a simple rhyme to remember. You might post it up in your tent or room:
>
> > 'Adolf's cunning, that's a cert,
> > So don't chatter, be alert.'[42]

At least this was not intended for public consumption, and again it showed the determination not to give an inch.

Indeed, for all the apprehension about invasion, the national outlook and the strength of the army had been revolutionised since the dark days after Dunkirk. Mobility had been dramatically improved. Artillery and anti-tank guns were deployed more effectively. The front-line units in the Home Forces had received effective wireless equipment for the first time, while the War Office had also established an army broadcasting station to provide reliable information. As the historian David Newbold has pointed out, most divisions now had '75 per cent of their proper complement'[43] of artillery and anti-tank guns, although there were still shortages of light machine guns, mortars and Bren carriers. The total number of tanks in the Home Forces in mid-September was 748, the best of them a match for the German medium tanks. Brooke's total force now amounted to twenty-seven divisions, with his reserves for the eastern and southern coasts consisting five infantry divisions, an infantry brigade and two armoured or tank brigades.

In his history of the Second World War, Churchill recalled the powerful hopes for success engendered by Brooke's forces:

> In the last half of September we were able to bring into action on the south coast front, including Dover, sixteen divisions of high quality of which three were armoured divisions or their equivalent in brigades, all of which were additional to the local coastal defence and could come into action with great speed against any invasion landing. This provided us with the punch or series of punches which General Brooke was well placed to deliver as might be required; and no one was more capable.[44]

The Cabinet expected that those pugnacious qualities were about to be put to the test. In the penultimate week of September, invasion fever reached its climax. Earlier in the month, Sir Samuel Hoare, the British ambassador in Madrid, had passed to the Foreign Office information 'from a reliable source, just returned from Berlin', that the invasion was certain to take place on 'the 21st of the same month'.[45] The government took the news seriously. Even Churchill, for so long dismissive of the threat in private, began to wonder whether the invasion might actually happen.

On the night of 20 September, over dinner at Chequers, Ismay, Colville and the prime minister talked about the 'possibility of the Germans using poison gas' in their landings. According to Colville's account, Churchill 'is doubtful whether the invasion will be tried in the near future, but says that every preparation has been made. He is becoming less and less benevolent towards the Germans . . . and talks about castrating the lot.'[46]

The sense of imminent crisis was compounded early on the morning of Sunday 22 September, when Downing Street received from Lord Lothian, the British ambassador in Washington, an urgent telegram claiming that, based on information passed to the White House, the invasion 'will take place at 3pm this afternoon'.[47] Britain's moment of fate appeared to have arrived.

All naval and army commands in the vulnerable areas were telegraphed the news about the Washington report. From the Nore, Admiral Drax sent the stirring message to his flotillas: 'In the past 2000 years there have been only two successful invasions of Britain: by Julius Caesar and William I in 1066. Another attempt may be shortly expected, but the defence will be stronger than ever.'[48]

Foreign Secretary Anthony Eden, who that weekend was staying in his cottage near Folkestone overlooking the English Channel, remained sceptical. As he wrote in his memoirs, he was telephoned at his cottage by Churchill with the message that 'President Roosevelt had telegraphed saying that three o'clock was zero hour for the German invasion. If I thought I should come back, he would give me dinner. I replied that it was wet and blowing and I felt quite safe. I went to the top of the hill which overlooked the Channel and afterwards sent a further message, reporting that it was so rough that any German who attempted to cross the Channel would be very sea-sick.'[49] Later on Sunday, it turned out that Washington had got their invasions mixed up. The attack referred to was not the German one against England, but the Japanese one against Vichy-held Indo-China, which indeed began on 22 September.

Soon after this farcical episode, there was a tangible slackening in the tension. With each day that Hitler failed to come, the belief spread that the invasion had been abandoned. As early as 23 September, just the day after the Washington alarm, the Soviet ambassador Ivan Maisky reported to Moscow, 'People are becoming increasingly doubtful here whether the Sausage Dealers [Soviet code for the Germans] will invade.'[50]

Evidence began to arrive of the German fleet's gradual dispersal. Six destroyers and a torpedo boat that had been photographed at Cherbourg appeared a few days later to have left the port. On 28 September, British Intelligence admitted that there was a 'cessation of movement of shipping' to the Channel ports, but said that this could be interpreted as a sign that 'an advanced state of preparedness has been reached.'[51] Such an interpretation did not match the evidence from RAF reconnaissance over the following days. In the harbour at Flushing, the barges were reduced from 140 to just 45, with a similar pattern in Ostend. There were also steady reductions in the number of vessels noticed in Calais and Boulogne.

In the press some began to state openly that the crisis had passed and that defence troops should therefore be deployed to other duties. According to the *Spectator* magazine on 27 September, as a result of the Blitz, 'some services, the air raid wardens in particular, are working under an immense strain. They are in perpetual danger, their hours are too long and their numbers in some localities are too few. At the same time, there are tens of thousands of soldiers all over the country doing nothing but standing by, pending the development of more active military operations.'[52]

The Associated Press Agency struck a more positive note: 'Military circles in London are looking to a rapidly approaching winter with what they cautiously term "reasonable confidence" and a feeling that the worst of the air onslaught is over. By the spring they expect to see Britain so much stronger that the invasion threat will have been completely reversed, leaving the Nazis much more concerned over how to repel the invasion rather than how to make one.'[53]

Ironically, for the only time in the Second World War, at that particular moment Hitler and Churchill had the same goal in common. Neither had ever really believed in the invasion, but now both wanted to maintain the threat for their own interests. The Führer thought, with some justification, that the pantomime of preparations kept the British armed forces tied down even when they were badly needed elsewhere, like in the Atlantic to counter the U-boat threat or in the Mediterranean to tackle the Italian navy. According to the US military attaché General Raymond Lee, writing in his diary, Hitler depended on the bluff to keep his own men occupied: 'It is being done in order to make a show of invasion before the German troops who line the other side of the Channel and who, from all reports, are getting fed up with the war, since they had a categorical pledge from Hitler that it would all be over this autumn.'[54]

Churchill, too, felt that the invasion threat kept the public united and the armed forces alert, as well as giving him a justification to press Roosevelt for more support. Tellingly, just two days after the Washington telegram farce, the US government agreed to supply 250,000 rifles to Britain. More than a week later, Churchill wrote to Roosevelt to warn that there could be no complacency. 'I cannot feel that the invasion danger has passed. The gent has taken off his clothes and put on his bathing suit, but the water is getting colder and there is an autumn nip in the air. We are maintaining the utmost vigilance.'[55]

He took the same line in his speech to the House of Commons on 8 October, when he gave high praise to the armed forces, especially the RAF fighters, for deterring the Germans thus far and allowing the British 'to feel easier in ourselves'. But he warned, 'Do not let us be lured into supposing that the danger is past. On the contrary, unwearying vigilance and the swift, and steady strengthening of our forces by land, sea and air, which is in progress, must be maintained.'[56] In keeping with this approach, Churchill continued to highlight for his military and political colleagues certain regular pieces of intelligence, particularly the Bletchley Park decrypts from the Luftwaffe.

Typically a decrypt explained that the '2nd German airfleet asked for the provision of two tankers each filled with approximately 250,000 gallons of aviation fuel to be held in readiness for S plus 3 day [the third day of the invasion operations against the UK] at Rotterdam and Antwerp.'[57] In the same vein, a source told military intelligence that a German 'anti-aircraft regiment received orders to carry out embarkation and disembarkation exercises at Gravelines on 13 October. The exercises were to include the passing of barges through locks and the approach to the shore as well as actual landing.'[58]

Germany could not maintain the charade indefinitely. Hitler needed some of his forces in other theatres like the Balkans and Scandinavia and, above all, in the preparation for the great offensive against Russia in 1941. Indeed, it was the demands of the forthcoming Barbarossa campaign that may have fuelled German reluctance to carry on with the Battle of Britain, according to Jodl, who told a group of gauleiters in December 1943, 'No one could take it upon himself to allow the German Air Force to bleed to death in view of the struggle which lay before us against Soviet Russia.'[59] On 12 October, nearly a month after he had announced the indefinite postponement of the invasion, Hitler confirmed that Operation Sea Lion would not be considered again until the following spring.

Despite this talk of a possible revival in early 1941, all his senior officers knew that the scheme had died a death, given the way in which the Russian campaign came to dominate all military planning. At a conference three days later with Mussolini at the Brenner Pass, Hitler explained that 'the decisive factor' in the abandonment of Sea Lion had been 'poor weather; only five consecutive days of clear skies were needed, but they did not come'. It was an implausible explanation, but Hitler tried to appear as bellicose as ever by talking of new campaigns in Gibraltar and Egypt, new weapons, accelerated military production, telling Il Duce, 'It is still imperative to look for means to get at Britain without invasion.'[60]

Like the decision on postponement, the final confirmation of the abandonment of Operation Sea Lion did not immediately filter back to Britain. Although the tension had been radically reduced in recent weeks, there were still lingering fears that, even in the unfavourable autumnal weather, Hitler might stage an audacious strike.

Then, on 27 October, the government received proof that the invasion was off. Inevitably it came from a Bletchley Park decrypt of a Luftwaffe message, which ordered the dismantling of loading bays that had been built in Holland for Sea Lion. That day, Group Captain Winterbotham, based at Bletchley, had the satisfaction of passing the news of Sea Lion's abandonment to Churchill and the Cabinet, as he recalled in a post-war interview for the Imperial War Museum.

We got a very important signal from Hitler to the loading point organisation in Holland, where they were going to load all their planes. He gave permission for them to be dismantled. It was tantamount to saying that the invasion was off. That signal I sent straight through to Churchill and the Chiefs of Staff.

That evening, Churchill ordered a conference in the Cabinet rooms and I was ordered to go along as the producer of this signal. It was one of the most extraordinary moments of my life. There were all the Chiefs of Staff, a few secretaries, the PM and General Ismay and my chief, Stewart Menzies. This signal was in front of Churchill. He asked, 'Gentlemen, we would like to know what this really means.' Menzies asked me to respond. I pointed out that if these loading bays were dismantled, then the invasion force would not have its proper air support and that Hitler had in fact given up the idea of invasion. Churchill looked at me and then turned to the Chief of the Air Staff. 'May I have your views?'

Newall replied, 'That is entirely our view. With the dismantling of these bays, the invasion is off.'

Everyone then sat back in their seats. Churchill also sat back, pulled out a big cigar, lit it and then said, 'Well, gentlemen, let's see what is happening upstairs.'

There was a terrific blitz going on. The whole of Carlton House Terrace was in flames, the bombs were dropping and Churchill came up, smoking his cigar and wearing his tin hat. He was in his boiler suit. In front of the door to the underground Cabinet rooms was a concrete screen, and everyone tried to prevent him going up because there was so much metal flying about. Not a bit of it. I can see him today with his hands on his stick, smoking his cigar, with the Chiefs of Staff and Ismay behind. And he said, 'My God, we'll get the buggers for this.'[61]

The next few days brought further intelligence that the invasion had definitely been abandoned. According to a War Office summary at the end of the month: 'Nearly every recent report from secret and political sources received recently indicates that invasion of UK has been either abandoned or postponed until 1941.'[62]

For the first time in the war, the will of the Reich had not prevailed. Until Sea Lion, no German advance had been halted. Now the Nazi war machine had shown its fallibility. On occasions Hitler tried to put on a brave face on the colossal setback that the Reich had endured, claiming he was prepared for a long struggle. He declared in November 1940, 'If Britain declares that this war shall go on, I am quite indifferent. The war will go on until we finish it and we shall finish it – of that we can be sure. Believe me, it will end with our victory.'[63] He sometimes even went through the masquerade that he was about to revive Sea Lion, as the paratrooper leader Kurt Student recalled from a visit to the Führer in January 1941 that once more displayed Hitler's ambivalence and ignorance about Britain.

He had no clear, determined will towards Britain. He said to me, 'The

British Empire has shown in its long and stormy colonial history that it is not only the biggest but the best-administered colonial Reich. The British are better colonial administrators than Germans and other people. If I destroy this Empire, 500 million yellow, brown and black natives will become leaderless. Murder and death will stalk and the whole world will go to pieces. So I must proceed very carefully.'

To Student this proved that the invasion preparations had always been just an affectation. 'Hitler was a past master at the art of pretence. He did it sometimes even with his closest collaborators.' During their talk, the Führer's mood suddenly changed and he referred to Britain as 'the chief enemy'. Then he talked again of invasion, with Student pointing out that the south coast was now too well defended. At this, Hitler walked over to a map on the wall, drew a circle round Taunton and told Student, 'Here your paratroopers could go into action.' Student concluded that it was another of the Führer's fantasies, especially with the Russian campaign so near.[64]

On other occasions, however, Hitler recognised what a catastrophe Operation Sea Lion had turned out to be. His despondency was all too rational. He had not only emboldened Britain, but was now faced with the prospect of fighting on two fronts, something he had always sought to avoid. With Britain unconquered, he would have to keep huge numbers of troops and aircraft in Western Europe and in Norway, as well as a naval force in the Atlantic.

His own general Erich von Manstein grasped the long-term strategic disaster into which Hitler had plunged the Reich through the failure of Operation Sea Lion, commenting: 'If Hitler jibbed at fighting the battle with Britain at the hour most favourable to himself, Germany must sooner or later land in an untenable position.'[65] In a paper to the War Cabinet at the end of September 1940, Lord Beaverbrook predicted just this outcome. 'If we can prevail until the winter months, the Americans will come into the war and the issue will be settled in our favour.'[66]

Against what had seemed overwhelming odds, Britain had indeed prevailed. Although the struggle ahead would be long and hard, the deterrence of Operation Sea Lion was the beginning of the end for the Reich. With that soaring eloquence that had done so much to sustain Britain through the long months of mid-1940, Churchill perfectly captured the significance of what had been achieved by the British nation when he spoke to the Commons on 5 November, after the confirmation of Sea Lion's abandonment. 'The plain fact that an invasion, planned on so vast a scale, has not been attempted in spite of the very great need of the enemy to destroy us in our citadel and that all these anxious months, when we stood alone and the whole world wondered, have passed safely away – that fact constitutes in itself one of the historic victories of the British Isles and is a monumental milestone in our onward march.'[67]

In May 1940, when the German threat to Britain first arose, Duff Cooper was on a sea voyage back from France to Plymouth. As he wrote to a friend, the first sight of the coast brought a surge of deep affection for his homeland. 'There suddenly was England under my eyes – Cornish fields, little white cottages, the coastguard station, small roads running down into coves by the sea. I was so foolishly moved, perhaps just because it was unexpected. I think I should die if we had to surrender.'[68] It was precisely that spirit of patriotism, so widely felt, that helped to save the nation in its moment of greatest danger.

Acknowledgements

There are a number of people I wish to thank for their help with this book. I am grateful to the staff of the National Archives at Kew, the Imperial War Museum, the British Library, the Churchill Archives Centre at Churchill College Cambridge, the London Metropolitan Archives, the British Newspaper Library at Colindale, the Cambridge University Library, and the Liddell Hart Centre for Military Archives at King's College London. I am also indebted to Dr Mathias Strohn for not only carrying out research on my behalf at the German military archives in Freiburg, but also giving me guidance on the strategy of the Wehrmacht at the time. Chris Vyner provided me with a host of insights into the local history of east Kent in 1940, while the indefatigable Peter Devitt of the RAF Museum helped me gain a deeper understanding of Bomber Command in 1940.

The excellent team at John Murray did sterling work in putting, my original, bloated manuscript into publishable form, as well as organising the photographs and the publicity. So I wish here to express my deep thanks to Roland Philipps, Caroline Westmore, Lyndsey Ng, Juliet Brightmore, Nick de Somogyi and Douglas Matthews for all their hard work on my behalf. In addition, I sincerely appreciate the heroic job performed by Celia Levett in reducing the text to a manageable size and in editing the copy so skilfully. My superb agent Bill Hamilton, who first came up with the idea of a book on Operation Sea Lion, gave me encouragement and wise advice throughout.

Finally, I am, as always, profoundly grateful to my wonderful, beautiful wife Elizabeth, who remained a constant source of support throughout the two long years it took to write this book. Her tolerance and devotion through this period were amazing, especially at the times when completion of the manuscript never looked to be within sight.

Tragically, just before I finished, my dear cousin Katharine Kinney died suddenly. She was a remarkable woman in the prime of her life, full of energy, curiosity and optimism. Through her bold sense of adventure and unflagging resolution, she exuded the sort of spirit that ensured Britain's survival in 1940. It is to her memory that this book is dedicated.

Illustration Credits

Notes

Introduction: 'He is coming!'

1. Peter Townsend, *Duel of Eagles*.
2. William Shirer, *Berlin Diary 1939–1941*.
3. Ibid.
4. Figures from, Kurt Assmann, 'Operation Sea Lion', Official History 1947, National Archives CAB 101/347.
5. James Lucas, *Reich: World War II through German Eyes*.
6. Report by GHQ Home Forces, 5 September 1940, National Archives HW 48/1.
7. Alex Danchev and Daniel Todman, *The Alanbrooke War Diaries 1939–1945*.
8. Martin Gilbert, *Finest Hour: Winston Churchill 1939–1941*.
9. Charles Messenger, *The Last Prussian: A Biography of Gerd von Rundstedt*.
10. Kesselring to Basil Liddell Hart, June 1957, Liddell Hart Archives 15/15.
11. Ronald Wheatley, *Operation Sea Lion*.
12. Walter Ansel, *Hitler Confronts England*.
13. Mark Rowe, *Don't Panic: Britain Prepares for Invasion*.
14. Michael Glover, *Invasion Scare 1940*.
15. Norman Longmate, *If Britain Had Fallen*.

Chapter 1: 'Walking with destiny'

1. Erich Raeder, *My Life*.
2. Colonel Roderick Macleod and Denis Kelly (eds), *The Ironside Diaries 1937–1940*.
3. Pound to Forbes, 20 February 1940, Cunningham Papers, BL Add 52565.
4. Diary entry for 6 May 1940, Liddell Hart Archives, LH II/1940/Part 2.
5. Alex Danchev and Daniel Todman (eds), *Field Marshal Lord Alanbrooke: War Diaries 1939–45*.
6. Macleod and Kelly (eds), *The Ironside Diaries*.
7. W.H. Thompson, *Sixty Minutes with Winston Churchill*.
8. Gilbert, *Finest Hour*.
9. Ironside to Colonel Roderick McCleod (undated), Fuller Papers, King's College Archive, 4/9.
10. Carlo D'Este, *Warlord: A Life of Churchill at War 1874–1945*.
11. Taylor Downing, *Churchill's War Lab*.
12. David Dilks (ed.), *The Diaries of Sir Alexander Cadogan 1938–45*
13. Robert Rhodes James (ed.), *The Diaries of Sir Henry Channon*.
14. John Lukacs, *Blood, Toil, Tears and Sweat*.

Chapter 2: 'Last Desperate Venture'

1. Leo McKinstry, *Lancaster*.

2. Slessor to Brigadier J.N. Kennedy, 25 September 1939, National Archives WO 193/697.

3. David Newbold, 'British planning and preparation to resist invasion on land', King's College, 2012.

4. Churchill to Sir Samuel Hoare, 8 October 1939, quoted in S.P. Mackenzie, *The Home Guard*.

5. Rowe, *Don't Panic*.

6. Kirke Papers 9/1.

7. Diary of Sir Basil Liddell Hart, 7 May 1940, Liddell Hart Archives, II/1940 Part 1.

8. Memorandum on attack on the United Kingdom, January 1940, National Archives WO 199/1690.

9. Report by Southern Command, 7 February 1940, National Archives WO 199/1690.

10. Newbold, 'British planning'.

11. Air staff note, 23 May 1940, National Archives WO 199/1705.

12. Tizard to Ismay, 16 May 1940, National Archives CAB 21/1472.

13. Report by William Strang, Foreign Office, 29 April 1940, National Archives CAB 21/1472.

14. Report to the United Kingdom representative in Eire, 15 May 1940, National Archives WO 193/141.

15. Report by R.H. Denning, Director of Operations at the War Office, National Archives WO 193/141.

16. Report to HQ, Salisbury, 14 May 1940, National Archives WO 199/1705.

17. Newbold, 'British planning'.

18. Glover, *Invasion Scare*.

19. Newbold, 'British planning'.

20. Warren F. Kimball, *Churchill & Roosevelt: The Complete Correspondence*.

21. John Barnes and David Nicholson (eds), *Empire at Bay: The Leo Amery Diaries 1929–45*.

22. Paul Addison and Jeremy Craig (eds), *Listening to Britain*.

23. S.P. MacKenzie, *The Home Guard*.

24. Newbold, 'British planning'.

25. Glover, *Invasion Scare*.

26. McKenzie, *The Home Guard*.

27. Hugh Purcell, *The Last English Revolutionary: Tom Wintringham 1898–1949*.

28. Frank and Joan Shaw, *We Remember the Home Guard*.

29. Interview with William Kellaway, Imperial War Museum sound archive 11283.

30. Shaw, *We Remember the Home Guard*.

31. Midge Gillies, *Waiting for Hitler*.

32. Shaw, *We Remember the Home Guard*.

33. Gillies, *Waiting for Hitler*.

34. Shaw, *We Remember the Home Guard*.

35. Ibid.

36. Rowe, *Don't Panic*.

CHAPTER 3: 'THESE PERSONS SHOULD BE BEHIND BARBED WIRE'

1. Dilks (ed.), *The Diaries of Sir Alexander Cadogan 1938–45*.

2. Jonathan Pile, *Churchill's Secret Enemy*.

3. Major Gerhard Engel, *At the Heart of the Reich*.

4. Glover, *Invasion Scare*.

5. Stuart Hylton, *Careless Talk: The Hidden History of the Home Front 1939–45*.

6. Gillies, *Waiting for Hitler*.

7. Sir John Wheeler-Bennett, *John Anderson: Viscount Waverley*.

8. Brian Simpson, *In the Highest Degree Odious*.

9. Martin Gilbert, *The Churchill Documents: Never Surrender. May 1940–December 1940*, vol. 15.

10. Memorandum by the Home Secretary, 17 May 1940, National Archives CAB 67/6/31.

11. Simpson, *In the Highest Degree Odious*.

12. Nigel West (ed.), *The Guy Liddell Diaries*.

13. Richard Griffiths, *Patriotism Perverted*.

14. 'The Fascist', *IFL* magazine, October 1934.

15. Statement to Home Office by Anna Wolkoff, 22 May 1940, National Archives KV 2/840.

16. Bryan Clough, *State Secrets: The Kent-Wolkoff Affair*.

17. Recollection by Kent's Russian acquaintance, P.F.R. Sabline, 16 July 1940, National Archives KV 2/543.

18. Text of coded letter to Joyce from McNab, 2 April 1940, National Archives KV 2/842.

19. Clough, *State Secrets*.

20. Ibid.

21. Churchill to Roosevelt, 15 May 1940, Gilbert, *The Churchill Documents*, vol. 1.

22. Roosevelt to Churchill, 17 May 1940, Gilbert, *The Churchill Documents*, vol. 1.

23. Churchill to Roosevelt, 18 May 1940, Gilbert, *The Churchill Documents*, vol. 1.

24. Memorandum from Knight, 19 May 1940, National Archives KV 2/840.

25. Memorandum from Knight, 21 May 1940, National Archives KV 2/840.

26. Metropolitan Police Report, 22 May 1940, National Archives KV 2/840.

27. Transcript of interview with Tyler Kent, 20 May 1940, National Archives KV 2/543.

28. Report by Norman Kendall, 20 May 1940, National Archives KV 2/543.

29. Bullitt to Robin Campbell, 10 June 1940, National Archives KV 2/543.

30. Report by Inspector Pearson, 25 June 1940, National Archives KV 2/841.

31. F.H. Hinsley and C.A.G. Simkins, *British Intelligence in the Second World War*, vol. 4.

32. Addison and Craig (eds), *Listening to Britain*.

33. A.J.P. Taylor, *English History 1914–1945*.

34. Diary entry, 23 May 1940, John Colville, *The Fringes of Power: Downing Street Diaries*, vol. 1.

35. *Hansard*, 22 May 1940, vol. 361.

36. Interview with Klaus Ernst Hinrichsen, Imperial War Museum sound archive 3789.

37. Hinsley and Simkins, *British Intelligence*.

38. West (ed.), *The Guy Liddell Diaries*.

39. Ibid.

40. Paper for the War Cabinet, 25 May 1940, National Archives CAB 66/7/48.

41. Report by Desmond Morton to Churchill, 30 May 1940, National Archives PREM 7/7.
42. Archibald Ramsay, *The Nameless War*.

CHAPTER 4: 'FACING UP TO THE POSSIBILITY OF INVASION'

1. Intelligence report, 30 May 1940, National Archives AIR 40/1637.
2. Newbold, 'British planning'.
3. Diary entry, 2 July 1940, Macleod and Kelly (eds), *The Ironside Diaries*.
4. Gilbert, *The Churchill Documents*, vol. 15.
5. Newbold, 'British planning'.
6. Gilbert, *The Churchill Documents*, vol. 15.
7. Chiefs of Staff paper, 25 May 1940, National Archives CAB 66/7/48.
8. Gilbert, *The Churchill Documents*, vol. 15.
9. Diary entry, 7 May 1940, Liddell Hart LH II/1940 Part 1.
10. Winston Churchill, *The Second World War*, vol. 2.
11. Diary entry, 27 May 1940, Macleod and Kelly (eds), *The Ironside Diaries*.
12. Henry Wills, *Pillboxes: A Study of UK Defences*.
13. Ibid.
14. Rowe, *Don't Panic*.
15. Memorandum from War Office, 25 May 1940, National Archives WO 199/1695.
16. Newbold, 'British planning'.
17. Circular from the War Office, June 1940, National Archives WO 199/1695.
18. Angus Calder, *The People's War*.
19. Circular from Southern Command, 15 July 1940, National Archives WO 199/1698.
20. Memo from the Ministry of Transport, 25 May 1940, National Archives WO 199/1695.
21. Catherine Pearson (ed.), *E.J. Rudsdale's Journals of Wartime Colchester*.
22. Addison and Craig (eds), *Listening to Britain*.
23. Memorandum from Cadogan, 25 May 1940, National Archives, PREM 7/2.

CHAPTER 5: BRING ENGLAND TO ITS KNEES

1. Newbold, 'British planning'.
2. Ansel, *Hitler Confronts England*.
3. Quoted from letter to Basil Liddell Hart from General Gunther Blumentritt, June 1957, Liddell Hart 15/5.
4. Ian Kershaw, *Hitler 1936–1945: Nemesis*.
5. Wheatley, *Operation Sea Lion*.
6. Egbert Kieser, *Operation Sea Lion*.
7. Raeder, *My Life*.
8. Wheatley, *Operation Sea Lion*.
9. Charles Burdick and Hans-Adolf Jacobsen (eds), *The Halder War Diary 1939–1942*.
10. Joachim Fest, *The German Resistance to Hitler*.

11. Wheatley, *Operation Sea Lion*.
12. Ibid.
13. Ibid.
14. Kieser, *Operation Sea Lion*.
15. Burdick and Jacobsen (eds), *Halder War Diary*.
16. Ibid.
17. Raeder, *My Life*.
18. Ansel, *Hitler Confronts England*.
19. Colville, *The Fringes of Power*.
20. Macleod and Kelly (eds), *The Ironside Diaries*.
21. Ibid.
22. Danchev and Todman (eds), *Alanbrooke: War Diaries*.
23. Letter to Basil Liddell Hart, 16 May 1949, Liddell Hart Archives 15/15.
24. Letter to Basil Liddell Hart, 13 May 1950, Liddell Hart Archives 15/15.
25. Andrew Roberts, *The Storm of War*.
26. Letter to Basil Liddell Hart, 22 June 1949, Liddell Hart Archives 15/15.
27. Major Gerhard Engel, *At the Heart of the Reich*.
28. Ansel, *Hitler Confronts England*.
29. Article by Basil Liddell Hart in *John Bull Magazine*, 13 May 1950.
30. Note to Basil Liddell Hart, June 1949, Liddell Hart Archives 15/15.
31. Hastings Ismay, *The Memoirs of General Lord Ismay*.
32. Gilbert, *The Churchill Documents*, vol. 15.
33. Interview with Sandy Frederick, Imperial War Museum sound archive 19804.
34. Diary entry for 25 May 1940, Danchev and Todman (eds), *Alanbrooke: War Diaries*.

CHAPTER 6: 'WE SHALL FIGHT ON'

1. Gilbert, *Finest Hour*.
2. Morton to Churchill, 23 May 1940, National Archives PREM 7/7
3. Gilbert, *Finest Hour*.
4. Ibid.
5. Roy Jenkins, *Churchill*.
6. Gilbert, *The Churchill Documents*, vol. 15.
7. Gilbert, *Finest Hour*.
8. Jenkins, *Churchill*.
9. Ibid.
10. Churchill, *The Second World War*, vol. 2.
11. Hugh Dalton, *The Fateful Years*.
12. Jenkins, *Churchill*.
13. Julian Thompson, *Dunkirk: Retreat to Victory*.
14. Interview with Patrick Barrass, Imperial War Museum sound archive 27185.
15. Richard Havers, *Here is the News: The BBC and the Second World War*.
16. Interview with Sandy Frederick, Imperial War Museum sound archive 19804.
17. Danchev and Todman (eds), *Alanbrooke: War Diaries*.
18. Sean Longden, *Dunkirk: The Men They Left Behind*.
19. Addison and Craig (eds), *Listening to Britain*.

20. Interview with Sandy Frederick, Imperial War Museum sound archive 19804.
21. Virginia Nicholson, *Millions Like Us*.
22. Ibid.
23. Interview with Dennis Mulqueen, Imperial War Museum sound archive 17377.
24. D'Este, *Warlord*.
25. Gilbert, *The Churchill Documents*, vol. 15.
26. Ibid.
27. Gilbert, *Finest Hour*.
28. Rhodes James (ed.), *Diaries of Sir Henry Channon*.
29. Nigel Nicolson (ed.), *Harold Nicolson: Diaries and Letters: 1939–45*.
30. Roberts, *The Storm of War*.
31. Macleod and Kelly (eds.), *The Ironside Diaries*.
32. Paper by Dennis Wheatley, 25 June 1940, National Archives W0199/973

CHAPTER 7: 'DROWN THE BRUTES IS WHAT I'D LIKE TO DO'

1. Dalton, *The Fateful Years*.
2. Max Hastings, *Finest Years: Churchill as Warlord 1940–45*.
3. Basil Collier, *The Defence of the United Kingdom*.
4. Nigel Hamilton, *The Full Monty: Montgomery of Alamein 1887–1942*.
5. Newbold, 'British planning'.
6. Telegram from Chiefs of Staff, 31 May 1940, National Archives WO 199/566.
7. 'Notes on Invasion', paper from GHQ Home Forces, 6 June 1940, National Archives WO 199/1705.
8. Vansittart to Morton, 3 June 1940, National Archives PREM 7/7.
9. Memo from the Director of Naval Intelligence, 5 June 1940, National Archives ADM 223/484.
10. Macleod and Kelly (eds), *The Ironside Diaries*.
11. 'Report on Preparations for Defence', GHQ Home Forces, 4 June 1940, National Archives WO 199/1712.
12. Peirse to Ismay, 25 May 1940, National Archives CAB 21/1472.
13. Shirer, *Berlin Diary*.
14. Field Marshal Albert Kesselring, *The Memoirs*.
15. *Sunday Express*, 13 May 1951.
16. Samuel W. Mitcham, *Eagles of the Third Reich*.
17. Derek Robinson, *Invasion 1940*.
18. Ibid.
19. Kurt Assmann, 'Operation Sea Lion', Official History 1947, National Archives CAB 101/347.
20. Gilbert, *Finest Hour*.
21. Peter and Leni Gillman, *Collar the Lot*.
22. Dilks (ed.), *Diaries of Sir Alexander Cadogan*.
23. Christopher Andrew, *The Defence of the Realm*.
24. Colville, *The Fringes of Power*.
25. Danchev and Todman (eds), *Alanbrooke: War Diaries*.
26. Ibid.
27. *Hansard*, 16 June 1940, vol. 36.

28. Colin Smith, *Fighting Vichy*.
29. Hastings, *All Hell Let Loose*.
30. Malcolm Brown, *Spitfire Summer*.
31. Ansel, *Hitler Confronts England*.
32. Ibid.
33. Engel, *At the Heart of the Reich*.
34. Ansel, *Hitler Confronts England*.
35. D'Este, *Warlord*.
36. Glover, *Invasion Scare*.
37. Correspondence of Christopher Mayhew, Liddell Hart Archive, Mayhew 1/2.
38. Jenkins, *Churchill*.
39. D'Este, *Warlord*.

CHAPTER 8: 'MAKING BRICKS WITHOUT MUCH STRAW'

1. Kimball (ed.), *Churchill & Roosevelt: The Complete Correspondence*.
2. Ibid.
3. Churchill to the Cabinet, 16 June 1940, National Archives CAB 120/10.
4. Newbold, 'British planning'.
5. Interview with Patrick Barrass, Imperial War Museum sound archive 27185.
6. Joshua Levine, *Forgotten Voices of the Blitz and the Battle for Britain*.
7. Summary of Home Defence forces, 13 June 1940, National Archives AIR 75/7.
8. Newbold, 'British planning'.
9. D'Este, *Warlord*.
10. David Collyer, *Deal and District at War*.
11. Philip Warner, *Auchinleck: The Lonely Soldier*.
12. Danchev and Todman (eds), *Alanbrooke: War Diaries*.
13. Report of the Combined Intelligence Committee, 22 June 1940, National Archives AIR 40/1137.
14. Report by Major General H.P. Whitefoord, 22 June 1940, National Archives ADM 223/484.
15. Report of the Combined Intelligence Committee, 27 June 1940, National Archives AIR 40/1637.
16. Zaleski to Halifax, 29 June 1940, National Archives CAB 120/438.
17. Interview with Ernie Faulkner, Imperial War Museum sound archive 19823.
18. Robin Brooks, *Kent and the Battle of Britain*.
19. Norman Longmate, *The Real Dad's Army*.
20. General Raymond Lee, *The London Observer*.
21. *If the Invader Comes*, 19 June 1940, National Archives CAB 21/1473.
22. Addison and Craig (eds), *Listening to Britain*.
23. Virginia Nicholson, *Millions Like Us*.
24. *The Times*, 20 June 1940.
25. *The Times*, 5 July 1940.
26. Norman Moss, *Nineteen Weeks*.
27. Newbold, 'British planning'.
28. Quoted in Alfred Draper, *Operation Fish*.
29. Rowe, *Don't Panic*.

30. Ibid.
31. Glover, *Invasion Scare*.
32. Interview with Brigadier Harry Hopthrow, Imperial War Museum sound archive 11581.
33. Newbold, 'British planning'.
34. War Office paper by Dennis Wheatley, 1 July 1940, National Archives WO 199/973.
35. Verbatim note of meeting with LDV commanders, National Archives WO 199/3244A.
36. Report by Laurence Carr, Assistant CIGS, 11 June 1940, National Archives WO 185/1.
37. Moss, *Nineteen Weeks*.
38. Interview with William Kellaway, Imperial War Museum sound archive 11283.
39. John Warwicker, *With Britain in Mortal Danger*.
40. Jack Yeatman, BBC World War 2 People's Archive A4048120.
41. Minutes of Ministry of Supply meeting, 28 June 1940, National Archives WO 185/1.
42. Stephen M. Cullen, *In Search of the Real Dad's Army*.
43. Stuart Macrae, *Winston Churchill's Toyshop*.
44. Ibid.
45. Diary entry for 8 August 1940, Danchev and Todman (eds), *Alanbrooke: War Diaries*.
46. Radio Broadcast by Franklin Roosevelt, 29 December 1940, in David M. Kennedy, *Freedom from Fear*.
47. Moss, *Nineteen Weeks*.
48. Macleod and Kelly (eds), *The Ironside Diaries*.
49. GHQ Operational Instruction No. 3, 15 June 1940, National Archives ADM 223/484.
50. Ibid.
51. Churchill to Eden, 25 June 1940, quoted in Gilbert, *The Churchill Documents*, vol. 15.
52. Ironside to the War Cabinet, 19 June 1940, quoted in Newbold, 'British planning'.
53. Minutes of the Chiefs of Staff Committee, 25 June 1940, National Archives CAB 79/5.
54. Figures taken from Henry Wills, *Pillboxes: A Study of UK Defences*.
55. Minutes of the Vice-Chiefs, 26 June 1940, National Archives CAB 79/5.
56. Minutes of the Chiefs of Staff, 26 June 1940, National Archives CAB 79/5.
57. Ibid.
58. Note by the Chiefs of Staff, 27 June 1940, National Archives CAB 80/13.
59. Newbold, 'British planning'.
60. Gilbert, *The Churchill Documents*, vol. 15.
61. Churchill to the Chiefs of Staff, 28 June 1940, National Archives CAB 80/13.
62. Diary entry, 29 June 1940, Macleod and Kelly (eds), *The Ironside Diaries*.
63. Ibid.
64. Ironside to the Chiefs of Staff, 3 July 1940, National Archives CAB 21/1472.
65. Private undated note, Kirke Papers 9/2.

CHAPTER 9: 'OUR BACKS ARE AGAINST THE WALL'

1. Notes for speech by Sir Hastings Ismay, 1944, Ismay Papers 1/5.
2. Addison and Craig (eds), *Listening to Britain.*
3. Interview with Hilda Cripps, Imperial War Museum sound archive 18377.
4. Stuart Hylton, *Careless Talk: The Hidden History of the Home Front 1939–45.*
5. Gillies, *Waiting for Hitler.*
6. Jonathan Croall, *Don't You Know There's a War On?*
7. Interview with Rose Rosamund, Imperial War Museum sound archive 5361.
8. Interview with Mary Whiteman, Imperial War Museum sound archive 9730.
9. Dr Edith Summerskill, 'Let the Children Go', *Star,* 15 June 1940.
10. Newbold, 'British planning'.
11. Egbert Kieser, *Operation Sea Lion.*
12. Gillies, *Waiting for Hitler.*
13. J.B. Priestley, BBC broadcast, 14 July 1940.
14. Gillies, *Waiting for Hitler.*
15. *Daily Mirror,* 15 July 1940
16. Longmate, *If Britain Had Fallen.*
17. William Shawcross, *Queen Elizabeth the Queen Mother.*
18. Statement to the Commons, *Hansard,* 10 July 1940.
19. Ronnie Scott (ed.), *The War Diaries of Colonel Rodney Foster.*
20. Diary entry for 29 June 1940, Colville, *The Fringes of Power.*
21. Paper from the Chiefs of Staff, 19 June 1940, National Archives CAB 80/13.
22. Home Office paper to all Chief Constables, 29 June 1940, National Archives CAB 93/3.
23. Stuart Hylton, *Careless Talk.*
24. Interview with Klaus Ernst Hinrichsen, Imperial War Museum sound archive 3789.
25. Ibid.
26. Richard Toye, *Lloyd George & Churchill.*
27. John Barnes & David Nicholson (eds), *The Empire at Bay: The Leo Amery Diaries 1929–1945*
28. Glover, *Invasion Scare.*
29. Thomas Munch-Petersen, 'Common sense not bravado: the Butler–Prytz interview of 17 June 1940', *Scandia* (1986), vol. 52:1.
30. Ibid.
31. Ibid.
32. Ibid.
33. Diary entry, 10 May 1940, Colville, *Fringes of Power.*
34. Message from the prime minister, 3 July 1940, National Archives CAB 66/8.

CHAPTER 10: 'A UNIFIED IRELAND UNDER THE
GERMAN JACKBOOT'

1. Letter from Blumentritt to Sir Basil Liddell Hart, June 1957, Liddell Hart Archive, LH 1940 Part II.
2. Tim Pat Coogan, *De Valera.*

3. Memorandum from Eire's External Affairs Department, 28 June 1940, NAI DFA Secretary Files No. 207.
4. John Bowman, *De Valera and the Ulster Question 1917–1973*.
5. Ibid.
6. Memorandum from Eire's External Affairs Department, 28 June 1940, NAI DFA Secretary Files No. 207.
7. Bowman, *De Valera and the Ulster Question*.
8. Memorandum from Eire's External Affairs Department, 28 June 1940, NAI DFA Secretary Files No. 207.
9. Bowman, *De Valera and the Ulster Question*.
10. Report on Eire from the Chiefs of Staff, 20 June 1940, National Archives, CAB 66/8.
11. Brian Barton, *Brookeborough: The Making of a Prime Minister*.
12. Ibid.
13. John Bowman, *De Valera and the Ulster Question 1917–1973*.
14. John J. Turi, *England's Greatest Spy: Eamon De Valera*.

CHAPTER 11: 'IT IS REPUGNANT TO ABANDON BRITISH TERRITORY'

1. Gilbert, *Finest Hour*.
2. Letter of 4 June 1940, Gilbert, *The Churchill Documents*, vol. 15.
3. Letter of 5 June 1940 from Ismay, Gilbert, *The Churchill Documents*, vol. 17.
4. Winston G. Ramsey, 'Operation Ambassador', *After the Battle* (1981), no. 32.
5. Peter Haining, *Where the Eagle Landed*.
6. Nicholas Rankin, *Churchill's Wizards: The British Genius for Deception 1914–1945*.
7. Gilbert, *The Churchill Documents*, vol. 15.
8. Ramsay, 'Operation Ambassador'.
9. Barry Turner, *Outpost of Occupation*.
10. Charles Cruickshank, *The German Occupation of the Channel Islands*.

CHAPTER 12: 'TO THE LAST SHIP AND MAN'

1. Raeder, *My Life*.
2. Paper by Captain Cecil Harcourt, 29 May 1940, National Archives ADM 11/10566.
3. Forbes to the Admiralty, 4 June 1940, National Archives ADM 11/10566.
4. Forbes to Pound, 15 June 1940, National Archives ADM 116/4654.
5. Notes of Admiralty meeting, 29 June 1940, National Archives, AIR 7/57.
6. Notes of Admiralty meeting, 29 June 1940, National Archives AIR 7/57.
7. Paper to Chiefs of Staff, 2 July 1940, National Archives CAB 80/14.
8. Minutes of Chiefs of Staff Committee, 9 July 1940, National Archives CAB 80/14.
9. Basil Liddell Hart, *The German Generals Talk*.
10. Anthony J. Cumming, *The Royal Navy and the Battle of Britain*.
11. Geoff Hewitt, *Hitler's Armada*.

12. Pound to War Cabinet, 22 June 1940, Dudley Pound Papers, DUPO 5/3.
13. Note of Admiralty meeting, 7 June 1940, Dudley Pound Papers, DUPO 5/1.
14. William Langer, *The Challenge of Isolation*.
15. Ibid.
16. Glover, *Invasion Scare*.
17. *Hansard*, 25 June 1940.
18. Diary entry, 23 June 1940, Colville, *The Fringes of Power*.
19. Glover, *Invasion Scare*.
20. Ibid.
21. Note from Admiral Dudley North, October 1940, Dudley Pound Papers, DUPO 5/5.
22. Robin Brodhurst, *Churchill's Anchor: Admiral of the Fleet Sir Dudley Pound*.
23. Ibid.
24. Gilbert, *Finest Hour*.
25. Anne Chisholm and Michael Davie, *Beaverbrook: A Life*.
26. Memoir of Paymaster Ronald Phillips, HMS *Hood* Association website, www. hmshood.com.
27. Interview with Morgan Morgan-Giles, Imperial War Museum sound archive 11237.
28. Addison and Craig (eds), *Listening to Britain*.
29. Diary entry, 4 July 1940, Colville, *Fringes of Power*.
30. Gilbert, *Finest Hour*.
31. Tim Clayton and Phil Craig, *Finest Hour*.

Chapter 13: 'We hurl it back, right in your evil-smelling teeth'

1. Ansel, *Hitler Confronts England*.
2. Dilks (ed.), *The Diaries of Sir Alexander Cadogan*.
3. Report from Sir David Kelly to the Foreign Office, 8 July 1940, National Archives CAB 66/8.
4. *Hansard*, 4 July 1940.
5. Ansel, *Hitler Confronts England*.
6. Galeazzo Ciano, *Ciano's Diary 1937–1943*.
7. Kershaw, *Hitler*.
8. Ansel, *Hitler Confronts England*.
9. Ibid.
10. Memorandum from Jodl, 30 June 1940, Liddell Hart Archives, LH 15/15/11.
11. Diary entry, 30 June 1940, Burdick and Jacobsen (eds), *Halder War Diary*.
12. Ansel, *Hitler Confronts England*.
13. Kurt Assmann, 'Operation Sea Lion', Official History 1947, National Archives CAB 101/347.
14. Richard Brett-Smith, *Hitler's Generals*.
15. Peter Schenk, *The Invasion of England 1940*.
16. Lucas, *The Reich*.
17. Wheatley, *Operation Sea Lion*.
18. Robinson, *Invasion 1940*.

19. Jak P. Mallmann Showell (foreword), *Führer Conferences on Naval Affairs 1939–1945*.
20. Ibid.
21. Memorandum from Jodl, 12 July 1940, Liddell Hart Archives, LH 15/15/11.
22. *The Times,* 15 July 1940.
23. Mallmann Showell (foreword), *Führer Conferences on Naval Affairs 1939–45*.
24. Wheatley, *Operation Sea Lion*.
25. Naval staff war diary, 21 July 1940, quoted in Wheatley, *Operation Sea Lion*.
26. Ibid.
27. Kurt Assmann, 'Operation Sea Lion', Official History 1947, National Archives CAB 101/347.
28. Robinson, *Invasion 1940*.
29. Paul Schmidt, *Hitler's Interpreter*.
30. John Lukacs, *The Duel*.
31. Ibid.
32. Shirer, *Berlin Diary*.
33. Ibid.
34. Schmidt, *Hitler's Interpreter*.
35. Rankin, *Churchill's Wizards*.
36. Shirer, *Berlin Diary*.
37. Addison and Craig (eds), *Listening to Britain*.
38. Colville, *The Fringes of Power*.
39. John Lukacs, *The Duel*.
40. Mallmann Showell (foreword), *Führer Conferences on Naval Affairs*.
41. Ansel, *Hitler Confronts England*.

CHAPTER 14: 'TO DEFEND OUR OWN LITTLE PATCH OF ENGLAND'

1. Michael Glover, *Invasion Scare*.
2. Gilbert, *Finest Hour*.
3. Ibid.
4. Ibid.
5. Report by MI14, 3 July 1940, National Archives WO 193/141.
6. Dilks (ed.), *The Diaries of Sir Alexander Cadogan*.
7. Diary entry, 11 July 1940, Colville, *Fringes of Power*.
8. Report to the Joint Intelligence Committee, 10 July 1940, National Archives AIR 40/1637.
9. Report to the Joint Intelligence Committee, 12 July 1940, National Archives AIR 40/1637.
10. Report from Admiral Drax, 9 July 1940, National Archives WO 193/14.
11. R.V. Jones, *Most Secret War*.
12. *The Times*, 15 July 1940.
13. Diary entries for 1 and 8 July 1940, Macleod and Kelly (eds), *The Ironside Diaries*.
14. Memorandum from Churchill, 9 July 1940, National Archives ADM 223/484.
15. Memorandum from Pound, 10 July 1940, National Archives ADM 223/484.
16. Minute by Churchill, 15 July 1940, National Archives ADM 223/484.
17. Note of Pound's meeting with ministers, 15 July 1940, National Archives CAB 65/10/8.

18. Macleod and Kelly (eds.), *The Ironside Diaries*.
19. Ismay to Home Defence Executive, 1 July 1940, National Archives CAB 113/20.
20. Field Marshal Bernard Law Montgomery, *Memoirs*.
21. Hamilton, *The Full Monty*.
22. Report by the Home Defence Executive, 11 July 1940, National Archives CAB 113/20.
23. Harold Nicolson, *Diaries 1939–1945*, entry for 20 July 1940.
24. Gilbert, *The Churchill Documents*, vol. 15.
25. Longmate, *If Britain Had Fallen*.
26. D.M. Clarke, 'Arming the Home Guard 1940–44' (Cranfield University, 2011).
27. *The Times*, 15 July 1940.
28. Cullen, *In Search of the Real Dad's Army*.
29. Memoir by Jack Yeatman, BBC World War 2 People's Archive, A4048120.
30. Column in *News Chronicle*, 6 January 1941.
31. S.P. Mackenzie, *The Home Guard*.
32. Gilbert, *Finest Hour*.
33. Mackenzie, *The Home Guard*.
34. Ibid.
35. Memoir of Eric Hart, BBC World War 2 People's Archive A1137566.
36. Memo by Alan Brooke, 12 July 1940, National Archives WO199/1697.
37. Montgomery, *Memoirs*.
38. Ibid.
39. Ibid.
40. Churchill to Ironside, 8 July 1940, National Archives CAB 120/438.
41. Collyer, *Deal and District at War*.
42. Sir John Slessor, *The Central Blue*.
43. Charles Stewart (ed.), *The Reith Diaries*.
44. Churchill, *The Second World War*.
45. Danchev and Todman (eds), *Alanbrooke: War Diaries*.
46. Ibid.
47. Ironside to Colonel Roderick McCleod, 9 January 1941, Fuller papers 4/9.

CHAPTER 15: 'A MENACE TO THE SECURITY OF THE COUNTRY'

1. Interview with Jean Shipton, Imperial War Museum sound archive 22578.
2. Interview with Ken Holland, Imperial War Museum sound archive 12015.
3. Interview with Alf Pack, Imperial War Museum sound archive 2813.
4. Interview with Anthony Eden, Imperial War Museum sound archive 2811.
5. Calder, *The People's War*.
6. *Glasgow Herald*, 11 July 1940.
7. Gillies, *Waiting for Hitler*.
8. Hylton, *Careless Talk*.
9. Richard North, *The Many Not the Few*.
10. Helen Millgate (ed.), *Mr Brown's War*.
11. Addison and Craig (eds), *Listening to Britain*.
12. Hylton, *Careless Talk*.
13. Sir Harry Hinsley and C.A.G. Simkins, *British Intelligence in the Second World War*.
14. Ibid.

15. Stephen Dorrill, *Blacklist*.
16. Morton to the Prime Minister, 10 July 1940, National Archives, PREM 7/6.
17. Churchill to Sir Edward Bridges, 11 July 1940, National Archives HO 45/25767.
18. Minutes of War Cabinet, 22 July 1940, National Archives HO 45/25767.
19. Home Office file on Fuller, National Archives HO 45/25569.
20. A.J. Trythall, *Boney Fuller*.
21. Anthony John Trythall, *'Boney' Fuller: The Intellectual General*.
22. Report by Home Office, 22 September 1940, National Archives KV 22/2146.
23. Note by Home Office, December 1940, National Archives KV 2/793.
24. Home Office report on the Duke of Bedford, 5 December 1941, National Archives KV 2/793.
25. Ibid.
26. File on the Thomases, National Archives HO 45/25569.
27. File on Else Varicopulos, National Archives HO 45/25569.
28. File on Katherine Rouse, National Archives HO 45/25569.
29. File on Professor J.E. Daniel, National Archives HO 45/25569.
30. File on Paul Durrell, National Archives HO 45/25568.
31. File on Edward Baker, National Archives HO 45/25568.
32. Letter to the Suffolk Chief Constable, 6 June 1940, National Archives HO 45/25568.
33. Adrian Searle, *The Spy Beside the Sea*.
34. Ibid.
35. Ibid.
36. Ibid.
37. Ibid.

CHAPTER 16: 'HIDE THEM IN CAVES AND CELLARS'

1. Richard Holmes, *Churchill's Bunker*.
2. Diary entry, 20 September 1940, Colville, *The Fringes of Power*.
3. Handwritten note by Churchill, National Archives PREM 7/2.
4. Steve Fox, 'The Cabinet War Room and Subterfuge', www.burlingtonbeyond.co.uk.
5. Comer Clarke, *England Under Hitler*.
6. Sarah Bradford, *George VI: The Reluctant King*.
7. Interview with Malcolm Hancock, Imperial War Museum sound archive 7396.
8. Interview with Brigadier Harry Hopthrow, Imperial War Museum sound archive 11581.
9. Williams to Duty Officer, Cabinet War Room, 7 July 1940, National Archives CAB 21/2637.
10. Joint Intelligence Committee to Williams, 7 July 1940. National Archives CAB 21/2637.
11. Clark, *England Under Hitler*.
12. Ibid. There was also a shortened version of his passage on Begus in a serialised article in the *Sunday Chronicle*, 22 March 1959.
13. Hugh Montgomery-Massingberd and Christopher Sykes, *The Great Houses of England and Wales*.

14. John Connell, *Auchinleck*.
15. Sir Owen Morshead, *Windsor Castle*.
16. Ibid.
17. Marion Crawford, *The Little Princesses*.
18. Tate online archive, 'The War', www.tate.org.uk/archivejourneys.
19. Raymond Lee to William Gibson, Keeper of the National Gallery, 27 April 1940, National Gallery file NG 290.
20. Davies to Gibson, 5 June 1940, National Gallery file NG 59/2.
21. Gibson to Davies, 28 May 1940, National Gallery file NG 59/2.
22. Suzanne Bosman, *The National Gallery in Wartime*.
23. Draper, *Operation Fish*.
24. Memo from S. Gilmour of the Admiralty, 18 May 1940, Bank of England Archives C43/242.
25. Draper, *Operation Fish*.

CHAPTER 17: 'THE SEA ITSELF BEGAN TO BOIL'

1. Vera Brittain, *Testament of Youth*.
2. League of Nations Treaty Series, vol. 94.
3. Minutes of War Cabinect, 30 May 1940, National Archives ADM 116/4654.
4. Diary entry for 22 July 1940, Danchev and Todman (eds), *Alanbrooke: War Diaries*.
5. Memo by War Office, 1 July 1940, National Archives WO 193/732
6. Ibid.
7. Report by Air Raid Precautions Department, 8 December 1939, National Archives HO 144/21584.
8. Report by F.L. Fraser, 15 July 1940, National Archives HO 144/21584.
9. Report by Intelligence Branch, 6 June 1940, National Archives HO 144/21584.
10. Plan by the War Office, 27 July 1940, National Archives WO 193/732.
11. Minutes of War Cabinet, 4 October 1940, National Archives CAB 79/7.
12. Paper by Dill, 15 June 1940, National Archives WO 193/732.
13. Paper by Anderson, 16 June 1940, National Archives WO 193/732.
14. Paper by Collins, 27 June 1940, National Archives WO 193/732.
15. Memo by Churchill, 30 June 1940, National Archives WO 193/732.
16. Figures from War Office report, 8 July 1940, National Archives WO 193/732.
17. Minutes of RAF Chemical Warfare Committee, 14 September 1940, National Archives AIR 2/5200.
18. RAF note, 11 September 1940, National Archives AIR 2/5200.
19. Minutes of RAF Chemical Warfare Committee, 14 September 1940, National Archives AIR 2/5200.
20. Memo by Slessor, 10 August 1940, National Archives AIR 2/5200
21. Ibid.
22. Meeting of Chiefs of Staff, 27 September 1940, National Archives CAB 70/7.
23. *Oxford Dictionary of National Biography*.
24. Minutes of Home Defence Executive, 27 June 1940, National Archives CAB 63/170.

25. Hankey's memorandum to Churchill, 1 July 1940, National Archives CAB 63/170.
26. Hankey to Ismay, 1 July 1940, National Archives CAB 63/170.
27. Morton to Hankey, 5 July 1940, National Archives CAB 63/170.
28. Report on Dumpton tests, 3 July 1940, National Archives CAB 63/170.
29. Sir Donald Banks, *Flame over Britain*.
30. Ibid.
31. Thorne to Lloyd, 10 July 1940, National Archives CAB 63/170.
32. King to Brigadier A.G.B. Buchanan, 10 August 1940, National Archives WO 199/433.
33. Report on mobile fire ejector, 18 July 1940, National Archives CAB 63/170.
34. Memory of Fred Hilton, BBC World War 2 People's Archive, tape A8090471.
35. Banks, *Flame over Britain*.
36. Ibid.
37. Hankey to General Sir Robert Haining, 31 July 1940, National Archives CAB 63/170.
38. Harris to General Sir Robert Haining, 30 July 1940, National Archives CAB 63/170.
39. Banks, *Flame over Britain*.
40. Ibid.
41. Report by Simpson, 28 August 1940 National Archives ADM 1/10753.
42. James Hayward, *The Bodies on the Beach*.
43. Ibid.

CHAPTER 18: 'FOUL METHODS HELP YOU KILL QUICKLY'

1. Interview with Tom Andrew, Imperial War Museum sound archive 14834.
2. Warwicker, *With Britain in Mortal Danger*.
3. Joshua Levine, *Forgotten Voices of the Blitz and the Battle of Britain*.
4. Peter Fleming, *Operation Sea Lion*.
5. David Lampe, *The Last Ditch*.
6. Warwicker, *With Britain in Mortal Danger*.
7. John Warwicker, *Churchill's Underground Army*.
8. Lampe, *The Last Ditch*.
9. Ibid.
10. Jacob to Ismay, 22 June 1940 National Archives CAB 21/1473.
11. Dan Cruickshank, *Invasion: Defending Britain from Attack*.
12. Paget to Cabinet Office, 30 July 1940, National Archives CAB 120/241.
13. Clarke, *England Under Hitler*.
14. Ibid.
15. Interview with Peter Boulden, Imperial War Museum sound archive 13615.
16. Levine, *Forgotten Voices of the Blitz*.
17. Gubbins's advice to intelligence officers, 17 July 1940, National Archives CAB 120/241.
18. Figures from War Office Progress Report, July 1940, National Archives CAB 120/241.
19. Fleming, *Operation Sea Lion*.
20. Levine, *Forgotten Voices of the Blitz*.

21. Bernard Lowry and Mick Wilks, *The Mercian Maquis*.
22. Interview with Tom Andrew, Imperial War Museum sound archive 14834.
23. Warwicker, *With Britain in Mortal Danger*.
24. War Office memorandum, 4 September 1940, National Archives CAB 120/241.
25. Colin Gubbins, *The Partisan Leader's Handbook,* National Archives PREM 3/223.
26. Guidance for Scout Patrols, GHQ Home Forces, 17 August 1940, National Archives CAB 120/241.
27. Lowry and Wilks, *The Mercian Maquis*.
28. Levine, *Forgotten Voices of the Blitz*.
29. Cullen, *In Search of the Real Dad's Army*.
30. Warwicker, *With Britain in Mortal Danger*.
31. Longmate, *If Britain Had Fallen*.
32. Warwicker, *With Britain in Mortal Danger*.
33. MacLeod to Churchill, 23 July 1940, National Archives CAB 120/241.
34. Churchill to Eden, 25 August 1940, National Archives CAB 120/241.
35. Progress report from War Office, 4 September 1940, National Archives CAB 120/241.
36. Arthur Ward, *Resisting the Nazi Invader*.

CHAPTER 19: 'THE FÜHRER ORDERS AN ABDUCTION
TO BE ORGANISED AT ONCE'

1. Costello, *Ten Days that Saved the West*.
2. *Guardian*, 29 June 2002.
3. Stephen Dorril, *Blackshirt*.
4. Chisholm and Davie, *Beaverbrook*.
5. National Archives MEPO 3/17/13.
6. Report by Maxwell Knight, 24 April 1941, National Archives KV 2/842.
7. Costello, *Ten Days that Saved the West*.
8. Report to Cadogan, 7 July 1940, National Archives FO 1093/23.
9. Gilbert, *Finest Hour*.
10. Ibid.
11. Telegram, Churchill to Duke of Windsor, 4 July 1940, National Archives FO 371/24249.
12. Michael Bloch, *Operation Willi*.
13. Duke of Windsor to Major Gray Phillips, 9 July 1940, National Archives FO 371/24249.
14. Duke of Windsor to Churchill, 18 July 1940, National Archives FO 371/24249.
15. Lord Lloyd to the Duke of Windsor, 18 July 1940, National Archives FO 371/24249.
16. Gilbert, *Finest Hour*.
17. Churchill to the Duke of Windsor, 20 July 1940, National Archives HO 144/20324.
18. Bloch, *Operation Willi*.
19. Ibid.
20. Ibid.
21. Ibid.

22. Jimmy Burns, *Papa Spy*.
23. Churchill to the Duke of Windsor, 24 July 1940, National Archives HO 144/23024.
24. Duke of Windsor to Churchill, 26 July 1940, National Archives HO 144/23024.
25. Churchill to the Duke of Windsor, 27 July 1940, National Archives HO 144/23024.
26. Gilbert, *Finest Hour*.
27. Schellenberg, *Memoirs*.
28. Costello, *Ten Days that Saved the West*.
29. Duchess of Windsor, *The Heart Has its Reasons*.
30. Costello, *Ten Days that Saved the West*.
31. Schellenberg, *Memoirs*.
32. Bloch, *Operation Willi*.
33. Ibid.
34. Selby to the Foreign Office, 2 August 1940, National Archives HO 144/23024.
35. Bloch, *Operation Willi*.

CHAPTER 20: 'THE DAYS ARE NUMBERED FOR THOSE BUMS OVER IN ENGLAND'

1. Shirer, *Berlin Diary*.
2. War diary entry for 5 September 1940, quoted in Wheatley, *Operation Sea Lion*.
3. Kesselring, *Memoirs*.
4. Führer Directive No. 16, 16 July 1940, archive of Defence Academy of the United Kingdom.
5. Ibid.
6. 'Kurt Assmann, 'Operation Sealion', Official History 1947, National Archives CAB 101/347.
7. Ansel, *Hitler Confronts England*.
8. Burdick and Jacobsen (eds), *Halder War Diary*.
9. Ansel, *Hitler Confronts England*.
10. Wheatley, *Operation Sea Lion*.
11. Führer Directive No. 17, 1 August 1940, Liddell Hart Archives 15/15/11.
12. Memorandum from Keitel, 1 August 1940, Liddell Hart Archives 15/15/11.
13. Egbert Keiser, *Operation Sea Lion*.
14. Burdick and Jacobsen (eds), *Halder War Diary*.
15. Lucas, *Reich: World War II Through German Eyes*.
16. Postwar interview with Admiral Theodor Krancke, undated, Liddell Hart Archives 9/24/219.
17. Schenk, *The Invasion of England*.
18. Interview with the journalist Milton Shulman, quoted in Richard Brett-Smith, *Hitler's Generals*.
19. Postwar interview with Admiral Theodor Krancke, undated, Liddell Hart Archives 9/24/219.
20. Ansel, *Hitler Confronts England*.
21. Schenk, *The Invasion of England*.
22. Ibid.

23. Ibid.

24. Ansel, *Hitler Confronts England.*

25. Recollection of E. Roseke, German Military Archives MSG 2/17741.

26. Recollection of E. Roseke, German Military Archives RH 26/1002/3.

27. Recollection of E. Roseke, German Military Archives MSG 2/17741.

28. Wheatley, *Operation Sea Lion.*

29. Situation report by Alfred Jodl, 13 August 1940, Liddell Hart Archives 15/15/11.

30. Wheatley, *Operation Sea Lion.*

31. Kurt Assmann, 'Operation Sea Lion', Official History 1947, National Archives CAB 101/347.

32. Report of IV Army Corps, 30 July 1940, German Military Archives RH 29/16/11.

33. Instructions on Operation Sea Lion, 30 August 1940, German Military Archives RH 29/16/1208.

34. Kurt Assmann, 'Operation Sealion', Official History 1947, National Archives CAB 101/347.

35. Chroniknet.de, online transcript of speech.

36. Karl Fuchs, Your Loyal and Loving Son: *The Letters of Tank Gunner Karl Fuchs 1937–1941.*

Chapter 21: 'All that for tuppence and an orange'

1. Pile, *Churchill's Secret Enemy.*

2. Report to Combined Intelligence Committee, 7 August 1940, National Archives AIR 40/1637.

3. Keith Jeffrey, *MI6: The History of the Secret Intelligence Service 1909–1949.*

4. Combined Intelligence Committee report, 31 August 1940, National Archives AIR 40/1637.

5. Report by Major G.S. Whitefoord, 19 August 1940, National Archives WO 199/911A.

6. Ibid.

7. Report to Amery, 15 August 1940, British Library PZ 4581/40.

8. Lee, *London Observer.*

9. Addison and Craig (eds), *Listening to Britain.*

10. Ibid.

11. *East Anglian Daily Times*, 10 August 1940.

12. Glover, *Invasion Scare.*

13. Broadcast reported in *Daily Telegraph*, 22 July 1940.

14. Appreciation by GHQ Home Forces, 15 August 1940, National Archives WO 199/1700.

15. Paper to the War Cabinet, 17 August 1940, National Archives CAB 66/10/50.

16. Paper by Admiral Burrough, 7 August 1940, National Archives ADM 223/484.

17. Glover, *Invasion Scare.*

18. Telegram to Combined Intelligence Committee, 20 July 1940, National Archives HW 48/1.

19. Report to the Home Security Committee, 21 August 1940, National Archives CAB 93/5.

20. *Hansard*, 20 August 1940.
21. 'Red herrings for the Luftwaffe', *Flight*, 29 November 1945.
22. Shirer, *Berlin Diary*.
23. Recollection of Kenneth Webb, 6 October 2004, BBC World War 2 People's War archive, tape A6043367.
24. Cunningham to Pound, 19 August 1940, Cunningham Papers ADD52563.
25. Addison and Craig (eds), *Listening to Britain*.
26. Newbold, 'British planning'.
27. Venona transcript, 22 August 1940, National Archives, HW 15/43.
28. Newbold, 'British planning'.
29. Ibid.
30. Ibid.
31. Note in Ismay Papers, 20 October 1945, Ismay 3/4/9.
32. Interview with Colonel William Watson, Imperial War Museum sound archive 10420.
33. Memorandum by Southern Command, 21 July 1940, National Archives WO 199/1698.
34. Duncan Grinnell-Milne, *The Silent Victory: September 1940*.
35. Churchill to Roosevelt, 15 May 1940, Kimball (ed.), *Churchill & Roosevelt: The Complete Correspondence*.
36. Churchill to Roosevelt, 31 July 1940, Kimball (ed.), *Churchill & Roosevelt: The Complete Correspondence*.
37. Lee, *London Observer*.
38. Anthony Cave Brown, *Wild Bill Donovan: The Last Hero*.
39. Paper by J. Balfour, 'Bases for Destroyers 1940', National Archives FO 800/433.
40. Ibid.
41. Churchill to Lothian, 3 August 1940, Gilbert, *The Churchill Documents*, vol. 15.
42. *Hansard*, 4 June 1940.
43. Paper by J. Balfour, 'Bases for Destroyers 1940', National Archives FO 800/433.
44. Kimball (ed.), *Churchill & Roosevelt: The Complete Correspondence*.
45. Ibid.
46. Paper by J. Balfour, 'Bases for Destroyers 1940', National Archives FO 800/433.
47. Ibid.
48. Diary entry, 31 August 1940, Colville, *The Fringes of Power*.
49. Diary entry, 17 August 1940, Ciano, *Diary 1937–1943*.

CHAPTER 22: 'A NEW ARISTOCRACY OF GERMAN MASTERS WILL HAVE SLAVES'

1. *Daily Telegraph*, 22 February 2009.
2. Directive signed by von Brauchitsch, 9 September 1940, German Military Archives RW 35/241.
3. *Life* magazine, 9 December 1940.
4. Order 'Concerning the organisation and work of the military administration of England', 9 September 1940, German Military Archives RW 35/241.
5. Directive signed by von Brauchitsch, 9 September 1940, German Military Archives RW 35/241.

6. Order 'Concerning the organisation and work of the military administration of England', 9 September 1940, German Military Archives RW 35/241.
7. Longmate, *If Britain Had Fallen*.
8. 'Guide to behaviour in England', 9 September 1940, German Military Archives RW 35/241.
9. Lampe, *The Last Ditch*.
10. Announcement regarding occupied territory, German Military Archives RW 35/241.
11. Notice of the introduction of German law in the Occupied English territories, German Military Archives RW 35/241.
12. Lampe, *The Last Ditch*.
13. Ibid.
14. Announcement, 9 September 1940, Liddell Hart Archives LH 15/15.
15. Information taken from Derek S. Hart, *Dangerous Coastline 1939–45*.
16. Hannah Arendt, *Eichmann in Jerusalem* (1963).
17. Clarke, *England Under Hitler*.
18. Comer Clarke, 'Britain's girls as sex slaves', *Sunday Pictorial*, 6 April 1959.
19. Comer Clarke, 'We find blacklist boss', *Sunday Pictorial*, 29 March 1959.
20. Walter Schellenberg, *Invasion 1940*.
21. Lampe, *The Last Ditch*.
22. Nicolson (ed.), *Harold Nicolson: Diaries and Letters*.
23. *Guardian*, 14 September 1945.
24. Noël Coward, *Future Indefinite*.
25. Schellenberg, *Invasion 1940*.
26. Ibid.
27. Nigel West, introduction to Schellenberg, *Invasion 1940*.
28. Clarke, 'We find blacklist boss', *Sunday Pictorial*, 29 March 1959.
29. *Daily Mail*, 28 December 2011.
30. Hayward, *Double Agent Snow*.
31. William Bliss, article on the Kent spies, *Daily Express*, 14 June 1941.
32. Terry Crowdy, *Deceiving Hitler*.
33. *After the Battle* (1976), vol. 11.
34. Terry Crowdy, *Deceiving Hitler*.
35. Special Branch report, 22 November 1940, National Archives KV 21/1452.
36. William Bliss, article on the Kent spies, *Daily Express*, 14 June 1941.
37. West (ed.), *The Guy Liddell Diaries*.
38. 'The Spy from the Sky', Denton History website.
39. Hayward, *Double Agent Snow*.
40. Ibid.
41. Ibid.
42. West (ed.), *The Guy Liddell Diaries*.
43. J.C. Masterman, *The Double-Cross System*.
44. Hayward, *Double Agent Snow*.
45. Searle, *The Spy Beside the Sea*.
46. Statement by John Donald, 6 February 1941, National Archives KV 2/1701.
47. Statement by PC Grieve, 6 February 1941, National Archives KV 2/1701.

48. Interview with John Simpson, *After the Battle* (1976), vol. 11.
49. William Merrilees, *The Short Arm of the Law.*
50. West (ed.), *The Guy Liddell Diaries.*
51. Report by Home Office counsel, 1 April 1941, HO 1442/1636.
52. William Jowitt, *Some Were Spies.*
53. Editor's note, *After the Battle* (1976), vol. 11.
54. West (ed.), *The Guy Liddell Diaries.*

CHAPTER 23: 'ONE GIGANTIC CONFLAGRATION'

1. Statistics from Basil Collier's official history, *The Defence of the United Kingdom.*
2. James Holland, *The Battle of Britain.*
3. Calder, *The People's War.*
4. Gillies, *Waiting for Hitler.*
5. Longmate, *Island Fortress.*
6. Peter Stansky, *The First Day of the Blitz.*
7. Roberts, *The Storm of War.*
8. Order signed by Keitel, 3 September 1940, archive of the UK Defence Academy.
9. Wheatley, *Operation Sea Lion.*
10. Report of Combined Intelligence Committee, 1 September 1940, National Archives AIR 40/1637.
11. Report of Combined Intelligence Committee, 3 September 1940, National Archives AIR 40/1637.
12. Danchev and Todman (eds), *Alanbrooke: War Diaries.*
13. Paper from GHQ Home Forces, 5 September 1940, National Archives HW 48/1.
14. Report to C-in-C Home Fleet, 6 September 1940, National Archives WO 193/14.
15. Gillies, *Waiting for Hitler.*
16. Meeting of the Chiefs of Staff Committee, 7 September 1940, National Archives CAB 80/18.
17. Ibid.
18. Interview with Patrick Barrass, Imperial War Museum sound archive 27185.
19. Recollection of Major R.F. Hall, BBC World War 2 People's War archive, tape A4543670.
20. Rowe, *Don't Panic.*
21. Gillies, *Waiting for Hitler.*
22. Glover, *Invasion Scare.*
23. Rowe, *Don't Panic.*
24. Gilbert, *Finest Hour.*
25. Minutes of Chiefs of Staff Committee, 9 September 1940, National Archives CAB 80/18.
26. Report of the Combined Intelligence Committee, 10 September 1940, National Archives AIR 40/1637.
27. Minutes of the War Cabinet, 11 September 1940, National Archives CAB 65/15/3.
28. Gilbert, *Finest Hour.*
29. Danchev and Todman (eds), *Alanbrooke: War Diaries.*
30. Recollection of Sir Hastings Ismay, speech, 24 October 1941, Ismay Papers 1/7.
31. Recollection of Sir Hastings Ismay, speech, 30 June 1949, Ismay Papers 1/7.

32. Minutes of Chiefs of Staff Committee, 10 September 1940, National Archives CAB 65/15/3.
33. Wheatley, *Operation Sea Lion*.
34. Walter Gorlitz (ed.), *The Memoirs of Field Marshal Wilhelm Keitel*.
35. Ansel, *Hitler Confronts England*.
36. Hewitt, *Hitler's Armada*.
37. Grinnell-Milne, *The Silent Victory*.
38. *Yorkshire Post*, 17 September 1940.
39. Daily report, 16 September 1940, German Military Archives RH 29/16/11.
40. Ulrich Steinhilper and Peter Osborne, *Spitfire on my Tail*.
41. Glover, *Invasion Scare*.
42. Hylton, *Careless Talk*.
43. Rhodes James (ed.), *The Diaries of Sir Henry Channon*.
44. Nicolaus von Below, *At Hitler's Side*.
45. Kurt Assman, 'Operation Sea Lion', March 1947, National Archives CAB 101/347.
46. Burdick and Jacobsen, *The Halder War Diary 1939–45*.

CHAPTER 24: 'THE EXTRAORDINARY GRAVITY OF BRITAIN'S PRESENT SITUATION'

1. Haining, *Where the Eagle Landed*.
2. Ibid.
3. Hayward, *The Bodies on the Beach*.
4. Haining, *Where the Eagle Landed*.
5. Millgate (ed.), *Mr Brown's War*.
6. Colin Perry, *The Boy in the Blitz*.
7. Addison and Craig (eds), *Listening to Britain*.
8. Memories of Ronald Ashford, 'The secret war at Shingle Street', website.
9. Report in *Sunday Dispatch*, 1 November 1944.
10. Shirer, *Berlin Diary*.
11. Haining, *Where the Eagle Landed*.
12. Ibid.
13. *The Times*, 21 October 1940
14. Fleming, *Operation Sea Lion*.
15. *Hansard*, 18 November 1946, vol. 430,
16. Peter Haining, *Where the Eagle Landed*
17. Hayward, *The Bodies on the Beach*.
18. Report by anonymous staff officer, 15 September 1942, National Archives WO 199/573.
19. Report of Naval Intelligence Division, 26 November 1941, National Archives ADM 199/2477.
20. Churchill, *The Second World War*.
21. Inspired Rumours Weekly reports, National Archives FO 898/70.
22. Ibid.
23. Hayward, *Bodies on the Beach*.
24. John Baker White, *The Big Lie*.
25. Sefton Delmer, *Black Boomerang*.
26. James Hayward, *The Bodies on the Beach*.

27. Baker White, *The Big Lie*.
28. Lucas, *World War II Through German Eyes*.
29. James Hayward, *Myths and Legends of the Second World War*.
30. Desmond Morton to Churchill, 27 June 1940, National Archives PREM 7/2.
31. Draper, *Operation Fish*.
32. Augustus Agar, *Footprints in the Sea*.
33. Interview with Morgan Morgan-Giles, Imperial War Museum sound archive 11237.
34. Levine, *Forgotten Voices of the Blitz*.
35. Report on Operation Lucid, October 1940, National Archives PREM 3/264.
36. Interview with Morgan Morgan-Giles, Imperial War Museum sound archive 11237.
37. Ibid.

CHAPTER 25: 'WE KNEW FAR TOO LITTLE OF ENGLAND'

1. Basil Liddell Hart, 'RAF will decide our fate', *Sunday Pictorial*, 18 August 1940.
2. Burdick and Jacobsen (eds), *The Halder War Diary 1939–1942*.
3. Ciano, *Diary 1937–1943*.
4. *Daily Telegraph*, 16 September 1940.
5. *Daily Mirror*, 16 September 1940.
6. *Daily Express*, 16 September 1940.
7. North, *The Many Not the Few*.
8. Adolf Galland, *The First and the Last*.
9. XXII AK, evening report, 16 September 1940, German Military Archives RH 29/16/11.
10. Wheatley, *Operation Sea Lion*.
11. *Daily Express*, 13 May 1951.
12. Order signed by Keitel, 17 September 1940, archive of the Defence Academy of the UK
13. Order signed by Keitel, 19 September 1940, archive of the Defence Academy of the UK.
14. Kurt Assmann, 'Operation Sea Lion', Official History 1947, National Archives CAB 101/347.
15. Raeder, *My Life*.
16. Ansel, *Hitler Confronts England*.
17. Robinson, *Invasion 1940*.
18. Kurt Assmann, 'Operation Sea Lion', Official History 1947, National Archives CAB 101/347.
19. Note by Ismay of Doenitz's views, recorded 20 October 1945, Ismay Papers 2/1.
20. Kurt Assmann, 'Operation Sea Lion', Official History 1947, National Archives CAB 101/347.
21. *Daily Express*, 13 May 1951.
22. *Irish Defence Journal*, January 1949.
23. Minutes of the Chiefs of Staff Committee, 17 September 1940, National Archives CAB 79/6.
24. Churchill to Colonel Jacob, 16 September 1940, National Archives CAB 120/438.
25. Minutes of the Chiefs of Staff Committee, 17 September 1940, National Archives CAB 79/6.
26. Joint Planning Staff paper, 17 September 1940, National Archives CAB 8418/454.
27. Gilbert, *The Churchill Documents*, vol. 15.
28. Geoffrey Field, *Blood, Sweat and Toil: The Remaking of the Working-Class 1939–1945*.
29. North, *The Many Not the Few*.

30. *Daily Mirror*, 18 September 1940.
31. Perry, *The Boy in the Blitz*.
32. Longden, *Blitz Kids*.
33. Martin Gilbert, *The Churchill Documents*, vol. 15.
34. Danchev and Todman (eds), *Alanbrooke: War Diaries*.
35. Pound to Cunningham, 20 September 1940, Cunningham Papers ADD 52563.
36. 'Barge concentrations', report to the Admiralty, 21 September 1940, National Archives MT 6/2755.
37. Report on 'Seelöwe', Wing Commander Winterbotham, 10 October 1940, National Archives HW 48/4.
38. Instruction by GHQ, Home Forces, 19 September 1940, National Archives WO 193/14.
39. Admiralty instruction, 22 September 1940, National Archives ADM 116/4654.
40. Montgomery to Auchinleck, 15 September 1940, National Archives WO 199/1712.
41. Paget to Auchinleck, 24 September 1940, National Archives WO 199/1712.
42. Text of pamphlet, 'What would you do, chum?', 19 September 1940, National Archives WO 199/1977.
43. Newbold, 'British planning'.
44. Churchill, *The Second World War*.
45. Air Ministry paper on the history of Operation Smith (Sea Lion), 19 October 1940, National Archives HW 48/4.
46. Colville, *The Fringes of Power*.
47. Kimball (ed.), *Churchill & Roosevelt: The Complete Correspondence*.
48. J.P. Foynes, *The Battle of the East Coast*.
49. Anthony Eden, *The Reckoning*.
50. Venona transcript, 23 September 1940, National Archives HW 15/43.
51. Report by British Intelligence, 28 September 1940, National Archives WO 199/911A.
52. *Spectator*, 27 September 1940.
53. Associated Press Agency, quoted in the *Daily Telegraph*, 7 October 1940.
54. Lee, *The London Observer*.
55. Kimball (ed.), *Churchill & Roosevelt: The Complete Correspondence*.
56. Gilbert, *The Churchill Documents*, vol. 15.
57. Intelligence report of 9 October 1940, National Archives WO 199/911A.
58. Intelligence report of 12 October 1940, National Archives WO 199/911A.
59. Jodl speech, 11 December 1943, Ismay Papers 3/4/9.
60. Burdick and Jacobsen (eds), *The Halder War Diary*.
61. Interview with Group Captain Frederick Winterbotham, Imperial War Museum sound archive 7462.
62. Report by the War Office, 31 October 1940, National Archives WO 193/141.
63. Quoted by Basil Liddell Hart, personal memorandum, Liddell Hart Archive, LH II/1940/Part 3.
64. *Daily Express*, 13 May 1951.
65. Erich Manstein, *Lost Victories*.
66. North, *The Many Not the Few*.
67. *Hansard*, 5 November 1940.
68. Alfred Duff Cooper, *Old Men Forget*.

Bibliography

PRIMARY SOURCES

Admiralty papers (National Archives)
Air Ministry papers (National Archives)
Alanbrooke papers (King's College Archives)
Bank of England reports and correspondence (Bank of England Archives)
Brannan, Dorothy (BBC World War 2 People's Archive A4551383)
Cabinet papers (National Archives)
Chandler, Francis (RAF Museum)
Clark, Sir Kenneth (National Gallery Archive)
Cunningham, Admiral Andrew (British Library)
Davies, Martyn (National Gallery Archive)
Dill, Sir John (King's College Archives)
Forbes, Admiral Sir Charles (British Library)
Foreign Office papers (National Archives)
Fox, Steve (www.burlingtonandbeyond.co.uk)
Fuller, Major-General, J.F.C. (King's College Archives)
Gearing, Daphne (BBC World War 2 People's Archive A3295488)
German Military Records (Bundesarchiv, Freiburg)
Gibb, Sergeant Eric (RAF Museum)
Hall, Major R.F. (BBC World War 2 People's Archive A4543670)
Harrison, Ronald (RAF Museum)
Hart, Eric (BBC World War 2 People's Archive A1137566)
Hilton, Fred (BBC World War 2 People's Archive A8090471)
Home Office papers (National Archives)
India Office papers (British Library)
Irish Foreign Policy papers (National Archives of Ireland)
Ismay, Sir Hastings (King's College Archives)
Kirke, Walter (King's College Archives)
Kirwan, Dermon (BBC World War 2 People's Archive A8259825)
Krancke, Admiral Theodor (King's College Archives)
Liddell Hart, Basil (Liddell Hart Archives)
London County Council papers (London Metropolitan Archives)
London County Council Education Department papers (London Metropolitan Archives)
Loosemore, Jose (BBC World War 2 People's Archive A2127133)
Mayhew, Christopher (King's College Archives)
Ministry of Supply papers (National Archives)

National Gallery papers (National Gallery Archives)
OKW Directives (Defence Authority of the UK)
Pound, Admiral Sir Dudley (Churchill College Archives)
Prime Minister's papers (National Archives)
Rogers, Sergeant Richard (RAF Museum)
Roswarne, Flying Office Vivian (RAF Museum)
Venona transcripts (National Archives)
War Office papers (National Archives)
Webb, Kenneth (BBC World War 2 People's Archive A6043367)
Wintringham, Tom (King's College Archives)
Yeatman, Jack (BBC World War 2 People's Archive A4048120)

Audio Interviews

Andrew, Tom (Imperial War Museum tape 14834)
Barrass, Patrick (IWM tape 27185)
Body, Richard (IWM tape 13614)
Boothby, Robert (Thames TV archive)
Boulden, Peter (IWM tape 13615)
Butler, Rab (IWM tape 2742)
Chandler, Eric (IWM tape 11036)
Clark, Ernest (IWM tape 1993)
Cripps, Hilda (IWM tape 18337)
Eden, Sir Anthony (IWM tape 2811)
Faulkner, Ernie (IWM tape 19823)
Frederick, Sandy (IWM tape 19804)
Garside, Geoffrey (IWM tape 12196)
Hancock, Malcolm (IWM tape 7396)
Hinrichsen, Klaus Ernst (IWM 3789)
Holland, Ken (IWM tape 12015)
Hopthrow, Brigadier Harry (IWM tape 11581)
Kay, Ernie (IWM tape 19851)
Kellaway, William (IWM tape 11283)
Lyttelton, Oliver (IWM tape 2739)
Melville, Sir Ronald (IWM tape 13708)
Morgan-Giles, Morgan (IWM tape 11237)
Mulqueen, Dennis (IWM tape 17377)
Myers, Thomas (IWM tape 10166)
Pack, Alf (IWM tape 2813)
Peroni, Douglas (IWM tape 3866)
Priestley, J.B. (IWM tape 2805)
Rosamund, Robert and Rose (IWM tape 5361)
Shipton, Janet (IWM tape 22578)
Spears, General Sir Edward (IWM tape 2714)
Thornton, Leslie (IWM tape 10421)
Warton, Harry (IWM tape 8322)
Watson, Colonel William (IWM tape 10420)

Whiteman, Mary Walker (IWM tape 9730)
Winterbotham, Group Captain Frederick (IWM tape 7462)

PUBLISHED SOURCES
Books

Addison, Paul & Jeremy Craig (eds), *Listening to Britain* (2011)
Agar, Augustus, *Footprints in the Sea* (1961)
Alexander, Colin, *Ironside's Line* (1999)
Andrew, Christopher, *The Defence of the Realm* (2009)
Angell, Stewart, *The Secret Sussex Resistance* (1996)
Ansel, Walter, *Hitler Confronts England* (1960)
Arendt, Hannah, *Eichmann in Jerusalem* (1963)
Baker White, John, *The Big Lie* (1955)
Banks, Sir Donald, *Flame over Britain* (1946)
Barnes, John and David Nicholson (eds), *The Empire at Bay: The Leo Amery Diaries 1929–1945* (1988)
Barry, Tom, *Guerrilla Days in Ireland* (1955)
Barton, Brian, *Brookeborough: The Making of a Prime Minister* (1988)
Bearse, Ray and Anthony Read, *Conspirator: The Untold Story of Churchill, Roosevelt & Tyler Kent, Spy* (1991)
Beckett, Francis, *The Rebel Who Lost His Cause* (1999)
Beevor, Anthony, *The Second World War* (2012)
Bekker, Cajus, *Hitler's Naval War* (1974)
Below, Nicolaus von, *At Hitler's Side* (2010)
Best, Geoffrey, *Churchill and War* (2005)
Bird, Keith, *Erich Raeder: Admiral of the Third Reich* (2006)
Bishop, Patrick, *Battle of Britain: A Day to Day Chronicle* (2009)
Blake, Robert and William Roger Louis, *Churchill: A Major New Assessment* (1994)
Bloch, Michael, *Operation Willi* (1986)
Bond, Brian (ed.), *Chief of Staff: The Diaries of Sir Henry Pownall, 1933–40* (1973)
Bosman, Suzanne, *The National Gallery in Wartime* (2008)
Bowman, John, *De Valera and the Ulster Question 1917–1973* (1989)
Bowyer, Michael J.F., *The Battle of Britain* (1990)
Boyle, Andrew, *Trenchard* (1962)
Bradford, Sarah, *George VI: The Reluctant King* (1990)
Brayley, Martin, *The British Home Front 1939–45* (2005)
Bret, David, *Gracie Fields* (2010)
Brett-Smith, Richard, *Hitler's Generals* (1976)
Breuer, William B., *Daring Missions of World War II* (2001)
Brodhurst, Robin, *Churchill's Anchor: Admiral of the Fleet Sir Dudley Pound* (2000)
Brooks, Robin, *Kent and the Battle of Britain* (2009)
Brown, Malcolm, *Spitfire Summer* (2000)
Bunting, Madeline, *The Model Occupation* (1995)
Burdick, Charles and Hans-Adolf Jacobsen (eds), *The Halder War Diary 1939–1942* (1988)

Burleigh, Michael, *The Third Reich: A New History* (2000)

Burns, Jimmy, *Papa Spy* (2010)

Butler of Saffron Walden, Lord, *The Art of the Possible* (1971)

Calder, Angus, *The People's War: Britain 1939–1945* (1969)

Cameron, A. Bryce, *Under Sand, Ice and Sea* (1999)

Cantwell, John D., *The Public Record Office 1838 to 1950* (1991)

Casey, Steven, *Cautious Crusade* (2004)

Cave Brown, Anthony, *Wild Bill Donovan: The Last Hero* (1982)

Chisholm, Anne and Michael Davie, *Beaverbrook: A Life* (1992)

Churchill, Winston, *The Second World War: Volume 2* (1949)

Ciano, Galeazzo, *Ciano's Diary 1937–1943*

Clarke, Comer, *England Under Hitler* (1961)

Clayton, Tim and Phil Craig, *Finest Hour* (1999)

Clough, Bryan, *State Secrets: The Kent-Wolkoff Affair* (2005)

Collier, Basil, *The Defence of the United Kingdom* (1957)

Collyer, David G., *Deal and District at War* (1995)

Colville, John, *The Fringes of Power: Downing Street Diaries*, vol. 1 (1985)

Connell, John, *Auchinleck* (1959)

Coogan, Tim Pat, *De Valera* (1993)

Corrigan, Gordon, *Blood, Sweat and Arrogance* (2006)

Cosgrave, Patrick, *R.A. Butler* (1981)

Costello, John, *Ten Days that Saved the West* (1991)

Coward, Noël, *Future Indefinite* (1954)

Crawford, Marion, *The Little Princesses* (1950)

Croall, Jonathan, *Don't You Know There's a War On* (1989)

Crowdy, Terry, *Deceiving Hitler* (2008)

Cruickshank, Charles, *The German Occupation of the Channel Islands* (2004)

Cruickshank, Dan, *Invasion: Defending Britain from Attack* (2001) Cullen, Stephen
    M., *In Search of the Real Dad's Army* (2011)

Cumming, Anthony J., *The Royal Navy and the Battle of Britain* (2010)

Dallek, Robert, *Franklin Roosevelt and American Foreign Policy 1932–1945* (1979)

Dalton, Hugh, *The Fateful Years* (1957)

Danchev, Alex and Daniel Todman (eds), *Field Marshal Lord Alanbrooke: War Diaries
    1939–1945* (2001)

Deighton, Len, *Blood, Tears and Folly* (2007)

Deighton, Len and Ian Hawkins, *Destroyer* (2005)

Delmer, Sefton, *Black Boomerang* (1962)

D'Este, Carlo, *Warlord: A Life of Churchill at War 1874–1945* (2008)

Dilks, David (ed.), *The Diaries of Sir Alexander Cadogan 1938–1945* (1971)

Doenecke, Justus D., *Storm on the Horizon* (2000)

Donnelly, Larry, *The Other Few* (2004)

Dorril, Stephen, *Blackshirt* (2006)

Downing, Taylor, *Churchill's War Lab* (2010)

Draper, Alfred, *Operation Fish* (1979)

Duff Cooper, Alfred, *Old Men Forget* (1953)

Easom, S. (ed.), *The History of Newmarket*, vol. II (2000)

Eccles, Sybil and David, *By Safe Hand: Letters 1939–42* (1983)

Eden, Anthony, *The Reckoning* (1965)

Edgerton, David, *Britain's War Machine* (2011)

Engel, Major Gerhard, *At the Heart of the Reich* (2005)

Erickson, John (ed.), *Invasion 1940* (2000)

Erskine, Ralph and Michael Smith, *The Bletchley Park Codebreakers* (2011)

Evans, Richard, *The Third Reich at War* (2008)

Fenby, Jonathan, *The Sinking of the Lancastria* (2005)

Fest, Joachim, *The German Resistance to Hitler* (1994)

Field, Geoffrey, *Blood, Sweat and Toil: The Remaking of the Working-Class 1939–45* (2012)

Fleming, Peter, *Operation Sea Lion* (1957)

Foot, M.R.D and J.M. Langley, *MI9: Escape and Evasion 1939–1945* (1979)

Foot, William, *The Battlefields that Nearly Were* (2007)

Fox, Jo, *British Domestic Propaganda during World War II* (2013)

Foynes, J.P., *The Battle of the East Coast* (1994)

Fraser, General Sir David, *Wars and Shadows* (2003)

French, David, *Raising Churchill's Army* (2001)

Fuchs, Karl, *Your Loyal and Loving Son: The Letters of Tank Commander Karl Fuchs 1937–1941* (2003)

Galland, Adolf, *The First and the Last* (1982)

Garfield, Simon, *We are at War* (2006)

Gilbert, Martin, *Finest Hour: Winston Churchill 1939–1941* (1983)

——, *The Churchill Documents: Never Surrender May 1940–December 1940* (2011)

Gillies, Midge, *Waiting for Hitler* (2006)

Gillman, Peter and Leni, *Collar the Lot* (1980)

Glover, Michael, *Invasion Scare 1940* (1990)

Gorlitz, Walter (ed.), *The Memoirs of Field Marshal Wilhelm Keitel* (1965)

Griffiths, Richard, *Patriotism Perverted* (1998)

Grinnell-Milne, Duncan, *The Silent Victory September 1940* (1958)

Grossjohann, Georg, *Five Years, Four Fronts* (2005)

Guderian, General Heinz, *Panzer Leader* (1953)

Haining, Peter, *Where the Eagle Landed* (2004)

Hamilton, Nigel, *The Full Monty: Montgomery of Alamein 1887–1942* (2001)

Hands, Michael and John Spearman, *The Coldstream Guards*

Hart, Derek S., *Dangerous Coastline 1939–1945* (2009)

Harvey, John (ed.), *The Diplomatic Diaries of Oliver Harvey 1937–1940* (1970)

Hastings, Max, *Finest Years: Churchill as Warlord 1940–45* (2009)

——, *All Hell Let Loose* (2012)

Haufler, Hervie, *The Spies Who Never Were* (2006)

Havers, Richard, *Here is the News: The BBC and the Second World War* (2007)

Hayward, James, *The Bodies on the Beach* (1994)

——, *Myths & Legends of the Second World War* (2003)

——, *Double Agent Snow* (2013)

Hewitt, Geoff, *Hitler's Armada* (2008)

Hinsley, F.H. and C.A.G. Simkins, *British Intelligence in the Second World War*, vol. IV (1990)

Hoare, Adrian, *Standing up to Hitler: The Story of the Norfolk Home Guard* (1997)

Holland, James, *The Battle of Britain* (2010)

Holmes, Richard, *The World at War* (2007)

——, *Churchill's Bunker* (2009)

Holt, Thaddeus, *The Deceivers: Allied Deception in the Second World War* (2004)

Howard, Michael and John Sparrow, *The Coldstream Guards 1920–1946* (1951)

Hylton, Stuart, *Careless Talk: The Hidden History of the Home Front 1939–45* (2001)

Ismay, Hastings, *The Memoirs of General Lord Ismay* (1960)

Jeffrey, Keith, *MI6: The History of the Secret Intelligence Service 1909–1949* (2010)

Jeffreys-Jones, Rhodri and Andrew Lownie, *North American Spies* (1991)

Jenkins, Roy, *Churchill* (2001)

Jones, R.V., *Most Secret War* (1978)

Jowitt, William, *Some Were Spies* (1954)

Judd, Denis, *George VI* (1982)

Keegan, John, *The Second World War* (1997)

—— (ed.), *Churchill's Generals* (1991)

Kennedy, David, *Freedom From Fear: The American People in Depression and War 1929–1945* (1999)

Kershaw, Alex, *The Few* (2006)

Kershaw, Ian, *Hitler 1936–1945: Nemesis* (2001)

Kesselring, Field-Marshal Albert, *The Memoirs* (1953)

Kieser, Egbert, *Operation Sea Lion* (1997)

Kimball, Warren (ed.), *Churchill & Roosevelt: The Complete Correspondence*, vol. 1 (1984)

King, Greg, *Wallis: The Uncommon Life of the Duchess of Windsor* (1999)

Knappe, Siegfried with Ted Brusaw, *Soldat* (1999)

Lampe, David, *The Last Ditch* (1968)

Langer, William, *The Challenge of Isolation* (1952)

Lee, General Raymond, *The London Observer* (1972)

Lemay, Benoit, *Erich von Manstein: Hitler's Master Strategist* (2011)

Levine, Joshua, *Forgotten Voices of the Blitz and the Battle for Britain* (2006)

Liddell Hart, Basil, *The German Generals Talk* (1948)

Linge, Heinz, *With Hitler to the End* (2009)

Longden, Sean, *Dunkirk: The Men They Left Behind* (2009)

——, *Blitz Kids* (2012)

Longmate, Norman, *The Real Dad's Army* (2010)

——, *If Britain Had Fallen* (2012)

Lovat, Lord, *March Past: A Memoir* (1979)

Lowry, Bernard, *British Home Defences 1940–45* (2004)

Lowry, Bernard and Mick Wilks, *The Mercian Maquis* (2002)

Lucas, James, *Reich: World War II through German Eyes* (1987)

Luck, Colonel Hans von, *Panzer Commander* (2003)

Lukacs, John, *The Duel* (1991)

——, *Five Days in London, May 1940* (1999)

——, *Blood, Toil, Tears and Sweat* (2008)

McCamley, N.J., *Saving Britain's Art Treasures* (2003)

McCanne, Lieutenant Colonel Randy, et al., *Operation Sea Lion: A Joint Critical Analysis* (2002)

MacCarron, Donal, *Wings over Ireland* (1996)

McKay, Sinclair, *The Secret Life of Bletchley Park* (2010)

MacKenzie, S.P., *The Home Guard* (1995)

McKinstry, Leo, *Spitfire: Portrait of a Legend* (2007)

——, *Lancaster* (2009)

Macleod, Colonel Roderick and Denis Kelly (eds), *The Ironside Diaries 1937–1940* (1962)

Macrae, Stuart, *Winston Churchill's Toyshop* (1982)

Mallmann Showell, Jak P. (foreword), *Führer Conferences on Naval Affairs 1939–1945* (1990)

Maier, Klaus A., Hans Umbreit et al., *Germany and the Second World War*, vol. 2 (1991)

Manstein, Field Marshal Erich von, *Lost Victories* (1958)

Martienssen, Anthony, *Hitler and His Admirals* (1948)

Masterman, J.C., *The Double-Cross System* (1972)

Merrilees, William, *The Short Arm of the Law* (1966)

Messenger, Charles, *The Last Prussian: A Biography of Gerd von Rundstedt* (2012)

Middleboe, Penelope et al. (eds), *We Shall Never Surrender: Wartime Diaries 1939–1945* (2011)

Millgate, Helen (ed.), *Mr Brown's War* (1999)

Mitcham, Samuel W., *Eagles of the Third Reich* (2007)

Mitchell, John, *Churchill's Navigator* (2010)

Montgomery, Field Marshal Bernard Law, *Memoirs* (1958)

Montgomery-Massingberd, Hugh and Christopher Sykes, *The Great Houses of England* (1994)

Morgan, General Sir Frederick, *Peace and War* (1961)

Morshead, Sir Owen, *Windsor Castle* (1951)

Mosley, Leonard, *Backs to the Wall* (1971)

Moss, Norman, *Nineteen Weeks* (2004)

Nicholson, Virginia, *Millions Like Us* (2011)

Nicolson, Nigel (ed.), *Harold Nicolson: Diaries & Letters: 1939–45* (1967)

North, Richard, *The Many Not the Few* (2012)

O'Halpin, Eunan, *Spying on Ireland* (2008)

Olson, Lynne, *Citizens of London* (2010)

Orwell, George, *The Orwell Diaries* (2010)

Osborne, Mike, *Defending Britain* (2004)

Overy, Richard, *Goering: Hitler's Iron Knight* (2012)

Owen, James and Guy Walters, *The Voice of War* (2004)

Parker, R.A.C., *Struggle for Survival: A History of the Second World War* (1989)

Paxman, Jeremy and Robert Harris, *A Higher Form of Killing* (1982)

Pearson, Catherine (ed.), *E.J. Rudsdale's Journals of Wartime Colchester* (2010)

Pelling, Henry, *Winston Churchill* (1974)

Perry, Colin, *The Boy in the Blitz* (2000)

Peters, Charles, *Five Days in Philadelphia* (2005)

Pile, Jonathan, *Churchill's Secret Enemy* (2012)

Pimlott, *Hugh Dalton* (1985)

Poppel, Martin, *Heaven and Hell: The War Diary of a German Paratrooper* (2008)

Pugh, Martin, *Hurrah for the Blackshirts* (2005)

Purcell, Hugh, *The Last English Revolutionary: Tom Wintringham 1898–1949* (2004)

Raeder, Erich, *Grand Admiral* (1960)

Ramsay, Sir Archibald, *The Nameless War* (1952)

Rankin, Nicholas, *Churchill's Wizards: The British Genius for Deception 1914–1945* (2008)

Reeves, Anne and David Ewe, *Sheep-Keeping and Lookers' Huts on Romney Marsh* (1998)

Reynolds, David, *From Munich to Pearl Harbor* (2001)

Rhodes James, Robert (ed.), *The Diaries of Sir Henry Channon* (1967)

Richards, Denis, *RAF Bomber Command in the Second World War* (1995)

Roberts, Andrew, *The Holy Fox* (1992)

——, *The Storm of War* (2009)

Robinson, Derek, *Invasion 1940* (2005)

Rolfe, Mel, *Hell on Earth* (2006)

Rose, Norman (ed.), *Baffy: The Diaries of Blanche Dugdale* (1973)

Roskill, Stephen, *The Navy at War 1939–1945* (1960)

——, *Hankey: Man of Secrets* (1974)

——, *Churchill and the Admirals* (1977)

Rowe, Mark, *Don't Panic: Britain Prepares for Invasion, 1940* (2010)

Searle, Adrian, *The Spy Beside the Sea* (2012)

Schellenberg, Walter, *Invasion 1940* (2000)

Schenk, Peter, *The Invasion of England 1940* (1990)

Schmidt, Paul, *Hitler's Interpreter* (1951)

Scott, Ronnie (ed.), *The War Diaries of Colonel Rodney Foster* (2012)

Sebag-Montefiore, Hugh, *Dunkirk: Fight to the Last Man* (2006)

Shaw, Frank and Joan, *We Remember the Home Guard* (2012)

Shawcross, William, *Queen Elizabeth the Queen Mother* (2009)

Shirer, William, *Berlin Diary 1939–1941* (1941)

Simpson, Brian, *In the Highest Degree Odious* (1992)

Skidelsky, Robert, *Oswald Mosley* (1975)

Slessor, Sir John, *The Central Blue* (1956)

Smith, Colin, *England's Last War Against France* (1999)

Smith, Jean Edward, *FDR* (2007)

Smith, Victor, *Front-Line Kent* (2001)

Smithies, Edward, *Aces, Erks, and Backroom Boys* (2002)

Stafford, David, *Roosevelt & Churchill: Men of Secrets* (1999)

Stansky, Peter, *The First Day of the Blitz* (2008)

Steed, R.H.C. (ed.), *Hitler's Interpreter by Dr Paul Schmidt* (1950)

Steinhelper, Ulrich and Peter Osborne, *Spitfire on my Tail* (1990)

Stewart, Charles (ed.), *The Reith Diaries* (1975)

Storey, Neil R., *The Home Guard* (2009)

Stowe, Leland, *How Britain's Wealth Went West* (1963)

Sutton, Terry, *Dover in the Second World War* (2010)

Taylor, A.J.P., *English History 1914–1945* (1965)

Taylor, Fred (ed.), *The Goebbels Diaries 1939–41* (1982)

Thompson, Major-General Julian, *Dunkirk: Retreat to Victory* (2008)

Thompson, W.H., *Sixty Minutes with Winston Churchill* (1953)
Thorpe, D.R., *Eden* (2003)
Thurlow, Richard, *Fascism in Britain: A History 1918–1985* (1987)
Townsend, Peter, *Duel of Eagles* (1970)
Toye, Richard, *Lloyd George & Churchill* (2007)
Turi, John J., *England's Greatest Spy: Eamon De Valera* (2009)
Turner, Barry, *Outpost of Occupation* (2010)
Trythall, Anthony John, *'Boney' Fuller: The Intellectual General* (1977)
Ward, Arthur, *The Battle of Britain* (1989)
——, *Resisting The Nazi Invader* (1997)
——, *Churchill's Secret Defence Army* (2013)
Warner, Philip, *Auchinleck: The Lonely Soldier* (1982)
Warwicker, John, *With Britain in Mortal Danger* (2002)
——, *Churchill's Underground Army* (2008)
Watts, Norman, *In Case of Invasion: Panic or Peace* (1940)
Weeks, John, *Men Against Tanks* (1975)
West, Nigel (ed.), *The Guy Liddell Diaries* (2005)
West, Nigel and Madoc Roberts, *Snow* (2011)
Wheatley, Ronald, *Operation Sea Lion* (1958)
Wheeler, Harold and Alexander Broadley, *Napoleon and the Invasion of England* (1908)
Wheeler-Bennett, John, *John Anderson: Viscount Waverley* (1962)
Williams, Charles, *Pétain* (2005)
Williamson, Alan, *East Ridings Secret Resistance* (2004)
Wills, Clair, *That Neutral Island* (2007)
Wills, Henry, *Pillboxes: A Study of UK Defences* (1985)
Windsor, The Duchess of, *The Heart has its Reasons* (2012)
Winter, Paul, *Defeating Hitler* (2012)
Wood, Ian S., *Britain, Ireland and the Second World War* (2010)
Wyburn-Powell, Alun, *Clement Davies: Liberal Leader* (2003)
Young, Kenneth (ed.), *The Diaries of Sir Robert Bruce-Lockhart* (1980)
Ziegler, Philip, *King Edward VIII* (1990)

Articles and Theses

Angus, Ian, 'The history of WWII invasion committee war books', 1999 (www.britannia.com)
Arnold, Ralph, 'Home forces' (*Blackwood's Magazine*, June 1959)
Ashford, Gary, 'The story of Shingle Street' (www.shford.fslife.co.uk)
'The Auxiliary Units history' (www.coleshillhouse.com)
Blumentritt, General Gunther, 'Operation Sea Lion' (*Irish Defence Journal*, June 1949)
Boyd, David, 'British equipment losses at Dunkirk', 4 January 2009 (www.wwiiequipment.com)
Caygill, Marjorie, 'The British Museum at war' (*British Museum Magazine*, summer 1990)
Clarke, D.M., 'Arming the Home Guard 1940–44' (Cranfield University, 2011)

Clonan, Tom, 'What if: Hitler's invasion of Ireland' (Dublin Institute of Technology, January 2010)

Crowcroft, Robert, 'The Labour Party and the impact of war' (University of Leeds, 2007)

Cumming, Anthony, 'The air marshal versus the admiral' (*Journal of the Historical Association*, April 2009)

Denton History, 'The spy from the sky' (www.tinycc/dentonhistory)

Fairhead, Huby, 'Decoy sites: wartime deception in Norfolk and Suffolk' (www. aviationmuseum.net)

Fox, Steve, 'The Cabinet War Room and Subterfuge' (www.burlington beyond.co.uk)

Freeman, David, 'Churchill & Eamon De Valera: a thirty year relationship' (Paper to Conference on 'Churchill and Ireland', 2009, University of Ulster)

Gordon, Dr Andrew, 'New perspectives on the Battle of Britain', 21 September 2010 (www.critical-reaction.co.uk)

Kappes, Irwin J., 'Mers-el-Kebir: a battle between friends' (www.military historyonline.com)

King, Gilbert, 'The monocled World War II interrogator', 23 November 2011 (www.smithsonian.mag)

Kluiters, F.A.C. and E.Verhoeyen, 'An international spymaster and mystery man: Abwehr officer Hilmar G.J. Dierks and his agents' (www.such-im-dunklen.de)

Liddell Hart, Basil, 'Why did Hitler order the stop' (*John Bull Magazine*, May 1950)

Munch-Petersen, Thomas, 'Common sense and not bravado: the Butler–Prytz interview of 17 June 1940' (*Scandia*, 52, 1986)

Newbold, David, 'British planning and preparation to resist invasion on land' (King's College, 2012)

Parker, Larry, 'Sea Lion versus Overlord' (www.militaryhistoryonline.com)

Phillips, Paymaster Sub-Lieutenant Ronald G., 'Destruction of the French fleet at Mers El-Kebir' (www.hmshood.com)

Ramsey, Winston G., 'The German spies in Britain' (*After the Battle*, 11, 1976)

——, 'Operation Ambassador' (*After the Battle*, 32, 1991)

'Red herrings for the Luftwaffe', *Flight*, 29 November 1945

Wise, Robert, 'Wargaming Operation Sea Lion' (*Airfix Magazine*, December 1975)

Index

Ranks and titles are generally the
highest mentioned in the text